CW00347484

Sparta

Sparta

Unfit for Empire 404–362 BC

by

Godfrey Hutchinson

Frontline Books, London

To Oliver, Torquil and Mathilda

Sparta: Unfit for Empire
This edition published in 2014 by Frontline Books,
an imprint of Pen & Sword Books Ltd,
47 Church Street, Barnsley, S. Yorkshire, S70 2AS

ISBN: 978–1–84832–222–6

CIP data records for this title are available from the British Library

For more information on our books, please visit
www.pen-and-sword.co.uk, email info@frontline-books.com
or write to us at the above address.

Printed and bound by CPI Group (UK) Ltd, Croydon, CR0 4YY
Typeset in Garamond by Wordsense Ltd, Edinburgh

Contents

CONTENTS

Illustrations

Plates

Maps

Battle Plans

Glossary

agoge	the training and educational programme for Spartans
acropolis	the upper or higher city that served as a citadel
anastrophe	Spartan battlefield manoeuvre for folding back a phalanx wing
aspis	hoplite shield
boiotarch	an elective office within the Theban-led Boiotian confederacy. Office holders were expected to be generals in times of war
ekklesia	assembly
enomotia	a Spartan army unit of forty men
enomotarch	officer commanding an *enomotia*
ephor	senior Spartan magistrate, elected for one year
gerousia	the judicial and governing council of Sparta
harmost	Spartan governor of a colony
hegemon	position of leadership
helot	servile agricultural worker on a Spartan farm or estate holding a position in society between slave and freedman
hippeis	the chosen 300 serving as a Spartan king's bodyguard
homoioi	one of the names for a Spartan citizen
hoplite	heavy infantryman and a component of the phalanx
hypomeiones	inferiors, members of the class below full citizenship in Sparta
lambda	the insignia on a Spartan hoplite's shield. The Greek letter L (λ)
lochos	Spartan army unit of 640 men at full strength
lochagos	commander of a *lochos*
mora	Spartan army unit of 1,280 men at full strength
mothax	inferiors who were put through the *agoge* by wealthy friends

navarch	Spartan commander of the fleet and any associated land forces
neadamodeis	new citizens. *Helots* freed in return for armed service
oligarchy	government by a minority group
peltasts	light-armed troops used initially as skirmishers but transformed by the reforms of Iphikrates
pentekostys	Spartan army unit of 160 men
perioikoi	free communities living in Lakonia and Messenia.
phalanx	the close formation in depth of interdependent hoplites
polemarch	commander of a *mora*.
rhetra	an adopted decision of the *ekklesia* (strictly speaking, a saying)
Spartiate	full Spartan citizen
syssition	Spartan military messes; there were several locations for the nightly meals, depending on the group the individual had joined
tagos	elected ruler of Thessaly
tresantes	cowards in the face of battle. These 'tremblers' lost their citizen status

Acknowledgements

SPECIAL THANKS MUST GO TO the anonymous reader. He was meticulous in his examination of my text and made several very useful suggestions. Originally the structure of the book was one in which an excursus was interposed between chapters, wherein cumulative aspects of the background to the period were given. Reluctantly, I was persuaded by him to gather these together in the form of Appendices to achieve a continuous narrative for what is now the first section of the book. Any errors or omissions remaining are my own.

I am indebted to the support and advice given to me over the years by Michael Leventhal, initially at his father's publishing house, Greenhill, and now at Frontline. I have also appreciated the splendid transfer of information conducted initially by Stephen Chumbley and then by Kate Baker during the preparation of this publication. Thanks must also be given to Joanna Chisholm for the meticulous presentation of the text and to Shona Andrew for the excellent cover design.

I am greatly appreciative of the company of friends and family I enjoy when on field trips in Greece examining topography, battlefields and sites in preparation for my publications. All may not share my degree of enthusiasm but always show great humour and patience.

I have continued to profit from the generous and spontaneous support of Valerie Jones and Geoffrey Watson on a variety of technical matters.

A grant from the Royal Literary Fund gave me the opportunity to gather additional material for the revision of the original draft of this book.

Photographs, maps and battle plans were initially prepared by the author.

Introduction

> Nothing short of a complete revolution in the Spartan state could have
> rendered her essay in empire a success; but the narrow Spartan system
> was too narrowly based in the narrow Spartan character to suffer such
> a revolution.
>
> J. B. Bury, A History of Greece

THIS IS A MILITARY HISTORY of the period between the end of the
Peloponnesian War (404 BC) and the Battle of Second Mantineia (362 BC)
and, as the title suggests, covers the successive *hegemon*ies of Sparta and Thebes. At
the close of that war Sparta found itself in a position of ascendancy unprecedented
in its history. The maritime Aegean empire of Athens was now added to the
leadership Sparta enjoyed in mainland Greece.

One focus was the growing enmity between Sparta and Thebes, the leading
city of the Boiotian Federation, and one of Sparta's allies during the Peloponnesian
War. That enmity led to Sparta's inexorable slide from being the dominant land
power in the Greek world for two centuries, to having the eventual status of a
second-rate power at the hand of Thebes. All this happened in a matter of forty
years, a time span almost coinciding with the reign of Agesilaos, one of the kings
of Sparta.

The text gives the reader the broad sweep of the ever-changing alliances that
occurred throughout the period, but its main concern lies with military operations.
What, until relatively recent times, has traditionally been viewed as a formalised
method of Classical hoplite warfare is often belied by close examination of sources.
The opinion that battles were fought between two armies on plains, usually after

provocation by the invading force or by mutual agreement, is more romantic than actual. The tradition stems from observations made well after the Classical period even by greatly respected historians such as Polybios (XIII. 3. 2–6) living some 200 years after the beginning of the period under discussion. Pitched battle was not the regular currency of Greek warfare and, when it did occur, was sometimes the result of accident, surprise or expediency. It was easy for a strong city-state to bully one that was weaker. To destroy crops or capture livestock may have been a gross annoyance and economically damaging. However, it did not always result in the men of the attacked area coming out from behind their walls for a formal contest of arms, much as that might have been the desire of the invaders. Such meetings on plains were more often between larger coalitions and are certainly the pattern for the period under review. Much of what has come to be regarded as the 'rules of play' will be seen, in Appendix 6, to emanate more from shared religious observance – notably followed more meticulously by Spartans than by others.

Within the narrative there are detailed analyses that concentrate on actions, tactics and manoeuvres. These show the continuing development of auxiliary forces and their co-operation and tactical use in a variety of actions. Then, as now, commanders sought to put their opponents at a disadvantage by ruse, manoeuvre and speed of movement. So, too, the increasing use of mercenaries and citizen training brought additional skills to armies, allowing other states to challenge the supremacy of Spartan arms with greater confidence.

This study seeks to draw attention to the limitations or opportunities presented by topography and its effect on campaigns and battles. Of course, the topography of Greece dictated that any contest between heavy infantry in close formation would require to be fought on plains, but the invading forces had first to traverse the mountainous terrain that separated one plain from the next. It was often in such areas that a column of hoplites was at its most vulnerable, usually from lighter-armed troops. Passes could easily be blocked and manned by the defenders. One of the most obvious differences between the generalship of two Spartan kings, Agesilaos and Kleombrotos, is that the former always secured the pass of entry well prior to his invasions of the Boiotian plain, whereas the latter omitted to do so on more than one occasion.

Success or failure of command is examined, and questions of training and the sustaining of morale given scrutiny. To those with knowledge of current British Army Doctrine the two set battles fought by the Theban Epaminondas show recognisable use of dislocation and disruption. In Agesilaos we have a commander skilled in manoeuvre, deception, deployment and dislocation, and, in Antalkidas, a Spartan commander who successfully achieved the objective of the strategy agreed by his state with superb efficiency. Other able commanders such as the Thebans Pelopidas and Ismenias, the Spartan Teleutias, and the Athenians Chabrias and Iphikrates are given attention, as is the unnamed incompetent Spartan commander in the debacle of Lechaion.

Today, ancient Sparta is often viewed as a strange society. Indeed, it was unique in the Greek world of ancient times. However, it was no less Greek than other states. It shared the same gods as its neighbours and was perhaps more pious than many. Sparta was no more belligerent than any other and, while it can be accused of committing atrocities on its own enslaved population and that of Messenia to maintain its security, it in no way matched the recorded atrocities committed by such states as Athens and Thebes on fellow Greeks. How far the influence of King Agesilaos on foreign policy is to blame for Sparta's downfall is still a matter for debate.

The book is divided into two sections. The chapters of the first part carry the narrative of the period under scrutiny. The appendices deal with background information to the period.

Our sources, following the example of Thucydides, are as concerned with sieges, ambushes, opportune attacks and the economic effects of agricultural depredation on an enemy. Xenophon, in particular, is eager to give details of minor engagements occurring in locations other than on a plain.

Of the main sources used, only two are contemporary to the period under discussion. Some papyrus fragments by an unknown historian, the *Hellenica Oxyrhynchia,* would appear to have been intended to be a continuation of Thucydides' unfinished history. Xenophon obviously shared that intention, picking up where Thucydides had left off. The points at dispute between these two sources are dealt with in the main text.

Main Sources

Xenophon (Xen.)

Agesilaos (Ages.)　　　　　　　　　*Constitution of the Lacedaimonians*
Anabasis (Anab.)　　　　　　　　　*Hellenika (Hell.)*

Horsemanship	*Memorabilia (Mem.)*
Hunting	*The Cavalry Commander*
Kyropaideia (Kyro.)	

Plutarch (Plut.)
Lives of:

Agesilaos (Ages.)	*Kleomenes (III)*
Agis (IV)	*Lykourgos*
Alkibiades (Alk.)	*Lysander (Lys.)*
Artaxerxes	*Pelopidas (Pelop.)*

Diodoros (Diod.)
Histories Books XIV–XVI

Anon.
Hellenica Oxyrhynchia (Oxy.)

Lesser-Used Sources

Aeneas *Tacticus*	Nepos *Agesilaos, Lysander*
Aristotle *Politics*	Pausanias (Paus.)
Asklepiodotos *Tactics* (Ask.)	Polyainos
Athenaios (Ath.)	Polybios (Pol.)
Frontinus (Front.)	Thucydides (Thuc.)

To avoid much page-turning, ancient source references are given within the text. Modern commentaries are present within the endnotes of each chapter and the select bibliography. Unless otherwise stated, quotations from the ancient sources use the translation in the Loeb Classic series.

Other than the unknown *Oxyrhynchia* historian, Xenophon is the only significant surviving contemporary source for our period. Xenophon's own life is very worthy of attention. Born of an aristocratic background, possibly, in 429 BC and shortly after the start of the Peloponnesian War, he came under the influence of Sokrates in his youth. He not only lived through this momentous period but also participated in some of the major events within it. He accompanied Kyros the

Younger's army in the latter's attempt to take the Persian throne from his brother. With the death of Kyros at the Battle of Kounaxa and the subsequent treachery of the Persian satrap Tissaphernes that removed the command structure of the undefeated 'Ten Thousand' Greeks, Xenophon found himself elected as one of the replacement generals.

His account of the epic return of the Greeks from the heart of the Persian Empire is the subject matter of his *Anabasis*. When safely arrived at the coast, he, with a significant proportion of the Greek army remaining under his command, undertook mercenary service with the Spartans, now at war with Persia.

When the Spartan king, Agesilaos, was recalled from Asia Minor to face the coalition of Thebes, Athens, Korinth, Argos and others, Xenophon and the mercenaries accompanied him on the journey from Asia Minor to fight on the Spartan side in the Battle of Koroneia in 394 BC.

His service to Sparta was recognised and he was allowed to settle on an estate near Skylous, just south of Olympia. He continued to serve Sparta throughout the Korinthian War and knew most of Sparta's leading men, including Agesilaos. In consequence, he was privy to information which, without his writings, would be unavailable. His two sons were educated in the Spartan *agoge*.

After Leuktra, in 371 BC, he was obliged to leave his estate, which had passed from Spartan control. Still an exile from Athens, he settled in Korinth. There, it is highly likely that he observed the Theban incursions into the Peloponnese. Later, with Athens now in alliance with Sparta, Xenophon was able to return to his homeland.

The *Hellenika* must be described as Xenophon's personal view of the events occurring during the period. Although he can justly be accused of Spartan bias, he does not pull his punches when criticising his host country's actions when necessary. Both the breaking of the oath that all cities should be free by the occupation of Thebes, and the adoption of imperialism, are condemned in stark terms, and cited as causes for the Spartan misfortune at Leuktra. To Xenophon this was impiety.

Of his other writings, the *Anabasis* is very detailed in matters military and reads like an adventure story. His essays on *Horsemanship* and *The Cavalry Commander* give us a clear insight into equine care and those problems with which a cavalryman had to contend. The *Constitution of the Lacedaimonians* gives information on the Spartan education system, the role of the kings and some formation changes made when on campaign. Although a rather ponderous text to read, the *Kyropaideia* (*'The Education of Kyros'*), a fictional and idealised account of Kyros the Great, gives much detail of Spartan military practice that would otherwise be lost to us. Even so, it must be recognised that, famous as Sparta is, we know much less about this strange society than we do of Athens.

The reader will note some differences in the spelling of proper names and places between the main text and passages quoted from the Loeb translations of the sources. These usually concern my preference for a closer reflection of the Greek rather than the often-employed Latinised treatment. The ancient Greek alphabet did not contain a 'c' so that the 'k' is retained in such names as Korinth and Antalkidas.

Some maps and battle plans are slightly modified versions of those used in my earlier publications.

Godfrey Hutchinson, Staindrop, 2014

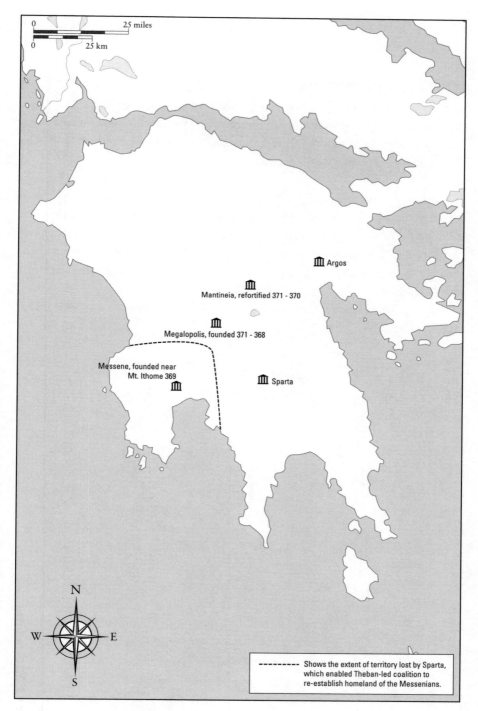

MAP 1 *Encirclement of Sparta*

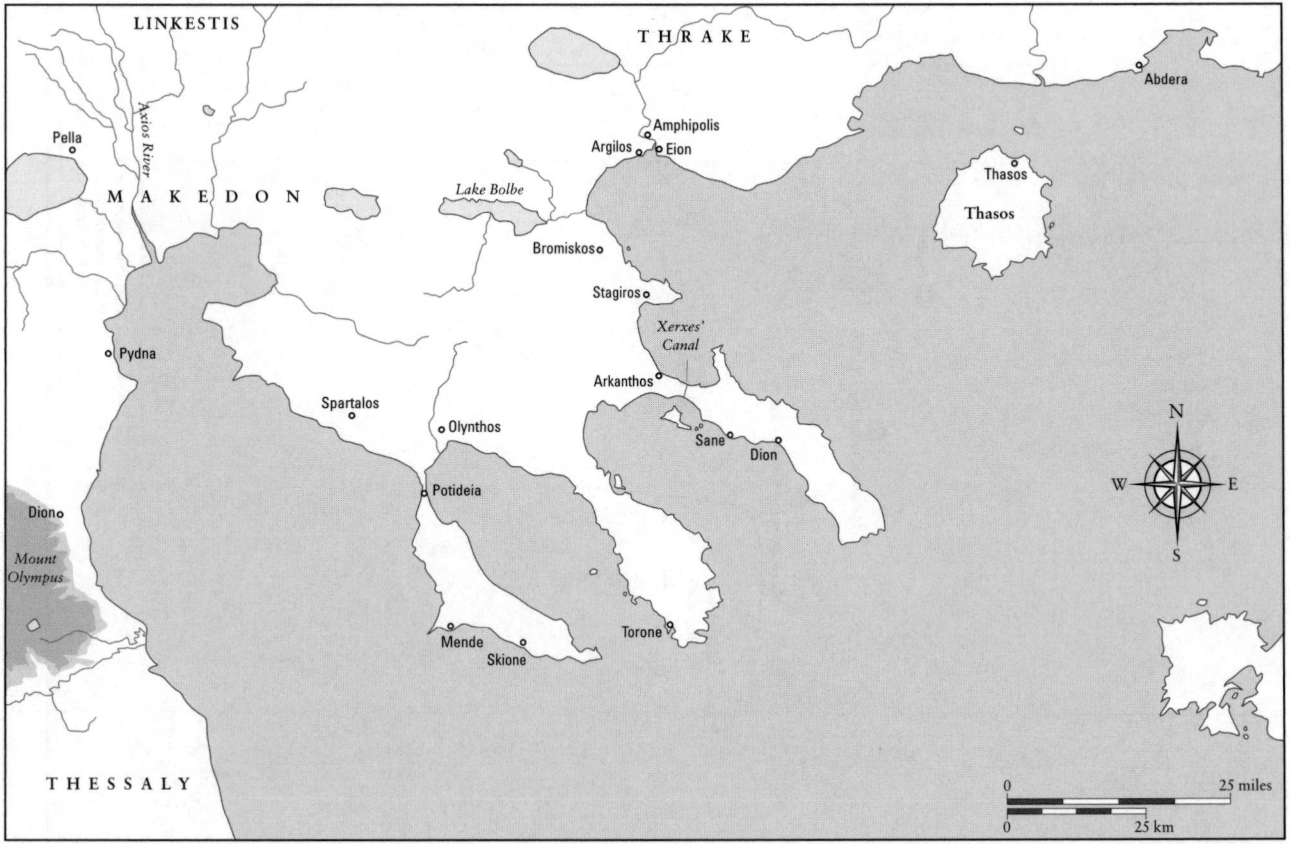

THRAKE

Abdera

Thasos
Thasos

LINKESTIS

MAKEDON

Axios River

Pella

Pydna

Dion
Mount
Olympus

THESSALY

Lake Bolbe

Amphipolis
Eion
Argilos

Bromiskos

Stagiros

Arkanthos

Xerxes'
Canal

Sane

Dion

Torone

Spartalos

Olynthos

Potideia

Mende

Skione

N
E
S
W

25 miles

25 km

0

0

MAP 2 *Northern Greece*

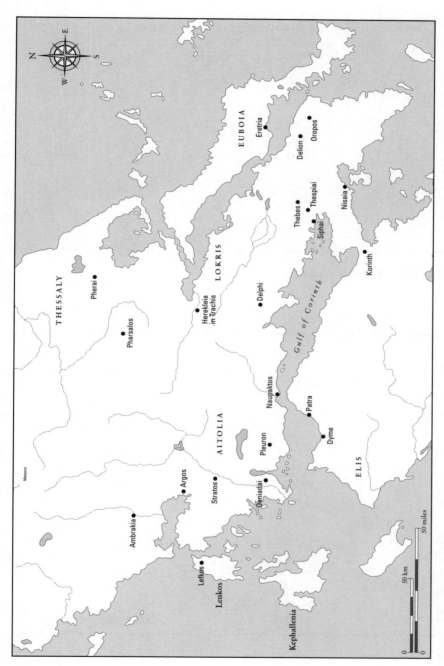

MAP 3 *Central and north-western Greece*

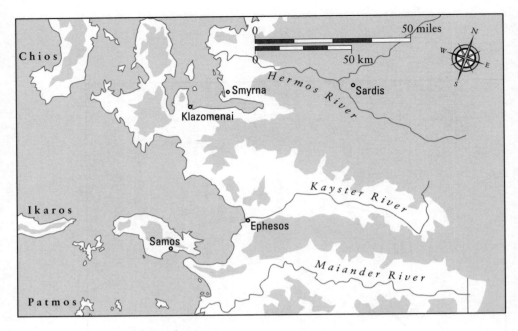

MAP 4 *Area of the Sardis campaign*

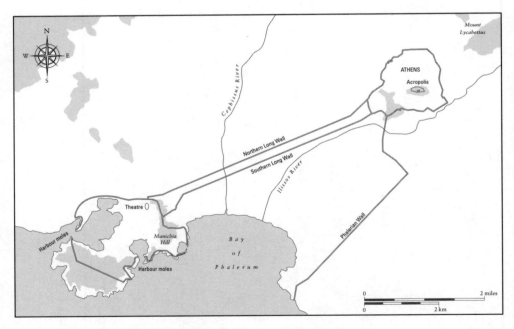

MAP 5 *The defences of Athens and its harbours*

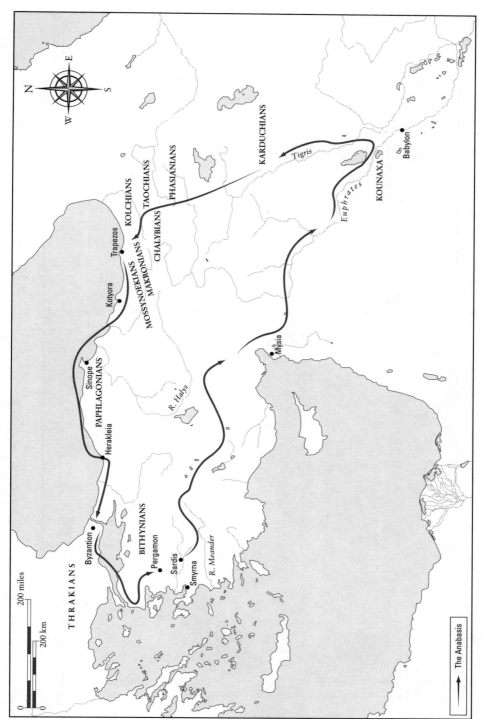

MAP 6 *The Anabasis*

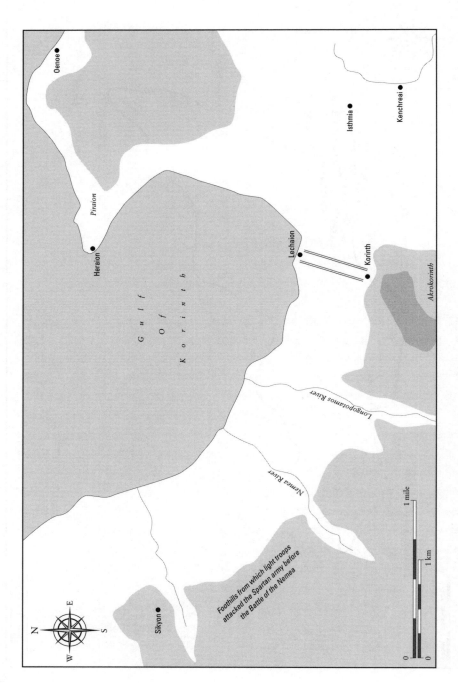

MAP 7 *Area around Korinth with the city linked to its port by walls*

CHAPTER 1

From the Peace to the Outbreak of Hostilities with Persia

The 'Beloved City' of Pericles had become a tyrant, her nature poisoned
by war, her government a by-word in Greece for brutality.

Gilbert Murray, *Five Stages of Greek Religion*

THE YEAR 404 BC SAW the end of the Peloponnesian War, the twenty-seven-year conflict that had created turmoil in most parts of the Greek world. What could then have been a transition to a more settled world was soon to display clear evidence to the contrary. Sparta's victory should have led to the freedom of those cities within the Athenian Empire and those on the Asian littoral. Such had been one of the proclaimed purposes for undertaking the conflict that had destroyed the ever-growing power of Athens, the fear of which had been the underlying reason to cause Sparta and its allies to go to war. In an ideal world Sparta could have been expected to oversee the peaceful resumption of whatever local constitutional arrangement was decided upon by the populations of the former members of the Delian League. Having done so, and guaranteeing protection to these cities, Sparta could have nobly withdrawn to its position within its Peloponnesian alliance amid the plaudits of the Greek world.

This was not to be, for the price of victory was the apparent abandonment of Greek cities on the Asian littoral to the Persians in return for their help in the later period of the war. Whether there was a hope that, with the death of Dareios in 404 BC a few months before the final surrender of Athens, the agreement would in some way alter the outcome is conjectural. There is much still to be clarified in the matter of arrangements between individuals such as Kyros the Younger and

1

Lysander, the victor at Aigospotami. The tacit support of Sparta for Kyros' attempt to usurp the Persian throne was no doubt given in recognition of his unstinting financial help to the Spartan cause in the last years of the Peloponnesian War. There may also have been the hope that the Asian Greek cities could enjoy some form of autonomy had he been successful, thereby giving credibility to Sparta's original claims.

To Sparta's credit, it resisted demands to destroy Athens from allies such as Thebes, Korinth and others: 'The Lacedaemonians, however, said that they would not enslave a Greek city which had done great service amid the greatest perils that had befallen Greece' (Xen. *Hell.* II. 2. 20).

The extent of the allied demands is not wholly clear from our sources.[1] They may well have gone so far as to mirror those practised during the war by Athens when dealing with obdurate foes – namely, the destruction of fortifications, the execution of all adult males and the enslavement of women and children. Whatever the case, Sparta was having none of this. The demands required Athens to destroy the city walls and those of Peiraieos, to reduce the fleet to a token force of twelve ships, to permit exiles to return, and to accept the usual terms of an alliance. This meant that it should follow Sparta on land and sea and have the same friends and enemies. At the Spartan assembly, where this decision was reached, there is a hint of rebuke for the Thebans in the Spartan comment that they would not make slaves of the people of a city that had served Greece so well in the past. This reference to Athens' resistance against Persia when the freedom of Greece was at risk would remind the delegates present that Thebes had fought on the side of Persia at the Battle of Plataia.

Rather than destroy Athens, Sparta had brought it into alliance. Possibly the geographical proximity of Boiotia and a concern that expansion southward would be a temptation to Thebes was a factor in the decision. Korinth and Thebes in particular, although still technically within the Spartan-led Peloponnesian League, continued to display an increasingly provocative attitude to Spartan leadership. Even as the war had come to an end in 404 BC, Thebes had misappropriated the sacred tithe for Apollo from the spoils of war held at the fortification of Dekeleia, to the north of Athens, and due to be dedicated at Delphi at the close of hostilities (Xen. *Hell.* III. 5. 5). The Boiotians had benefited greatly from their raids into Attika in both goods and slaves during their garrison duties at Dekelia and possibly expected further reward at the cessation of hostilities. Tensions between members of the Peloponnesian League continued over the following years with Thebes being suspected, correctly, of increasing arrogance and influence.

Now the possessor of a powerful fleet unrivalled in the Greek world, Sparta faced the problem of its maintenance. Tribute from its new empire was the obvious solution. However, personal possession of coinage in great quantity within its borders, whether of silver or gold, was prohibited under the laws of Lykourgos. In its place debased iron in the form of heavy bars was the traditional means of exchange. Obviously, in the winning of the war, Sparta had used Persian subsidies to pay its growing mercenary forces both on land and sea. However, with tribute flowing into Sparta, peculation was soon to become evident and the laws of Lykourgos had to be adapted to make such tribute the property of the state and not of the individual. This proved impractical; there is evidence that imbalances between rich and poor accelerated the loss of citizen rights that had been a growing concern for some years. Since the Spartans had by law traditionally avoided wealth in any form other than land, and living a conservative and relatively simple life, exposure to the wealth to be seen in the eastern Aegean in the later years of the Peloponnesian War must have turned more than a few heads.

The most obvious example to be recorded is that of Gylippos. He had been the saviour of Syrakuse after being sent by Sparta to command its forces against the Athenians during their abortive siege. Commissioned by Lysander to escort a large amount of currency to Sparta at the end of the war, Gylippos undid the bottom of each sack and took a significant quantity of coins before sewing it up again. His theft was discovered when the sum in each sack was found not to agree with the amount shown on the note placed in the top of the sack. His house was searched and the cache was discovered under the roof (Plut. *Lys.* 16). Although peculation is unlikely to be an inherited trait, Gylippos' father, Kleandridas, had gone into exile rather than face the death sentence awaiting him at Sparta for taking bribes *c.*446 BC (Plut. *Perikles* 22).

So, at the outset of empire, it can be seen that Sparta had innate problems, suggesting it was unsuitable for the task it had taken upon itself. Without appropriate constitutional change its society was imploding. The ever-decreasing citizen population was generally of naive and conservative character, conditioned by tradition to maintain a massive *helot* population under severe restraint. Some proved subject to avarice or a desire for power when exposed to the opportunity.

There seemed, at the very outset, little to commend Sparta for the imperial role it undertook.

Overall, the population of Lakedaimon and Messenia was large and relatively stable. The decline in citizen numbers had its constitutional cause. Tentative measures had been taken during the Peloponnesian War to give *helots* freedom in return for military service. An example of this was of the *helots* serving under Brasidas (424–422 BC). This practice grew over the closing years of the Peloponnesian War and, during the narrative of the period covered in this book, references will appear of increasing numbers being employed in this way. Though free and with local autonomy in their new communities, the *helots* were never to enjoy the exclusive rights of a Spartan citizen. This was only tinkering and did little or nothing to make the life of the serf communities any better or willing to support the state. It also did not address the obvious constitutional issue – that of the inferiors (for the structure of Spartan society, see Appendix 1). A number of this group had shared the training of the *agoge* and were of a calibre to sustain the proven reputation that the Spartan hoplite was the best in the Greek world. The resentment felt at their reduced status could have been removed if measures had been taken for their reinstatement as full citizens by land redistribution. It would also have given greater security against any *helot* uprising rather than encouraging the internal plots involving inferiors that appeared from time to time at Sparta. We have already seen the example of avarice in the case of Gylippos. The desire for power was exemplified by the arrogant conduct of the regent Pausanias, the victor at Plataia, nearly eighty years earlier. Its recurrence within our period, later to be discovered in the case of Lysander, is indicative.

Lysander's very personal settlement of affairs in those cities now 'liberated' from the Athenian Empire was to set up narrow oligarchies. These boards of ten exercised the governance of their cities and were supported by a garrison under the command of a *harmost*. They soon proved unpopular. The majority of those in power took advantage of their position to enrich themselves and oppress many under their rule. Lysander had hoped to build for himself a wide client base of support throughout the Aegean. While the garrisons remained, each local populace was notionally free to choose its own constitutional form. Nonetheless, these cities were very much under the control of a new imperial master.

Within Sparta itself there were clear signs of factionalism at the start of its imperial period. King Pausanias and some *ephors* of that time were clearly against

Lysander's settlement and possibly fearful of his growing power base that had the appearance of a personal fiefdom. They were unhappy with the great influx of coined monies pouring into the city or accruing to Lysander's clients throughout the empire. The compromise reached by the factions to allow coined money to continue to come as tribute to Sparta for use only by the state proved uncomfortable. Presumably such coinage was for use in hiring mercenaries and building ships etc., and the hope that citizens would continue to use only the traditional crude iron currency in their dealings was overly optimistic. Significant personal wealth in anything other than land was anathema to Lykourgos' law.

With the peace, Athens was governed by an oligarchy backed by a Spartan garrison. Lysander, now at the height of his power and influence, formulated this policy. The rule of the 'Thirty', as it came to be known, was short lived. Civil unrest was provoked in the city by the Thirty's repressive rule and often inhuman treatment of their fellow Athenians; their actions were frequently motivated by personal gain. Death and confiscation of wealth and property were commonplace. Many of the lucky men who retained their lives fled to Megara, Korinth and Thebes where, despite its call for the destruction of Athens, Thebes gave refuge to Athenian democrats.[2] In so doing, Thebes appeared happy to cause discomfort and annoyance to Sparta. The ingredients of civil war at Athens were firmly in place, and the first significant action came from the exiles at Thebes.

Thrasyboulos, who had been a gifted Athenian commander during the latter part of the Peloponnesian War, led a small following of about seventy men from Thebes and took the fortress of Phyle, north of Athens, in the foothills of Mount Parnes. The response of the Thirty was immediate, and hoplites and cavalry moved against Thrasyboulos' exiles. The Athenians' first assault was repulsed and a decision was reached to lay siege to Phyle with the intention of starving its occupants into submission. All this had occurred in fine weather conditions, but this was soon to change. Prolonged and heavy snow persuaded the forces of the Thirty to return to Athens. On their march, a number of the camp followers lost their lives to opportunistic attacks from the exiles, whose numbers were steadily increasing. In Athens the defence of the outlying farms around Phyle became a concern and the majority of the Spartan garrison, together with two divisions of Athenian cavalry, were committed to the task of denying their opposition the chance to plunder. The Athenians made camp near Phyle where, by this time, the number of exiles had grown to 700 men. Thrasyboulos made a night march to within half a mile of the Athenian camp and remained there until dawn. As those in the encampment rose from their sleep and went about their preparations for the day, the exiles made a rapid advance on them. Casualties were immediate in the surprise attack, and the survivors took to flight. The pursuit was relentless and no fewer than 120 infantry were killed. Returning to the deserted camp, the exiles erected a battle trophy, quickly collecting arms and baggage thereafter, and were back in Phyle before the remainder of the cavalry from Athens arrived on the scene. All that they could do was to supervise the gathering up of the bodies of the fallen before returning to the city.

This development unnerved the Thirty. Their insecurity led them to the conclusion that some place of retreat was needed in the event that the control of Athens slipped from their grasp. The choice of location fell upon Eleusis, easily reached within half a day from Athens. Taking cavalry with them, the Thirty, under their leader Kritias, pretended that the visit was to assess the number of residents so that a protecting garrison for them could be arranged. On being registered, each townsman passed through the south gate of the town where cavalry, stationed on either side of the gate, seized and bound them. Thereafter, they were taken to Athens and handed over the 'Eleven', a group of minor magistrates responsible for the confinement and execution of prisoners. At a gathering of all those favouring the Thirty, Kritias addressed the assemblage. 'We, gentlemen,' said he, 'are establishing this government no less for you than for ourselves. Therefore, even as you will share in honours, so also you must share in the dangers. Therefore you must vote condemnation of the Eleusinians who have been seized, that you may have the same hopes and fears as we' (Xen. *Hell.* II. 4. 8). In this way, the guilt for the following injustice was shared by all those associated with the oligarchy.

Meantime, the number of exiles at Phyle had reached over a thousand. In a night march this force reached the port of Athens. When news of its arrival came to the Thirty they immediately mobilised a force of cavalry and hoplites along with the Spartan garrison and advanced on Peiraieos. Not having sufficient men to man the walls of the town, Thrasyboulos took up a position on a hill on the eastern side of the town.

On their arrival at the marketplace the oligarchs formed in line of battle to the depth of fifty ranks, seemingly unusual for the time. Given their greater number, this depth was most probably forced upon them by the restrictive conditions they had to face in their uphill advance and not for any tactical reason. There is evidence

6

for this at Xen. *Hell*. II. iv. 11–12. Having described the oligarchs' formation as filling the road, the source continues:

> As for the men from Phyle, they too *filled* the road, but they made a line not more than ten hoplites in depth (emphasis added).
>
> Behind this formation there were peltasts and and javelineers and, significantly, stone-throwers. 'And of these there were many, for they came from that neighbourhood.' (Xen. *Hell*. II. 4. 11)

The uphill advance of the oligarchs was met by showers of missiles that they were unable to counter to any effect because of the gradient. Then, as they were protecting themselves from these attacks, the hoplite exiles charged on them and pursued the broken enemy downhill. The oligarchs lost around seventy men. In the presumption that their greater number would prevail, they had ignored the time-honoured avoidance of an uphill attack on an enemy and paid the price. The victors stripped the armour from the fallen, taking their arms, no doubt, to equip those of their followers who lacked weapons.

Two interesting facts emerge from our source: one before battle, and the second when hostilities ended. The advice from the exiles' seer that their attack should not start before one of their side had suffered a wound or death led to the seer himself charging upon the enemy alone and being killed. By his personal sacrifice he fulfilled the condition of his own advice, no doubt made after portents had been taken. His action demonstrates the piety of many Greeks at that time. The second occurred when the bodies of the dead were being given back. At that point, 'many on either side mingled and talked with one another' (Xen. *Hell*. II. 4. 19). One of the exiles, who was a herald to the Eleusinian mysteries, addressed both victors and vanquished. He questioned the reasons for their being driven from the city and pointed to their kinship and former comradeship during the Peloponnesian War. All this, he declared, had been changed by the Thirty and their actions, and he regretted the deaths that had occurred that day. Those of the Thirty who had survived did not wish their followers to hear these things and ordered them back to Athens.

Kritias had been killed in the battle and the die was now cast. Dissension broke out in the city, with those who had the most to fear from reprisals arguing against any accommodation with the exiles. They deposed the Thirty, who withdrew to Eleusis with some followers, and replaced them with the Ten, representing each of the ten tribes. Even so, the Ten had to use their cavalry to patrol outside the city walls to prevent defections to the exiles. They patrolled on foot as hoplites during the night and, with the coming of daybreak, on horseback. Undoubtedly, these duties would have been undertaken by alternating cavalry squadrons, with the daytime patrols also being employed in attacking foraging parties of exiles.

Many more exiles arrived in Peiraieos and attacks were made on Athens' defensive walls. Matters had now become so worrying that ambassadors from both Eleusis and Athens were sent to Sparta. They requested help against the exiles, who they claimed had come out in revolt against Sparta. Aid was swiftly forthcoming. Lysander was appointed as commander of land forces with his brother Libys as *navarch* of the fleet. The intention was to repeat the operation that had ended the Peloponnesian War, by blocking all supplies to the exiles by land and sea.

With Lysander gathering allied land forces and mercenaries at Eleusis, King Pausanias was busy 'politicking' at Sparta. Xenophon (*Hell*. II. 4. 29) declares that Pausanias was jealous of Lysander, who, 'by accomplishing this project, would not only win fame but also make Athens his own'. This may be part of the case but, whatever Pausanias' arguments, they had support from others in authority who had concerns about the rapid accumulation of power and influence by Lysander. Three of the five *ephors*, the senior Spartan magistrates, agreed that Pausanias should be sent out to take command, as was usual when a Spartan king took to the field. Quickly, a Lakedaimonian army set out with its allies. Significantly, both Thebes and Korinth refused to serve.

With his camp established close to Peiraieos, Pausanias sent ambassadors to the exiles with an order that they should return to their homes. His intention to proceed with a light touch is indicated in Xenophon's comment: 'when they refused to obey him, he attacked them, at least so far as to raise the war cry, in order that it might not be evident that he felt kindly toward them' (Xen. *Hell*. II. 4. 31).

Having achieved nothing, he took two *morai* and some Athenian oligarchic cavalry towards the shoreline to investigate the best position at which a wall could be built to seal off the exiles. Pausanias' force was attacked as it returned to camp. It can be presumed that this attack was made by light-armed troops because he ordered the cavalry to attack them in turn, supported by those of his hoplites who were under thirty years of age and therefore the fleetest of foot. He followed with the main body of hoplites. In the pursuit, almost thirty of the exiles fell and the remainder managed to reach the theatre of Peiraieos. There, the greater part of the exiles had gathered, arming themselves in readiness for combat. The light-armed section of this assemblage charged upon the pursuers. Many of the latter are described as being wounded by the missile fire of peltasts, slingers and archers. As the Lakedaimonians fell back, but still in order, the attack on them increased in vigour. The report that two Spartan *polemarch*s fell at this time indicates that Pausanias and the main body of hoplites had now joined their comrades. Thrasyboulos with his hoplites came quickly to reinforce his numerous light-armed force and formed up eight deep as a protecting screen behind which the missile throwers continued their attack. Outnumbered and under duress, Pausanias withdrew just over half a mile and took up a position on a hill. He sent messengers to his camp with orders that the forces there should come to his support.

Having gained a little respite, possibly because Thrasyboulos did not relish an attack uphill and wisely remained at the foot of the hill, Pausanias arranged his troops in 'an extremely deep phalanx'. This formation was very likely dictated by similar conditions to those of the earlier battle between the oligarchs and the exiles on the hill of Munichia. Restrictions in the available space for deployment, whether by buildings, natural features, or a mixture of both, must have caused the adoption of depth to permit a narrower front.

The following downhill charge was met by the Athenian exiles, and fighting at close quarters ensued, shield on shield. It is evident that the Athenian line buckled under the weight of the massed push (*othismos*) of the Spartan phalanx: 'In the end some of them were pushed into the mire of the marsh Halion and others gave way; and about one hundred and fifty of them were slain' (Xen. *Hell.* II. 4. 34).

What followed proves fascinating. Pausanias, through the use of covert messages, instructed both exiles and oligarchs to send ambassadors to him and the *ephors*. He also defined the proposals that those ambassadors should bring with them. This offered an opportunity for both parties to achieve rapprochement; they followed Pausanias' advice and surrendered themselves to the will of Sparta. When the representatives of both sides were sent to Sparta, the governing body there, having heard them, sent a group of fifteen Spartans to assist Pausanias with the peace proposals. It was agreed that Athenians should 'be at peace with one another'. The only exceptions to this agreement were those men who had been members of the Thirty and its successor bodies. All these past leaders were excluded from the amnesty.[3] Anyone in the city who had fear – presumably of reprisal – was

9

permitted to settle at Eleusis as long as they registered their name within ten days. How many chose to do so is unclear but the number may have been considerable.

King Pausanias had finally resolved the problem and supported the establishment of the traditional democracy hitherto enjoyed by Athens. The undoing of the initial settlement made by the victorious Lysander reflects a marked difference of opinion among those Spartans who normally shaped policy and possibly, as remarked earlier, some jealousy of Lysander on the part of the kings (see Xen. *Hell.* II. 4. 29–30). Proof of this can be found in the initial support of three of the five *ephors* for Pausanias' expedition to Athens, and also in the support the two *ephors* gave to Pausanias' policy for the resolution of the problem: 'Now Naucleidas also, who was an *ephor*, was pleased to hear this. For, as it is customary for two of the *ephors* to be with a king on a campaign, so in this instance Naucleidas and one other were present, and both of them held to the policy of Pausanias rather to that of Lysander' (Xen. *Hell.* II. 4. 36).

Sadly, Pausanias did not return to Sparta to receive plaudits for his achievement from all his countrymen. The supporters of Lysander had been enraged by this alternative solution to the Athenian problem which was not the one they had desired. Pausanias found himself arraigned before the *gerousia* on charges appertaining to his conduct of the campaign and its outcome. He was fortunate to avoid an adverse outcome, but this action showed a marked division in Spartan policy (Pausanias. III. 5. 2), as did the cancellation of Lysander's arrangements for the governance of those territories under Spartan control in Asia Minor.[4]

Sparta now turned its attention to long-standing grievances. During the Peloponnesian War, Elis had defected from the Spartan-led league of allies and had entered into an alliance with Athens. Sparta wanted to extract revenge for this action but added further charges against Elis, citing the banning of Sparta from competing at the Olympic Games and that the Spartan King Agis had been forbidden from making sacrifice to Zeus at the sanctuary. In truth, the Spartans wanted to bend Elis to their will and to that end they provoked hostilities by demanding that certain of its towns should be independent. Elis refused, and Agis led an army in an invasion into its northern territory from Achaia in 402 BC. Agis had not penetrated far when an earthquake occurred, prompting the king to disband his forces and return to Sparta.

The Eleans were relieved and immediately sent to those city-states they knew to be averse to Sparta but had no success in raising support. Within the year another

10

ban, or call-up, was called in Sparta and Agis, at the head of an army containing Athenians among the allies, but again without the support of Thebes or Korinth, invaded Elis once more. Agis started his campaign from Aulon in the south of Elean territory. With no opposition to his activities being offered, he was able to range widely throughout Elean territory, plundering at will. So successful was he that many other Arkadians and Achaians joined his forces in hope of personal gain. Towns readily came over to Agis and, following a violent and unsuccessful insurrection in Elis, the party that lost to the Commons fled to the Spartan army. At the end of the campaign these exiles were left at Epitalion, a few miles to the west of Olympia, which received a garrison and governor. For the remainder of the campaigning season and well into the winter, Lysippos, the governor of Epitalion, used the exiles and his garrison to continue plundering the area. Eventually, Elis sought to come to terms. It was made to accept the independence of towns to the south and north of Elis and considerable tracts of the territory hitherto under its control.

All this is covered in Xen. *Hell.* III. 2. 21 to III. 2. 31. Whereas Diodoros makes no mention of Agis' invasions, he does, however, report an invasion of Elis by Pausanias (Diod. XIV. 17. 4–17) that, in turn, fails to be given coverage by Xenophon, who may have been otherwise preoccupied at the time by involvement in Kyros the Younger's attempt on the Persian throne (See Appendix 2).

Diodoros' description notes the absence of Korinthian and Boiotian contingents from the Spartan-led army. Pausanias entered Elean territory by way of Arkadia, quickly winning support from small towns and then moved further west to capture Pylos, situated but a short distance away from the city of Elis. Moving on Elis itself, Pausanias made preparations to lay the city under siege. Pausanias was unaware that the Eleans had received support from Aitolia. The 1,000 Aitolians would, in all likelihood, be peltasts, coming as they did from a rugged area where such combatants were the best suited to the conditions. They were guarding the *gymnasion* and, early in the siege, when a certain laxity was observed in the behaviour of the besiegers, the Aitolians and many of the Eleans made a surprise concerted attack on the Lakedaimonians. So unexpected was the sortie that the besiegers lost around thirty men.

Pausanias lifted the siege shortly after and pillaged the area around the city. He set up small walled garrisons throughout Elis and over-wintered with his army near the coast to north of the city of Elis, in Dyme.

Later in Diodoros, a report is made of what must have been an extension of Pausanias' activities although he is not mentioned by name:

> The Eleans, because they stood in fear of the superior strength of the Lakedaimonians, brought the war with them to an end, agreeing that they would surrender their triremes to the Lakedaimonians and let the neighbouring cities go free. And the Lakedaimonians, now that they had brought their wars to an end and were no longer concerned with them, advanced with their armies against the Messenians, of whom some were settled in an outpost on Cephallenia and others in Naupactus, which the Athenians had given them, among the western Locrians. Driving the Messenians from these regions, they returned the one outpost to the inhabitants of Cephallenia and the other to the Locrians. (Diod. XIV. 34. 1–3)

The Athenians, at the end of the siege of Ithome, had settled the Messenians at these places in the 460s following the Messenian *helot* uprising against the Spartans. Thereafter, the Messenians had helped Athens control the outlet of the Korinthian Gulf during the Peloponnesian War. Given that Dyme was located opposite the island of Kephallenia at the mouth of the Korinthian Gulf and Naupaktos was inside the narrows, it seems unsurprising that the opportunity to be rid of these troublesome settlements was taken.

Although the descriptions of the Elean campaigns give us little in the way of actions to analyse, they provide a clear example, in modern terms, of sequencing and tempo.[5] The lesson of the Elean War would not have been lost on its future adversaries.

At around the time of these campaigns Sparta took a crucial decision to help Kyros the Younger in his attempt to displace Artaxerxes, his brother, and make the throne of Persia his own. Without his financial support in the last years of the Peloponnesian War it would have proved difficult for Sparta to achieve control of the sea and thereby eventual victory. The help offered seems a little meagre for such an enterprise, in terms of 700 hoplites and a fleet of thirty-five ships for what was ostensibly a land operation. Nonetheless, Sparta had committed itself to the enterprise and had to live with the consequences of its failure when Kyros lost his life at the Battle of Kounaxa. The epic fighting return of the 'Ten Thousand' Greek mercenaries from the heart of the Persian Empire is recounted in Xenophon's *Anabasis* (see Appendix 7).

With the completion of the Elean War, Agis had travelled to Delphi to offer the sacred tithe from the booty taken during the conflict, but he fell ill on his journey home and died soon after, in Sparta. Lysander and his adherents may have seen a setback to their ambitions when Pausanias and his following were early in the ascendant. However, it is quite clear that Lysander had regained much of his influence at the time of the accession of Agesilaos, the half-brother of Agis, who was preferred over the late king's son (see Appendix 1). His support for his former lover at that time was pivotal.

What is very clear from our sources is that both Thebes and Korinth were displaying a growing spirit of independence. As members of the Peloponnesian League they were acting in a very provocative manner in withholding their obligations to that body. It is likely that Korinth was becoming increasingly under Theban influence and had been persuaded to join it in its absence from the army in the campaigns in Attika and Elis. Other incidents in the next few years show a growing antipathy to Sparta before outright confrontation was reached.

Such are some of the indications that all did not augur well for the new imperial power. However, the first major problem was to emanate not from Greece but from Persia.

Endnotes

1   C. D. Hamilton, in Laurence A. Tritle (ed.), *The Greek World in the Fourth Century: From the Fall of the Athenian Empire to the Successors of Alexander*, London and New York, NY, Routledge, 1997, chapter 3, cites four sources in support of the claim that Sparta was urged by the Thebans and Korinthians 'to execute all adult males, enslave the women and children, and destroy the city itself'. Scrutiny of these will show that only Xen. *Hell.* II. 2. 20 gives partial support to this view but makes no mention of executing adult males. Hamilton's opinion probably relies on previous Athenian practice in the matter of captured populations, but that is not to deny the very vehement attitudes of Sparta's allies.

2   See Simon Hornblower, *The Greek World 479–323* BC, London, Methuen, 1983, pp. 182–3, where he persuasively explains the Theban help given to Athenian democrats following on from their original demand for the destruction of Athens and the enslavement of the population.

3   P. Cartledge, *Sparta and Lakonia*, London, Routledge, 1979, 2nd edn 2002, p. 231 suggests that this is the first recorded amnesty in history.

4   For the abandonment by Sparta of the narrow oligarchies set up by Lysander, see A. A. Andrewes, 'Two notes on Lysander', *Phoenix*, vol. 25 (1971), pp. 206 ff.

5   DCDC, *Operations: Army Doctrine Publication, Vol. I*, Army Publications, Marlborough, 2010, available at www.dcdc.dii.r.mil.uk, 0324 f & I, under 0301: Operational Art I, the skilful employment of military force to attain strategic goal through the design, organisation, integration and conduct of campaign and major operations.

CHAPTER 2

Sparta at War with Persia

Since Konon was in alliance with Pharnabazos when Agesilaos was laying
Asia waste, he persuaded the Persian to send money to the political leaders
of the cities of Hellas, in order that, after receiving it, they might persuade
their fatherlands to begin the war against the Spartans.

Polyainos, *Strategemata* I. 48. 3, Phillip Harding trans.

SPARTA'S INVOLVEMENT IN KYROS' ATTEMPT on the Persian throne had
angered Artaxerxes. The Greek Ionian cities, which had revolted from
Tissaphernes to Kyros, were now threatened by the operations Tissaphernes
undertook to effect their recovery. His position in the west of the Persian Empire
had been enhanced to the level hitherto enjoyed by Kyros, and he was now second
only to the Great King himself.

In desperation the cities turned to Sparta for protection. Unusually for Sparta,
it was quick to respond to the plea. With the altered view of Persia's military
power following the achievements of the Ten Thousand, Sparta entered the
conflict with confidence. Thibron was dispatched with an army in the summer
of 400 BC. Freed *helot*s to the number of 1,000 were included in the 5,000-strong
allied force, indicating Sparta's now embedded reliance on troops from this human
resource. Thibron also enlisted those mercenaries of the Ten Thousand who had
not returned to their homes but had chosen to remain in Asia in the hope of
further employment. They probably numbered around 6,000 under the command
of Xenophon. This proved to be a conflict that lasted for almost fourteen years,
400–387 BC.

Garrisons and *harmost*s (governors) were placed in the Greek cities with little effective resistance from Tissaphernes. Although Thibron appears not to have been the most exciting of commanders, he proved successful in laying the foundation of a secure Spartan protectorate on the Asian littoral. With this achieved, his successor, Derkylidas, continued to expand Sparta's control both inland and to the north. Xenophon suggests that this expansion was made more for personal reasons than in following specific Spartan policy:

> Besides, Derkylidas was an enemy of Pharnabazos from earlier days; for after
> he became governor at Abydos at the time when Lysander was admiral, he was
> compelled, as a result of his being slandered by Pharnabazos, to stand sentry
> carrying his shield – a thing which is regarded by Lacedaimonians of character as
> a disgrace; for it is a punishment for insubordination. (Xen. *Hell.* III. 1. 9)

Derkylidas had made a truce with Tissaphernes so that he would be unhindered when he moved against Pharnabazos. Technically, Tissaphernes' status was superior to that of Pharnabazos. Had it not been for personal enmity, his duty should have been to aid his fellow satrap, not least for the security of the empire. The growing tendency for satraps to act as individual rulers was later to see several revolts from the Great King.

Such had been Derkylidas' success that he also secured the protection of the Greek cities of the Chersonese from Thrakian incursions by rebuilding the earth wall across the peninsula built earlier by the Athenians.

All this was possible because the western satraps were at odds with each other and neither had a force of infantry capable of withstanding the Greek phalanx. Divided, they were convenient foes. It was only when the two satraps at last agreed to come together that peace terms between Sparta and Persia were sought. Under a truce, the proposals were carried to Sparta, and by Tissaphernes to the Great King. The circumstances gave Derkylidas little choice. He had heard that the satraps had moved their combined forces into the area of Ephesos, and he moved to give his allies protection. As he approached, Derkylidas found himself confronted by the opposing army in battle order, made up of Karian, Persian, and eastern Greek infantry at its centre, with large forces of cavalry on both wings. He ordered the phalanx to be drawn up eight deep and protected his wings with peltasts and the few cavalry he had. It was obvious that he was willing to engage. However, while the forces that had come with him from the Peloponnese, and presumably

16

the mercenaries under Xenophon, were ready to fight, the Greek allies from the islands and coastal cities deserted in large numbers. Those who stayed gave the impression that they would not remain in their positions for long. Luckily these defections had been hidden from the Persians by the high corn growing in the region. Had it not been so, Tissaphernes and Pharnabazos would have taken the opportunity to launch an attack on the depleted forces, despite their knowledge of the efficacy of Greek hoplites. Tissaphernes, in particular, would have clear memories of Kounaxa and its aftermath.

A conference was proposed by Tissaphernes at which Derkylidas appeared accompanied by his most impressive-looking men. His bluff succeeded and achieved an honourable pause in hostilities without losing anything already gained. Pharnabazos used the truce to go to the Great King, both to make complaints against Tissaphernes and to be successful in persuading him to finance the equipping of a fleet. He hoped, by this means, to wrest control of the sea from Sparta. The satrap had the vision to realise that this had become a strategic necessity. The Athenian, Konon, was suggested as the commander of the new fleet (Diod. XIV. 39. 1–4). Konon had sought refuge in Kypros after Lysander's decisive victory at Aigopotamai that ended the Peloponnesian War. He had escaped with around ten ships, fearing to return to Athens, where he would certainly have been put on trial (Diod. XIII. 106. 6). He had now been given an opportunity to win honour and serve Athens' interests. Kypros had been given the task of supplying 100 ships and, in the course of these preparations, Konon took forty ships and sailed north to Kilikia on the mainland to make preparations. Thereafter, he sailed to Lake Kaunos, an inland stretch of water reached from the coast via an easily navigable river. There he found himself blockaded by a Spartan fleet of 120 vessels under its *navarch* Pharax, who also laid siege to the neighbouring settlement. The arrival of Pharnabazos with a relieving army saw Pharax forced to return to his base at Rhodes.

However, in the space of a year, 397 BC, the Spartan *ephors* moved from a position of protecting the traditional constitutions of the Ionian Greeks in the hope that their autonomy might be secured, to a reinvigorated war footing against Persia.

This was prompted by reports that the Persian king was preparing a fleet of 300 warships in Phoenicia. Xenophon puts Lysander at the heart of Sparta's response. He is said to have assessed that Sparta would be the stronger at sea, presumably on the basis of superior seamanship. Numerically, however, the opposition would be very substantial. He suggested that the new king, Agesilaos, be put at the head of land forces and, on the king's agreement, 6,000 allied troops and 2,000 freed *helots* were assembled. In addition, thirty Spartiatai, including Lysander, were selected to accompany Agesilaos to act as advisers and officers (Xen. *Hell.* III. 4. 2).

Xenophon also gives an additional reason for Lysander's desire to go to Asia. He saw the opportunity to re-establish the oligarchies that he had set up in the cities at the close of the Peloponnesian War and which had been dismantled by the *ephors* of the time. To do so would give him additional influence to counterbalance that of King Pausanias and those of his persuasion.

The start of the expedition began inauspiciously. In making a sacrifice reminiscent of Agamemnon's at Aulis before setting out for Troy, Agesilaos found the ceremony disrupted by horsemen sent by the chief magistrates of Boiotia. Agesilaos is described as being greatly angered (Xen. *Hell.* III. 4. 4) but the reason for the action is given clarity in Plutarch's *Life of Agesilaos*. In the Boiotian tradition such a sacrifice on their soil should have been carried out by the Boiotian official designated for the purpose. Agesilaos had contravened this custom by having his own seer officiate. Although the incident seems trivial when compared with the larger scenario, it serves Xenophon well to give evidence of the continuing fractious relationship between Sparta and Thebes.

On arrival at Ephesos, Tissaphernes sought a truce so that Agesilaos' proposals that the Greek cities in Asia should have their independence could be sent to the king. Xenophon makes it clear (*Hell.* III. 4. 7) that Tissaphernes arranged the truce so that additional forces could be sent to him, and also that Agesilaos was aware of his attempt to deceive. He was happy to take the time of the truce to integrate his newly arrived force with those Spartan-led troops already in Asia. Time was also needed to settle local political misgivings which had been aroused by the changing edicts of the *ephors*. Significantly, on his arrival in Asia, Agesilaos demanded greater direct participation in the war from the Greek cities of Asia Minor.

The return of Lysander to Asia Minor proved so popular that the relationship between Agesilaos and Lysander was soured. Petitioners went first to Lysander rather than to the king and he appeared to enjoy far more influence than Agesilaos. The king had to take firm measures to assert his authority. He did this by refusing any petition brought to him by Lysander on behalf of another, and removing him from the immediate vicinity by sending him to the Hellespontine area. Lysander eventually returned to Greece at the end of the year, leaving Agesilaos with his influence and leadership unchallenged.

With the arrival of additional forces, Tissaphernes now openly threatened Agesilaos with war unless he and his forces left Asia. Unperturbed, Agesilaos made arrangements as if he was about to invade Karia. Apart from the river plain of the Maiander, this area was not wholly suitable for cavalry. It was this factor, together with the received intelligence that Agesilaos had arranged for cities to the south of Ephesos on the route to Karia to be contacted to provide markets, which led Tissaphernes to place his infantry in Karia. As already indicated, the terrain there was not appropriate for cavalry operations and Tissaphernes led his numerous cavalry into the plain of Maiander near the northern border of Karia, where it could be more effectively deployed.

Agesilaos, however, went in the opposite direction, unopposed for much of the time, capturing cities and gathering booty as he went. No details of his route are given except for the report of a small cavalry action near Daskyleion. Using that clue, we can surmise that he had campaigned up to and within Hellespontine Phrygia, the satrapy of Pharnabazos.

Although brief, the description of that cavalry engagement proves highly informative. Agesilaos' cavalry were in advance of the main body and had gone to the crest of a hill to survey what lay ahead. It so chanced that a cavalry force of Pharnabazos commanded by his brother, Bageios, and Rathines had taken the same decision from the opposite direction. The two groups faced each other at a distance of about 400 feet. The Greeks were formed up in a phalanx and the barbarians in a deep column with a front of twelve. It was the Persians who charged first. The following sentences are significant: 'When they came to a hand-to-hand encounter, all the Greeks who struck anyone broke their spears, while the barbarians, being armed with javelins of cornel-wood, speedily killed twelve men and two horses. Thereupon the Greeks were turned to flight' (Xen. *Hell*. III. 4. 14).

The shorter weapon with a stronger shaft is noted to have proved the better technology. Persia was renowned at this time for its effective cavalry arm.

Agesilaos came up with his infantry to retrieve the situation and the Persians suffered one casualty. On the following day, at the usual daily sacrifice, livers without lobes indicated an inauspicious outcome unless operations were changed. He therefore abandoned the expedition and returned to the coast. He was also persuaded by the event that, unless he acquired an effective cavalry arm, he would be unable to take the offensive in the plains: 'he resolved that this (*the cavalry*) must be provided, so that he might not have to carry on a skulking warfare' (Xen. *Hell*. III. 4. 15). From this comment by Xenophon, who was serving in a position of command under Agesilaos, we have the firm indication that the king was seeking to move wholly to the offensive.

With this in mind, he made it the responsibility of the richest men within his protectorate to produce horses, with the proviso that, if the men themselves were not serving, they were to provide a fully equipped rider in their place. In late winter, the army gathered again at Ephesos and training was undertaken for all contingents. Prizes were given to all who excelled, and the whole city was given over to munitions manufacture. Morale improved, particularly when Agesilaos ordered captured Persians to be sold naked at the slave markets. As those to be displayed in this way are described as being: 'white-skinned because they never were without their clothing, and soft and unused to toil because they always rode in carriages, [the Greeks] came to the conclusion that the war would be in no way different from having to fight with women' (Xen. *Hell*. III. 4. 19).

Obviously, Agesilaos was highly selective of those men chosen to be displayed. Sparta had attempted to conclude an alliance with the ruler of Egypt, who was in revolt from the Persian Empire. He, in turn, had gifted a large quantity of grain and equipment for a hundred triremes. Meanwhile, a revolt had occurred in Rhodes where the ruling oligarchs were replaced by democrats.[1] Konon is reputed to have given assistance in this change of governance that lost Rhodes as an ally of Sparta and a base for its fleet. Konon had gathered additional ships for his fleet and forced the convoy of grain and naval equipment on route from Egypt to Sparta to land their cargoes at Rhodes (Diod. XIV. 79. 7).

With a newly formed cavalry of worth, and all sections of the army in a state of readiness and high morale, the king made it known that he 'would immediately lead them by the shortest route to the best parts of the country' (Xen. *Hell*. III. 4. 20).

Tissaphernes again came to the wrong conclusion. He assumed that Agesilaos had announced this intention with the purpose of misleading him and that, this time, his true goal was the invasion of Karia. Once more he positioned his forces in the areas they had occupied during the previous year: the infantry in northern Karia and the cavalry in the plain of the Maiander River. Whether this was sheer accident and luck for Agesilaos is debatable. He had maintained the initiative since his arrival, done nothing precipitate, and it is highly likely that he was purposely providing misinformation to his enemy. Now, with Tissaphernes with his cavalry to the south, he went north from Ephesos, them east into the plain of Sardis.

So far the account of these years has been based mainly on the evidence of Xenophon. Now, consideration must be given to sources that are in conflict with his evidence, particularly in relation to the Battle of Sardis. These are to be found in Diodoros and *Hellenica Oxyrhynchia*.[2] The differences seem to outweigh the similarities so greatly that the differing descriptions seem more to suggest two separate engagements. Only an agreement on the approximate location of the battle may lead us to believe that the two contrasting versions describe the same conflict. The differences concern the tactics, the direction of the Greek response in terms of attack, the route taken by Agesilaos, and the participating forces.

Starting with the version found in the work of the Oxyrhinchos historian,[3] which was followed by Diodoros (*Oxy.* XI. 3–XII. 1 and Diod. XIV. 80. 1–5), we find Agesilaos advancing through the river plain, taking plunder as he went. Tissaphernes followed with a large force of cavalry and infantry. In Diodoros 10,000 cavalry and 50,000 infantry are given but he is notorious for exaggerating numbers. The text of the *Oxyrhynchia* is incomplete at this point but the size of the Persian force would have been considerably larger than that of Agesilaos. The Persians cut off any Greeks separated from the main body when seeking plunder.

Diodoros claims that Agesilaos organised his men in a 'square'. This is no doubt a reference to the 'hollow square' formation in which the baggage and light troops marched within the protection of hoplites. Despite recording the formation as having been adopted until Agesilaos could attack his pursuers, Diodoros follows this by saying that the plundering continued even up to the environs of the city of Sardis where Agesilaos 'turned back'. Early in the return journey he sent Xenokles ahead with a force of 1,400 men to set up an ambush in a wooded area. The following morning Agesilaos broke camp and marched until he had passed the ambush point. The enemy continued harassing his rearguard in no sort of order and Agesilaos turned his army to face the Persians. Having engaged, he signalled to those in ambush to make their attack on the Persian rear. The Persians broke and fled and were pursued, suffering 6,000 dead and the capture of 'a multitude of prisoners' (Diod. XIV. 80. 4). The Persian camp was taken and pillaged. Again, Diodoros exaggerates numbers, for his source, the Oxyrhynchos historian, describes Persian losses as 600 dead.

Xenophon's version starts with the claim that Agesilaos took the shortest route to the best parts of the country. While this does not go against the possibility that it is in agreement with the Oxyrhynchos historian and Diodoros, it could provide an alternative route that did not follow the Kayster River. The Greek army travelled for three days without opposition, taking what they chose from the area. The following day saw the cavalry of the Persians make contact. Their general had ordered his baggage train to cross the Paktolos River and make camp. This put them on the opposite bank to that of the Greeks. The Persians killed a considerable number of the Greek camp followers engaged in gathering plunder before Agesilaos ordered his cavalry to go their rescue. The Persians are described as forming 'an opposing line, with very many companies of their horsemen' (Xen. *Hell*. III. 4. 22).

Agesilaos saw also that the Persian cavalry, although large, had no supporting forces. Herein lies a key element. The purpose of the cavalry pursuit would have been to make contact with the Greek army and slow its advance until the Persian infantry could join them. Persian cavalry was highly effective and in such numbers that it could limit the damage that a marauding army could achieve. The fact that Agesilaos made his response immediately on seeing the lack of supporting arms to the Persian cavalry indicates that he was well aware of the fact that the Persian infantry would take some time to join them.

Agesilaos moved his phalanx forward and ordered his cavalry to attack with the support of the first ten-year classes of hoplites running together with the peltasts in close support. He followed on behind with the main body. Initially the Persians sustained the attack of the enemy cavalry but were routed when the other Greek forces came to contact. Pinned down against the river, some tried to cross it but were killed, while the remainder managed to effect an escape to Sardis. The Persian camp was taken and some peltasts set about looting it. However, Agesilaos saw to it that his army surrounded the whole camp so that all booty, to the value of seventy talents, could return with him to Greece. Thereafter, Agesilaos led his army south from Sardis, bypassing the plain of the Kayster and taking plunder from the plain of the river Maiander.

The knowledge that Xenophon was on this expedition gives his version the greater credibility. Another difference between the sources lies in the fact that Tissaphernes is described as commanding the Persians in the field in the

Oxyrhynchos/Diodoros account whereas, in Xenophon, he was in Sardis at the time of the battle.

Such was the anger of the Great King and so great his suspicion that Tissaphernes was culpable of causing the ongoing difficulties that he sent Tithraustes to take his place. Tithraustes arrested and beheaded Tissaphernes.[4] The new satrap made a peace offer to Agesilaos, offering autonomy to the Greek Asian cities if he withdrew from Asia Minor. It was agreed that, until news was received from Sparta, Agesilaos would stay in Asia Minor, removing his forces from Tithraustes' satrapy and carrying on campaigning in Hellespontine Phrygia. He was assisted in his enterprise by a gift of thirty talents from the satrap for provisions.

It may come as a surprise to some readers that one commanding satrap within a supposedly unified empire would acquiesce to another satrapy being attacked. This is to discount the growing rivalry between those courtiers who had been sent out to administer a province. So long as they raised the annual tribute required of them, the satraps were left much to their own devices and showed little concern for their neighbouring colleagues. As alluded to earlier, personal ambition was to bring about a spate of satrap rebellions in the middle of the fourth century.

Agesilaos' campaign in Phrygia was wide ranging. It is difficult to perceive an overall strategy other than to cause extreme discomfort for Pharnabazos. Agesilaos is not reported as having with him siege engines, and Xenophon's comment that he 'gained possession of cities, some by force, others by their voluntary surrender' (Xen. *Hell*. IV. 1. 1) does not wholly convince. The reason for the doubt lies with the elaborate description of the training and manufacture of armaments made the previous winter in Ephesos in which mention of such engines would have been expected. Xenophon's enthusiasm is not matched by the description of Agesilaos' activities at this time by the Oxyrhychos historian.

Nonetheless, there can be no doubt that Agesilaos caused serious discomfort to the Great King. The loss of revenue, first from Tissaphernes' satrapy and then from that of Pharnabazos was causing much more than local annoyance. Hellespontine Phrygia suffered severe depredation and Pharnabazos could do little to stop it. Agesilaos had received news from Sparta giving him licence to continue as he thought fit, and was given authority over the fleet. He now had an unprecedented command on both land and sea. He ordered additional triremes to be built by coastal and island cities, resulting in an increase of 120 vessels to the fleet. This was to counter the threat posed by the gathering of 300 or more triremes in Phoenicia at Persia's command. Agesilaos appointed his brother-in-law Peisander as its commander, and he supervised the preparations while Agesilaos was on campaign. Had Lysander not returned to Sparta, he would have been the obvious candidate for the position of *navarch*.

One foray was much more extended than its predecessors and attracted additional support as it progressed. The route taken is debatable. Through the good offices of a certain Spithridates, who had earlier been brought by Lysander to Agesilaos, an alliance was made with Otys, king of Paphlagonia, a semi-independent region adjacent to Phrygia, who supplied peltasts and cavalry to Agesilaos.

Little opposition was met on Agesilaos' campaign; rather, opportune attempts to cause the Greek army discomfort are reported in our sources. One such occasion occurred near Pharnabazos' headquarters at Daskyleion. The villages in its area were looted and winter quarters were set up by Agesilaos. Foraging continued without hindrance until Pharnabazos attacked groups of men with a force made up of two chariots and 400 cavalry. About 700 Greeks gathered together but were scattered by the scythed chariots before they could come into any sort of order. Persian cavalry rode down nearly 100 men, the remainder seeking refuge with the main army (Xen. *Hell.* IV. 1. 17–19). Soon after, Spithridates gained knowledge of where the enemy had made camp. Herippidas, a Spartiate, made a successful raid upon it, and much booty was taken, though the astute Pharnabazos made his escape, along with many of his followers. Herippidas then made a cardinal error in his treatment of the Asian allies. He saw to it that all the plunder they had collected was taken from them and added to that collected by the Greeks. This was designated to be passed on to those appointed to sell it. Feeling bitter and dishonoured by this action, Spithridates and the Paphlagonians left during the night and made their way to Sardis, where they placed themselves in the hands of Ariaios. They hoped that Ariaios would intercede for them. Ariaios had served under Kyros the Younger but defected to Artaxerxes after the Battle of Kounaxa and had been forgiven his initial disloyalty. This was the first and only loss of Asian allies sustained by Agesilaos.

For some inexplicable reason, Agesilaos passed through the difficult country of Mysian Olympos and came to terms with the local inhabitants. There were alternative easier routes but, having chosen to pass this way, Agesilaos found his rearguard attacked and sustained fifty or so casualties. Seemingly the Oxyrhynchos historian has a liking for stratagems and describes an ambush in reprisal (*Oxy.*

XXI. 2–3). The following day, Agesilaos left some of the mercenaries who had served with Kyros in a position of ambush and continued on his way with the main force. The Mysians, thinking they could repeat their success, set off in pursuit, only to be attacked in their turn by those in ambush. Having sustained 130 casualties and taken up their dead under truce, the Mysians no longer caused problems for the Greeks.

At *Hell.* IV. 1. 32–3, Xenophon reports a meeting under truce between Agesilaos and Pharnabazos. The latter reminded the king of the unswerving service he had given to Sparta in the last phase of the Peloponnesian War and asked him if the damage Agesilaos was causing to his satrapy was an honourable response by Spartans to the support and favours earlier received from him. This proved effective and the Spartans present felt shamed. Agesilaos then asked him to become an ally, but Pharnabazos replied, 'if the King sends another as general and makes me his subordinate, I shall choose to be your friend and ally; but if he assigns the command to me, so strong – it seems, is the power of ambition – you may be well assured that I shall war upon you to the best of my ability.' At this, Agesilaos acknowledged the honour of Pharnabazos and undertook to leave the satrap's territory and avoid making future attacks upon it so long as there were other targets at hand.

Some may wonder what all this marching through Asia Minor was achieving. A closer look at the circumstances facing Agesilaos on his arrival to the area may suggest a reason. Despite the successes of Derkylidas, he faced the problem of turning the timid population of the Greek cities into viable allies. He needed the additional manpower. This required training, the building of morale and campaign experience that would bring with it a realistic appreciation of the likely opposition for the newly recruited men. All this took time and, to his credit, Agesilaos was successful in all of his targets. He constructed a strong and growing army, with each of its successes in the field bringing ever-greater confidence. Xenophon's claim that the king was planning a major offensive into the interior is believable.

Matters moved on apace. Tithraustes now realised that Agesilaos was intending to stay in Asia. In typical Persian manner he sent a Rhodian called Timokrates with fifty talents of silver to mainland Greece with the intention of fomenting problems nearer to home for the Spartans. With anti-Spartan factions in the ascendancy, Thebes, Korinth and Argos accepted the monies and set about persuading others to their opinion. Xenophon claims that Athens received no financial inducement but was eager to take this opportunity to reassert its ascendancy (Xen. *Hell.* III. 5. 2).

Probably not unconnected with this move was the arrangement for the Athenian Konon to travel to the interior for an audience with the Great King. Tithraustes had given him 220 talents to settle the overdue pay for the men of his fleet who were near revolt, and arranged a war-chest of 700 talents at Sardis (*Oxy.* XIX. 2–3). Konon had successfully evaded the Spartan fleets for the nine years since his escape from Lysander's devastating attack on the Athenian fleet at Aigospotami. Not daring to return to Athens for fear of being tried and executed as some of his predecessors had been, Konon continued to ply the seas with his growing fleet, causing the Spartans occasional annoyance as already noted in the case of the island of Rhodes. According to Diodoros (XIV. 81. 4–6), Konon was well received by the Great King and given joint command of the fleet with any Persian of his choosing. His choice fell on Pharnabazos. It is more likely, however, that Pharnabazos was Artaxerxes' selected commander and Konon was to be co commander.

Back in mainland Greece, a territorial dispute arose between Phokis and Lokris, reputed to have been engineered by the Thebans. Thebes made the most of the opportunity to create problems for Sparta's ally Phokis by impeding the possibility of any arbitration to settle the matter (*Oxy.* XVIII. 2–4). We are given more detail in the *Hellenika Oxyrhynchos* than in our other available sources. The Thebans overran Phokis and ravaged the countryside but achieved little success in attacks on several towns and, in the attempt on Hyampolis, which had strong defences, they lost eighty men. However, damage to crops and outlying properties must have been considerable.

Sparta's firm reaction was to raise two armies. Lysander was sent with a small force to Phokis, where he made further musters and summoned other allies from central Greece. King Pausanias marched north with an army from the Peloponnese with the intention of making a junction with Lysander's army near Haliartos for a joint attack on that city. Thebes' influence in Boiotia was not as secure as it would have liked and its rival, Orchomenos, was won over to the Spartan side by Lysander.

The sources supply varied detail but are generally in agreement. Diodoros' account is brief. Plutarch, in his *Life of Lysander* (28), recounts that Pausanias was expected to enter Boiotia from the direction of Mount Kithairon, with Lysander marching south towards their target. On his way Lysander is claimed to have ravaged Lebadeia and to have sent a message to Pausanias telling (not requesting) him to make the march from Plataia to Haliartos, where he intended to arrive himself at daybreak. The message is said to have been intercepted and taken to Thebes.[5] A force of their new Athenian allies was entrusted with the defence of Thebes while the Thebans themselves marched to Haliartos. Arriving there before Lysander, they sent part of their forces into the town.

Xenophon treats the episode at some length in a balanced and credible manner. Chapter 5 of Book III is almost entirely dedicated to the Spartan–Theban conflict. The *ephors* sent Lysander to Phokis, ordering him to go to Haliartos and to take with him Phokians, Oetaions, Malians, Ainians and Herakleiots. These last would come from the colony set up by the Spartans during the Peloponnesian War near the Malian Gulf. Pausanias, as king, is described clearly as the intended commander-in-chief and was to appear at Haliartos on an agreed day.

In addition to following his instructions, Lysander was successful in detaching Orchomenos from Thebes. Meantime, Pausanias waited at Tegea while Peloponnesian allies gathered. The anti-Spartan leaders, Ismenias and Androkleidas in Thebes (the names are taken from the Oxyrhynchos historian) who had instigated the Phokian/Lokrian problem, sent representatives to Athens. There, the assembly was persuaded to support them against the Spartans and it was Thrasyboulos[6] who passed the decision to the ambassadors.

Pausanias moved north into Boiotia. Of the Spartan allies, Korinth refused to take part and it is possible that Sparta already knew of Athens' defection. Lysander arrived at Haliartos ahead of Pausanias and instead of waiting for the king's arrival approached the wall of Haliartos, arguing that if it was to revolt from the Thebans it would have its independence. He was obviously unaware of an allied presence in the town and it was this that probably persuaded the Haliartans to remain loyal. Their refusal of Lysander's offer was followed by an attack on the walls by Lysander. It is likely that, from their elevated positions on the walls, the defenders were aware of approaching Theban forces and resisted until the relief force came up and engaged Lysander's army. Xenophon's comment, 'Whether it was that they fell upon Lysander unawares, or that he saw them coming and nevertheless stood his ground in the belief that he would be victorious, is uncertain,' leaves us to wonder that Lysander seemed unaware of the position of opposition forces when, under the circumstances, their presence nearby would have been expected.

Lysander lost his life and his army was routed. In the pursuit the Thebans suffered significant losses when their opposition, having reached higher and rougher ground, turned on them and drove them from the incline with a mixture of missiles and stones rolled down the hill. The Theban loss of 200 men equated with those they had inflicted on their enemy during the battle.

More may lie behind the events than is directly mentioned in our sources. Lysander was known to be a careful commander. During the latter part of the Peloponnesian War he had carefully prepared financial support for his Aegean fleet and seen that it was well manned and eminently seaworthy. He had avoided conflict unless he was sure that the possibility of success was heavily weighted in his favour. However, there was a character flaw. His appalling behaviour when passing the command to Kallikratidas at the end of his year's tenure of the office of *navarch* could well have endangered eventual Spartan success. His pique at this juncture, and the impediments that he put in place to discomfort his successor,[7] served to signal that he was possibly more concerned about his own glory than the success of the state he served (Xen. *Hell*. I. 6. 1–12). There was evidence of enmity between Lysander and Pausanias dating back to 403 BC (Xen. *Hell*. II. 4. 29), at the time of the struggle between the democrats and the oligarchs. The king's intervention and his actions that saw the eventual return of democracy to Athens replaced the tyranny of the Thirty that had been set up by Lysander. Pausanias had been supported in his policy by the two accompanying *ephors* who were, obviously, in disagreement with the existing policy of Lysander (Xen. *Hell*. II. 4. 36). This, together with the replacement of the arrangements made by Lysander in his settlement of the cities of the former Athenian Aegean empire, would not sit well with Lysander.

Lysander, arriving earlier than Pausanias at Haliartos, did not wait for him as arranged. It is not inconceivable that he was seeking to settle matters himself before the king's appearance and thereby be able to claim total credit for the operation.

There followed the arrival of Pausanias. This, too, seems to have been unexpected by his enemies. One would have expected the presence or movements of large numbers of men to be detected early enough for countermeasures to be taken. Pausanias did not advance upon them immediately, as might have been expected. No reason is given, and on the following day, with the arrival of Athenian hoplites, the Thebans formed up with them in battle line.

28

Pausanias discussed the option of joining battle or recovering the dead under truce with his fellow Spartiatai.[8] The decision to adopt the latter course was taken on the following grounds:

> Considering that Lysander was dead and that the army under his command
> had been defeated *and was gone*, while the Korinthians had altogether refused
> to accompany them and those who had come were not serving with any spirit;
> considering also the matter of horsemen, that the enemy's were numerous while
> their own were few, and, most important of all, that the bodies lay close up to the
> wall, so that even in the case of victory it would not be easy to recover them on
> account of the men upon the towers. (Xen. *Hell*. III. 5. 23; emphasis added)

The phrase 'and was gone' indicates that the survivors of the beaten army of Lysander had not stayed in the vicinity. They had presumably fled homeward. It is obvious that the original Spartan plan was that action would be taken after the junction of the two forces. Without the presence of this force, and taken together with the other reasons given, Pausanias was probably correct in his decision. His reward, however, was that he was summoned to trial on a capital charge. He did not appear to answer the charges against him, but fled to Tegea, where he remained in exile, reputedly writing a revision of the Spartan constitution. At the trial he was condemned to death in his absence.

Those in Sparta would not be wholly unaware of the contrasting opinions of Pausanias and Lysander. Whether the differences went further and were also personal is unknown. The command of an army was always in the hands of one of the kings, should he be present. Had Pausanias arrived before Lysander's abortive attack, Lysander could well have been alive for several years more. As it was, allowing a junction of the two forces would have put Lysander in a position subordinate to the king. We can only guess whether Pausanias was late or that Lysander, having arrived earlier, chose to make an attempt on the city so that, if successful, plaudits would be reserved for him alone. In the final analysis, Pausanias was tried in his absence on three charges. The first, for arriving at Haliartos later than Lysander, the second, that he had not given battle to recover the dead, and had acquired them under truce. Planned junctions of forces could never be guaranteed,[9] and we have already seen the cogent reasons for Pausanias' non-engagement. The third charge shows the latent resentment still festering, some eight years after the event: that Pausanias had come to an accommodation with the Athenian democrats when he could have destroyed them in Peiraeios in 403 BC (Xen. *Hell.* II. 4. 29–39). This last action had been approved by the *ephors* and the assembly at Sparta. They had sent a commission of fifteen Spartans to assist Pausanias in making a final settlement between the democrats and the oligarchs at Athens. Despite this official endorsement at the time, in 395 BC those of Lysander's persuasion were in the ascendant and were petty enough to allow this matter to resurface in their desire for revenge. At the heart of the issue, given further evidence, overweening pride lies behind Lysander's precipitate action (see Appendix 1).

The consequences of Haliartos should not be underestimated. Sparta had competent commanders, but to lose three in just under two years was a serious matter, particularly when two of them, Agis and Pausanias, were kings, and Pausanias' successor was underage.

The major consequence of this disastrous incident was the recall of Agesilaos from Asia Minor.

Endnotes

1 P. R. McKechnie and S. J. Kern (trans.), *Hellenica Oxyrhynchia,* Warminster, Aris & Phillips, 1988, XV. 1–3; thereafter referred to as *Oxy.*

2 The unknown author of the *Hellenica Oxyrhynchia* was a fourth-century historian. Fragments of papyri were discovered in Egypt from 1906 onwards, and it is always hoped that others will come to light. Whereas Plutarch follows the text of Xenophon, Diodoros follows that of the *Oxyrhynchos* historian. The differences found between the two traditions caused doubts to be raised about the integrity of Xenophon's account. While admitting the bias and possible over-statement of Agesilaos' intentions while in Asia, the fact that Xenophon was campaigning with the king and derived his material at first hand must tip the balance in support of his account of the Battle of Sardis. The *Oxyrhynchos Hellenica,* however, provides us with information not covered in Xenophon's *Hellenika,* notably the Theban Constitution and an alternative treatment of the Battle of Notion in the Peloponnesian War. Where the *Oxyrhynchia* is more secure in chronology than Xenophon is in the treatment of activities on the Greek mainland just prior to the Korinthian War.

3 McKechnie and Kern.

4 For detailed analyses of the Battle of Sardis, see J. K. Anderson, 'The Battle of Sardis in 395 BC', *California Studies in Classical Antiquity,* vol. 7 (1974), pp. 27–53, and V. J. Gray, '*Two different approaches to the Battle of Sardis in 395 BC*', *California Studies in Classical Antiquity,* vol. 12 (1979), pp. 183–200.

5 The two commanders must have prearranged the meeting place of the two armies in

Sparta before they left. The intercepted message, if indeed it existed, may have been necessary because Lysander had completed his preparations earlier than expected.

6   Thrasyboulos was a prominent Athenian commander during the latter part of the Peloponnesian War. He was instrumental in ridding Athens of the oligarchy of the Thirty and later served Athens well in the northern Aegean before his violent death near Aspendos in 389 BC.

7   See Godfrey Hutchinson, *Attrition: Aspects of Command in the Peloponnesian War*, Stroud, Spellmount, 2006, pp. 194–5.

8   With reference to the retrieval of the dead see P. Vaughn, 'The identification and retrieval of the Hoplite dead', in V. D. Hanson, (ed.), *Hoplites: The Classical Greek Battle Experience*, New York and London, Routledge, 1991.

9   In 423 BC, the Athenian generals Demosthenes and Hippokrates devised a plan to divide the forces of Boiotia with the aid of sympathetic Boiotians. Land forces under Hippokrates were to proceed north to Delion, and Demosthenes was to sail to Syphai in southern Boiotia with forces gathered from Akarnania and Naupaktos. An error was made on the agreed date of the start of operations. This, together with the plan being betrayed to the Spartans, who, in turn, informed their Boiotian allies, led to the Athenian defeat at Delion by the undivided forces of Boiotia. See Thucydides IV. 89.

CHAPTER 3

The Nemea

Up in freeborn hardihood,
Soldiers born of Spartan blood!
Guard your left with shields a-swinging;
High the gallant spear-shafts flinging.
Hoard not life nor stint to pay:
Such was never Sparta's way.

Tyrtaios; C. M. Bowra trans.

BOIOTIAN SUCCESS AT HALIARTOS IN 395 BC emboldened those states that held grievances against Sparta and set in train a sequence of events that led to a formidable coalition of the most powerful city-states in opposition to Sparta. They were likely to have been negotiating with each other heartened by the monies from Persia mentioned in the previous chapter. Xenophon (*Hell.* IV. 2. 1) notes the formation of the alliance, but Diodoros gives more detail from IV. 82. The four main powers, Thebes, Athens, Argos and Korinth, set up a joint council at the Isthmos of Korinth with the intention of prosecuting hostilities against Sparta. Their first measure was an attempt to detach allies of Sparta from their adherence to the Peloponnesian League. They were successful in adding all the cities of Euboia, the Leukadians, Akarnanians, Ambrakiots and Chalkidians to their number, but were unable to persuade other states geographically within the Peloponnese.

The council of allies at Korinth appears to have been a permanent institution throughout hostilities. With its early aims achieved, although the chronology cannot be confirmed, it is likely that it was at this time that the council responded to a call for assistance from Medios of Larissa against Lykophron of Pherai. The council committed 2,000 Argive and Boiotian hoplites under Ismenias, the Theban general. With their assistance Medios captured Pharsalos in southern Thessaly, overcoming the Spartan garrison there. Leaving Medios in possession of Pharsalos, Ismenias led his forces further south and captured the Spartan colony of Herakleia in Trachis. This was achieved by treachery. Certain of the inhabitants facilitated the troops' entry to the town at night and, once within the walls they selectively massacred the Lakedaimonians while other Peloponnesians were permitted to leave with such belongings as they could carry. This was done, no doubt, in an attempt to foster goodwill in those states still within the Peloponnesian League in the hope that they might consider switching alliance.

Herakleia was resettled by Trachinians, and a section of the Argives remained as a garrison. In what was to prove to be a cleansing of Spartan influence in Thessaly and central Greece, Ismenias went on (according to Diodoros) to persuade the neighbouring Ainianians and Athamanians to secede from their support of Sparta. He is purported to have then recruited nearly 6,000 additional troops from the immediate area and possibly from Lokris further south. It was just as well that he did, as a Phokian army under the command of the Spartan Alkisthenes arrived on the scene. After a battle for which we are given no details of the action, Ismenias proved to be the victor.

Matters were going well for the alliance at Korinth. They had control of the Isthmos entry to the Peloponnese and proceeded to amass troops there early in 394 BC. Sparta had not been idle while this new threat developed. Hearing that its new enemies had received Persian monies, Sparta sent messages to Agesilaos in Asia Minor to return to the aid of the homeland. Naturally this proved a great disappointment to him but, being a loyal servant of the constitution, he immediately set about making arrangements to respond to his recall. Xenophon suggests that just prior to the receipt of his instructions from Sparta, Agesilaos was preparing a spring offensive against the heart of the Persian Empire (Xen. *Hell.* IV. 1. 41). He had, after all, disrupted contact between the western satraps and their suzerain. If the substance of Xenophon's claim is true, this may account for the vehemence of Agesilaos' attitude and actions against Thebes from this time on.

In Spartan eyes the need to recall Agesilaos was pressing. Sparta recognised the difficulties that could arise in fighting on two fronts. As Pausanias was now living in exile, his underage son, Agesipolis, who had succeeded to the throne of the Agiadai, was not eligible for this duty. That role now fell to his guardian, Aristodemos.

After appointing Euxinos as governor and leaving a force of 4,000 with him in Asia Minor, Agesilaos (Xen. *Hell*. IV. 2. 5) set out on his return to Sparta with a considerable force. At about the same time the presiding *ephor*s at Sparta called the ban to assemble their forces (Xen. *Hell*. IV. 2. 9) for a march to the Isthmos.

There, the position of the alliance appeared to be extremely strong but could soon be the subject of assault from two armies approaching from two directions. This realisation made it clear that action must take the place of prevarication and merely waiting for additions to their forces.

When news arrived of the Spartan mobilisation, the alliance at Korinth was already discussing tactics for the coming engagement. At one of its sessions a certain Korinthian, Timolaos, outlined an enlightened proposal to his colleagues that is fully reported by Xenophon, who obviously recognised the merit in his argument (Xen. *Hell*. IV. 2. 11–13). Timolaos urged the allies to advance immediately with the intention of bringing the Spartans to battle, either within Lakedaimon itself, or as near to the Spartan homeland as possible. If the alliance adopted this course of action the Spartans would not be able to add to their strength as they moved north, picking up allies on the way. He likened the Lakedaimonians to a river that is small at its source but grows in power as it proceeds. Similarly, a nest of wasps is best dealt with when all the insects are in the nest rather than to attack it when they are already outside their home. His suggestion was adopted by all in the assembly. However, despite time being of the essence for a successful outcome to be achieved in the plan, they squandered any advantages they may have had by going on to discuss, at considerable length, matters ranging from the depth and consequent length of the phalanx when in battle line, to the question of leadership.

Meantime, the inexorable advance of the Spartans continued, with significant additions to their forces as they proceeded north through allied territories. The tactical discussions of their enemy had taken so much time that, although the allliance had eventually marched south to reach Nemea, the Spartans were already at Sikyon to their north-west. On discovering this, the coalition army fell back towards Korinth, sending their light-armed troops towards Sikyon in the hope of harrying and slowing the Spartan advance. Indeed, as Spartans and their allies moved east towards Korinth, they were subject to missile attack on their right unshielded side from these light-armed troops on higher ground and suffered significantly. The attacks continued until the Spartans eluded their tormentors by moving down to the coastal plain, wreaking great damage as they went. Aristodemos, the young king's guardian, commanded the Spartan army.

It has been persuasively established[1] that the battlefield was on the plain between two watercourses. Between Sikyon and Korinth there are three riverbeds: Asopos, the largest near Sikyon, then, to the east, the Nemea, and near Korinth, the smallest, Longopotamos. The coalition forces had, by this time, established camp on the Korinthian side of the last named watercourse, using it as a natural defence for their position. The Spartans, having crossed the Nemea, set up camp a little over a mile away (Xen. *Hell.* IV. 2. 15 has ten stadia) from their enemy.

Xenophon goes on to enumerate the strengths of the opposing sides and begins his lists with hoplite numbers. Beginning with the Spartan army, Xenophon suggests there were around 6,000 Lakedaimonian hoplites. This means that five *morai* were present. We have no evidence of how many age groups were called for service by the Spartan ban but, in these worrying times, it is likely to have been thirty-five of the forty year groups, which would give each *mora* 1,120 men and a total of 5,600 hoplites. Adding to that figure the 300 *hippeis* (royal guard), we arrive at a figure of 5,900 heavy foot-soldiers. A total of 3,000 Eleans were present with their immediate neighbours being the Tryphylians, Akrorians and Lasionians, 3,000 Epidaurians, Troezenians, and Halians and Hermionians, and 1,500 Sykonians. No numbers are given for the Tegeates or Mantineians despite Xenophon indicating at *Hell.* IV. 2. 13 that their contingents joined the Spartans on the march north. Further, the Tegeates are specifically mentioned in the battle line adjacent to the Spartans and facing four of the Athenian tribes (Xen. *Hell.* IV. 2. 19). This suggests that around 2,500 Tegeates were present and, with Mantineia able to field an even larger number, the total from the two states could have been 6,000 hoplites. Diodoros (XIV. 83. 1–2) is unhelpful in his very brief mention of the battle. A further contingent from Pellene is mentioned at Xen. *Hell.* IV. 2. 20, but this is unlikely to have numbered more than 500 hoplites and faced the men of Thespiai. Total numbers for the Achaians including the Sikyonians may well have been 3,000, described as being directly opposite the Boiotians in the battle itself.

A necessary digression is needed at this point. Although the combined numbers of the Achaians seem too few (*c.*3,000) to face the 5,000 Boiotians, Xenophon (*Hell.* IV. 2. 18) notes that the depth of sixteen agreed upon by the coalition for the overall phalanx was unilaterally greatly increased in the case of the Boiotians, which would reduce the frontal length of their phalanx. At the Battle of Delion in 424 BC the Thebans had adopted a depth of twenty-five and if, at Nemea, this was the depth decided upon by the Boiotians, the front for this contingent would have been one of 200 shields. This front would have been matched by the Achaians with a phalanx with a depth of ten. However, Xenophon – like most soldiers of his day – would know of the Delion depth and it is not out of the question that his reference to the very deep formation adopted by the Boiotians implies an even greater depth than the twenty-five suggested here. After all, it was only twenty-three years later that the Thebans appeared at Leuktra with a depth of fifty ranks.

We have no evidence for the depth or depths of the Spartans and their allies. Lakedaimonian cavalry was present to the strength of around 600,[2] with 300 Kretan archers and 400 slingers. Xenophon makes mention that the men of Phleious were not present. This city, a long-term ally of Sparta, had a sacred obligation elsewhere at that time and its absence from conflict was perfectly acceptable under a holy truce. Time after time such occasions are reported in our sources, demonstrating the piety of the Greek world and its capacity to give priority to this aspect of life.

The coalition forces were made up of 6,000 Athenian, 7,000 Argive, 5,000 Boiotian, 3,000 Korinthian and 3,000 Euboian hoplites. They fielded a strong cavalry consisting of 800 Boiotians, 600 Athenians, 100 Chalkidians and fifty from Opuntian Lokris. Numbers are not given for the light-armed troops from Korinth, Ozolian Lokris, Malia and Akarnania but Xenophon hints that they were substantial. He also remarks that the forces of Orchomenos, now an ally of Sparta, were absent from the Boiotian federation's contribution.

In what was to be the largest number of hoplites contesting the field up to that time the coalition hoplites approximated 24,000 as against those of Sparta and its allies at around 19,000. Given those figures, and with superior numbers of cavalry and light troops, the coalition could be assumed to have been confident, but this seems to be questioned by Xenophon at *Hell.* IV. 2. 18. There, he remarks on the reluctance of the Boiotians to contemplate battle when their position in line was to be on the left wing and directly opposite the Spartans, who always held the right wing in their armies. The inference is that each of the major coalition members held command in turn, probably on a daily basis, and that the ensuing battle was certainly not immediate. When the Boiotian time to command arrived, possibly a day later at the earliest, they immediately ordered an advance on the basis of propitious sacrifices.

Despite the shortened front of their phalanx, the unnamed Boiotian commander possibly assumed that the considerable numerical superiority of the whole army gave it room to attempt an outflanking of the enemy left. This led them gradually and purposely to move to the right as the advance proceeded.[3] Xenophon notes that the integrity of the line was preserved despite the fact that the Athenians, now on the left wing, were aware that they were at risk of suffering a similar outflanking by the Spartans.

The land between the armies is described as being overgrown and the Spartans only became aware of the enemy advance when the latter struck up the paian. This also suggests that no effective observers or lookouts were in place. There is no hint of confusion in the Spartan response. Orders were immediately given and the battle line was formed. The Spartans led off to the right in like manner to the Boiotian advance so that, just before the clash of the two armies, the Athenians found themselves significantly outflanked. Xenophon is quite specific in numbering only six, rather than the intended ten, Athenian tribes being directly opposite the Lakedaimonian right; the other four were now facing the Tegeates. The Athenian position was further exacerbated by their adoption of the agreed phalanx depth of sixteen, the Spartan line being possibly eight or twelve deep at most. Depth becomes an irrelevance when an overlap of 300 or more shields has been achieved and the distance between the two opposing forces has become only 150 yards. As was their custom, the Spartans made sacrifice to Artemis Agotera and then immediately came to battle.

On the other wing the Boiotians had achieved their objective of outflanking their opposition. The oblique advance to the right of both armies had seemingly brought advantage to each respective right wing. However, this is only part of the answer to the winning of an engagement; the outcome relies on what the commander requires next of the forces under him. Herein, the professionalism of the Lakedaimonians can be seen in sharp contrast to that of their adversaries.

Except for the brave men of Pellene who fought and held up the Thespians, all other allies of the Spartans were successfully overcome and, on breaking, were pursued from the field of battle. Even the four Athenian tribes who were opposite the Tegeates were successful in this initial part of the engagement. Those Spartans facing the Athenians had more than contained the enemy attack and those enjoying the overlap wheeled to their left to take the six Athenian tribes in flank and rear. Many Athenian casualties were sustained before the remnant was able to escape. Maintaining their formation, the Lakedaimonians swept from right to left of the battlefield, taking each now-disordered phalanx of the opposition in turn as it returned from the pursuit of Spartan allies. First the Argives, then the Korinthians and finally the Thebans were taken on their unshielded side. Such was the discipline of the Spartan phalanx that no opposition to them in this phase of the battle could be mustered.

At *Hell.* IV. 2. 22, Xenophon records that the leading *polemarch*, the commander of a *mora*, had been about to wheel again to attack the Argives frontally. He was persuaded otherwise when someone in the ranks called out to him to let the leading ranks pass by and attack the remainder in flank as they sought to escape. This made sense and avoided another wheeling manoeuvre. It also shows that, despite the great discipline of the Spartans, it was possible for subordinates to offer advice that was acted upon by their superior officers. This is reminiscent of another proffered piece of advice given to King Agis when campaigning in Mantineian territory (Thuc. V. 65. 2) during the Peloponnesian War.[4] Just such a manoeuvre as the *polemarch* almost attempted at the Nemea to face the returning enemy frontally was put into effect later that year by Agesilaos at Koroneia, but more on that later.

And so the lateral advance of the Lakedaimonians continued across the field, bringing carnage to successive enemy units. The only parts of the coalition forces to escape relatively unscathed were the four Athenian tribal regiments who had been in pursuit of the Tegeates as the Lakedaimonians swept across the field. These Athenians presumably made a safe withdrawal behind the Spartan line of advance after they had passed by in their sweep across the field. No mention is made of the Euboians in this phase of the battle and they too could well have enjoyed the same good fortune in safe withdrawal if the Spartan advance had passed across the Euboian line of escape as they returned from pursuit. If that was the case, their position in the battle line must have been adjacent and immediately to the right of the Athenians.

Casualties were considerable on both sides. Diod. XIV. 83. 2 plausibly suggests that from the Spartan-led army, 1,100 fell whereas their enemy lost 2,800. As a result of Spartan tactics, initially successful contingents of the coalition forces were decimated, while on the Spartan side their allies took a heavy beating. Of the Spartans themselves it was reported to Agesilaos, now at Amphipolis on his return from Asia Minor, that they had suffered only eight fatalities. There can be no

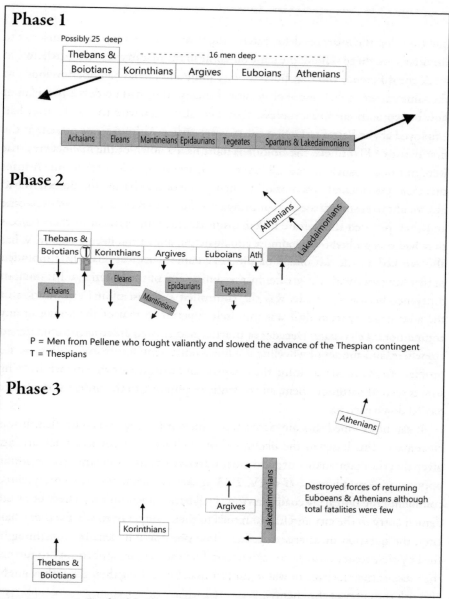

Phase 1

Possibly 25 deep

| Thebans & | - - - - - - - - - - - 16 men deep - - - - - - - - - | | | |
| Boiotians | Korinthians | Argives | Euboians | Athenians |

| Achaians | Eleans | Mantineians | Epidaurians | Tegeates | Spartans & Lakedaimonians |

Phase 2

Athenians

Lakedaimonians

| Thebans & | | | | | |
| Boiotians | T | Korinthians | Argives | Euboians | Ath |

P

| Achaians | Eleans | Epidaurians | Tegeates |

Mantineians

P = Men from Pellene who fought valiantly and slowed the advance of the Thespian contingent
T = Thespians

Phase 3

Athenians

Lakedaimonians

Argives

Destroyed forces of returning
Euboeans & Athenians although
total fatalities were few

Korinthians

Thebans &
Boiotians

BATTLE PLAN 1 *Battle of the Nemea. In Phase 1, both right wings make purposeful moves to the right to achieve an outflanking of the opposition. In phase 3, the sweep from right to left over the battlefield gave the Spartans the opportunity to take the enemy contingents in flank as they returned from the pursuit of the Spartan allies. Most casualties were sustained by Argives, Corinthians and Boiotians.*

question that the Spartans deliberately sought to outflank their enemy just as the Boiotians sought to achieve the same outcome in the first phase of the battle. What made the difference was that Boiotian discipline and tactics had not developed to the same extent as their more professional enemy. They had no developed plan of how to exploit their initial success. They were still stuck with the tactics they had employed at the Battle of Delion thirty years earlier. Although not present at the first Battle of Mantineia, the Boiotians must have known of the manoeuvres that were put opportunely in train. Unlike the Spartans, who had learnt much from this almost accidental outcome of the first phase of that battle, the Boiotians had not sought to ensure victory by adopting a similar plan. Rather, they had overcome and then pursued the defeated. Perhaps in the heat and elation of their success they had succumbed to the almost ritualistic pursuit of the fleeing enemy. What also worked to the advantage of the Lakedaimonians was that their intended outflanking was made the greater by the similar aim of the Boiotians. The obvious difference between the two was the controlled and disciplined exploitation of the advantage. Spartan drill was infinitely superior to that of the armies of any contemporary city-state. Decades of practice had created an expertise unmatched elsewhere, and the act of wheeling the line from a temporarily fixed point was no problem to them. Maintaining the evenness and integrity of the line while doing so was second nature to them, all the while responding to the orders as they were passed down each file.

It can be assumed that any Spartan pursuit was limited and controlled, as was customary. This lessened the likelihood of any successful counterattack arising, given that the maintenance of good order was paramount. Concerning their fleeing opponents, Xenophon, at *Hell.* IV. 2 23, makes an interesting and unexplained comment. The retreating coalition troops fell back on Korinth for safety but were denied entry to the city and had to return to their camp. Given what was to occur later, the question must arise whether those pro-Spartan elements remaining in the city were temporarily in the ascendant. Did they see an opportunity to further the cause of their faction, or was it just fear that, by opening their gates, they might also risk the entry of the enemy?

The victors went through the usual ritual of setting up a trophy. After such a momentous victory it is significant that nothing had changed. The coalition was still in command of the Isthmos and the Spartans and their allies remained contained by land within the Peloponnese.

Xenophon's description of the battle may well satisfy some with its broad-brush handling of the engagement, but on close scrutiny there remains a great deal unreported. Having taken the trouble to list the forces ranged on each side, he wholly omits any mention of cavalry or light troops once battle was joined. What we have from him is solely an account of a hoplite contest. This in part reflects the attitude to auxiliary forces in the early and middle Classical period. The hoplite was supreme. He it was who, in the company of his fellow citizens, came against a similar interdependent formation in a clash of arms face to face. In such terrifying circumstances it is no wonder that those who sought to kill from a distance, e.g. javelineers, archers, slingers and even cavalry, were regarded as being of less import both militarily and sometimes socially. There were certain exceptions to this general observation. The cavalry of Athens was well regarded but this was probably more due to the fact that it was almost wholly made up of the well-to-do citizens, who could afford to maintain horses. The same may be said of Thebes and Thessaly but not of Sparta. Sparta's horse-owning citizens chose to serve as hoplites leaving their mounts to be ridden by lower orders.

Other factors to be considered must include the rise of the citizen class in city-states. The expectation was that the citizen would make himself immediately available to fight in defence of his community, not least through self-interest, but also through his sense of belonging to a community and sharing in the responsibility for maintaining its welfare. It was easier for the heavily armoured men to adopt a close-packed formation against similarly organised opposition in a relatively brief but savage confrontation in which personal weapon skills could be of a limited nature. How much more difficult, and perhaps expensive, it was for a state to organise and train specialist forces such as archers and slingers. These needed time and regular practice to acquire and hone the necessary skills. So what was the auxiliaries' part in this battle? To attempt an answer, we need to start by examining their function in hostilities.

The light-armed forces, archers, slingers and peltasts were essentially involved in the delivery of missiles. Often they were involved in skirmishing between lines before the onset of the opposing phalanxes opened the main struggle. At this point they would retire to the wings to help screen the flanks of their hoplites. Archers and slingers could sometimes range along the rear of their phalanx, sending volleys over the heads of their own hoplites into the ranks of those of the enemy. Javelineers or peltasts were usually much fleeter than hoplites and could be quite devastating in pursuit of broken and retreating combatants. It has already been noted how effective they had been in harassing the Spartan advance from Sikyon. In the case of the Battle of the Nemea there was insufficient time prior to this battle for the customary preliminary skirmishing. The Lakedaimonian forces and their allies had quickly to come into line only after hearing the paian of the advancing coalition forces. In such circumstances, the light-armed of both armies would most probably have been on the wings.

Cavalry, too, could prove to be a damaging nuisance to an opposing phalanx prior to the clash of the two sets of heavy infantry. With cavalry riding up to within casting distance of an enemy line, the discharge of javelins could be more than just an irritant, particularly when, after the cast, the rider retired, only to return for a repeat attack. If there was additional support from peltasts the combined effectiveness could sometimes prove a formidable problem to the much slower hoplite formation.[5] Indeed, the Thebans further developed their strong cavalry arm by interspersing *hamippoi,* light-armed spearmen, as a partner to each rider. They ran alongside or, by holding onto the horse's tail, were hauled to the area of contact where, in combination, they could exploit any weakness in the enemy line. Pursuit of a broken enemy and screening of flanks in an advance were the most common duties to be expected of cavalry at this time. They were also used as scouts when the need to locate the enemy arose. What is certain is that no cavalry force alone could hope for success against an unbroken formation of hoplites. At the Nemea, for the same reasons given for the light-armed above, the cavalry of both sides would also be on the wings.

To return to the question of their likely roles in the battle we must deal with the anticipated activities of the screening forces of each wing. That to the right of the Boiotians is the most predictable. It would have been made up of about 800 Boiotian cavalry, some of the best in Greece, with probably the unspecified number of light-armed serving with the Korinthians. Following the onset of battle and the quick collapse of their opponents' left and centre, these auxiliaries would play a significant part in the lengthy pursuit. Fighting more as individuals than in formation against a rabble, encumbered by heavier equipment, their task would be made easier by the targets of unprotected backs. Others of the pursued would cast aside their heavy shields in an attempt to escape, thereby making themselves the more vulnerable when overtaken and forced to make a final stand. Obviously, the more mobile cavalry could range further afield to ride down hoplites from their enemy's centre too.

On the other wing there were probably far fewer of the light-armed serving alongside the combined 750-strong cavalry force of the Athenians, Chalkidians and Opuntian Lokrians. Nonetheless, they were a formidable force, but, with the considerable Spartan overlap, they were faced with the sight of the impenetrable array of spears of the Lakedaimonian phalanx. It would be understandable that the coalition cavalry would have withdrawn in good order before contact, but there is some evidence that some did not do so. Monuments set up later in Athens testify to the valour of Athenian cavalry in the battle. One in particular, the funeral monument to one of five cavalrymen, Dexileos by name, can be seen today and was found near the Dipylon Gate.[6] It depicts a young man astride a rearing horse in the act of spearing a fallen hoplite. It has been suggested that this, together with a memorial list honouring eleven cavalrymen including Dexileos, was set up by one of the Athenian tribes.[7] All but one, who fell later at Koroneia, commemorate the casualties of the Nemea. There may have been others, now lost or destroyed, set up by some of the other tribes, the possibility of which suggests that, initially, some heroic resistance not mentioned in our sources had taken place.

At the start of the battle the coalition forces would have had a front of just under a mile. This was much the distance which the Lakedaimonians had to traverse, killing as they went and maintaining their formation. To appreciate fully the critical advantage of sustaining such discipline in the ranks, one only has to realise that 6,000 well-ordered Lakedaimonian hoplites put to rout some 15,000 of their enemy on their passage across the battlefield in the second phase. It also illustrates the vulnerability of hoplites when attacked on their unshielded side.[8] Hence over the years a natural drift to the right of a phalanx to preserve its less protected side, which had resulted in an accidental outflanking, came to be adopted as a definitive tactical movement to achieve the same result. There can be little doubt that the Boiotians intended from the outset to do the same. They, and the great majority of their allies, wrought havoc among their opponents of the left wing and centre in the initial phase. It was their over-enthusiastic and overlong pursuit that brought about their downfall. One can imagine their dismay as individuals, now, in no sort of order and spread out over a considerable area, each turning on giving up their pursuit, only to discover the Spartan phalanx threatening to cut off their retreat.

Meantime, Agesilaos pressed on with his return.

Endnotes

1 See J. F. Lazenby, *The Spartan Army*, Warminster, Aris & Phillips, 1985, pp. 135–6. Lazenby cites support from W. K. Pritchett, *Studies in Ancient Greek Topography*, vol. II, Berkeley, CA and Los Angeles, CA, University of California Press, 1969, p. 78.

2 In the Loeb translation 'περι εξακοσιου' is mistranslated and given as 'about seven hundred' as opposed to around 600.

3 G. Cawkwell's second note at the foot of p. 198 of the Penguin translation of Xenophon's *Hellenika* is perhaps a little too indulgent of the possible reasons for the Boiotian lead to the right: 'Xenophon imputes cowardice and bravado to the Boiotians but it is evident that when they had their turn as commanders, they seized the chance and fought a battle which Xenophon perhaps did not understand; for the concentration of force and the oblique movement to the right seem to foreshadow their tactics at Leuctra.' To further assert that it foreshadows the tactics at Leuktra is surely pressing the issue too far. Until Leuktra, any engagement in which Thebans and their fellow Boiotians were involved against Spartans saw the former avoiding any possible confrontation with Spartans in the opening phases of an engagement. The action at Tegyra was unavoidable and does not represent the usual hoplite clash between two armies.

4 This was the case of an older and more experienced combatant shouting to King Agis that he could not make amends for a previous error by committing another. See Hutchinson, *Attrition*, p. 107.

5 A number of examples relevant to the use of the light-armed and cavalry in this period are given in the first two sections of Godfrey Hutchinson, *Xenophon and the Art of Command*, London, Greenhill, 2000.

6 M. N. Tod, *Greek Historical Inscriptions*, Oxford, Clarendon Press, 1933, rev. edn 1948, vol. 2, p. 105.

7 Tod, vol. 2, p. 104.

8 Thucydides V. 71. 1 notes the natural drift of the phalanx to the right on advancing. This was the outcome of the hoplite at the extreme right of the line seeking to protect his unshielded side. Naturally the man on his left moves with him in order to maintain his own protection from his neighbour's shield, and this is repeated along the front. Several instances of attacks on the unshielded side are known. Two of the most successful are Brasidas' surprise attack on Kleon's forces at Amphipolis (Thuc. V. 10. 6) and the final action described in Chapter 5.

CHAPTER 4

The Return of Agesilaos and the Battle of Koroneia

The Ideal General
Not for me the general renowned nor the well groomed dandy.
Nor he who is proud of his curls or is shaven in part;
But give me a man that is small and whose legs are bandy,
Provided he's firm on his feet and is valiant in heart.

Archilochos; A. Watson Bain trans.

SETTING OUT FROM ASIA MINOR, Agesilaos crossed the Hellespont and appears to have taken much the same route as the Persians did at the time of their great invasion of 480 BC. Details of this journey are given in the writings of both Plutarch and Xenophon with the latter making mention that Agesilaos completed it in a month compared to the year it had taken Xerxes. The disparity of the forces must be noted, however. Xerxes' much larger force of well over a quarter of a million men, when combining the army, naval personnel, and baggage carriers and attendants, must have posed immense logistical problems, the ready solution of which must leave us in admiration of the Persian commissariat. Xenophon was still serving with Agesilaos and his account must be given due weight.

Passing through Thrake, the land between the Hellespont and Makedon, negotiating with each tribe in turn, the king enjoyed co-operation and unimpeded passage – with one sole exception. Diodoros claims that the Trallians demanded 100 talents of silver and 100 women in return for safe conduct through their territory.[1] The king is reputed to have told them to come and try to take what they demanded. On continuing his march, he found the Trallians impeding his onward journey. He is said to have engaged and easily destroyed their forces. It was at Amphipolis that Agesilaos received the news of the victory at the Nemea. Derkylidas, who had taken part in that battle, had been sent post haste with the news. He was ordered by Agesilaos to proceed to Asia Minor to spread the good news to those cities who had supplied him with troops for his present assignment and to assure them that, if successful in his undertakings in Greece, he would return to them thereafter (Xen. *Hell*. IV. 3. 2–3).

After passing through Makedon, Agesilaos made a point of ravaging Thessaly, now in sympathy and loose alliance with the coalition. Thessaly itself was not always unified in its purpose, being regionally controlled by families competing for control of the whole, and often without one person sufficiently dominant to become *tagos* (elected ruler) of all Thessaly. Plut. *Ages*. 16, reflecting elements possibly from the Theban tradition not found in Xenophon's monograph, gives us information that the king sent envoys to Larissa with the intention of achieving a friendly passage and possibly in the hope of gaining the city's support. The envoys were arrested and imprisoned. Despite being urged to lay siege to the city the king negotiated terms for the envoys' release. This was sensible: speed was of the essence and the undertaking of a siege would have unduly delayed Agesilaos' army in its march southward. Its presence was sorely needed to counter the continued threat from Sparta's enemies at the Isthmos.

Thereafter, a large cavalry force that continuously harried the rear of his army hampered Agesilaos' progress through Thessaly. Cavalry were most easily raised in plains or lowland areas of good grazing. These plains were also best suited to the deployment of this arm so that Thessaly, with its large and almost totally level plain, produced the best cavalry in Greece. From the geographical references in our sources, it seems that the eventual engagement took place in the southernmost area of the plain to the south of Larissa. To counter these attacks, Agesilaos adopted a defensive formation that he had employed at Sardis (Diod. XIV. 80. 1): a hollow square that gave protection to baggage, accompanying non-combatants and the light-armed within a shield wall of hoplites.[2] To the front and rear he placed cavalry.

The Thessalians probably attacked in sequential waves discharging javelins and avoiding direct contact. After retiring, each wave would return for another assault. When the attacks continued unabated, and the speed of the march slowed markedly as a result, Agesilaos committed the cavalry in the van to join those in the rear, retaining only those who were in his immediate vicinity. Agesilaos now had the cavalry force in a position where it was capable of taking both offensive and defensive action, particularly with hoplite support. In such circumstances it is not surprising that the opposing bodies of cavalry came into battle formation. From that very act it can be assumed that, although no numbers are given for either side, the opposing cavalry forces must have been fairly equal. In view of the fact that Agesilaos' cavalry had hoplite support, the Thessalians refused the challenge, turned and began a slow retreat. Agesilaos, unimpressed by the caution shown by his own cavalry in its equally slow and measured pursuit, sent those cavalrymen who were still with him to join their fellows at the rear. They had orders for the unimaginative cavalry commander to launch an attack at such speed that the Thessalians would have insufficient time to turn to meet the charge.[3]

The attack was so wholly unexpected that many of the Thessalians had no time to make a complete turn to face their enemy. They were captured or killed; those who did manage to face about fell fighting, among them the Thessalian cavalry commander Polycharmos. There followed a complete rout, with the remainder being pursued, overtaken or captured. The pursuit must have been long because the surviving Thessalians did not stop until they had reached the Othrys mountains, well to the south of Pharsalos.

In his writings Xenophon sometimes presumes knowledge of detail in his anticipated readership. He would be aware that the majority of his contemporaries would have known of differing formations, often at first hand. In his description we have the two bodies of cavalry forming up against each other and it is easy to assume that both would adopt the same or similar arrangement. However, there were regional differences, often reflecting skills in horsemanship. Some were adopted for tactical reasons, and that most favoured by the Thessalians was the rhomboid with a wedge to the front and the rear. This probably allowed them to face about to facilitate a withdrawal while still in formation, with the original front wedge becoming that of the rear. There was also the possibility of wheeling so that either flank could become van or rearguard. While there is no evidence one way or the other within our sources for the specific arrangements adopted, it seems sensible to follow that of habit. Agesilaos' cavalry most probably adopted a rectangular formation not dissimilar to a phalanx, as was customary in the southern states.[4] The speed of Agesilaos' cavalry attack must have been superbly timed to deny the Thessalians sufficient time to reform.

Although Plutarch declares that Agesilaos led his cavalry into battle, this is unlikely and negates the need for him to send orders to the rear for the manner of the action that was adopted. Had he led the force, Xenophon, who was present, would have undoubtedly reported this action of his hero. As it is, both sources are in agreement that this victory, by a force raised and trained by Agesilaos over highly esteemed proponents of the art of mounted action, was a significant achievement and one of which the king could be truly proud.

After setting up a trophy to the victory, the army crossed the Othrys mountains within a day and marched south by the easiest route through Thermopylai. There is no record of any attempt being made to recapture the original Spartan colony of Herakleia in Trachis on the way, or of any attempt by its inhabitants to impede passage. It can be assumed that time was of the essence, for Plutarch (*Ages*. 17) offers information not recorded by Xenophon, but which must be addressed with caution. A certain Diphridas, an *ephor*, had come from Sparta to meet Agesilaos with orders to move immediately into Boiotia. Plutarch also adds that this had not been Agesilaos' original intention until he had gathered reinforcements. The passage is suspect and is at odds with what he is reported to have done next in this source. He is supposed to have sent for the two *morai* notionally on duties at Sikyon. To have sent for both *morai* would have left Sikyon virtually undefended. If we are to believe that the *ephor* travelled to meet him, he may have come with the single *mora* reported by Xenophon to have travelled north from Korinth (Xen. *Hell*. IV. 3. 15). To reach Agesilaos, the *mora* from the area of Korinth would have crossed over the Korinthian Gulf, possibly disembarking at Aigosthena. At the same reference half of the Spartan *mora* stationed at Orchomenos joined Agesilaos, along with their Orchomenian allies. These reinforcements joined the king prior to his arrival in Boiotia.

Although it would be unusual for only one instead of two of the five highest officers of state to be in attendance on the king, this can be explained by the fact that the king was returning from campaigning overseas. It would have been far more convincing, considering the difficult circumstances, for any message sent by the *ephor*s to have been dispatched in the usual way – namely, a parchment strip wrapped around a rod. The commander, who received only the parchment and who was in possession of a rod of exactly the same dimensions as that of the *ephor*s, could decode the message by wrapping the aforesaid parchment around his rod. If the parchment strip fell into the hands of an enemy it would take them a great deal of time to achieve the correct dimensions of a rod to could give them the subject of the message.

Agesilaos most probably reached Boiotia by crossing the Kallidromos mountains, a relatively low range by Greek standards, with two or three possible routes from east to west available for an army proceeding in column. The most likely is that which passes Pharygai (near modern Mendhenitsa) in order to avoid the narrow coastal strip of that time. Alluvial deposits over more than 2,000 years from the rivers Spercheios, Melas and Asopos have advanced the coastline by more than three miles. Today's coastal plain would be unrecognisable to an ancient. At that time, unless some local agreement for passage was achieved, there would always be the possibility of harassment from missiles to the unshielded side from hostile Lokrians on the foothills further south.

Having reached the central plain, Agesilaos gathered his Phokian allies and advanced to the border of Boiotia. There, news came to him of the defeat of the Lakedaimonian fleet at Knidos.[5] The battle occurred near that settlement, situated on the mainland north of the islands of Sime and Rhodes. It would appear that Pharnabazos and Konon, with more than ninety triremes, heard of the Spartan fleet at Knidos and purposely sought it out (Diod. XIV. 83. 5). The same source goes on to describe how the Spartan *navarch*, Peisander, having first put in at Physkos, set sail with eighty-five warships and 'fell in' with the enemy fleet, gaining an advantage over the leading vessels. However, when the Persian triremes under Pharnabazos appeared in close formation, Peisander's allies on the left wing turned and fled shoreward. Losses to the Spartan-led fleet are recorded at fifty triremes with 500 crewmen captured. Peisander lost his life in the conflict.

Our other major source, Xenophon, calls into doubt the odds against Peisander given by Diodoros: 'Pharnabazos who was admiral, was with the Phoenician ships, while Conon with the Greek fleet was posted in front of him. *And when Peisander, in spite of his ships being clearly fewer than the Greek ships under Conon,* had formed his line of battle against them, his allies on the left wing immediately fled' (Xen. *Hell.* IV. 3. 11–12; emphasis added). The loss of this battle proved a heavy cost for Sparta to bear. Sparta lost control of the Aegean and with it influence in the islands and much of the Asian littoral.

At the same time that the news had been given to Agesilaos a partial eclipse had occurred. This natural portent could have had an adverse effect on the morale of his army, particularly if the truth of the battle was to become known. So with special regard to those who had come with him from Asia, Agesilaos chose to declare that a victory had been won, at the cost of the life of the commander. Agesilaos proceeded to make sacrifice in celebration, probably in the area of Orchomenos, where he picked up the Spartan and Orchomenian contingents alluded to above. With them, he advanced due south towards Thebes, through country that gave him the option of moving either in column or, if necessary, in line of battle with Lake Kopais, then undrained, to the left. Skirmishing took place, as cavalry and peltasts of both sides probed and made contact; those under the king's command emerged victorious. The main opposing forces met near Koroneia north of Thebes.

Unlike at the Battle of the Nemea, one can only guess the numbers of each side. None of the sources gives any guidance on this matter other than identifying those who were present. However, by using the figures of the coalition given for the earlier battle, and applying common sense to those of Agesilaos' army, a reasonable estimate can be achieved.[6] From Asia Agesilaos had brought with him what remained of the *neadamodeis*, *helot*s who had been given their freedom in return for military service. At the beginning of Agesilaos' Asian campaign they had been 2,000 strong. Those allies that were with Agesilaos from the very beginning and embarked at Aulos must have still numbered over 5,000 men. The remnant of the so-called 10,000 mercenaries that had been commanded by our major source, Xenophon, in the aftermath of the failed attempt on the Persian throne by Kyros the Younger, had found employment under Sparta. Earlier casualties and the dispersal of some to their homelands would have led to a reduction of this force to possibly 4,500. The one and a half *morai* would have given an additional 1,800 and, at a conservative estimate, the hoplites of the Orchomenians and Phokians would have mustered 4,000. At no point do our sources give an idea of the number of hoplites from the Greek Asiatic cities, but a considered guess would put these at around 3,000. The Spartiate Herippidas commanded these and the mercenaries. At *Hell*. IV. 3. 15, Xenophon also makes mention of additional troops garnered from those Greek cities in Europe on the route of his return. Hoplite strength could have been around 19,000 men. He is specific in giving significant superiority in peltasts to Agesilaos and judges the cavalry of both sides as being of equal strength.

As the Battle of the Nemea had been such a recent event the coalition forces would have been spared major problems of recruitment. Knowing of Agesilaos' return, they had the less onerous task of moving a little further to the north to protect Thebes and their position at Korinth, to attempt to impede any attempt by the king to return to the Peloponnese. As expected, its army reflected those who had participated at the Nemea, with the addition of Ainianian light troops and contingents from both Opuntian and Ozolian Lokris. Numbers for the Euboians were probably 3,000, much as they had been at the Nemea where they, together with four Athenian tribes, had escaped the Lakedaimonian lateral sweep across the battlefield. The Athenians, despite the losses suffered by the six tribal regiments opposed to the Lakedaimonians at the Nemea, would again probably field 6,000 hoplites. The required replacements to bring their numbers up to the original strength were derived from Attika, which had a common border with Boiotia. As the coming battle was to take place in Boiotia, Boiotian casualties at the Nemea could have been made good by additional local recruitment. This would have given a similar, or even larger, number of Boiotian hoplites than were fielded in the first battle and suggests that there were between 5,000 and 6,000 present. However, the losses suffered earlier by the Argives and Korinthians, together with the need to leave a secure line of defence at Korinth, would have reduced their available numbers. It is suggested, therefore, that 4,000 Argives and 2,000 Korinthians participated at Koroneia. Both Lokrian peoples probably added no more than 2,000 men, some of whom may well have been light troops. A hoplite strength of just over 20,000 seems a reasonable estimate of the coalition heavy infantry.

At *Ages.* II. 9, Xenophon notes that, to both sides, the opposing lines appeared to be of equal strength. Visually it may have appeared that both lines were of equal length but, since no depths to sections of battle lines are available in our sources, it perhaps indicates that the Thebans had adopted their customary practice of forming up to a greater depth and consequent shorter front than their allies. This would partly explain the apparent equality in the length of the lines when considering any relatively small disparity in hoplite numbers.

Limited information is available concerning the disposition of each battle line (Xen. *Hell.* IV. 3. 16; *Ages.* II. 9). The Argives were on the coalition left wing, directly opposed to Agesilaos, who commanded the Lakedaimonians; the Thebans of the Boiotians were on their own right wing, opposite the Orchomenians. Where the various other groups appeared in each line is wholly a matter for speculation with one exception. Xenophon, who was present at the battle, was able to describe all phases of the action. In so doing he must have been with the victorious section of the Spartan-led army throughout. As he had been with the mercenaries from the Ten Thousand, he would still be serving as an officer with its remnant now serving

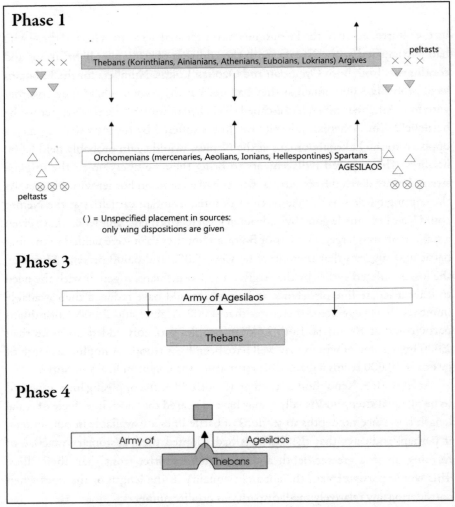

BATTLE PLAN 2 *Battle of Koroneia. The Argives flee before enemy contact in phase 1. In phase 2, the Thebans defeat the Orchomenians and go on to plunder Agesilaos' camp. Elsewhere all the forces in Agesilaos' phalanx are victorious. In phase 3, both sides now face each other in the opposite direction. Significant carnage occurred in phase 4, in which some Thebans achieve a breakthrough and Agesilaos is wounded. It is to be noted that the Thebans adopted an unusually compact formation for their phalanx, the depth of which is unknown.*

under Herippidas. This firmly suggests that the mercenaries took up station in the line to the immediate left of the Lakedaimonians.[7] This is confirmed at Xen. *Hell.* IV. 3. 18, where, after the first phase of the battle had been completed, some mercenaries are described as garlanding Agesilaos.

Both sides advanced to engage; the coalition forces had Mount Helikon to their rear. Xenophon remarks of a profound silence descending on both lines (*Hell.* IV. 3. 17; *Ages.* II. 10). This silence persisted until the opposing lines were about 200 metres apart, at which point the Thebans raised their paian. As the armies closed, those forces under Herippidas surged forward from the phalanx and quickly put those facing them to flight. On the right, this action, together with the sight of the advancing Lakedaimonians, obviously unnerved the Argives. They fled to the safety of Mount Helikon before contact was made. From Xenophon's account it is obvious that little or no pursuit was made. Soon, with the enemy's centre broken and their left wing in full retreat, Agesilaos' men were already congratulating their leader. However, the euphoria was tempered by the news that the Thebans had broken the Orchomenians and had reached the Lakedaimonian baggage train.

Agesilaos' immediate response was to put his troops in order and make an advance upon the Thebans. Translations describe his next action as wheeling his phalanx, which gives the impression of a manoeuvre similar to that made at the Nemea. In Xenophon's account, however, he uses the word εξελιξασ, which suggests an 'unfolding' and may also describe a countermarch. The initial phase of the battle had seen the coalition army to the south of that of Agesilaos. Now it was necessary to reverse the direction for the next advance so that Agesilaos' army moved back towards its own baggage train. To achieve this, a familiar drill would be put into operation. All men in each file except the 'file closer' would make an about-turn. This would appear to make the file leader the original rearmost man in the file. While the file closer remained motionless in his place, the file leader would step to one side, and then march forward, followed by each man in turn so that all would be in their original order. With an about-turn by the file closer the whole phalanx would now be facing in the opposite direction, in its original formation, and be ready to engage the enemy.[8] Such a drill would put Agesilaos towards, but not at, the new left wing and this would not necessarily be a disadvantage. His new place would in all probability be in opposition near to the command point of the Theban phalanx, where fighting would be fiercest. This probably accounts for the number of wounds he received in this phase of the battle.

Although our sources make no mention of it, there may have been a need to traverse the battlefield to be in a position to attack the Thebans. It is unlikely that the newly arranged phalanx faced right and marched in column before facing left to meet their returning enemy. If that was, indeed, necessary, it is more probable that a positive lead to the left – in like manner to that which was made to the right in the initial advance at the Nemea – achieved the objective of putting the phalanx between the returning Thebans and their point of safety. At *Hell*. IV. 3. 19, Xenophon remarks that the king could have taken the safer option of allowing the Thebans to pass by and to attack them in flank and rear as they sought safety on their return. As it was, Agesilaos took the option that the *polemarch* at the Nemea had been persuaded against. He met the Thebans head-on and has been criticised for doing so.[9]

Agesilaos must have had a reason for ordering such a confrontational battle order and we will examine what that purpose might have been later. Even Xenophon, a commander of great experience, notes that he did not take the safest option of attacking the Thebans as they passed by (Xen. *Hell*. IV. 3. 19). So the second phase of the battle took place:

> he (Agesilaos) made a furious frontal attack on the Thebans. Thrusting shield against shield, they shoved and fought and killed and fell. There was no shouting, nor was there silence, but a strange noise that wrath and battle will produce. In the end some of the Thebans *broke* through and reached Helikon, but many fell during the retreat. (Xen. *Ages*. II. 12; emphasis added)
>
> Finally, some of the Thebans *broke* through and reached Mount Helicon, but many were killed as they made their way thither. (Xen. *Hell*. IV. 3. 19; emphasis added).

At *Ages*. 18, Plutarch remarks that such was the resistance of the Thebans that the Spartan-led forces were obliged to part their ranks to allow the enemy passage through the gap (see also Polyainos II. 1. 19 and Frontinus *Strategemata* II. 6. 6). In Plutarch's description there followed attacks on the Theban flank and rear until they reached Helikon, reportedly proud that they were still undefeated. They had, however, fought their way from the battlefield. Interestingly, Plutarch in his *Life of Pelopidas* XVII also describes an action at Tegyra between Thebans and Spartans of 375 BC wherein he claims the Spartans also opened their ranks to allow the Thebans to pass through after an attack had been made on the command position which had seen the deaths of the two commanding *polemarchs*. This, too, though possible for well-drilled Lakedaimonians, poses problems, as it is difficult to conceive that, in the midst of any savage conflict, an order to open ranks could have been successfully and safely completed. Being a Boiotian from Chaironeia, Plutarch may well be presenting a tradition more favourable to his countrymen.

There can be little doubt that the Thebans breached the line by weight and brute force. As has been mentioned, some Thebans were forced through or 'fell through' the Spartan line.

The breakthrough would not have been immediate, but would still have been early enough to avoid being attacked in flank by any overlap wings of Agesilaos' force. It is possible that in the second phase the Thebans had adopted their now habitual formation in great depth, although we have no record of the number of ranks chosen. Xenophon describes them as being in close order with locked shields with about two feet between the shoulders of adjacent men in the ranks. Whatever the depth, the front rank and, to a lesser extent, the second rank would have been the only hoplites in direct fighting contact with the enemy. To them, as was the lot of their opposing front ranks, fell the unenviable task of stabbing and thrusting for their very survival while all the time being compelled by the pressure from behind to hold their place or be killed. This takes incredible courage or confidence: courage and strength in those Theban hoplites called from their farms to take their place in the phalanx; and for the Spartiatai and their followers the confidence in their soldierly skills dedicated to their training for war.

The ranks behind would have placed their shields against the backs of those in front of the opposing formations and pushed, much in the manner of a rugby scrum. The famous call attributed to Epaminondas at Leuktra in 371 BC for one more step forward is also evocative of this similarity. Many have been persuaded that the more ranks a formation possessed the greater the pushing power. This is debatable, however. In experiments of troops in column it was commented:

> suppose your first rank stops at the moment of shock: the twelve ranks of the
> battalion, coming up successively, would come into contact with it, pushing
> it forward . . . Experiments made have shown that beyond the sixteenth the
> impulsion of the ranks in the rear has no effect on the front, it is completely taken
> up by the fifteen ranks already massed behind the first.[10]

Diodoros at XIV. 84. 2 gives casualty figures of more than 600 for the coalition forces and 350 for Agesilaos' army. Although he is often unrealistic concerning numbers, this could well be a good reflection of actuality. Xenophon says nothing of casualties on his own side, but notes that many of the enemy were killed as they sought safety on their retreat to Mount Helikon (Xen. *Hell.* IV. 3. 19).

Fighting had been extremely fierce near Agesilaos' position and he sustained many wounds, giving us further evidence of commanders still 'leading from the front' in this period. Victory was his, but as he lay within the battle line, some cavalry came with news that about eighty armed Boiotians, who had been unable to join their fellows in the breakthrough, had taken sanctuary in a nearby temple dedicated to Athena Itonia. With the battle over, the king gave orders that these Thebans should be allowed to go unmolested, wherever they wished, in accordance with his duty of piety to the gods. Particularly resonant is Xenophon's description of the battlefield after hostilities:

> Now that the fighting was at an end, a weird spectacle met the eye, as one
> surveyed the scene of the conflict – the earth stained with blood, friend and foe
> lying dead side by side, shields smashed to pieces, spears snapped in two, daggers
> bared of their sheaths, some on the ground, some embedded in the bodies, some
> yet gripped by the hand. (Xen. *Ages.* II. 14)

The broad picture of the battle is clear in sources thanks to Xenophon's presence there, but the lack of essential detail is an irritant. The key to Agesilaos' success lay in the tactical control of Spartan commanders of Lakonian forces resisting an overlong pursuit of retreating enemies in the first phase of a battle. This gave them the additional time necessary to organise their men for the crucial second phase.

The following morning the army was drawn up as for battle by the *polemarch*, Gylis, with orders from Agesilaos to set up a trophy. Shortly afterwards Theban heralds arrived seeking a truce and permission to acquire the Theban dead for burial, thereby admitting defeat.

Although the coalition forces still had a viable army it can be assumed that they would not easily commit themselves to another battle. They could, however, impede any attempt to pass Helikon. In addition, there can be no doubt that the king had suffered severe wounds, and it was perhaps his physical condition that led him to choose to go home, leaving the command of the army with Gylis. Gylis chose or was ordered to withdraw from Boiotia to allied Phokis, thereby relieving any pressure on the Boiotians.

Returning now to the possible reasons for Agesilaos' adoption of a directly confrontational formation in the second phase, we find there are several. In the absence of evidence, it is up to the individual to decide which, either singly or in combination, led the king to choose the more difficult way.

First, there is the question of wounded pride. Thebes had been an awkward partner in the Peloponnesian League at the time of the Peace of Nikias and again following the defeat of Athens in 404 BC, as is described in Chapter 1. On a personal level, the Thebans, in his expedition to Asia Minor, had not supported Agesilaos. They had refused to commit troops and had disrupted his ceremonial leaving of the Greek mainland. This would have given Agesilaos grounds for an act of revenge, but the present writer would discount this from being the reason for his thinking within the battle. Personal dislike of Thebans may well have been foremost in his mind but there is more to his adoption of this extremely confrontational approach.

The second reason is a desire to cause as much damage as possible to Theban manpower and thereby perhaps persuade them to leave the coalition. Exactly 100 years before, in 494 BC, Kleomenes of Sparta confronted an Argive army at Sepeia (near modern Nauplion).[11] By both fair means and foul, the Argives suffered a catastrophic loss of over 6,000 men. The deaths of so many citizens gave rise to tremendous political turmoil, with power at Argos being taken by former slaves. It was almost fifty years before the citizen population fully recovered. In consequence, the neutrality of Argos in the Persian War was an understandable outcome. Had the Thebans suffered severe casualties in the second phase, the Boiotians might well have left the war now that the power of Thebes, their dominant partner, been diminished.

With Thebes and their fellow Boiotians out of the coalition, Attika would be open to invasion, and unwalled Athens could soon be brought to terms – countering the consequences at sea stemming from the Battle of Knidos. Any opposition from the remaining major coalition partners, Argos and Korinth, would evaporate.

Third, and probably the most likely, was the question of booty. Agesilaos had been informed that the Thebans had raided the baggage train. This had undoubtedly been given a guarding force, but it would have been easily overcome by the numerically superior Thebans. Agesilaos would therefore be unsure whether or not a considerable part of the product of his Asiatic campaign was being carried off. The only way to ensure that it could be saved was to seal off any escape route. When confronted by a battle line blocking an avenue to survival, the Thebans would have relieved themselves of any encumbrance in order to save their skins. Unlike at the Nemea, the Thebans did not have the option of attempting an escape while being attacked in rear and flank. Being faced with a solid wall of heavy infantry directly blocking their path they had no choice but to reform and to fight for their salvation. Desperation can lead either to collective panic or to acts that are regarded as superhuman.[12] That the latter proved to be the case also gave the Thebans the confident knowledge that in future they could break a Lakedaimonian battle line, for there can be little doubt that they forced a breach. Agesilaos eventually departed for Delphi.

The many wounds suffered by Agesilaos reinforce the idea that an attack on the area of the battle line containing the command position could achieve unexpected results; this appears to have informed future Theban planning at Tegyra and Leuktra. Another lesson is that in the usual hoplite battle where the right wing of both armies overcomes its opposition, an overlong pursuit or greed for looting a baggage train by one side is usually disastrous. This may have been the thinking behind the Spartan habit of only having a limited and controlled pursuit of enemy forces. In any case, such looting as was undertaken by a Spartan army was on behalf of the state, not for personal gain unless the loot was edible.

However, even with two victories on the battlefield under their belt in a relatively short time, the Spartans had achieved nothing in reducing the stranglehold which the coalition held at the Isthmos. Sparta's allies at the Nemea had been severely mauled and, after Koroneia, it was now faced with the prospect that, once the result of the Battle of Knidos became common knowledge, the Greeks from Asia would leave the army. The position was relatively unchanged, and the age when the hoplite battle could achieve an effective result for the victors would seem, until Leuktra, to be at an end.

In the aftermath of the battle Gylis led the army into allied Phokis from where he invaded Lokris. No force came against him and, for much of the time several villages suffered looting of foodstuffs and anything of value that could be carried away. On the day of withdrawal from Lokrian territory the Lakedaimonians were acting as a rearguard rather than the light-armed and were attacked as evening approached (Xen. *Hell.* IV. 3. 22). The Lokrians were obviously light-armed troops, described as throwing stones and javelins. Despite the fact that they would be more mobile than Spartan heavy infantry, they were initially counterattacked by the Lakedaimonians and several were killed. The Lokrians now switched tactic, giving up the pursuit of the rear, and occupied the heights flanking the right of the path of withdrawal. From there they showered missiles into the unshielded side of the Spartan column. Again, the Lokrians were pursued, presumably by the younger hoplites, this time up an incline. On retiring, some Spartans fell because of the uneven nature of the terrain and the difficulty in seeing where they were in the encroaching darkness. All the while the Lokrians kept up the barrage with such success that, had not those already in camp and at dinner come to the rescue, all were in danger of being wiped out. Among the casualties were Gylis and seventeen other Spartiatai, full Spartan citizens.

Agesilaos proceeded under escort to Delphi, where he offered the customary tithe of one-tenth to the god Apollo. The sum was huge for its time. No less than 100 talents, enough to keep a fleet of sixty triremes with over 7,000 men in action for nearly two months. From Delphi, Agesilaos went down to the coast and took ship over the Korinthian Gulf, possibly from what is now modern Itea. The absence of a belligerent follow-up to Koroneia in Boiotia, or a march south to contest the position of the coalition at Korinth, proved to be the reasons for the ensuing protracted nature of the Korinthian War.

Endnotes

1   Also Plutarch. *Ages.* 16. However, Xenophon, who accompanied the king on this journey, makes no mention of this in his monograph on Agesilaos or in his *Hellenika*.

2   The first recorded use of this formation was in the Peloponnesian War by Brasidas for a withdrawal (Thuc. IV. 125. 2–3). See also Hutchinson, *Attrition*, p. 85. In the case of Spartan use, the younger and fleeter hoplites briefly left their positions in the ranks to make short pursuits of any light-armed missile throwers. Such a formation could only be preserved over an open route with no narrows or obstacles. See Hutchinson, *Xenophon*, p. 63. Another less successful use of the hollow square was in the attempted Athenian retreat from Syrakuse (Thuc. VII. 78. 2); see Hutchinson, *Attrition*, p. 163 for the tactics employed against this formation. See also Xen. *Anabasis* III. 2. 36, for Xenophon's proposal for the adoption of this formation.

3   The account of the engagement is given very similar treatment in Xenophon's

Hellenika and *Agesilaos.*

4   There was also a single-wedge formation said to derive from the Scythians. This was later adopted by Epaminondas at the Battle of Second Mantineia and was strengthened by the presence of intermingled peltasts (*hammipoi*) See also Robert E. Gaebel, *Cavalry Operations in the Ancient Greek World*, Norman, OK, University of Oklahoma Press, 2002, p. 118. Also Ask. *Tactics* VI. 1–5.

5   Victor D. Hanson, *A War Like No Other*, London, Methuen, 2005, p. 291 notes that 'the historians Cratippus and Theopompos felt that the Peloponnesian War did not really end until 394' and goes on to state that 'the Spartan fleet was defeated by Athens at the sea Battle of Cnidos (394).' Much the same is to be found in Hanson, *A War Like No Other*, p. 31. No mention is made of any Persian involvement on either page. The Persian-built fleet manned by mercenaries paid for with Persian monies and commanded by the Persian satrap Pharnabazos, together with the Athenian Konon with his smaller fleet also funded by Persia, defeated the Spartan fleet at that location. The prime mover to rid Aegean waters of Spartan triremes was Pharnabazos. Up to this time, for a period of eight years, Konon had studiously avoided returning to Athens in case charges were brought against him in connection with the disaster at Aigospotami. It was only his success prior to Knidos that led to a softening of Athenian opinion of Konon. Diodoros XIV. 39. 2–3 clearly mentions the 'King's fleet'. Xen. *Hell.* IV. 3. 11 names the two commanders.

6   Another persuasive argument on numbers present at the battle is made by Lazenby, *The Spartan Army*.

7   This has led me to change the organisation of both battle lines within their wings slightly from that which appeared in the battle plans for the Battle of Koroneia. See Hutchinson, *Xenophon*, pp. 260–1.

8   The drill is based on that described in *Tactics* by Asklepiodotos, who lived in the first century BC. He indicates this movement of men as the Lakonian drill alongside the Makedonian countermarch and that of the Kretan and Persian countermarch at X. 14.

9   Lazenby, *The Spartan Army*, p. 146 criticises Agesilaos for acting in this manner.

10 Ardent du Picq, *Battle Studies*, vol. 2 *Roots of Strategy*, trans. J. N. Greely, Mechanicsburg, PA, Stackpole Books, 1987, p. 169.

11 Herodotos VI. 79.

12 Sun Tzu, *The Art of War*, trans. Yuan Shibing with a foreword by Norman Stone, London, Wordsworth Editions, 1993, p. 116: 'Leave a way of escape to a surrounded enemy, and do not press a desperate enemy too hard.' The Chinese general Sun Tzu lived at about the time of the Persian Wars, some ninety years before the Battle of Koroneia. It is a pity that his military manual was not available to Agesilaos.

CHAPTER 5

The Battle Between the Walls

Sparta
Spear-points of young men blossom there:
Clear-voiced the Muses' songs arise;
Justice is done in open air,
The help of gallant enterprise.

Terpander; C. M. Bowra trans.

FOLLOWING THE NAVAL VICTORY OVER the Spartan fleet at Knidos, the Persian satrap Pharnabazos with Konon, the Athenian admiral, brought over to their side the cities of the Asian littoral and many of the islands. Irritatingly for the Spartans, they did this by pledging autonomy to those cities and islands, the very issue that the Spartans had tried to achieve by both diplomatic and military means.[1]

Derkylidas, who had earlier met Agesilaos at Amphipolis with news of the victory at the Nemea, had been sent by the king to convey the good news to the Asiatic cities. With the defeat at Knidos he found it expedient to go to Abydos. There he persuaded the citizens to remain loyal to Sparta. It was at this location that Lakedaimonian governors from cities captured by Pharnabazos' fleet sought refuge. From Abydos Derkylidas crossed over the short distance near the mouth of the Hellespont and made Sestos and the other eleven towns of the Chersonessos secure in their support of Sparta. Control of the land flanking the seaway posed a problem for Pharnabazos and, despite his best efforts, he was unable to dislodge his opposition.

In the following spring of 393 BC, Pharnabazos and Konon moved south and raided the coast of the southern Peloponnese, taking control of the island of Kythera. Just as in the Peloponnesian War, it became a refuge for escaping *helots* and a possible focus for the less privileged within Lakedaimon. Persian monies were given to the allies at Korinth by Pharnabazos for the continuation of the struggle, and Konon took funds from the satrap to Athens for the completion of the walls between Athens and Peiraieos,[2] a task begun in 395 BC. The Athenians were given additional manpower by most of their allies to achieve the objective more quickly.

It is evident from sources that firm endeavours were made by the Korinthians to gain control of the Korinthian Gulf. They used the monies left by Pharnabazos to supply crews for their ships and contested the waters with the Spartans. Although no information is given on any naval engagement, the Korinthians were initially successful, gaining control of much of the southern shore of the Gulf. The Spartans, however, were persistent and, despite losing a *navarch* and having his deputy return home because of wounds, were eventually successful under Herippidas in taking back Rhion at the mouth of the Gulf.

Over the next eighteen months the coalition continued to hold the Isthmos, repelling raids by the Spartans from nearby Sikyon. The repeated depredation was a great problem for the Korinthians. It was their territory and not that of their allies that suffered. It was they who appeared to suffer more casualties than their allies by having to live within the area of conflict. Add to this further Spartan success under Herippidas which gave Sparta full control of the seaways of the Gulf. The command of the Spartan fleet then passed to Agesilaos' half-brother, Teleutias, who continued to maintain unremitting pressure. It is not surprising, therefore, that opinion in Korinth concerning the continuance of the war should have become divided.

By 392 BC a sizeable element of the Korinthian population wished for a return to peace and association once again with the Peloponnesian League under Sparta. This proved alarming to those Korinthians who were the greatest beneficiaries of Persian largesse. They, together with the other members of the coalition, decided to do away with as many of the dissidents as possible. Xenophon accuses them of gross impiety for choosing the last day of a religious festival, that of Artemis Euklea, to carry out their action (Xen. *Hell.* IV. 4. 2). They had chosen that day because it was considered there would be more people in the marketplace, including many of those targeted for massacre.

On a signal, the slaughter began. Xenophon is graphic in his description of what followed:

> They drew their swords and struck men down, – one while standing in a social group, another while sitting in his seat, still another in the theatre, and another even while he was sitting as judge in a dramatic contest. Now when the situation became known, the better classes immediately fled, in part to the statues of the gods in the marketplace, in part to the altars; then the conspirators, utterly sacrilegious and without so much as a single thought for civilised usage, both those who gave the orders and those who obeyed, kept up the slaughter even at the holy places, so that some who even among those who were not victims of the attack, being right-minded men, were dismayed in their hearts at beholding such impiety. (Xen. *Hell*. IV. 4. 3)

As we know his political sympathies it is obvious from Xenophon's use of the word βελτιστοι (better men) that those who were killed were not, in his opinion, of a democratic persuasion.

There had been suspicions that something was afoot prior to the bloodletting. A number of the younger men had ensconced themselves in the gymnasium on the slopes of the Akrokorinth, the acropolis of the city. They heard the sounds of the killings and, when they were joined by some of the fleeing survivors, they fought off the pursuers together. This indicates that a not inconsiderable number had gathered there. Without warning, the top of a column fell to the ground for no obvious reason, there being no wind or earth tremor. Sacrifices were duly made to test the opinions of the gods and, on the advice of the seers who examined the entrails of the animals, the men came down from the Akrokorinth, crossed the boundary line of Korinthian territory, deciding to go into exile.

Many friends and female relatives followed them, pleading with them to return. Indeed, those holding power in the city promised under oath that they would come to no harm should they return. Some did so, despite the fact that the pledge was made by those already guilty of sacrilege. The number who chose exile is not given, but later, at Xen. *Hell*. IV. 4. 9, Xenophon enumerates 150 Korinthian exiles as taking part in the action described below. Those who had returned to Korinth are described as being unhappy with the governance of their city.

The chronology and detail of two of our sources – Xenophon, who gives much more detail, and whoever Diodoros was following – do not agree. Similarly, the viewpoint of each differs a little when referring to the political aspirations of the participants. Choosing the line of greater probability, it can be seen that there was a body of the Korinthian citizens supportive of a junction of the states of Argos and Korinth. Obviously, there was an opposition and this, in its more vociferous form, is seen in the attitude of the self-imposed exiles. There would be a groundswell of support for them from the more timorous citizens who had remained in the city following the atrocities.

The isopolity (merger) of Argos and Korinth that followed gave common citizen rights to both Argives and Korinthians in the enlarged state.[3] It cannot have been wholly comfortable for the Korinthians when the Argives thought it necessary to establish a garrison in their partner city. The fundamental first steps to union were likely to have been made in 392 BC, but its completion was not to occur until perhaps 389 BC. At *Hell.* IV. 4. 6, Xenophon states that it was in this year of 392 BC that the boundary stones between Argos and Korinth were removed and the combined territories called Argos.[4] Under such circumstances some dissidents within Korinth decided to take action.

The Spartan *polemarch*, Praxitas, who was stationed at Sikyon, was contacted by two Korinthians, Pasimelos[5] and Alkimenes. The two had crossed at least one river in spate to meet him. Praxitas was on the point of being relieved to return to Sparta but chose to remain when he heard their offer to help him gain entry to the land between the walls from Korinth to its port, Lechaion. Praxitas knew both men and is said to have trusted them. He arranged for the *mora* that was to return to Sparta to extend its stay at Sikyon, thereby giving him a total force of two *morai* when added to the relieving regiment.

Whether the two Korinthians were on a duty roster as guards, or managed to become so, is not clear. Nor is the method by which the Spartans were informed of the night on which the attempt was to be made. Obviously, Praxitas would not take both *morai* on the mission, needing a garrison to be left at Sikyon. More likely, his force contained his own *mora* with additional troops from the Sikyonians and the Korinthian exiles, giving a total of just over 2,000 men.

On arriving at the western wall, Praxitas made doubly sure that the entry through the gate would be safe by sending a man to check the prevailing conditions within. On being reassured, Praxitas moved his small army within the area between the walls that linked Korinth to its port of Lechaion, about one and two-thirds of a mile away. These walls are at their widest near the port, where there is about a mile between them. They are narrower nearer the city at about seven-eighths of a mile. Wherever the exact point of entry, Praxitas realised that his numbers appeared small when formed in battle line. Had it been drawn up eight or ten deep its front would have covered only about an eighth of a mile, thereby leaving ample space for an outflanking. Despite there being a garrison of Thebans in the port of Lechaion to his rear, Praxitas thought it politic to build a stockade with a ditch facing the city, for this was the point from which the greatest danger was to be expected.

Night passed, and the whole of the following day, without any enemy movement. However, by the next day, the Argives had arrived in force. Soon the coalition forces within the city emerged and deployed for battle. The Lakedaimonians were in their usual position on the right wing with the Sikyonians next in line, and, abutting against the eastern wall, the 150 Korinthian exiles. Against this line their significantly more numerous enemies organised themselves. Iphikrates and his mercenaries were on the right, facing the Korinthian exiles near the eastern wall, with the Argives to their left taking up the centre and part of the right. The Korinthians of the coalition occupied the left wing. This arrangement avoided setting the Korinthians on each side against each other.

In a short digression it must noted that at this time Iphikrates was just beginning to embark on the development of a type of soldier modelled on the light-armed peltast typical of the more rugged parts of Greece and Thrace that had featured in several actions in the Peloponnesian War. Mobility was the key to their success, particularly in conjunction with other armed units. They became highly successful on their own in terrain best suited to their tactic of repeated javelin attacks and retirals before an enemy could make physical contact. Iphikrates retained the javelins and lengthened the sword and spear, while at the same time making the protective clothing lighter. That longer spear allowed the newer form of peltast to outreach any hoplite opponent. His reforms and training brought into being a type of combatant whose capacities placed him between the hoplite model and the original peltast model. This new type was obviously the basis for further development by Phillip II of Makedon.

The coalition advance is described as being immediate. The Sikyonians were quickly put to flight by the Argives, who broke down the stockade and pursued them to the coast. Sikyonian casualties were heavy. In a vignette, Xenophon, at

Hell. IV. 4. 10, describes the action of Pasimachos, the Spartan cavalry commander. Taking a few of his men, he rode in in an attempt to bring relief to the Sikyonian allies. Arriving at the point where this secondary action was taking place, he and his men tied their horses to trees and took shields from the Sikyonians. They then advanced upon the Argives who, mistaking them for Sikyonians because of the sigma markings on their shields, attacked them with gusto. Brave as this action of the Lakedaimonians was, it appears to have been a rather pointless action unless it was intended to persuade the Sikyonians to rally. No doubt they fought well and caused a momentary problem to the Argives, but, as all lost their lives by this heroic gesture, one must question its wisdom.

Near the eastern wall, the exiles were successful against the mercenaries of Iphikrates. This can possibly be explained by the fact that the mercenaries were probably equipped as peltasts with a light shield and javelins and Iphikrates' reforms had not yet been fully implemented. As their enemy was most probably in the hoplite panoply of heavy infantry, the mercenaries would not be effective as part of a battle line where their mobility would be severely curtailed. With the Sikyonians being pursued to the coast and the Korinthian exiles in pursuit of the mercenaries to the very walls of Korinth, the Spartans moved from the protection of the palisade and marched across its line, keeping it to their left. The Argives realised that the Spartans were now moving to cut them off from the city. No mention is made of the opposing Korinthians of the coalition left wing and one must assume that they had joined with the Argives in the pursuit of the Sikyonians. The Spartans caught the Argives as they came through the breach in the stockade, killing those on the right as they passed by, unprotected on the unshielded side. The remainder of what was now a rabble near the eastern wall moved to gain the safety of the city, only to be faced by the returning Korinthian exiles. These last must have been in good order, for the more numerous Argives turned back in panic, only to be confronted by the Lakedaimonians yet again. What happened next is gruesomely described by Xenophon:

> Thereupon some of them, climbing up by the steps to the top of the wall, jumped down on the other side and were killed, others perished around the steps, being shoved and struck by the enemy, and still others were trodden under foot by one another and suffocated. And the Lakedaimonians were in no uncertainty about whom they should kill; for then at least heaven granted them an achievement

such as they could never have prayed for. For to have a crowd of enemies delivered into their hands, frightened, panic-stricken, presenting their unprotected sides, no one rallying to his own defence, but all rendering all possible assistance toward their own destruction, – how could one help regarding this as a gift from heaven? On that day, at all events, so many fell within a short time that men accustomed to see heaps of corn, wood, or stones, beheld then heaps of dead bodies. (Xen. *Hell*. IV. 4. 11–12)

At the port of Lechaion a similar fate befell the Boiotian garrison. Shortly afterwards the customary truce was established so that the defeated could reclaim their dead. Reinforcements arrived from the allies, and Praxitas, now wholly in control of the land between the walls, decided to dismantle part of those fortifications so as to make it possible for an army to make its way through the barriers. With his enlarged army, he entered the territory of Megara to the east of both walls and successfully assaulted Sidos and Krommyon. In both locations garrisons were established and, on returning, he fortified Epiekeia to protect the Sikyonians. This location has still to be identified, but must be in the intervening space between the western wall of the Korinth/Lechaion fortifications and the city of Sikyon. After completing these works he disbanded the army and returned to Sparta, presumably taking with him the *mora* which had been technically relieved earlier. Xenophon makes a telling comment at *Hell*. IV. 4. 14: 'From this time on large armies of citizens were no longer employed on either side, for the states merely sent out garrisons, the one party to Korinth, the other to Sikyon, and guarded the walls of these cities. Each side, however, had mercenaries, and with these prosecuted the war vigorously.'

The following year, 391 BC, saw the Athenians come in considerable numbers with the intention of rebuilding the walls from Korinth to Lechaion. Along with the army came masons, carpenters and labourers and very quickly the western wall was repaired to a high standard. Once this had been done they took a more leisurely approach to the re-establishment of the eastern wall. What is hard to understand is the Spartan attitude to this. When they had achieved the upper hand by the actions of Praxitas, why is there no record of attempts to disrupt the rebuilding, to sustain Spartan gains, or indeed to further develop the growing control of the area? It is as if the Spartans accepted success on the battlefield, but disregarded the necessity to maintain pressure on their opponents. To give up something cleverly won, by what would appear to be either neglect or sheer indifference, is difficult to understand. Indeed, the very purpose of all Spartan-led activity at this time should have been to destroy the blockade at the Isthmos.

Endnotes

1   See Hornblower, pp. 196–7.
2   See Tod, vol. 2, p. 107.
3   See R. A. Sealey, *A History of the Greek City States 700–338 BC*, Berkeley, CA, University of California Press, 1976, pp. 397–8.
4   J. B. Bury, *A History of Greece to the Death of Alexander the Great*, London, Macmillan, 3rd edn 1961 was a standard work for more than sixty years and sets the union between Korinth and Argos in 392 BC. However, the notes by George Cawkwell in Xenophon, *History of My Times* appear to prove that full union had not been achieved by the time of the winter 392/1 BC. Then, the peace negotiations record that Argos and Korinth were afforded separate ambassadors (Xen. *Hell.* IV. 8. 13). Two verses later there is a slightly ambivalent statement suggesting that, by accepting the principle of autonomy, the Argives would not be able to retain Korinth. Sealey, p. 393 concludes that at the time it was only a partial union.
5   Cawkwell, in Xenophon, *History of My Times*, pp. 208–9 suggests that Pasimelos was later well known to Xenophon. He goes on to state that the views of Pasimelos were prejudiced and may have coloured the account with regard to the union of Argos and Korinth. However, Xenophon would also know others who participated, such as Praxitas.

CHAPTER 6

The Disaster of Lechaion and the Activities in the North-West

A clever general, therefore, avoids an army when its spirit is keen, but attacks it when it is sluggish and inclined to return. This is the art of studying moods.

Disciplined and calm, to await the appearance of disorder and hubbub among the enemy – this is the art of retaining self-possession.

Sun Tzu, *The Art of War*, VII. 29 and 30; Y Shibing trans.

WITH PERSIA CONTINUING TO FAVOUR the coalition, and Sparta fearing the threat of *helot* insurrection posed by the enemy occupation of Kythera, a diplomatic attempt to defuse the crisis was made in 392 BC.

From Xen. *Hell.* IV. 8. 12, Xenophon records the mission of the Spartiate Antalkidas to the Persian Satrap Tiribazos with the aim of securing a peace between Sparta and Persia. He suggests that other causes for such an approach were the rebuilding of the long walls at Athens with Persian monies, and the Athenian admiral Konon's attempts to bring over islands and cities on the Asian littoral to Athens with a fleet provided and funded by Persia. The last point proved too good an opportunity to miss to alert the Great King of Athens' likely intentions.

Members of the coalition heard of this move and likewise sent their own representatives to Tiribazos – Konon among them. The Spartan case was made as follows:

Antalkidas said to Tiribazos that he had come desiring peace between his state and the King, and furthermore, just such a peace as the King had wished for. For the Lakedaimonians, he said, urged no claim against the King to the Greek

69

cities in Asia and they were content that all the islands and the Greek cities in general should be independent. 'And yet,' he said, 'if we are ready to agree to such conditions, why should the King be at war with us or be spending money? Indeed, if such terms were made, we could not take the field against the King, either; the Athenians could not unless we assumed the leadership, and we could not if the cities were independent.' (Xen. *Hell.* IV. 8. 14)

Obviously, and for differing reasons, this did not sit well with the coalition representatives. The Athenians feared that they would lose recently recovered Lemnos, Imbros and Skyros, the Thebans faced the prospect of the break-up of the Boiotian federation which Thebes headed, and the Argives knew this endangered the merging of their lands with those of Korinth.

Although no peace was agreed, there were significant gains for the Spartan side. Secretly, Tiribazos gave money to Antalkidas to support a Spartan fleet. Its purpose was to increase pressure on Athens and its allies so that they would be more susceptible to agreeing a future peace. More importantly, when the representatives were making their departure, Tiribazos arrested and imprisoned Konon, thereafter travelling to Artaxerxes to advise him of what had happened, and to seek his instructions. The king then sent Strouthas to take charge of his satrapy. He was obviously still angered by Sparta's aggression of recent years.

Back in Greece, shortly after the Battle between the Walls, the Athenian general Iphikrates led his peltasts on a series of operations against Sparta's Peloponnesian allies. Towns in Arkadia were subjected to attacks. Phleious suffered severe losses and the city put itself into the hands of a Spartan garrison for security, and those in Arkadia proved so fearful of the plundering operations of the peltasts that they were too afraid even to send out their hoplites against them. This fear may have arisen from the success of peltasts against hoplites from Mantineia, when the latter were broken by missile fire and some killed in the ensuing flight. The Spartans, with their base at the town of Lechaion, made several raids on the land around Korinth with one *mora* and the Korinthian exiles. No one from the city came out to meet them. Xenophon attributes this to the fact that some peltasts had, on occasion and over a considerable distance, been overtaken and killed by the younger Spartan's hoplites. These last could be ordered to leave the ranks and drive off javelineers. Despite being more heavily armoured, they had been so successful that the peltasts were averse to making an attempt against them. It was at this time that the rebuilding of the walls from Korinth to the coast was completed. An additional reason for the rebuilding is suggested by Xenophon at *Hell.* IV. 4. 18: the Athenians feared that, since the barrier at the Isthmos had earlier been breached, a similar success would permit a Lakedaimonian invasion of Attika.

Within the same year of 391 BC Agesilaos invaded Argive territory. This was probably a diversionary tactic that disguised his real intention, given the evidence immediately following in Xenophon. Unlike the Boiotians and Athenians, it will have been noted that the Argives had not put up any serious opposition to Spartan forces in recent engagements. They had been badly mauled at the Nemea, had fled the field of battle at Koroneia, and had been little less than a rabble when faced by the Lakedaimonians in the Battle between the Walls. In consequence, Agesilaos' invasion of the lands of Argos would be made with great confidence.

After extensive damage had been done to property without any reported opposition, he immediately moved north in a direct attack on the Korinthian long walls. It can have been no accident that his half-brother, Teleutias, made a simultaneous attack by sea on the naval dockyards and fleet at Lechaion. This must have been a carefully planned operation in which the arrival time of both forces was critical. Agesilaos' depredation of the Argolid, when taken together with his quick advance on Korinth, suggest that they were to serve two purposes: to exclude the possibility of support coming from Argos to Korinth at the time of its attack, and to disguise the main objective of the expedition.

The Korinthian fleet, dockyards and walls were captured. These joint operations show sophisticated planning. They gave Sparta complete control of the Korinthian Gulf and the free range of areas in all directions around Korinth. That city was, to all intents, isolated. It still had its garrison of mercenaries, but the possibility of operations with its allies was now much diminished. Now that the port of Lechaion was in Spartan control, the garrison in the adjacent Spartan-held town was probably increased before Agesilaos dismissed his allies and returned to Sparta with his Lakedaimonians.

It was probably early in the next year of 390 BC that the Korinthian exiles, stationed at Lechaion or Sikyon, informed Sparta that the Korinthians were relying on livestock being herded on the Peiraion.[1] Lying north of the Isthmos and north-north-east of Korinth, the area provided adequate pasturage. Although our sources do not expressly state as much, supplies for those in Korinth must have been very limited at this time. No foodstuffs could be brought to Korinth via the Korinthian Gulf with the long walls and the port and town of Lechaion now in Spartan hands. The Korinthian lands between the city and Sikyon were too dangerous to be cultivated or used for pasture. Perhaps the Akrokorinth provided some supplies but, in the report of the exiles mentioned above, it was clearly stated that many at Korinth now relied heavily on supplies of meat from the herds held on nearby Peiraion. In addition to the information given in the *Hellenika*, a further reason for attacking this area is to be found at Xen. *Ages.* II. 18. The Thebans had made a base at Kreusis on the northern shore of the Korinthian Gulf to the south of Thespiai. The base lay opposite the peninsula and, in the occasional absence of Spartan warships in the area, could ferry forces across the short waterway. Conveniently for the Thebans, Teleutias was with a Spartan fleet at Rhodes at this time (Xen. *Hell.* IV. 8. 25). However, an overland march from Kreusis to the Peiraion was possible within a day, admittedly over some rough terrain.

Once again, Agesilaos led forces north to the Isthmos. There, the Argives were celebrating the opening of the Isthmian games, hitherto the responsibility of Korinth. This says much for the increasing control of Argos over Korinth. The Argives had made sacrifice to Poseidon and had been about take breakfast but, yet again, fled from the approaching Spartans to Korinth. Agesilaos made no pursuit. He made camp within the area and gave sacrifice to the god, followed by sacrifices by the Korinthian exiles. The games now proceeded under his aegis but, when he left the Isthmos, the Argives returned and reran the whole series of contests with little difference in the outcome for victors or losers.

No indication is made in our source of where Agesilaos encamped when he left the Isthmos. It cannot have been too distant, and perhaps towards Peiraion itself, for he was able to assess, on moving towards it, that its approaches were heavily guarded. Among those with this responsibility would be Iphikrates and his peltasts, who would be most effective in the upland areas between the coastal strip and the mountains.

In a feint which was all too typical of his generalship, Agesilaos then made as if to move against Korinth itself. This had the desired effect in that many of the citizen body concluded that his approach suggested that some within were about to betray the city or surrender it to the enemy. They sent a messenger to Iphikrates requesting his return from guarding the Peiraion to give them greater security. On making camp near the city, the inference of Xenophon's text is that Agesilaos established lookouts, for a report was given that Iphikrates and his force of peltasts had passed the Spartan army during the night. His ruse having succeeded, Agesilaos reversed his pretended advance on Korinth and proceeded once again against the now-weakened defences of Peiraion.

It may surprise some that a city with substantial walls could have been in such fear from an attacking army. Hoplites were not the best troops with which to storm such fortifications. More usually, as the evidence from the Peloponnesian War attests, a city was either the object of betrayal by those citizens whose sympathies lay with the attackers and who organised their entry, or of a protracted siege. In the case of the Korinthians they had reason to feel insecure in light of the recent example of the Battle between the Walls.

Agesilaos encamped on the coastal strip near the thermal springs emerging at the foot of the Gereneia mountains. These heights lay to the east of the camp stretching north towards Oenoe. He secured the overlooking heights to deny them to any returning enemy peltasts. Here we have a strong indication in Xenophon's text that he himself was either a member of the expedition or received his information from reliable sources. At Xen. *Hell.* IV. 5. 4, he recounts an action by Agesilaos that shows his concern for the morale and well-being of his men. Those he had sent into the mountains were lightly clothed and unprepared for the chill of a night at altitude, even though it was summer. To discomfort them further, there had also been a hailstorm in the early evening. He organised ten or more men to carry fire in pots up to various high points by different routes. In such a way fires proliferated over the area and the soldiers were able to prepare their evening meal in relative comfort. This, and the considerable detail recounted later by Xenophon seems to be the product of direct observation rather than based on the report of others. Over the whole area those fires alerted those of the enemy – combatants, herders and the local population, particularly those of nearby Perachora who had not been aware of Agesilaos' approach – to their desperate position. They congregated in the Heraion[2] at the end of the blunt peninsula at the west of the Peiraion, presumably hoping that they might enjoy some protection from the sanctity of the place.

The following morning those occupying the heights came down to capture a fortified position at Oenoe and pillage the farms in the area. Much booty was taken, and those in the Heraion decided to put their fate in the hands of Agesilaos. Those who had been involved in the citizen massacre at Korinth were given to the Korinthian exiles. No record of their fate is available. The greater number of the remaining prisoners had come with portable property. Agesilaos' decision that everything else was to be sold is not wholly clear. No doubt a great amount of valuable booty was taken and disposed of. What is unclear is whether the prisoners themselves were sold into slavery. Certainly, this practice of selling fellow Greeks into slavery was fairly common during the Peloponnesian War, but this does not lie comfortably in this situation. Hitherto, Korinth had been a long-time ally of Sparta and to enslave part of its population, even under the conditions of the Korinthian War, was perhaps a step too far. It is more likely that only those already in servitude to the Korinthians were put up for purchase even though, at *Hell.* IV. 5. 8, Xenophon does not distinguish the status of the prisoners.

At *Hell.* IV. 5. 6, Xenophon states that many ambassadors arrived from several city-states. Only the Boiotians are named and they had come to seek a peace, but, given the timing, the other delegates are most likely to have been from other coalition states and cities such as Megara that were conveniently close to the area of the operation. Their arrival coincided with the evacuation of the prisoners under guard and the booty from the town. This spectacle gave Agesilaos the excuse to ignore the attempts of Pharax, the Spartan *proxenos*[3] to Thebes, to introduce the Theban embassy. While the procession continued, a horseman appeared whose sweating horse indicated the urgency of his mission. Disregarding those who asked him for his news, he made straight for Agesilaos and reported the disastrous outcome of an engagement near Lechaion (see below). So, from the euphoria felt at the outcome of the Peiraion expedition, Agesilaos' mood was radically changed.

Plutarch makes much of this episode. He infers that Agesilaos had watched his men looting the temple and this, together with his very obvious snub of the Boiotian delegation, led to the change of fortune:

> As he was watching his soldiers plundering the temple of its spoils, a delegation arrived from Thebes to sue for peace. But he had always hated Thebes, and this just gave him a good opportunity, as far as he was concerned, to show his utter contempt for the place, so when the delegates presented themselves before him he pretended he could not see them or hear them. But he soon got his come-uppance. (Plut. *Ages.* 22; Waterfield trans.)

There is no contemporary evidence that sacrilege was committed, and Xenophon, who was quick to report any transgression,[4] says nothing of this in either the *Hellenika* or his *Agesilaos*. For Agesilaos, a priest-king, to tolerate such behaviour is hardly believable. Plutarch, living more than 400 years after the event, and a Boiotian from Chaironeia, relied on other sources not as sympathetic to Sparta as Xenophon, and would reflect the Boiotian tradition.

Agesilaos immediately gave orders for the army to follow after him. Taking only his bodyguard and the senior commanders, and without refreshment, he made his way quickly towards the area of the engagement. Three horsemen met this force. They bore news that the bodies of the fallen had been recovered, which denoted that the Spartans had conceded defeat. The matter, for the moment, was closed, and Agesilaos led his army back to Peiraion.

The Theban envoys now made no reference to the peace settlement that would seem to have been their original objective. They asked only to be allowed to make their way into Korinth. Agesilaos would not permit this on the grounds that he knew that they only wanted to join their fellows there in celebration of the victory. He offered, instead, to take them with him to the environs of Korinth so that they could make an objective appraisal of the current situation. On the following day, after making sacrifice, he advanced upon the city.

The battle trophy was respected but every remaining fruit tree in the area was felled and burnt. No enemy force came out of the city to take up his challenge. This demonstrated to the Theban ambassadors that, even with the coalition success, nothing had changed in the overall control of the area. Thereafter, Agesilaos had the ambassadors transported back to Kreusis by sea and encamped near Lechaion.

We have sufficient detail to reconstruct the action in which coalition forces had prevailed against the Lakedaimonians near Korinth. Sparta's citizens were drawn from the five original villages of Kynosura, Pitana, Limnai, Mesoa and Amyklai. The first four villages were close enough to develop into Sparta itself but Amyklai was about five miles to the south. As a matter of honoured custom, the citizens of Amyklai returned home, even when on active duty, at the time of the festival of the Hyakinthia. And so it was that the *polemarch* at Lechaion arranged to escort the men of Amyklai safely past Korinth. Leaving the allies to defend Lechaion, he set out towards Sikyon with a *mora* each of hoplites and cavalry.

On approaching Sikyon the *polemarch* left the cavalry to continue escort duty for as far as the men of Amyklai required, after which the escort were to return. Xenophon notes that there were around 600 hoplites who were to make the return to Lechaion with the *polemarch* (*Hell.* IV. 5. 12). The number of hoplites in a *mora* varied, depending on the number of age groups at the call-up, or ban as it was known. A hoplite was liable for call-up from twenty-one to sixty years of age into one of six *morai*. This would produce a total of 1,280 men in each *mora*. However, as at the Nemea, for a major battle thirty-five age groups were mustered, giving an overall total for a *mora* of 1,120 hoplites,[5] leaving the oldest age groups at home. The actions around Korinth since the two great battles of the Nemea and Koroneia were of a much smaller scale. We are unaware of the number of age classes called up in successive years. The *mora* described as being stationed at Lechaion was obviously diminished in numbers by the departure of the men of Amyklai and possibly further depleted by garrisons supplied to Epiekeia, Sidos and Krommyon. Therefore, the apparently low figure of 600 men can easily be accounted for.

It is suggested that the *polemarch* and his men knew there were significant numbers of hoplites and peltasts within Korinth but, in view of recent events, they arrogantly assumed that none would dare to make an attack upon them (Xen. *Hell*. IV. 5. 12).

Observing the return of the Lakedaimonians without supporting auxiliaries, Kallias, the general of the Athenian hoplites, and Iphikrates, commanding the peltasts, decided that there was a strong case to attempt an attack. The Athenian hoplites came into battle line not far from the city and Iphikrates' peltasts made their attack. On their outward journey the Lakedaimonians would have had their shielded side towards Korinth. Now, on their return, their unshielded side was exposed on the march past the city. Iphikrates' men had success from the start, killing and wounding several. The first ten of the age groups, being nimbler and speedier than their fellows, were ordered by the *polemarch* to attack the peltasts. Iphikrates had obviously given strict orders to his men that they should retire early before the pursuing hoplites could make contact. In such a way the peltasts suffered no casualties. To compound matters further, when the Spartans gave up the pursuit, the peltast attack was resumed, catching them in disorder because of the differing speeds of individual hoplites. The attack from those who had been initially pursued was this time on the Spartan rear, and by other peltasts on their unprotected right flank. This brought ten further casualties to the Lakedaimonians. The *polemarch* increased the number of age classes to fifteen but to no avail. Such was the discipline of Iphikrates' peltasts that more Spartan casualties resulted.

It was at this point that the Spartan cavalry came up. To be joined by a more mobile and speedy retaliatory force should have made a difference. The cavalry joined the hoplites in the pursuits and one would have expected the horsemen to have used their superior speed to run down retreating peltasts. However, for some unaccountable reason, the cavalry maintained an even front with their hoplites in both failed attack and retreat. In this way the cavalry became subject to the same treatment from peltast counterattack.

With diminishing numbers and suffering ever more confident attacks, the Spartans retired to a hill about 400 yards from the sea, but still over a mile from Lechaion along the coast. They had made progress on their journey, but at what cost? The attacks continued with the Lakedaimonians unable to cause any damage to their enemies. Those in Lechaion saw what was happening and some boats were sent along the coast until they were in alignment with the hill. At the same time the beleaguered Spartans saw the Athenian hoplites advancing towards their position. This proved too much for them and they broke and ran. Some are described as going directly into the sea, presumably in the hope of being picked up by the boats, while others made their escape with the cavalry. The losses to the Lakedaimonians that day were significant and were put at 250 dead.

It can be seen that Iphikrates' peltasts could be a highly effective force even on level ground when supported in their turn by the presence of heavy infantry in reasonable proximity. Obviously, the pursuing young Spartans would not wish to come up against an unbroken line of supporting hoplites should the peltasts retire towards the heavy infantry under Kallias, and therefore they retired before this became a possibility. The morale-sapping experience of seeing comrades fall to an enemy who was always just out of reach must have been severe. As observed earlier in this chapter, young Spartans had often been able to pursue and catch peltasts when ordered to do so by leaving their line, but this time they were up against a thoroughly trained force. Under Iphikrates' training regime his men had become as fit as the young Spartan hoplites. This gave them the advantage in mobility over their more encumbered enemies. The peltasts maintained a suitable distance between themselves and their pursuers. Earlier, it was also noted that Iphikrates and his peltasts had been so successful in their raids in Arkadia that hoplites were unwilling to come out against them. It is highly probable that their successes there had emboldened them in this confident enterprise.

The true worth of auxiliary arms was now being tested and developed. Similarly, co-ordinated action involving more than one arm became increasingly frequent. We have already seen Agesilaos' use of cavalry when supported by hoplites; now it was the turn of peltasts to be given their day. While the richer city-states could bring in mercenaries for these specialist roles to supplement their needs, the smaller states could ill afford the expense to do this or to embark on the recruitment and training of such forces from their own populations. In difficult terrain auxiliaries such as peltasts and archers would obviously be at their most effective. However, except for the ultra-conservative commander, the days of using auxiliaries merely in skirmishing were numbered. In consequence, the trend to lighten the hoplite panoply in pursuit of greater mobility, which had started in the Peloponnesian War, continued.

It is a pity that we are left in ignorance of the name of the *polemarch* or of the Spartan cavalry commander, while the Athenian generals are immediately identified. Such is Xenophon's regard for incompetence.

Following the Athenian success at Lechaion, Agesilaos replaced the *mora* at Lechaion and took the defeated remnant with him back to Sparta. He was careful on his return journey to pass by Mantineia during darkness to avoid his men seeing the Mantineians jubilant at their misfortune. This is indicative of the attitude of some of Sparta's so-called allies at the time. From that time, the Korinthian exiles did not dare to pass between Lechaion and Sikyon by land and made such movements by boat along the coast. It is apparent that, in the absence of Agesilaos, the surrounding terrain of Korinth came under coalition control. Iphikrates took this opportunity to recapture all those garrisoned strongpoints in the area established by Praxitas and Agesilaos (Xen. *Hell.* IV. 5. 19), and so the see-saw nature of the conflict continued.

The next year, 389 BC saw another of Sparta's allies, Achaia, making complaints against Sparta. The Achaians had established control of Kalydon on the northern shore of the Korinthian Gulf at its very mouth. Now this city was under attack by Akarnanians, Athenians and Boiotians. The Achaians claimed that, while they had faithfully served the Spartan cause, Sparta had shown them little regard when assistance was most needed. They threatened to withdraw from the war unless the Spartans joined them in an expedition against the enemy. First Mantineia and now Achaia displayed the strains that were beginning to appear in the relationships between Sparta and its allies. The five *ephors* of that year, the *gerousia* and the assembly of citizens were agreed that they should mount a campaign. Such unanimity for the undertaking was probably prompted more by a desire to shore up allied support than for the enterprise itself. Of necessity, it put matters at Korinth on hold while this operation proceeded.

Agesilaos commanded the army that probably crossed over the short stretch of water between the Peloponnese and the coastal area near beleaguered Kalydon. It is unlikely that he took the shortest route between modern-day Rion and Andirion and his transports would have to keep a watchful eye out for the Athenian squadron of triremes based a little further to the north-west at Oeniadai. He took with him two *morai* of an unknown number of year classes, together with all available Achaian combatants. At his approach the enemy melted away and took refuge in their fortified towns and cities. An ultimatum was sent to the Akarnanians. Either they left the alliance with the Athenians and Boiotians or their lands would be totally laid waste. Their refusal to accept his order led Agesilaos to proceed on a slow march of devastation. This must have been very thorough, for his advance is reported as being no more than about a mile and a quarter a day. This proved to be only a stratagem and the Akarnanians were lulled into a false sense of security. So much so, that after about sixteen days, they emerged from the towns to continue cultivating their crops, bringing their livestock down from the highlands and concentrating them near a lakeside.

Assessing that an opportune time had now arrived, Agesilaos made a march of over twenty miles to arrive at the enclosed lowland area around the lake where the greater part of the Akarnanian cattle, horses and other goods had been gathered. This took his enemy completely by surprise. All stock was captured, together with many slaves tending the herds and, on the following day, everything was sold.

It is not wholly clear where this lakeside place was. Agesilaos was already perhaps twenty miles north-north-west of his initial landing point when he decided to make his rapid advance. Topographical detail is limited and considered guesswork is needed to come up with a likely area. Taking those stretches of water within the range of the march, one must discount Lake Trikhonis, and its neighbour, Lake Lysimakhia, lying as they did in Aetolian territory. If the advance was due north, the initial low-lying country is ideal for a rapid march with ample opportunity to deploy in battle line should the need arise. To the west of the Akarnanian capital Stratos is Lake Ozeros, which also must be discounted on the grounds that the surrounding countryside does not evoke any of the features in the later descriptions of the hostilities. However, to its north is Lake Ambrakia, south of Amphilokhia, and this proves to be the most obvious candidate in terms of topography.

Shortly after the sale, Akarnanian peltasts appeared in considerable numbers on the ridge above the slopes where Agesilaos had made camp. They subjected the Peloponnesian army to volleys of javelins and stones, forcing them to move to lower ground, whereupon the Akarnanians desisted and retired for the night, leaving the army with an opportunity to sleep, admittedly with well-posted sentries. The following day Agesilaos made to move out of the area of the lake. Moving south, he now had heights to the left and right. This is indicated by the fact that further attacks were made from higher positions on the right unshielded side of his column. These attacks were so successful that the army is described as being unable to proceed. The likelihood is that Agesilaos was forced to order his column to face right, presenting a line of protecting shields against their enemies. Just as on the previous evening, countermeasures proved ineffective. Pursuits from the ranks by younger hoplites and cavalry did no harm to the Akarnanians. Progress thereafter was extremely slow, and before the Peloponnesians were able to spill out into more open country a little further on, attacks were made from higher ground on both sides of their line of march. Here, the gradient to Agesilaos' left was less onerous and he decided to make an all-out attack on the assailants ranged on this side. The march was halted while sacrifice was made. The Akarnanians probably mistook this to be a sign of diminishing confidence by their enemy and redoubled their attacks, descending lower on the slopes and causing several Peloponnesians to be wounded.

It is obvious that orders had been given, and arrangements made, for what was to be a much more elaborate counterattack than usual. At the command, the first fifteen age classes of hoplites sprinted from the ranks, supported by cavalry, with Agesilaos advancing with the remainder of his forces in their rear. The command must have been calculated to coincide with the point at which the Akarnanian peltasts were at their closest, for they suffered considerable casualties in their attempts to make good their escape to higher and safer points. Many would have been ridden down by the charging cavalry and others overtaken by the fleet young hoplites over terrain more compatible to the pursuers than had been enjoyed hitherto. The Akarnanians had made the error of approaching too close to their enemy and too distant from a point for safe retreat.

At *Hell*. IV. 6. 11, Xenophon indicates that the hoplites of the Akarnanians were drawn up in order on the summit together with the majority of their hitherto uncommitted peltasts. It is likely that Agesilaos was aware of their presence before making his counterattack otherwise he would not have needed to follow after his younger hoplites and cavalry. His advance uphill continued. In all likelihood, the hoplites that had made the initial pursuit returned to their ranks. Only the cavalry continued with the attack and lost several men and horses to missiles and hoplite spears thrown from above as Agesilaos with the phalanx advanced behind them. Just prior to contact, the Arkananian phalanx lost its nerve and broke, despite having occupied an advantageous position. An uphill attack is much easier to repel by a determined and confident force even when numerically outnumbered. However, as past examples have shown, the inexorable and well-disciplined advance of a Spartan-led phalanx was something which had caused an opposition to break and run before contact, even on level ground. In the ensuing carnage no fewer than 300 Akarnanians lost their lives.

A comparison of this action with that at Lechaion shows some clear differences. The counterattack was obviously splendidly timed and is reminiscent of the cavalry action in Thessaly. The cavalry had been ordered to make use of its greater speed and is described as making a charge rather than maintaining the same pace as the pursuing hoplites. The commitment of fifteen age classes at the outset rather than the ten used by the *polemarch* on his first response near Lechaion probably gave those in pursuit a numerical advantage over their enemies. Finally, the remainder of the phalanx moving in support would add to the terror of the pursued and reduce the distance over which their own younger hoplites had to return to the relative safety of their ranks, had their counterattack foundered.

After setting up a victory trophy, the remainder of the time spent in Akarnania saw Agesilaos using his army to lay waste the countryside over a large area. There is more than a hint that the Achaians were becoming rather disenchanted with the king. Xen. *Hell.* IV. 6. 12–13 makes clear that assaults on cities were made at the instigation of the Achaians, with Agesilaos feeling under an obligation to make such attempts. At the end of the campaigning season, with no successes in such ventures, his preparations to return home were met with objections. The Achaians made it plain that they thought nothing had been achieved. They requested that Agesilaos continue the campaign so that the Akarnanians would have no opportunity to sow their crops. The king would have none of this, promising to lead another expedition the following year, adding that under such duress the more planting that the Akarnanians undertook the more they would come to wish for a peaceful outcome.

It was necessary to undertake the return to the Peloponnese by the shortest sea crossing to minimise the possibility of any attacks being made on them during their crossing by the Athenian squadron of triremes based at Oeniadai. Therefore, having been given permission to pass through Aitolian territory, Agesilaos led his army first east, and then south-east, over a difficult route to the coast.

The following year, on receiving the news that Agesilaos was preparing to invade once more, the Akarnanians sued for peace. It had become clear to them that Athens and Boiotia could afford them little protection. They realised that even a diversionary action in the Korinthian area, had it been undertaken, would bring them scant relief. In these circumstances they came to terms and joined the Spartan alliance. So it was that the coalition at Korinth lost its ally in the west. From an obligation that had arisen accidentally, Agesilaos had reduced pressure on his Achaian allies and further eroded the strength of his enemies.

Endnotes

1   Above the Isthmos is a large peninsula lying between the territories of Korinth and Megara. Within it, on the coast, to the north of the modern spa town of Loutraki, is the delightful Sanctuary of Hera Akraia alluded to by Xenophon at *Hell*. IV. 5. 5. The reference to a lake, just a few lines later, is most probably the stretch of water that still exists south of the Heraion and to the north of Loutraki. Today, it has a small channel to the Korinthian Gulf, making it a safe anchorage for yachts.

2   Between 1930 and 1933 the director of the British School of Athens, Humfry Payne, undertook excavations on the headland of Perachora. His reason for doing so was based on the very same texts that provide the narrative of this book. What he uncovered was a small town within which lay an important sanctuary. The following extract from Dylis Powell, *An Affair of the Heart*, London, Hodder & Stoughton, 1958 gives an idea of the place and its importance to archaeology: '[a] small but well-to-do town with temples and altars, marketplace and colonnade, roads, watch-towers, an elaborate system of water-storage. The foundations of a temple from the ninth century BC, of another from the eighth, of yet another from the sixth, fine architectural remains from the classical fifth and fourth centuries and the later, the so-called Hellenistic period of Greece – the discovery of these alone would have been a great reward. But it was the amassing, season after season, of beautiful and precious small objects, gifts offered to the goddess Hera in gratitude for favours or in entreaty for help, which brought distinction to the Perachora expedition. Little bronze statuettes of men and animals, birds and mythical creatures, ivory seals, ivory pins, little couchant animals of ivory, jewellery and scarabs, hundreds of terracotta figurines, fragments of exquisitely painted pottery to be counted not in hundreds but in hundreds of thousands – only the most famous had yielded so much miniature treasure.' Dylis Powell was the wife of Humfry Payne and was present throughout all

but the 1930 season of excavations.

3   The majority of Greek states had a person appointed to represent the interests of a particular city within his own. Successive members of a family often held this position of diplomatic contact. Alkibiades' family had looked after Spartan interests in Athens.

4   A good example is to be found at Xen. Hell. V. 4. 1. Xenophon claims that the seizure of the Theban acropolis, after Sparta had sworn that all cities would be independent, was the cause of the Spartan defeat at Leuktra. To him it was wholly a matter of divine retribution. If this was his view of the cause of the Leuktra disaster, he would surely have made a similar claim for that of the Lechaion, particularly if there had been actual desecration of temples.

5   For a very persuasive treatment of the structure and numbers of men within units in the Spartan army, see Lazenby, *The Spartan Army*, Chapter 1.

CHAPTER 7

Sparta's Struggle to Regain Supremacy in Greece

All warfare is based on deception.
Hence, when able to attack, we must seem unable;
when using our forces, we must seem inactive;
when we are near, we must make him believe
we are far away; when far away, we must make him
believe we are near.
Attack him when he is unprepared,
appear where you are not expected.
Sun Tzu, *The Art of War*, I. 18, 19 and 24; Y. Shibing trans.

SPARTA'S PRESENCE AS A NAVAL power in the eastern Aegean had diminished markedly after the Battle of Knidos. The Persian fleet of Pharnabazos under the command of Konon could effectively roam the seas with impunity. Derkylidas, who had been sent to Asia Minor by Argesilaos after he had delivered the news of the Spartan success at Nemea, was forced to flee to Abydos on the eastern shore of the Hellespont as Pharnabazos regained control of the coastal cities. Derkylidas quickly took Sestos on the opposite shore and was able to hold out against repeated attacks. The two cities served both as safe havens for refugees and as bases for Spartan-led forces in the area. Pharnabazos' policy of allowing local autonomy to the newly captured cities saw their governance range widely between autocratic regimes to democracy.

As the Korinthian War dragged on, with little but occasional skirmishing at the Isthmos between the antagonists, those of influence in Sparta came to the

84

realisation that some accommodation with Persia needed to be made. The aim was to persuade Persia to withdraw its financial support to the coalition and, ideally, to give its backing to Sparta. Pharnabazos' policy was working all too well.

Returning to the peace negotiations of 392 BC referred to in the previous chapter, when Sparta sent Antalkidas to Tiribazos in Asia Minor to attempt some accommodation with Persia, we find that Tiribazos seems to have held similar powers to those enjoyed hitherto by Tissaphernes and he supported the Spartan approach. The two main pivotal proposals were that the Greek cities on the Asian Aegean littoral and islands should remain under Persian control and that all other Greek cities (i.e. on mainland Greece) should be self-determining. Sparta's desire was to acquire support from Persia with the first, and, with the second, to break up the Theban-dominated Boiotian federation and the newly unified state of Argos Korinth.

Athens was quick to follow with her own deputation led by Konon and hard on their heels came ambassadors from Thebes, Korinth and Argos. Obviously the Spartan proposals alarmed them, and Tiribazos travelled to the interior to present them to the Great King. Meantime he had secretly given Antalkidas finance for the support of a fleet. In addition he arrested Konon on suspicion of acting against Persia's interests.

His mission to the Great King on behalf of the Spartans proved unsuccessful. Artaxerxes was firm in his opposition to the Spartans, not least for the depredations suffered by the western satrapies at the hand of Agesilaos. In consequence, Strouthas was sent down in place of Tiribazos in a clear display of pro-coalition bias (Xen. *Hell*. IV. 8. 17). Shortly after, Evagoras, the ruler of Kypros, rebelled from Persian rule.

Sparta then resumed hostilities with Persia. Thibron was sent to Asia Minor and quickly took some coastal cities and others in the Maiander river plain, and made his base at Ephesos. This second phase of the Spartan–Persian war provides nothing momentous in terms of military interest. No great battles were fought, but there are certain aspects of command, both good and bad, that are deserving of mention.

Xenophon records that the raiding operations carried out by Thibron were lacking in order and discipline and were largely opportune (*Hell*. IV. 8.18). It appears, from what follows, that while some few were undertaking a raid, Strouthas, who had noted the disorderly habit, appeared with a large cavalry force.

He attacked, and Thibron was killed while taking exercise throwing the discus. The Spartan-led forces appear to have been divided. The survivors of the attack escaped to allied cities, while the greater number were still in camp unaware that some of their comrades were absent on a raiding mission. The most damning comment ends the description: 'For frequently, as in this case also, Thibron undertook his expeditions without sending out orders'. Such laxity can never be excused, even if the enemy is held in contempt.

The loss of their commander in Asia led the Spartans to send Diphridas as a replacement. He proved more efficient than his predecessor and was taken to Asia by a small fleet under the command of Ekdikos. This fleet[1] was bound for Rhodes, where the democrats threatened to take total control of the island. Unfortunately, Ekdikos discovered that the opposition fleet outnumbered his by two to one. He retired to Knidos and the Spartans now sent out Agesilaos' brother Teleutias with the twelve triremes with which he had controlled the Gulf of Korinth to take over the sea command. On his voyage he captured an additional ten Athenian ships on their way to assist Evagoras of Kypros, who was still in revolt from Persia. Teleutias called at Knidos to collect the Spartan vessels there, and proceeded to Rhodes to give support to the pro-Spartan party.

What is significant here, as Xenophon points out, is the curious position in which both Sparta and Athens now found themselves:

> Both parties were acting in this affair in a manner absolutely opposed to their own interests; for the Athenians, although they had the King for a friend, were sending aid to Evagoras who was making war upon the King, and Teleutias, although the Lacedaemonians were at war with the King, was destroying people who were sailing to make war upon him. (Xen. *Hell*. IV. 8. 24)

Athens responded by placing a fleet of forty triremes under the command of Thrasyboulos to try to counter Sparta's recovery at sea. He early discarded his intention of sailing directly to Rhodes on the grounds that the enemy was well entrenched there, but not in a position to do much harm to Athens' allies. Instead, he sailed directly to the Hellespont. There, he achieved great success in reconciling the differences between the King of the Odrysians and Seuthes, who both controlled coastal regions of the northern Aegean, bringing them into alliance with Athens. His next move was made to Byzantion, where he caused the governance of the city to be changed from oligarchy to democracy and set up a system of duties to be paid by merchant ships sailing from the Euxine Sea, much to the benefit of the Athenian treasury. From there he sailed south to Lesbos, where he had success in detaching some cities from Spartan control. Much plunder and subscriptions of money were gathered to help pay for his men. He now set out with the intention of reaching his original target of Rhodes.

Calling at Aspendos, on the Asian mainland, he gathered a further financial contribution from that city. Unfortunately, his men set out on plundering expeditions after this gift and, in outrage, the Aspendians attacked at night and killed Thrasyboulos in his very tent. He had achieved a great deal in a short time, much to the alarm of Sparta.

The northern waters of the Aegean and the Propontis and much of the Hellespont were now, c.389 BC, giving support to Athens. Anaxibios, who arrived with three ships and enough money to hire 1,000 mercenaries, succeeded Derkylidas at Abydos. Despite the small forces he brought, Anaxibios pursued a vigorous policy, raiding and bringing over to the Spartan side several of Pharnabazos' cities. Damaging to Athens was his regular capture of merchant ships belonging to Athens or its supporters. Athens responded by sending Iphikrates to the region with 1,200 peltasts, many of whom had been trained by him and had served with him in the actions around Korinth. He established himself on the Chersonese, but could easily cross over to the Asian side of the Hellespont to harass Anaxibios.

A decisive point came when Iphikrates heard that Anaxibios had gone to Antandros with his mercenaries and 200 hoplites from Abydos. Antandros lies to the south of Abydos and Iphikrates correctly guessed that the Spartan's intention was to leave a garrison in that city. Determined to cause Anaxibios discomfort, Iphikrates crossed over at night to the south of Abydos and laid an ambush in a mountainous area on Anaxibios' return route. He also gave instructions that those triremes that had conveyed his forces over the Hellespont should sail at dawn up the strait as if they were going on one of their regular money-collecting trips.

Anaxibios' return through friendly country, in the mistaken knowledge that Iphikrates was sailing north up the Hellespont, is described as 'making his march in a rather careless fashion' (Xen *Hell.* IV. 8. 36). It is difficult to assess what exactly this comment really means, because later, the route is described as being through 'a long and narrow way'. Obviously, the location for the ambush had been carefully selected and transit through this area would have necessitated a march in narrow column at best. The attack was made when the hoplites from Abydos, in the vanguard, had reached the plain below, with the bulk of the force on the slope, and Anaxibios and the Lakedaimonians on the point of starting their descent. Bravely, Anaxibios fell fighting, along with a dozen governors from supporting cities. No help could come from below and the Lakedaimonian forces broke and were pursued along with those on the plain, right up to the environs of Abydos. Losses were severe: 200 men from Anaxibios' army died, along with around fifty of the hoplites from Abydos.

Back in Greece the Spartans encouraged raids on Attika from the island of Aigina and caused disruption to merchant shipping on its way to Athens. War on land for Sparta had to be restricted. To attempt a land invasion of either Thebes or Athens was inhibited by the forces at the Isthmos and the danger of leaving Argos to the rear of any Spartan advance. Marauding expeditions were therefore made to Argos by, first Agesilaos, and then Agesipolis. Much damage was done on each of the enterprises, and that of Agesipolis proves informative of an unusual tactic practised by the Argives, and of the interstate customs of hoplite warfare.

The calendars of city-states often differed from one another. It was possible to claim that, because of a sacred festival, no involvement in hostilities could be considered. Such holy times were respected, and it was possible that some states actually falsely claimed a religious festival to avoid an unwanted situation. The Argives were not averse to moving the dates of their festivals to suit their own ends. An example of this is the invasion made by them of the territory of Epidauros in 419 BC (Thuc. V. 54). More contemporary examples of respectful observation within the Korinthian War are the refusal of Phleious to serve at the Battle of the Nemea, and the return of the men of Amyklai for their festival of the Hyakinthia (Xen. *Hell.* IV. 5. 11). These last are likely to have been genuine, but Argos evidently had a history of self-serving manipulation of the calendar.

To circumvent such a possibility, Agesipolis, once the border sacrifices proved to be favourable, went first to Olympia and then to Delphi to consult both oracles:

> he went to Olympia and consulted the oracle of the god, asking whether it would
> be consistent with piety if he did not acknowledge the holy truce claimed by the
> Argives; for, he urged, it was not when the appointed time came, but when the
> Lacedaemonians were about to invade their territory, that they pleaded their
> sacred months. And the god signified to him that it was consistent with piety for
> him not to acknowledge a holy truce which was pleaded unjustly. Then Agesipolis

88

proceeded straight from there to Delphi and asked Apollo in his turn whether he also held the same opinion as his father Zeus in regard to the truce. And Apollo answered that he did hold quite the same opinion. (Xen. *Hell.* IV. 7. 2)

The order of the visits is interesting. Having received the approval of the senior god it would have been unusual for his son, Apollo, to arrive at a different conclusion. Also the king's personal involvement is significant, considering he had two appointees on his staff whose duties were to consult with sanctuaries on his behalf.

He returned to Phleious, where the army was assembled, and advanced on Argos via Nemea: 'And when the Argives realised that they would not be able to hinder the invasion, they sent, *as they were wont to do*, two heralds, garlanded, pleading a holy truce' (Xen. *Hell.* IV. 7. 3; emphasis added).

Needless to say, Agesipolis ignored their appeal. On the first evening of the incursion an earthquake occurred and his men thought that they would withdraw from Argos out of respect for Poseidon. Agesipolis reasoned that if Poseidon had been against an invasion, the earthquake would have taken place prior to their entry into Argive territory. The god was urging them on, and sacrifices were made to him the following day. Significant damage was achieved and, on one occasion, when his forces were very near the walls of Argos, some Theban cavalry were unable to reach the safety of the city because the defenders had closed the gates in fear that the Spartans might enter with them. The horsemen hugged the walls of the city, no doubt relying on the covering fire from the Argives manning the fortifications. Had Agesipolis' Kretan archers not been away seeking plunder at Nauplio, the Theban cavalry would have suffered greatly. Xenophon states that this incident happened 'when most of the Argives were away in Lakonia', suggesting that an attempt was being made to draw off Agesipolis by an invasion of Thyrean territory. By contrast to that of Argos, the piety of the Spartans is shown in their response to a lightning bolt that killed some men in their camp, and an adverse sacrifice on a proposal to set up a garrison position on the border. The king immediately withdrew from Argos and disbanded his forces.

In those small naval actions in and around the Saronic Gulf alluded to earlier there are two of more than passing interest. Naval operations at this time were quite diverse for the Spartans. Heirax had a fleet at Rhodes, and Antalkidas was sent to Ephesos with a fleet. On that journey he took with him additional triremes from the small fleet at Aigina. This small group of twelve ships then returned to Aigina, under the command of Gorgopas, while the greater number was dispatched north to Abydos by Antalkidas, under the command of Nikolochos. He ravaged Tenedos on his journey before being blockaded by the Athenians at Abydos. Gorgopas managed to reach Aigina after being pursued by an Athenian squadron commanded by Eunomos. The Athenians waited only a short time before sailing off. During that time Gorgopas and his men took their meal ashore but re-embarked on the departure of the Athenian squadron. With darkness coming, Eunomos led the way, showing a light so that those following would not lose contact. Unbeknown to him, Gorgopas followed at a distance where he could see the light but not be seen by the enemy. Further precautions were taken and it is obvious that these had been decided upon before the pursuit occurred: 'while his boatswains gave the time by clicking stones together instead of with their voices, and made the men employ a sliding motion of the oars'[2] (Xen. *Hell.* V. 1. 8).

With the Athenian squadron arriving at the coast of Attika, the timing of Gorgopas' attack could not have been better chosen. Part of the Athenian forces had disembarked, some were just coming to anchor, and the remainder were still on their approach to the shore. Gorgopas captured four triremes and took them back with his fleet to Aigina.

This action brought about a severe response. Athens dispatched Chabrias, ostensibly to give support to Evagoras in Cyprus. He added additional ships and hoplites to his initial force of 800 peltasts and ten triremes and made landfall on Aigina during the night. Disembarking with his peltasts, Chabrias set up an ambush and, as prearranged, the Athenian hoplites landed at daybreak and advanced to a position about three-quarters of a mile beyond Chabrias' ambush point. Taking immediate action following the news of the hoplite landing, Gorgopas advanced against them with the marines from his triremes, possibly to the number of about 100, and an unspecified number of Aiginetans. With him went eight Spartiatai who were on the island and all those freemen from the ships' crews who volunteered to join his force, bringing with them whatever arms came to hand. Although the total number of those under the command of Gorgopas is unknown, the casualties suffered indicate that it was a considerable force. Advancing on the Athenian hoplites, the Spartan-led vanguard had passed Chabrias and his concealed peltasts before the latter made a surprise missile attack. At the same time the Athenian hoplites advanced and attacked the Spartan vanguard. Gorgopas and presumably the Spartiatai were quickly killed and a rout ensued. The list of those who fell in this action proves it to have been a severe defeat for the Spartan cause. Apart from the commander and his companions, about 150 Aiginetans, a mixture of resident aliens on Aigina, and Lakedaimonian volunteer sailors to a total of about 200 fell. What is significant is the increasing use and effectiveness of peltasts becoming a major influence on the outcome of any action. Admittedly, these were those who had been exposed to the training and adaptations introduced by Iphikrates.

The effect of this defeat was considerable. Xenophon notes at *Hell.* V. 1. 13 that the Athenian shipping found themselves sailing the Saronic Gulf freely and claims that the Lakedaimonian sailors refused to follow the command of Eteonikos. He gives the reason as being a lack of pay, but avoids mentioning the plummet in morale that must have been a major cause for their unco-operative stance.

Sparta's response was obviously carefully thought through. Teleutias was reappointed to his earlier command, possibly on the grounds that he had enjoyed great popularity with the men hitherto. His reception by the men of the fleet is reported as being enthusiastic. Xenophon even goes so far as to report the content of a speech Teleutias supposedly made to his men in which he admits that he comes without money to pay them, but promises, among other things, to secure provisions and pay if they follow him and provide for themselves for a short time (Xen. *Hell.* V. 1. 14–18).

In a daring undertaking, typical of this commander, he sailed at night with his twelve triremes to the harbour of Athens, resting his men on the way. He was correct in his assumption that the Athenian would not anticipate such a move after the death of Gorgopas. Unlike a fleet at sea, the triremes in harbour would be largely unmanned, with the commanders and crews lodged ashore. He took up a position about two-thirds of a mile from the harbour entrance to give his men the opportunity to rest before dawn. With the coming of daylight the raid was made. Teleutias' orders appear to have been followed to the letter in that all his objectives were achieved. Athenian triremes were disabled, laden merchant vessels were taken in tow, the larger merchant ships were boarded and those found on them were taken. Indeed a number of merchants and ship owners were captured on the shore and taken aboard the Spartan ships.

Unsurprisingly, the Athenians were convinced that their harbour was captured but the attacking force was gone before Athenians from the city arrived. The captured merchant ships were sent to Aigina in a convoy guarded by four Spartan triremes. Teleutias, with the remaining warships, now sailed out of the harbour knowing that he had nothing to fear from the diminished and damaged Athenian naval presence. When his fleet was seen emerging from the harbour area it was apparently mistaken for an Athenian squadron, for he 'captured great numbers of fishing craft and ferryboats full of people sailing in from the islands' (Xen. *Hell.* V. 1. 23). He continued south down the coast of Attika and captured further corn-laden merchantmen near Cape Sounion.

Returning to Aigina, he 'sold his booty', and his followers were given a month's pay in advance, presumably also settling debts of any monies already owed. The 'booty' would contain all those who had been captured. Xenophon gives no details as to how these were disposed of and we must conclude that, in accordance with common practice at that time, those of means were ransomed, those from places whose loyalties might be moved to support Sparta were sent back to their islands, and those of known opposition to Sparta were sold as slaves.

It was an outstanding and audacious success in which there are no casualties reported from either attackers or attacked. Thereafter, Teleutias was able to raid at will and Aigina was again taking an active part in the war.

When Antalkidas had gone to Ephesos in 388 BC, leaving the fleet in the hands of Nikolochos, he had set off with Tiribazos to the Persian capital. On this occasion his diplomatic mission was successful, not least because of the Athenian help given to Evagoras. Sparta now had Persia as an ally once again.

Antalkidas had been a good choice as diplomat for the Spartans and he was to prove an extremely able commander. It is a pity that we know so little of his earlier career from our sources. He had obviously proved himself extremely effective in all he had done up to the point when he emerges as a major figure in charge of missions to the Persians.

On returning to the coast, early in 387 BC, he travelled north to Abydos by land because of the Athenian blockade there. He resumed command of the Spartan fleet at Abydos and, having let it be widely known that the people of Kalchedon, at the Bosphoros, had requested him to come to them, he led the fleet, by night, past the naval blockade and up the narrows of the Hellespont. His exercise in misinformation worked well on the Athenians who, on learning of his departure, sailed north and past him at his concealed anchorage at Perkote. Antalkidas now returned to Abydos so that the reinforcement of twenty triremes from Syrakuse and southern Italy could join him.

His intention to achieve a rapid increase in fleet numbers becomes obvious at this point. The larger force might make it possible to seize control of the grain route from the Black Sea on which Athens depended. At the tactical level the use to be made of the enlarged force was still in doubt but as the operation unfolded it became clear that it was carefully planned to take any opportunity presented. How the Spartan fleet of twenty-five vessels evaded the blockade is not known. We can only conjecture that no lights were used on board, and that there was little or no moon at this time. It is possible that the manner of their leaving was quietly achieved, much in the same manner as the pursuit of the Athenians by Gorgopas, described above.

While awaiting further ships from the satraps, Tiribazos and Ariobazanos,[3] eight Athenian triremes, possibly from the Athenian naval station at Thasos, were spotted sailing up the Hellespont. Their intention was to join and reinforce the Athenian fleet of thirty-two vessels known to be in the Hellespontine area. Antalkidas' orders were explicit. Manning the twelve fastest vessels from his fleet, he lay in concealment until the enemy had passed his position. His squadron of twelve set off in immediate pursuit. His sub-commanders were instructed not to engage with the hindmost of the enemy but to continue on their way until the leading vessels had been overhauled. With the capture of the foremost Athenian warships, those following lost heart and surrendered to the slower of Antalkidas' ships. All eight Athenian vessels were now in Spartan hands and the main Athenian fleet, well to the north in the Prokonessos, was denied the possibility of any early news of this disaster to their cause.

With the arrival of allied ships Antalkidas now had a fleet that greatly outnumbered any Athenian force that could be quickly sent against an enemy from the south. He had cleverly tricked the original Athenian blockading fleet into sailing north and any fleet coming from the south had no chance of effecting a junction with it now that his fleet was in complete control of the narrow waterway of the Hellespont.

What follows is reminiscent of the close of the Peloponnesian War. All merchant ships sailing from the grain-producing area around the Euxine Sea were forced to sail to ports friendly to Sparta or Persia. Athenian food supplies were once more endangered. This was achieved with little loss of life in a clinical and well-paced operation. If we are to read our source Xenophon accurately, Antalkidas had a clear aim in mind: to bring Athens under economic pressure, knowing that a previous similar event was still well within memory. That he did so, with such precision, without the attendant arrogance that was innate to Lysander, is testament to the character of the man. In Antalkidas we have a man of great ability in the fields of diplomacy, military planning, and the strategic and tactical use of resources.

The message was clearly understood by the Athenians: Persia's support was lost to them and they were again under the threat of starvation by Spartan control of the Hellespont. Their very territory was under constant attack by Spartan raiding parties controlling the Saronic Gulf. The city was ready to accept any peace. Its error in supporting Evagoras, its loss of control of home waters, and the danger of another period of attrition and starvation, led Athens to hear the terms sent down by the Great King to Sardis as the basis for agreement and cessation of hostilities.

On its side, Sparta was tired of protecting its loyal allies and watching for signs of disaffection among those it distrusted. Apart from Athens, those states that were members of the alliance against Sparta had good reason to hope for a cessation of hostilities. Argos had the evidence that its bluff, of claiming sacred dates as a protection against invasion, had been called. Korinth, in terms of its exiles and those disaffected remaining there, ostensibly under the rule of Argos, was desirous of separation. Perhaps only Thebes, the remaining member of the anti-Spartan alliance, with sufficient distance from the hostilities at the Isthmos and at sea, would be disappointed to come to a peace, even though the Thebans had suffered significant losses at the Nemea and at Koroneia and had lost control of Orchomenos. And so it was that, when the terms were delivered to the Greeks, the extremely interesting experiment in federalism which had taken place in Boiotia was under threat. In brief, the conditions laid down by the Great King were:

> King Artaxerxes thinks it just that the cities in Asia should belong to him, as well
> as Klazomenai and Kypros among the islands, and that the other Greek cities,
> both small and great, should be left independent, except Lemnos, Imbros, and
> Skyros; and these should belong, as of old, to the Athenians. But whichever of the
> two parties does not accept this peace, upon them I will make war, in company
> with those who desire this arrangement, both by land and sea, with ships and with
> money. (Xen. *Hell.* V. 1. 31)

Such is the essence, but not the detail, of what came to be known as the Peace of Antalkidas, or the King's Peace.

All the ambassadors returned to their cities. They were to meet, thereafter, at Sparta to voice their decisions. At this gathering all cities, with the exception of Thebes, took the oath to abide by the conditions of the resolution. Thebes' claim to accept on behalf of all the cities in Boiotia posed a problem. If all cities were to be autonomous then it was unacceptable that Thebes should take the oath on their behalf. They were told to return to their city to reconsider their position on the issue. Xenophon records that 'Agesilaos, however, on account of his hatred for the Thebans, did not delay' (Xen. *Hell.* V. 1. 33). A mobilisation was called and Agesilaos was at the muster point of Tegea when the Theban representatives returned, obviously post haste, to accept that the Boiotian cities should be independent. Similarly, Korinth and Argos were warned that, if the Argive garrison did not leave Korinth, war upon both would follow. This too was accepted and the Korinthians who had taken part in the massacre of their fellow citizens earlier in the Korinthian War left the city.

Endnotes

1   For the history and reconstruction of an ancient Greek warship see J. S. Morrison, J. F. Coates and N. B. Rankov, *The Athenian Trireme,* Cambridge, Cambridge University Press, 1986 – a fascinating account containing some reconstructions of battles. Of these, however, that of Arginusai is obviously incorrect. For alternatives to this important battle late in the Peloponnesian War see Donald Kagan, *The Fall of the Athenian Empire,* Ithaca, NY, Cornel University, 1987, Chapter 13; J. F. Lazenby, *The Peloponnesian War – A Military Study,* London, Routledge, 2004; and Hutchinson, *Attrition.* Kagan's account is ingenious but a little misguided when dealing with the Athenian centre in the line of battle. Lazenby and Hutchinson are broadly in agreement on a plausible reading of the sources concerning the battle lines although there are differences of emphasis in the detail.

2   Seamanship had reached a high level of sophistication. Indeed, reading of the knowledge of local winds used to advantage by the Athenian commander Phormio in 429 BC (see Thuc. II. 84) suggests that the tactical aspect of natural elements was an important issue. Much acquired knowledge of tides, currents and hidden hazards would be experiential and would be passed on. There would be nothing new in the measures taken for the concealment of his squadron by Gorgopas.

3   Pharnabazos, his predecessor, had gone to Susa to marry the Great King's daughter.

CHAPTER 8

Sparta at the Zenith of its Power in Mainland Greece

No general should fight a battle simply out of pique

Sun Tzu, *The Art of War*, XII. 18; Y Shibing trans.

Now that peace was fully endorsed by all, Sparta was in a position of total dominance. Sadly for Greece, Sparta's first actions proved to be small minded: 'the Lacedaimonians resolved, in the case of all among their allies who had been hostile during the war and more favourably inclined toward the enemy than toward Lacedaimon, to chastise them and put them in such a situation that they could not be disloyal' (Xen. *Hell.* V. 2. 1).

Just as at the end of the Peloponnesian War, Sparta's allies were reluctant to join it in teaching Elis a lesson for its recalcitrance, and withheld their support, Sparta pressed on with 'schooling' its supposed allies to its will. Sparta was slow to learn from its diplomatic errors and, now, twenty or so years later, it was embarking on a programme of discipline not too dissimilar from previously. Sparta had not wholly appreciated that its earlier actions with respect to Elis had eventually contributed to the establishment of the coalition that had led to the Korinthian War. This did not bode well for a settled future.

Mantineia was the first city to be targeted. The reasons given for disciplining this ally were various, but the desire to see the demolition of its defensive walls was uppermost. The various villages of Mantineia had joined together to form a city around 470 BC. Now Sparta was of the opinion that the misdeeds suffered from this ally should be punished. It was accused of supplying corn to Argos during the Korinthian War, of having withheld its contingent to Sparta's forces on the pretext of a holy truce, and of its troops having served half-heartedly when they were present. In addition, the people had shown pleasure at Sparta's misfortune at Lechaion: 'When he (Agesilaos) approached Mantineia, by leaving Orchomenos before dawn he passed by that city while it was still dark: so hard, he thought, would the soldiers find it to see the Mantineians rejoicing at their misfortune' (Xen. *Hell.* IV. 5. 18).

Mantineia was ordered to demolish its fortifications and, when this was refused, Agesipolis undertook command of the army sent against the city. The usual practice of ravaging the surrounding territory was undertaken without any positive response from the Mantineians. The king now ordered a trench to be dug around the city, with half the army digging and being protected from possible forays by the other half, posted between the diggers and the walls. With the trench completed, it was possible to add a circumvallation of the city.

The intention to conduct a siege was disappointed when Agesipolos learnt that Mantineia was well provisioned. Not wishing to prolong the expedition to the discomfort of both his state and its allies, Agesipolis struck upon the idea of building a dam to interrupt the flow of the river that ran through the city. This was done, not to deprive the inhabitants of water, but rather to cause damage within the conurbation. The placing of the dam at the point where the river issued from the city, rather than where it entered, indicates the intention.

As the waters rose, the sodden foundations crumbled, the walls cracked and reached a state of collapse as their support diminished. Faced with the prospect of becoming prisoners of war, the Mantineians agreed to pull down their walls. A further condition was added to Sparta's demands. If they were to have peace, the Mantineians had to disperse and live in smaller village communities. This was agreed, and those of the inhabitants who had supported Argos, together with the leaders of the democrats, were saved at the request of Agesipolis' exiled father Pausanias. Some sixty men went into exile. The aristocratic party now assumed governance, and each of the four new villages had its own Spartan officer sent to it at the time of an army muster. With the absence of any significant democratic presence, such musters proved to be less of a problem.

Phleious was the next to be targeted. This was at the opportunistic instigation of exiles who had duly noted what had happened at Mantineia. The mere threat of an expedition against them led to the Phliasians agreeing to the return of the exiles and, to the gift to them, of reparation.

In the following year, *c.*383/2 BC, a clear proof that the Greek mainland now regarded Sparta as its arbiter is seen in the arrival in Sparta of representatives from Akanthos and Apollonia. Using their time-honoured procedure of calling together their own assembly and their allies, these ambassadors were given a hearing. The problem they outlined was the threat posed by the city of Olynthos. Since the beginning of the century, this city had benefited from the weakness of Makedon.[1] It had gradually developed control over its neighbours in Chalkidike and then brought under its influence several cities in Makedon, including Pella – which was later to become Philip II's capital. Now the Akanthians and Apollonians were being given the unenviable choice of joining the Olynthian League willingly, or being forced to do so. Other cities in the area, still independent for the moment, were too fearful of Olynthos to send their ambassadors to Sparta.

The ambassadors also reported that that they had knowledge that Athens and Thebes were considering entering into alliance with Olynthos. This last point was a possibility in that, had there been action only against Makedon, this would not have breached the Peace of Antalkidas. However, there is more than a hint that the product of such an alliance would be a great problem if eventually turned against Sparta (Xen. *Hell.* V. 2. 15).

Here was a case of the continuing development of a federal power with Olynthos at its head.[2] It could easily be compared to Thebes' former control of the cities of Boiotia, with the exception of Orchomenos. The region was rich in resources and expansion eastwards was a realistic possibility.

The allies agreed that action should be taken and that an army to the total of 10,000 be raised. All allies were to supply men to an agreed number proportionate to their population, or to give funds in their place. The values were placed at three Aiginetan obols per day for each foot-soldier and quadruple that for any cavalryman. This allowed mercenaries to be hired and was not too dissimilar to the Athenian requirement of the previous century that its 'allies' provided ships or a monetary donation to an equivalent value. In the case of Athens this had led to many of its allies becoming tribute-paying 'subjects', as power inevitably became centralised on Athens herself. In the present case, any ally that made no contribution was to be fined by Sparta at a cost of two drachmas per day per man.

Urgency was added to the plans by the final words of the ambassadors. They recommended that, while the army was gathering, an advance force of sufficient operational strength should be sent as soon as possible. To that end, 2,000 men made up of *perioikoi, neadamodeis* and Skiritai set off under the command of Eudamidas. He was obviously appointed as commander-in-chief and requested of the *ephors* that his brother, Phoibidas, take charge of the muster and follow on after him with the rest of the army.

On arrival in Chalkidike Eudamidas garrisoned those cities requiring them and made Poteidaia, which voluntarily came over to him, his base. Poteidaia held a strategic position at the neck of Pallene, the westernmost of the three large peninsulas that stretch into the Aegean from the base of Chalkidike. It was only about five miles to the south of Olynthos and cut off this city from settlements on the peninsula such as Sane, Mende and Skione. The Spartans were therefore in a position to threaten any move made by the Olynthians against Akanthos to the east and Apollonia to the north. Under such conditions there was little likelihood that cities of the Olynthian federation would risk coming to the aid of Olynthos even if there was a desire to do so. The rolling country of the area suited hoplites and cavalry. It was less suitable for peltasts, unless operating in conjunction with supportive cavalry or hoplites to protect them from being run down by enemy cavalry. The terrain was not rough enough to impede cavalry or to give peltasts the protection to be employed as a singular arm.

What follows from this point makes Sparta's intentions clear. The opportunity to exercise authority in the north was eagerly taken. Critically, the action of Phoibidas, described below, on his journey north with the main army raises many questions. The foremost is whether his coming action at Thebes was opportunist or pre-planned. The present writer is of the opinion that Phoibidas acted on an opportunity, the possibility of which may not have been wholly unexpected and in which the involvement of Agesilaos in its planning cannot readily be discounted.

On his march north, Phoibidas encamped very close to the city of Thebes. He was there sufficiently long for Leontiadas, one of the two Theban *polemarch*s, to make a proposal to him for the capture of the Kadmeia.[3] Again, can this be wholly coincidental? The festival of Thesmophoria was soon to take place, wherein all the women of the city went to the Kadmeia, where the assembly was displaced to a stoa (a colonnaded building) in the *agora* (marketplace).

It is reported that Thebes had voted not to supply men or funds for the Spartan expedition (Xen. *Hell.* V. 2. 27). The timing of the proclamation is not known, but this would be yet another aggravation for Sparta. It could well be that Phoibidas had arrived with the expectation of receiving additional forces from

Thebes and that the vote took place around the time of his arrival. Certainly there were opposing factions in the city. That of Leontiadas supported Sparta, while that of the other *polemarch*, Ismenias, was adamantly opposed. This was the same Ismenias who had successfully rid Thessaly of Spartan influence and had taken the Spartan colony of Herakleia in Trachis in 394 BC.

The plan as outlined by Leontiadas was that the Spartan army should appear to carry on with its march and, when the assembly was convened in the market area, he would ride out and lead the Spartans back to the city. This he did and, in August of 382 BC, with the streets empty, the Kadmeia was taken. Presumably the women of the city were held temporarily as hostages while Leontiadas went to the assembly. There he had Ismenias arrested by Leontiadas' fellow conspirators while some of those who were of the same anti-Spartan opinion as Ismenias left the city. Those who remained, numbering 300, left soon after for Athens on learning that Ismenias was imprisoned in the Kadmeia.

Meantime, Leontiadas went to Sparta. There he found those in governance outraged by Phoibidas' unilateral action – not for the act itself, but because he had acted without the authority of the state in the matter. Agesilaos, no doubt personally delighted with the turn of events, made the point that:

> if what he (Phoibidas) had done was harmful to Lakedaimon, he deserved to be
> punished, but if advantageous, it was a time-honoured custom that a commander,
> in such cases, had the right to act on his own initiative. 'It is precisely this point,
> therefore,' he said, 'which should be considered, whether what has been done is
> good or bad for the state.' (Xen. *Hell.* V. 2. 32)

Leontiadas addressed the Spartan assembly and rehearsed the varying grievances that Sparta held against Thebes. He also referred to the alliance with Olynthos. Now, he insisted, danger was averted and the Spartans could look forward to fulsome support from Thebes.

Despite the outrage perpetrated on Thebes by Phoibidas, he was only fined.[4] We shall find him later in a position of command. It proved convenient to Sparta to maintain a garrison on the Kadmeia in support of the oligarchic party of Leontiadas, but pro-Spartan Xenophon recognised Phoibidas' action as a violation not only of the conditions of the peace but, more importantly, in disrupting a religious convention, as blasphemy.

Three representatives from Sparta and one from each of its allies made up a court that tried Ismenias. They found him guilty mainly on charges relating to receiving monies from Persia and being the cause of problems throughout Greece. He was executed and Thebes settled to a period of collaboration with Sparta.

The following year saw Teleutias appointed to the command of operations against Olynthos. On his steady and unhurried march north, he collected additional forces and ensuring no harm came to friendly states as he went. He sent a message to Amyntas, king of Makedon, to hire mercenaries and to pay monies to neighbouring dynasts so that they would enter into alliance. In such a way Amyntas would eventually regain those dominions lost to the Olynthians. Derdas of Elimeia was also persuaded to join the expeditionary force.

Teleutias' advance on Olynthos from his base at Poteidaia made no depredation of the enemy territory; these actions were reserved for his withdrawal. Having reached a position about a mile from the city, the army halted to come into battle line.

Teleutias positioned himself on the left wing for the reason that this put him directly opposite the city gate from which the enemy was now emerging. The phalanx therefore extended to his right, his own wing being screened by Derdas and his 400 cavalry, and that of the right wing by Theban, Makedonian and Lakedaimonian horse.

The Olynthian line formed up below their walls. It would appear that they had placed the whole of their considerable cavalry on their left from where they made an early attack. The Spartan cavalry commander was killed and the whole of Teleutias' cavalry on his right wing was put to flight. Now the hoplites on the right who had been adjacent to the defeated cavalry are described as giving ground, signalling the danger of a likely defeat for Teleutias. The lack of detail in sources leaves it in doubt as to whether the crumbling right wing was caused by flank attacks upon it by the victorious Olynthian cavalry or whether it was giving way against that part of its opposing hoplite phalanx, discussed further below. The day was saved by the opportune action of Derdas who quickly charged towards the city gates followed by the section of the phalanx under Teleutias. The Olynthian cavalry saw that they were in danger of being shut out of the city and made a dash for the gates. They suffered severely as they rode past Derdas and his men. Xenophon (*Hell.* V. 2. 42) adds that the Olynthian hoplites also reached the safety of the city with less proportionate casualties than their cavalry because of their proximity to the city walls. They would have been given sufficient covering fire from the walls for a relatively ordered retiral. It suggests that the Olynthian hoplites had not engaged and had remained in line beneath these walls. It would be the Olynthian cavalry, whose attack had carried them a considerable distance from their line, who had to run the hail of missiles from Derdas' men. With victory to Teleutias, the withdrawal saw trees felled, possibly to impede any easy attack on his rear as well as to create economic harm to Olynthian territory.

Throughout the remainder of the summer, both sides carried out raids. At the beginning of the campaigning season of 381 BC, presumably when allied forces were returning to Teleutias after the winter, Derdas had arrived at Apollonia with his men. They were taking refreshment when around 600 Olynthian cavalry raided the district. Derdas ensured that his men and their horses were at the ready, but hidden and quiet. With no opposition apparent, the Olynthians penetrated the surrounding homesteads and came almost to the gates of the city. They were obviously not in any specific order, but rather acting as marauding groups. With their proximity to the gates, Derdas' attack upon them had the advantage of surprise and good order. The Olynthians fled at the first sight of them. What is significant is that Derdas continued the pursuit for more than twelve miles, killing some eighty of the enemy. This in itself is impressive and had such an unnerving effect on the Olynthians that they remained near to their city, putting only the closest of their land under cultivation from that time on. The distance gives us the clear indication that the Apollonia mentioned is that almost due north of Olynthos and not Apollonia Mygdonia still further to the north-east on Lake Bolbe.

On the next occasion in which the Spartan-led army took the field it proceeded to destroy any crops and remaining trees around Olynthos, presumably in the hope of provoking an engagement. The Olynthians could have chosen to do nothing, but their response deserves careful attention. Their cavalry very deliberately came out of the city and crossed the nearby river. This watercourse, the river Retsinikia as it is known today, runs to the west of the city and is still fordable. Xenophon's description implies that their continued approach towards the marauding army was quiet and unhurried. Teleutias is reported to have been irritated by their courage and ordered his peltasts to make an attack upon them. It is to be noted that these peltasts went into the attack without support from another arm. The Olynthian cavalry did not wait for the attack but quietly returned over the river. The commander of the Olynthian cavalry proved to be an extremely able tactician.

102

When only a proportion of the peltasts had crossed the river in pursuit, he turned his cavalry and made a charge upon them. The peltast commander Tlemonidas was killed, along with more than 100 of his men. Presumably those who had not yet crossed, or who were in the process of doing so, were dissuaded from continuing the pursuit. Teleutias was now outraged and led the hoplites quickly forwards, meantime ordering both peltasts and cavalry to precede him and press the pursuit without respite. The Olynthian cavalry gained the safety of the city and the pursuers came too close to the city walls. There, as would be expected, they suffered missile attacks and were obliged to start their retiral in some disorder. At that point, the Olynthian cavalry made a timely reappearance, sallying forth with peltasts in support, adding to the confusion of the Lakedaimonian army, only to be followed by the Olynthian hoplites. These last, obviously in good order, quickly made an attack on the disordered phalanx of their enemy, presumably exploiting any gaps in their ranks. Much in the manner of Lysander at Haliartos, Teleutias lost his life in this action of 380 BC, and his army was routed. Survivors found sanctuary in neighbouring friendly cities and Xenophon notes that the Olynthians killed 'a vast number of men, including the most serviceable part of the army' (Xen. *Hell.* V. 3. 6).[5]

This was a considerable disaster for Spartan policy but Sparta determined to move quickly to regain the dominant position previously held. Olynthos was not to be allowed any opportunity for resurgence. To that end, Sparta gave the command to Agesipolis. Just as Agesilaos had been allotted thirty Spartiatai when in Asia Minor, the same number were given to his colleague. Xenophon indicates that within the muster were many volunteers from the more prominent *perioikoi* (Xen. *Hell.* V. 3. 9). He also adds at the same location the useful information that among the volunteers were men from other cities who had been sent by their parents as children to undertake the Spartan form of training and education. In addition, in the muster, we catch a glimpse of the illegitimate sons of Spartiatai, born most probably of *helot* women, who, although not citizens, enjoyed some, or all, of the training experiences of the *agoge*. The particular mention of such a group gives some indication of the continuing reduction in citizen manpower. There seems to have been enthusiasm for the expedition even among the allies, and Thessaly provided cavalry.

Of the allies, Phleious had readily contributed monies for the expedition but, with Agesipolis now in the north, went back on its word to make reparation to its former exiles (see above). Representatives of this group came with their complaints to Sparta. To compound the issue further, the democrats of Phleious fined these so-called restored exiles for approaching Sparta. Although Xenophon says that they were confident that Sparta would not send Agesilaos out against them, as it was the custom not to send both kings out of their territory at any one time, it was still perfectly possible to take action against them under another commander. As it was, Agesilaos was indeed given command by the *ephors*. After successfully sacrificing at Sparta's northern frontier, Agesilaos advanced and was met on the way by Phliasian ambassadors offering him sums of money as an inducement not to invade their territory. On his refusal, they agreed to do whatever he required of them. His response was that he could not trust the word of a people who had not honoured their previous agreement. He demanded that they put their citadel into his hands as they had done some ten years earlier when threatened by Iphikrates. At that time, when the danger to Phleious had passed, the Spartans had left both the city and its acropolis.

On their refusal, Agesilaos settled to a siege of the city. Even under these circumstances friends and relatives of the exiles managed to come out of the city and Agesilaos organised that common messes should be made among these Phliasians and that any of the newcomers, who were willing to serve in the army, should be provisioned, trained and armed. The exiles undertook the expense of this exercise and eventually produced a force of more than 1,000 hoplites. Nonetheless, Phleious held out for more than a year and a half, mainly through the efforts of a citizen called Delphion. He, with 300 followers, incarcerated those under suspicion of wishing to come to terms and forced the population to maintain strict guard over the city, often under guard themselves. He was successful in his sallies against those guarding the siege wall and it was only when he was faced with famine that he allowed an embassy to go to Sparta to ask for terms.

Agesilaos, as commander in the field, had the authority of the state to make any settlement he wished. Nonetheless, he allowed the embassy safe passage, but sent a message to Sparta to the effect that the final decision should be left to him. On the embassy's return to Phleious, Delphion and one other made their escape and Agesilaos left a garrison in the city. He ordered that fifty of the exiles and fifty of the hitherto besieged citizens should together decide who should be put to death.

At the time of early operations in that siege, Agesipolis, in the north, had marched upon Olynthos by way of Makedon. The usual depredations of the countryside followed without any attempt by the enemy to prevent them. Similar attacks were made against Olynthian allies and the important city of Torone, situated on the middle of the three peninsulas, Sithonia, was taken by storm. There, Agesipolis, caught a fever and died seven days later in the late summer of 380 BC. As he was a Spartan king, his body was preserved in honey and taken to Sparta to be interred. Polybiades took his place. He competently completed the job by compelling the Olynthians, now faced with famine, to sue for peace and dissolve its federation. Olynthos and its former allies took the customary oath to have the same friends and enemies as Sparta and to follow wherever it led. And so 379 BC saw the end of both the Phliasian and Olynthian affairs, but in the cause of the latter they had lost two of their ablest commanders. The return to Amyntas of the territories taken by the Olynthians in return for his help in the Olynthian war left him, without any curb in the area, to lay the foundation for the power Makedon was to become under his son Phillip II.

Although it had been dominant since the Peloponnesian War, Sparta was now at the pinnacle of its power. None in Greece was in a position to gainsay its diktat. It is at this specific point in Xenophon's account that he sets out what he obviously believes to be the direct cause of Sparta's eventual downfall:

> Now one could mention many other incidents, both among Greeks and barbarians, to prove that the gods do not fail to take heed of the wicked or those who do unrighteous things; but at present I will speak of the case which is before me. The Lacedaimonians, namely, who had sworn that they would leave the states independent, after seizing possession of the Acropolis of Thebes were punished by the very men, unaided, who had been thus wronged, Although before that time they had not been conquered by any single one of all the peoples that ever existed. (Xen. *Hell*. V. 4. 1)

To digress, the power of piety among the Greeks should never be underestimated. The Spartans themselves were probably the most pious of all Greek-speaking peoples but Xenophon, an Athenian, whose sympathies lay with his adoptive country while in exile, saw what most Greeks would agree was a violation of an oath which could well bring retribution from the gods. Today, it may appear hard to understand the depth of belief in ritual, sacrifice, the examination of entrails, divination, festivals to the gods, portents and oaths sworn in the name of the gods, yet Greek history is peppered with examples of such religious observance. A prime example is that reported by Thucydides, himself a possible minority sceptic, which took place in the Peloponnesian War some thirty-four years earlier. In 413 BC, when it was imperative that the Athenians, then in dire straits, leave the environs of Syrakuse, a lunar eclipse made their commander, Nikias, consult his seers and soothsayers. At their recommendation it was decided to delay the Athenian withdrawal for a period of three times nine days. This merely exacerbated the already desperate circumstances in which the Athenian expeditionary force found itself and inevitably set the seal on its annihilation. This is surely an extreme example of the need to observe divine wishes conquering the very strong urge for self-preservation. That the decision was accepted by over 30,000 men without reported dissent is illuminating.

The quotation above from Xenophon refers to the Thebans. As time went on, the pro-Spartan leaders at Thebes felt that they had to maintain their position by a policy of repression. They had the comfort that they had the Spartan garrison to aid them if any opposition appeared. The Spartans had been in occupation of the Kadmeia for nearly four years. Although no evidence of atrocities can be levelled against them, for it would not be in the Spartan character, it was those they supported who would seem to have eventually provoked their own downfall and led to the liberation of Thebes.

Our main sources differ, but those of Plutarch, the most detailed, and Xenophon are broadly in agreement, while that of Diodoros is not wholly logical.[6] Plutarch, a native of the Boiotian city of Chairoeia, reflects the Boiotian tradition even though he was writing some centuries after the occasion. His version of events reads more like a boy's adventure story, giving points in the narrative where almost all comes to grief.

Plutarch reports that Leontidas' party sent men to assassinate the leaders of the Theban exiles now living in Athens. They failed, and Sparta requested that Athens expel the exiles. This request is likely to have been made much earlier than the assassination attempts, but follows the report of them in Plutarch's sequence. The Athenians had refused the Spartan request, being grateful for the help received from the Thebans in giving succour to their own exiled democrats immediately after the Peloponnesian War. The attempts against the leaders of the exiles could well have provoked some reaction, but it is more likely that they had been awaiting any opportunity that presented itself.

Working through an intermediary called Phillidas, who had acquired the post of secretary to the Theban *polemarchs*, men in the city made arrangements with the exiles to attempt a coup. Pelopidas, of whom we will hear much later, is given a leading role in Plutarch's account but is not mentioned by Xenophon, whose leading figure is Melon. In brief, seven of the younger exiles volunteered to enter the city secretly, armed only with daggers. After approaching at night, they hid for the following day and entered the city along with those who had been working outside the walls. They then spent the night and the following day at the house of a leading citizen by the name of Charon. Meantime, Phillidas had suggested to the *polemarchs* that he would provide them and their friends present with 'the most stately and beautiful women there were in Thebes' at the customary celebration of the end of their term in office. Xenophon adds a personal touch at this point, 'And they – for they were that sort of men – expected to spend the night very pleasantly.' Plying the *polemarchs* with drink, Phillidas ensured that they were sufficiently under its influence before he acceded to repeated requests to bring in the women. He did this only after the *polemarchs* had agreed that no servants were to be present, otherwise, he said, the women would refuse to enter: 'Then he led in the supposed courtesans and seated them one beside each man. And the agreement was, that when they were seated, they should unveil themselves and strike at once' (Xen. *Hell.* V. 4. 6–7).

The deed done, Phillidas went with three men to Leontidas' home and, after gaining entry on the pretence of carrying a message from the *polemarchs*, dispatched him. He then went to the prison and gained entry by a similar ruse. The guard was killed, the prisoners released, armed, and marshalled near the shrine of Amphion. A proclamation was made calling for the Thebans to join them. Initially, this call was not wholly believed and it was not until daylight that hoplites and cavalrymen joined their fellows at the shrine.

Meanwhile, the Spartan garrison commander had managed to send for help to Thespiai and Plataia. As the Plataian cavalry approached the city they were repulsed with the loss of around twenty men. In support of the cause of the exiles, a force of Athenian volunteers under two generals had been at the border between the two states.[7] With the success of the operation thus far, these Athenians arrived and joined in an attack on the Kadmeia. It soon became apparent that this position was untenable and the Spartan *harmost* came to terms under the condition that his men could withdraw in safety, while keeping their arms. It is obvious in both descriptions of this withdrawal that there were quite a number of citizens among the body that retired from the citadel. Plutarch states that during the tumult of the night, when the exiles had made the proclamation, many had been so frightened by the noise and lights that they had taken refuge with the garrison. As they emerged from the safety of the Kadmeia, those citizens, who were perceived as political opponents, were killed and even their children were sought out and done away with. The luckier ones were those who were quietly rescued by the Athenians

Such was the vehemence often shown between political factions and one that had caused untold suffering for more than a century before. It is not a simple matter to accept that this was a battle between the ideologies of democracy and oligarchy. In any conflict support was usually given by each side to those in a city who proved most sympathetic to the cause of their current protector. It is well to remember, for those who champion the example of the democracy of Athens and her imitators, that it was Sparta that first recognised, well before others, the equality of its citizen body within a clearly defined constitution. To argue that they lived above a subservient population of *helots*, semi-autonomous *neadamodeis* and *perioikoi* is to overlook the fact that all Greek city-states depended on a large slave population. Just as Sparta denied common citizen rights to other groups, so also did Athens: e.g. metics and slaves. More than 20,000 slaves from Athens had escaped to Spartan-held Dekeleia in the later stages of the Peloponnesian War. Athens' only excuse was that slaves in Athens were usually foreigners and not fellow Greeks. Finally, in this short digression, it was a Spartan king, Pausanias, who restored democracy to Athens at the end of the Peloponnesian War.

Sparta's reaction to the event at Thebes was swift. The governor, who had given up the Kadmeia rather than holding out for the inevitable relief force which would have been sent, was tried and executed. An immediate ban was called and Agesipolis' successor Kleombrotos was given command. An interesting fact emerges in relation to this appointment. Agesilaos had been the first choice for the command. He had argued, however, that he was over sixty, beyond the age at which citizens were expected to serve beyond the borders of Sparta. The reasons for his reluctance at this time to take command are questionable, considering that, just over a year later, he was again in command of Spartan forces well beyond its frontiers. Perhaps credence can be given to Xenophon's comments: 'It was not, however, for this reason that he stayed at home, but because he well knew that if he was in command the citizens would say that Agesilaos was making trouble for the state in order that he might give assistance to tyrants, therefore he let them decide as they would about the matter' (Xen. *Hell.* V. 4. 13). Certainly the cautious conduct of Kleombrotos on this so-called campaign led his men to 'being vastly puzzled to know whether there was really a war between them and the Thebans, or peace' (Xen. *Hell.* V. 4. 16).

Nonetheless, the move north by a Spartan army, passing Athenian territory as it did, alarmed them sufficiently that they appear to have disowned the supportive actions taken by their volunteer force. They called the two generals to face charges, executed the one who appeared and exiled the wiser of the two who had chosen to leave the state rather than face trial. On hearing of this, Thebes became alarmed. It had, no doubt, counted on the continuing and even more fulsome support of Athens. Now it was alone.

Kleombrotos had left one of his client Spartiatai as governor of Thespiai with sufficient money to hire mercenaries. Although this may look as if it was similar to the subjection of Thebes, the appointment of Sphodrias was no doubt made as a protection for Sparta's ally against Thebes. It proved not to be a good choice.

Athens' own position had been quietly improving. Ever since the Battle of Knidos Athens had taken every opportunity to bring into alliance any state which appeared willing to enter into such an arrangement. An embryonic second Athenian league was growing, possibly as a result of islands such as Chios fearing interference from the Persian-controlled mainland nearby. It probably makes more sense to follow Diodoros in the absence of any substantive information from Xenophon. Diod. XV. 27. 3 informs us that support from places such as Chios, Byzantion, Rhodes and Mytilene was given to Athens. Others followed eventually during the following years, no doubt encouraged by the very different terms on which the league came to be founded, putting clear limits on any recurrence of the former Athenian Empire with its garrisons and settlers.[8] Cities on Euboia joined the league and eventually Thebes was drawn into an alliance with Athens as a protection against Sparta. All this was a gradual process. However, Diod. XV. 28. 4–5 indicates that Sparta was aware of unrest in its followers and of an apparent growing opposition. Well before the accretion of so many cities to the league it must have been a matter of concern in Sparta. There would be opinions among some citizens that a firm move should be made to curb the growing power base in its early stages.

It was probably for this reason, rather than as a consequence of Athenian support for the liberation of Thebes, that the Sphodrias outrage occurred. At *Hell.* V. 4. 20, Xenophon claims that the Thebans bribed Sphodrias to invade Attika, their intention being to force Athens openly to their side in the conflict with Sparta. This view is given support by Plutarch in his *Life of Pelopidas* XIV. There may have been gossip to this effect, but it is equally possible that Sphodrias saw an opportunity to emulate Phoibidas. After an early evening meal he led the forces at his disposal from Thespiai on a march, the object of which was the capture of Peiraieos. Dawn found him well short of his target and in the Thriasian plain. His presence was reported to those in Athens and the city was put on immediate alert. Realising that a surprise capture of the Athenian harbour district was now impossible, Sphodrias turned back, plundering stock and houses as he returned to Thespiai.

His raid occurred at a time when three Spartan ambassadors were present in Athens and they were arrested. They were only released when they convinced the Athenians that it would have been folly for them to be in the city at such a time had they had knowledge of what had been intended. Further, they predicted that Sphodrias would be brought to trial and put to death for his action. Sphodrias was, indeed, charged but failed to appear for trial. Incredibly he was acquitted. It was inevitable that there was a division of opinion on the matter within Sparta. Given Xenophon's lengthy explanation of how the acquittal came about (*Hell.* V. 4. 25–33), there is no doubt that the influence of Agesilaos was pivotal.

Examining Sphodrias' plan, it is easy to understand why he failed in the enterprise, if indeed his target was the port of Athens. The distance between Thespiai and Peiraieos is well over forty miles and over some difficult terrain. Anyone who knows the region well will appreciate that he had no chance of reaching his goal and, if he had, his men would have been too exhausted to be effective. This was a man of courage and ambition but little common sense.

It is understandable that his acquittal drove Athens firmly back into open alliance with Thebes. It can be assumed that, while Athens was comfortable to be in such an alliance, it would not have been so had Thebes held control over other Boiotian cities, as it had done before the King's Peace. Peiraieos was gated, and Athens accelerated its programme of shipbuilding.

Agesilaos, preferred at this time by Sparta over Kleombrotos, was prevailed upon to take the command against Thebes and hostilities began.

Endnotes

1 Hornblower, pp. 204–6 gives an invaluable insight into the political opportunism of Olynthos.

2 There is an obvious error in the text when it gives the hoplite strength of Olynthos. The gross underestimate of 800 is belied by the later numbers described in battle.

3 The Kadmeia was the citadel of Thebes. Although much lower than the Acropolis in Athens or the Akrokorinth at the Isthmos, it still dominates the land around it. See also Diod. XV. 1–3 and, for the contemporary view of Phoibidas' act and his punishment, Isocrates, *Panegyricus* 126.

4 Plutarch (*Life of Pelopidas* 6) puts the total of the fine at 100,000 drachmas, a considerable figure.

5 Xenophon also makes the point that a commander 'especially that, in dealing with enemies, to attack under the influence of anger and not with judgement is an absolute mistake. For anger is a thing which does not look ahead, while judgement aims no less to escape harm than to inflict it upon the enemy' (Xen. Hell. V. 3. 3–7).

6 Diod. XV. 25–7; Plut. *Pelop.* 7–12; Xen. *Hell.* V. 4. 1–12.

7 Diod. XV. 26. 1 states that the Athenian assembly approved of the dispatch of an army to support the Theban exiles. In weighing the evidence, scholars have shown division, but the balance is in favour of a volunteer force approved in principle, but not given formal approval. See also Hornblower, p. 209 for a supportive view of Diodoros.

8 Among the later additions to the league, which in total number nearly seventy, are Kerkyra, Kephalonia and Akarnania. Evidence of the original formal foundation of 377 BC is to be found in inscriptions of the period, see Tod, vol. II. nos 118, 121, 122 and 123.

CHAPTER 9

The Drift to Leuktra

> The direct cause of the decline of Sparta was the great power it won at
> Aigospotami and the resulting hubris. What came about in other places
> by defeat and factional fighting was achieved here by success – forced to
> rule over Greece with its fully developed individualism, this people too
> had to become individualised, and the Spartan spirit, already seriously
> undermined, was totally fragmented.
>
> Burckhardt, *The Greeks and Greek Civilisation*

THE 370S HAD STARTED WELL for Sparta. The Chalkidian League had
been crushed in 379 BC, and all seemed to be well under Sparta's control.
Within a year, however, the opportune recapture of the Kadmeia and the
subsequent expulsion of the Spartan garrison from Thebes proved unsettling,
but did not necessarily in itself provoke an insoluble problem. It was Sphodrias'
unilateral and unprovoked attempt to capture the port of Athens within the year
that drove Athens into alliance with Thebes and presented Sparta with a much
bigger problem.

Had Sparta dealt promptly with Sphodrias and punished him in a manner
acceptable to Athens, there would have been no breach between the two cities.
It was in Athens' long-term interest to have the Boiotian cities independent of
Thebes, and while this remained the case, Athens was prepared to make common
cause with Thebes against the Spartans.

Chabrias, one of Athens' most successful generals, joined the Theban, Gorgidas,
in the defence of Theban territory against Sparta. The latter is credited with the

foundation of the Theban Sacred Band,[1] made up of the 150 pairs of lovers, that was to prove so effective at Tegyra and Leuktra. This was a specialist force that quite soon became a crack unit in the Theban army. This corps was likely to have spent almost its whole time in mastering several manoeuvres not commonly expected of the main phalanx and these were soon to become evident in later actions.

There followed a clever defensive war. A trench and palisade was constructed around much of Theban territory in anticipation of future Spartan incursions. Little of great military consequence followed as successive Spartan invasions achieved little more than the destruction of crops when they managed to breach the defensive circuit. Sparta could not provoke the enemy to a formal field battle.

The tactics of Agesilaos' enemy initially prevented him from gaining access to the fertile areas under cultivation. Whenever he led his army along the stockade after breakfast, enemy forces moved ahead of him on the opposite side of the defences ready to resist any incursion. On one occasion, when Agesilaos withdrew to his camp, Theban cavalry came through the exits in the stockade and attacked the stragglers, killing a significant number of peltasts and some dismounted cavalry (Xen. *Hell.* V. 4. 39). As the appearance of the enemy became a post-breakfast routine, Agesilaos decided to make his advance at dawn before the expected arrival of the opposition. In such a way he gained easy access to the lands within the stockade and proceeded to devastate it right up to the walls of Thebes.

Towards the end of this first year's campaign the king fortified the city of Thespiai and left Phoibidas as its governor. From this base, Phoibidas made several raids to bring further depredation to the land around Thebes. These raids so provoked the Thebans that they invaded Thespian territory with their entire force. However, Phoibidas cleverly used his peltasts to cause discomfort to any who left the phalanx on the march. For this tactic to have worked, it must be assumed that the Theban advance was over rough terrain. So successful were the repeated attacks by the peltasts that the Thebans began to retreat, leaving the booty that they had gathered. Panic seemed to be emerging as the withdrawal proved to be much quicker than their initial advance. Phoibidas increased his attacks and ordered the Thespian hoplites to follow in battle order. It seems obvious that Phoibidas was seeking to cause maximum damage to the Thebans and convert his opportune attacks into a significant victory. However, some Theban cavalry, whose duty at that time would have been to screen the retreating rearguard of their army, found themselves trapped in an impassable ravine. They turned in desperation to make a counterattack, having no other alternative, and Phoibidas and a few of his pursuing peltasts were killed. They had been considerably ahead of their fellows in the pursuit and their deaths caused the remainder of the serving mercenaries to take flight. Coming on the advancing Thespian hoplites these survivors infected the heavy infantry with fear and they too withdrew rapidly to the protection of their city walls, despite no significant pursuit being made by the Thebans (Xen. *Hell.* V. 4. 42–6).

Sparta's reaction to this was merely to send out a replacement governor to Thespiai with an additional *mora* and wait until the following spring when Agesilaos launched his second invasion. Much of Boiotia remained under Spartan control with the cities garrisoned and in the hands of oligarchic government. The democratic element in each now made it their business to leave and go to Thebes (Xen. *Hell.* V. 4. 46).[2]

Agesilaos sent orders to the Thespian governor to secure Mount Kithairon before he had even made the frontier sacrifices in Lakonia. On effecting a safe passage and arriving at Plataia,[3] he sent further orders for a market to be made in Thespiai for his men, and for any embassies to gather there to await his arrival. This proved to be a successful ruse. The Thebans deployed their forces to guard the entry to their district from Thespiai while Agesilaos struck out in an unanticipated direction to Erythrai. After a march in one day that would normally have taken an army two days to complete, he entered Theban territory through the now unguarded entry point in the stockade that he had used the previous year.

Widespread damage was done before Agesilaos started his withdrawal from Theban territory: 'Meanwhile the Thebans came up quietly and formed in line of battle against him on the hill called Old Woman's Breast, with the trench and stockade in their rear, believing this was a good place to risk a battle; for the ground at this point was a rather narrow strip and hard to traverse' (Xen. *Hell.* V. 4. 50).

Presumably because of the narrowness of the approach the Thebans were drawn up many ranks deep. According to Xenophon, Agesilaos wisely decided not to make an uphill attack on the Thebans but led his army away from them in the direction of the city. This was an intelligent move because it achieved its desired objective. It provoked great alarm among the Thebans, who had left their city virtually undefended. They abandoned their position and rushed post haste towards Thebes, passing by on higher ground. As they passed, Agesilaos' *polemarchs* and their men successively attacked them. Despite suffering some casualties, the Spartan forces cleared their enemy from the hills. It was only at the very walls of their city that the Thebans reformed and threatened the pursuing Skiritan contingent. The Skiritai did not engage but retired and, because of this retiral, the Thebans, who had suffered considerably up to that point, set up a battle trophy. Such were the accepted rituals of Classical warfare.

Agesilaos withdrew in his own good time and made camp in the very place where the Theban army had been deployed for battle. The following day he made his way to Thespiai. On that journey some mercenary peltasts in Theban service attempted to harass his rear. They urged the Athenian general, Chabrias, to join them in their enterprise. Without his support, they were dispersed and ridden down by the Olynthian cavalry with the Spartan army that wheeled and charged upon them. Pursued uphill, many of the mercenaries were killed.

The mention of Chabrias towards the end of Xenophon's treatment of this occasion suggests that the Athenian forces were present probably throughout the entire foregoing episode. There is a passage in Diodoros that probably alludes to Agesilaos' refusal of battle and shows that each side had reasons for remembering the incident slightly differently. While, in Xenophon, Agesilaos recognised the problems to be faced in attempting to dislodge the Theban army from a very strong position and achieved his objective by his move towards the city of Thebes. Diodoros gives the location of the Theban position at about one mile from Thebes on the oblong-shaped crest of a hill and suggests that it was the disciplined appearance of Chabrias' mercenaries which dissuaded Agesilaos from attacking the position: 'Chabrias the Athenian, however, leading his mercenary troops, ordered his men to receive the enemy with a show of contempt, maintaining all the while their battle lines, and leaning their shields against their knees, to wait with upraised spear' (Diod. XV. 32. 2 to 33. 1).[4]

Diodoros omits the Spartan move on the city but does record that the Thebans and their allies under Chabrias were unwilling to come down from their position to contest the issue in the formal traditional terms of a hoplite battle.

From what is reported in our sources, it seems obvious that Agesilaos was regarded as being far superior to Kleombrotos as a general (Xen. Hell. V. 4. 35). On each of his two invasions of Theban territory he had ensured his entry into Boiotia by securing the passes over Kithairon before his main force left Spartan territory. Kleombrotos, however, who led the third invasion due to the ill-health of Agesilaos, was forced to abandon the enterprise because he had neglected to make similar preparations and found the passes occupied by the enemy. Had Kleombrotos proved to be as successful as his colleague and continued crop depredation for a third year, matters may have turned out differently, for it is apparent that Thebes was suffering from a severe shortage of corn towards the end of Agesilaos' second campaign. So much so, that the Thebans dispatched two ships to Pagasai with ten talents for the purchase of grain (Xen. *Hell.* V. 4. 56). These ships were intercepted by three Spartan triremes stationed at Oreos on the northern coast of Euboia. The 300 men with the Theban ships were imprisoned in the town's acropolis, but, such was the laxity of the Lakedaimonian commander, Alketas, that the prisoners escaped. Furthermore, they made themselves masters of the strong point which had hitherto been their prison and brought the local population to revolt against Sparta and, in due course, returned to Thebes with the much-needed supplies. These were the kind of unnecessary errors that allowed the Thebans to continue in their struggle. They also had the good fortune not to be further molested by Agesilaos, who continued to be too ill to continue in command.

Agesilaos had demonstrated the accepted practices of old-fashioned Classical warfare: the securing of entry points into enemy territory before invading and the depredation of crops in an attempt to bring the opposition either to battle or terms, carried out over more than one season. It had worked for city-states for well over a century and the most recent success of this strategy had been at Olynthos.

However, not only were circumstances changing, but so were personalities, and, with them, practices too. Pelopidas, one of the heroes at the liberation of Thebes, came to the command of the Sacred Band and, along with his philosopher friend Epaminondas, was regularly elected to the position of *boiotarch* over the coming years. They brought new tactical and strategic thinking to the practice of warfare.

Meantime, the citizen body of Sparta had continued to diminish. Its members, once the significant core of any Peloponnesian army with an unrivalled ability for tactical manoeuvre, had sunk to such a low figure that virtually all would have been obliged to be in some position of command over others so that tactical moves could be achieved. It is possible that within the limitations of phalanx warfare these manoeuvres were reproducible, after training, by the mercenaries and *perioikoi* on whom Sparta now greatly relied. Study of preceding hoplite battles, where Spartan forces were significant in number, show that it was always the Spartan phalanx which dealt the coup de grace against an enemy, while their allies were sometimes subjected to heavy casualties. However, as will be seen later, even when the number of Spartiatai appeared small they continued to be brigaded together in battle.[5]

After the failure of Kleombrotos to force entry into Theban territory and the subsequent easing of pressure on Thebes and its food supplies, Sparta's allies sought to redirect Sparta's efforts to breaking the alliance between Athens and Thebes. Their aim was to use the sea power of the Peloponnesian League to interrupt grain supplies to Athens, the strategy that, in the view of Sparta's allies, had twice before brought Athens to its senses (Xen. *Hell*. V. 4. 60).

Pollis, the *navarch* of the Spartan-led fleet of sixty-five triremes, caused problems to the security of Athens' supply route by his very presence in nearby waters. Supplies, however, still managed to arrive at the port of Athens. In response, Chabrias was put in charge of the Athenian fleet that sailed for Naxos, an ally of Sparta. In the battle that ensued, the eighty-five Athenian triremes were victorious. Losses for the Spartan fleet are put at twenty-four vessels with eight captured with their crews, as against the eighteen lost by the Athenians (Diod. XV. 35. 2). Although Diodoros' brief description may be a little fanciful in supposed detail, he does mention that Chabrias did not pursue the defeated fleet, choosing to collect his men, both living and dead, from the waters. This was probably because of his fear of suffering the same fate as the victorious commanders at the Battle of Arginusai in 406 BC who were condemned to death by the Athenian assembly for neglecting to save their fellows.[6]

The Battle of Naxos[7] gave Athens supremacy at sea. Thebes, on hearing of Spartan preparations to ship an army across the Korinthian Gulf in the following year, requested that Athens send its fleet around the Peloponnese to threaten coastal incursions (Xen. *Hell*. V. 4. 62). Athens duly obliged, and Timotheos, the son of Konon, sailed round the Peloponnese capturing the island of Kerkyra and entering into alliances with parts of Akarnania on the north-west mainland. A Spartan fleet under an energetic *navarch*, Nikolochos, attempted with little success to disrupt Timotheos' activities. As a result, Athens regained much of its former influence in the west.

Within this period significant changes were taking place. Athens extended its league to around seventy members. It wisely put in place provisos for the membership: no garrisons in the form of Athenian settlers were permitted to be set up, nor could any Athenian acquire property on any member territory. The finances in the form of contributions to the league were administered by Athens, the acknowledged leader. As a further safeguard to any extension of the kind of power which had led Athens to its unpopular empire of the last half of the fifth century,[8] a voting system was put in place. The allies had their own meetings separate from those of the Athenian assembly. Both organisations could put forward proposals but either could exercise a veto.

Sparta seems to have reorganised the league of which it was leader into nine geographical sections, presumably for the changing requirements of warfare. It was not enough to rely on the manpower of an area to provide for an army, and states could offer funds for the purchase of mercenary troops in their place. This now encompassed the greater part of the Peloponnese, a good portion of central Greece and the Chalkidian and some Thrakian cities in the north. Notable, however, was that Sparta's influence in Thessaly was minimal, but more on that below.

The failure of Kleombrotos' invasion, the incapacity of Agesilaos, and the change in the direction of hostilities persuaded on Sparta by its allies, gave Thebes a much-needed breathing space. Thebes used this time well and regained influence over most of the Boiotian cities, giving assistance to democrats in all but Orchomenos and Chaironeia, which remained under Spartan control.

Then Sparta suffered a notable reverse on land in 375 BC which, in several ways, can be seen as a prelude to Leuktra. Our sources for the engagement are Diodoros XV. 37, who gives a brief mention, with no tactical detail, and Plutarch's *Life of Pelopidas* XVI and XVII. The latter, having behind it the Boiotian tradition, gives us greater insight. It may also derive from the work of contemporary sources now lost to us such as Ephoros.[9] What must surprise us is that Xenophon makes no mention of the engagement whatsoever, but this omission, like others in his memoirs, may have been one of distaste and therefore deliberate.

Sparta had maintained a military presence at Orchomenos for a considerable time. Initially, it had consisted of four *morai* together with allies, but it is very likely that this was reduced to a rotational procedure consisting of two *morai*.

This can be substantiated by the mention of two *polemarch*s, Gorgoleon and Theopompos, as commanders. Pelopidas learnt that the Spartans had made an expedition to Lokris and saw an opportunity to try to take Orchomenos in their absence, or so the story suggests. It is more likely that depredation of crops and damage to possessions beyond the city's defences was the more realistic prospect. He discovered that replacement Spartan troops were present at Orchomenos and therefore withdrew his forces from the immediate area.

Although the exact location of the engagement is not wholly certain, a calculated guess can be made. The name of the small battle gives us our main clue. Tegyra is purported to have been a small city a little to the east of Orchomenos, possibly on the site of modern-day Pirgos. It was within the area under its control that this momentous collision took place. Pelopidas' return to Thebes could not have proceeded very far when he found his way barred by the Spartan-led force returning from Lokris. Its return journey almost certainly would have been made via the relatively easy route from the coastal region of Lokris directly to the north of Orchomenos. Near modern Atalandi the Kallidromos range becomes much gentler, rising to little more than 2,300 feet in rolling foothills. This route gave access to the uplands of the friendly Phokian plain, with easy marching thereafter, past Exarhos, before approaching the destination, Orchomenos.

The confrontation obviously came as a surprise to both forces. With no prospect of avoiding contact, Pelopidas ordered his cavalry up from the rear to join in a charge, followed by the Sacred Band, now arranged in close order. To make sense of the action one must examine the likely arrangements of each small army at the point when the surprise sighting of each was made. The Spartan-led force would have been marching in column. There is no mention of cavalry, but it is possible that they had mounted Orchomenians accompanying them. Pelopidas' order to his cavalry was most likely intended to harass and delay the enemy's opportunity to deploy in battle line, so that his much smaller force of hoplites could themselves deploy for an attack on a disordered line. The ploy appears to have been successful. His aim appears initially to have been to force his way through the Lakedaimonian phalanx. The precedent for this is to be found at the Battle of Koroneia but, if Plutarch and his sources are to be believed, this was to develop into an operation of both cavalry and infantry, a surprising tactic for the time. Given the disparity in numbers between the two forces, it was probably Pelopidas' only chance of success, and a desperate one at that. It was almost suicidal for cavalry to charge an unbroken phalanx but, when closely supported by a crack infantry unit, the prospect could be grudgingly recognised as less certain when made against a phalanx not yet in battle order. The point of attack was made on the command position and this, more than anything else, brought early success. Both Spartan *polemarchs* were killed early in the encounter, suggesting that they were in close proximity. This indicates they were both at the head of their respective columns marching in parallel. Deployment of these columns to left and right to form a battle line would have brought the commanders together at the outset but had not been completed as the Thebans attacked.

The part of the Lakedaimonian phalanx that had achieved some form of order opened its ranks to provide a corridor through which the Thebans could pass through to its rear. Had Pelopidas passed through the phalanx he could well have been re-engaged by a reformed Spartan phalanx or decimated by a measured pursuit in good order. It was important for him to achieve success while still holding the initiative.

'But Pelopidas used the path thus opened to lead his men *against those of the enemy who still held together*, and slew them as he went along, so that finally all turned and fled' (Plut. *Pelop.* XVII. 4; emphasis added). The phrase in italics strongly indicates that the phalanx was not fully formed. It seems highly likely from the description that, once the breach appeared, instead of proceeding through to the rear, Pelopidas caused his men to turn to take the Lakedaimonian line in the flanks that were now exposed on either side of the corridor. The slaughter would be greater on the Spartan right as the attack would be made on its unshielded side. The men on this side would be the first to break and run, to be followed by those men on their left, dismayed at the sight. The pursuit was limited and a battle trophy set up.

Taking nothing away from the Thebans in their moment of significant glory, the composition of their enemies is less than certain. The only certainty we have of full Spartan citizens taking part in this small battle is in the persons of the *polemarch*s. The remainder of the two under-strength *morai* could have been made up of inferiors, *perioikoi*, allies, mercenaries or a mixture of any of these four groups. No doubt well trained, they would lack the more immediate articulation of manoeuvre of fifth-century Spartan armies. Just as training of the Theban and other citizen bodies was improving the morale, discipline and efficacy of their armies, Sparta's shrinking citizen numbers made Sparta more reliant on others unable to quickly match former standards.

The result of this success was to ensure that the Sacred Band[10] was henceforward always maintained as a separate division and not diluted by placements within the main phalanx (Plut. *Pelop.* XIX. 3). The Thebans immediately invaded Phokis. Sparta acted quickly and strongly, by sending Kleombrotos with four *morai* to protect its ally. Little activity occurred between the armed forces and, in many ways, the opportunity for anything of significance to happen was pre-empted by the peace negotiated by Persia.

This pause was welcome to most parties. Athens was financially exhausted. Thebes had urged Athens to deploy its fleet in a manner which had deflected Sparta's attention from Boiotia to Kerkyra and the north-west (see above), but Athens had received no financial support from Thebes for those fleets and expeditions, despite the benefits the latter had derived from the arrangement. Athens was also concerned by the rise of Thebes' power. The latter had used this time to make significant gains in its attempt to re-establish its Boiotian confederacy. Those in the ascendant in Sparta also recognised the need for some accommodation with Athens. If this could be achieved, Thebes could be more than contained. The broker of the peace, Persia, would hope to benefit from the mercenaries that such an agreement would make available to it in its attempt to regain Egypt.[11]

Thebes, however, was most unhappy. Having rebuilt the framework of its confederacy more by force than persuasion, it was faced with the insistence in the terms of the peace that all cities were to be autonomous. Thebes was not yet in a position to do anything except lodge objections. It could do no other than swear to the peace in its name only, and those of its nascent confederacy were permitted to be independent once more. It may appear strange that under the same requirements both Athens and Sparta continued to hold sway over the cities traditionally under their control. But this peace merely sought to restore the position achieved by the Peace of Antalkidas in 387 BC, at the time of the dissolution of the Theban Confederacy.

In just over a year, hostilities between Athens and Sparta resumed. This is alleged to have been provoked by the Athenian admiral Timotheos (Xen. *Hell.* VI. 2. 2–4). He was recalled from Kerkyra to Athens following the establishment of the peace. On his journey back to Athens, he returned exiles to the island of Zakynthos, much to the annoyance of the populace. The Zakynthians made representation to Sparta. Convinced that Athens had acted illegally, Sparta arranged for a fleet of sixty triremes to be gathered from its coastal allies Leukas, Korinth, Ambrakia, Elis, Zakynthos, Achaia, Epidauros, Troezen, Hermion and Halion to add to its own contribution. Command was given to Mnasippos, who was given 1,500 mercenaries in addition to an unspecified number of Lakedaimonians.

His arrival on Kerkyra appears to have been unimpeded. Quickly taking control of the countryside, his men laid waste all cultivable areas. Livestock and slaves were captured in large numbers, before he established a camp for his soldiers on the landward side of the city, at a distance of about two-thirds of a mile from its walls. Furthermore, a camp was set up near the coast for the oarsmen, from where any approaching ships could be observed and intercepted. The crews from the sixty ships would number nearly 12,000 men, a not inconsiderable force. The city was completely sealed off by the addition of a blockade of the harbour.

With no incoming supplies the city soon suffered food shortages. By some means or other, a request was made to the Athenians for help, stressing the strategic importance of Kerkyra. Acting with admirable speed, Athens dispatched 600 peltasts, requesting Alkestes, the ruler of Epiros, whose territory lay on the mainland opposite to Kerkyra, to ferry them to the island. This was achieved by a night crossing and the 600 (500 in Diodoros) made their way successfully, without detection, from the countryside to the city. A further vote was taken to send a following task force of sixty warships under Timotheos.

In his previous command Timotheos had encountered a serious shortage of funds that had provoked problems for the payment of his crews. Unwilling to take the chance of sailing to Kerkyra with crews of lesser competence than those of his enemy, he sailed to the islands within the Athenian League to recruit the required complement. Concerned that Timotheos was wasting time, the assembly replaced him with Iphikrates, lately returned from service to the Persian king in Egypt (Xen. *Hell*. VI. 2. 13). He gathered a fleet of seventy ships and Xenophon gives details of the training and security measures Iphikrates put in place, by which his men improved their physical condition and achieved high morale and safety during their voyage round the Peloponnese. Some are deserving of mention, if only to indicate his superlative qualities as a commander.[12]

Iphikrates only used sails when there was a good breeze and an opportunity to give the rowers some respite. He ensured that there was a strict rotation of groups of men for rowing duties. At mealtimes, in the middle of the day and in the evenings, when it was necessary to go onshore, he formed the fleet parallel to the shore and made the crews race to make landfall. The winners, and those following close behind them, had the pick of the brushwood and water, and time for a leisurely meal. The laggards were left to forage further and had, as a result, a more hurried meal before they had to take to their ships again. The usual watches were set, but, perhaps there is innovation in Iphikrates' change in the deck watch. The masts were raised and lookouts placed at their tops. This increased the area over which approaching land forces or any enemy vessels at sea could be spotted. Signals were instituted to ensure readiness of manoeuvre to bring the fleet to battle order. The practice of these took place during the day and firmly suggests that these signals were visual and ensured the maintenance of near silence. On the occasions when encampment was made ashore in enemy territory, fires were not allowed within the camp but placed in forward positions so that any enemy approach could be seen. Iphikrates may have adopted this practice in imitation of the Thrakian habit of placing fires in advance of their pickets so that their numbers and exact location remained concealed.[13] In such a manner Iphikrates had his men spend more than the usual time at sea, and thereby made the voyage the quicker (Xen. *Hell.* VI. 2. 27–32).

Back in Kerkyra Mnasippos' blockade had brought about near famine. Many attempted to flee the city despite the Spartan commander's threat to sell any fugitives as slaves. The population was almost beyond desperation and, as it turned out, Mnasippos was not as comfortably prepared as he imagined himself to be. He had dismissed a portion of his mercenaries and owed the remainder at least two months' pay. In consequence, surliness and a perceived laxity in the performance of their duties ensued. Those inside the city had noted this change. They took the opportunity to sally forth to inflict casualties on their besiegers and capture some of them. Mnasippos ordered the officers of the mercenaries to marshal their men. They, in turn, declared that they were finding it difficult to maintain discipline: 'And when some captains replied that it was not easy to keep men obedient unless they were given provisions, he struck one of them with a staff and another with the spike of his spear' (Xen. *Hell.* VI. 2. 19).[14] Xenophon makes the point that Mnasippos had sufficient funds to pay his men. The suspicion that he was attempting to enrich himself at their expense cannot be avoided.

With such resentment in his forces, it is no surprise that the counterattack made on the Kerkyrans led to disaster. Having formed his men in line, Mnasippos easily dispersed his opposition. However, the Kerkyrans poured out from the city and attacked the 'end of the line', which presumably was the left of Mnasippos' phalanx. He himself would be positioned on the right, and the description that follows concerns an attempted manoeuvre at the opposite end of his formation. The sub-commander there obviously thought eight ranks was insufficient to withstand the onslaught. An attempt was made to increase the depth by employing a drill known as an *anastrophe*. This required those at the end of the line to face about, march by file to a point where they could make a left turn, and march along the rear of their fellows to a position where, with a further turn to the left, they came up behind the unmoving front. In this way they effectively doubled the depth of that part of their phalanx. This was a drill that was second nature to Spartans and, with Spartiatai as commanders, they probably assumed that, with training, allies and mercenaries could do the same.

Speed is of the essence for this manoevre's safe and successful completion when faced with an enemy attack. In this case the Kerkyrans caught them in the first part of the movement. They thought that the about facing of their enemy was a sign that they were withdrawing and attacked this section of the line. Those adjacent to this point were sufficiently dismayed and fled. Mnasippos found himself and his part of the line under increasing pressure as his enemies reformed and joined those already attacking him. Numbers told as more came from the city to join the fray. With the death of Mnasippos and the subsequent rout of his men, it was only the numbers of men within the Spartan camp that deterred the Kerkyrans from capturing it.

Mnasippos had been very efficient on his arrival in Kerkyra. He had quickly seen that an investment of the city was completed. His eventual problems possibly arose from greed, but whatever the reason, denying the troops their dues was deleterious to morale. With men holding a grudge, willingness to serve would be translated into slower response times to orders and this brought on disaster.

A trophy was set up and bodies returned under truce. Soon after, news came that Iphikrates was on his way and the Kerkyrans now started to prepare their ships for joint action. Hypermenes, the second-in-command to Mnasippos, now ordered the crews to man their triremes and dispatched them along with the transports filled with slaves and the product of pillage. What remained of the troops also embarked and managed to reach Leukas undetected and in safety.

Meantime news of Mnasippos' death had reached Iphikrates. He took the precaution of sailing in battle line until he reached the island of Kephalonia, to the south of Leukas and Kerkyra, in case the news was a ruse. While there, he heard that ten triremes had been sent from Syrakuse in support of the Spartan task force. He quickly set out for Kerkyra and, on arrival, set up lookouts that could signal their approach. Selecting twenty commanders in his fleet, he arranged that, on sighting the enemy, they should follow him immediately in their vessels. He further warned them that failure to do so speedily would be punished. Xenophon's description at *Hell*. VI. 2. 34 is explicit. It would appear that Iphikrates was not seeking to meet the enemy in open waters but close to their time of arrival and to make his attack 'when they were at anchor'. A further signal was to indicate when this had happened so that the operation could proceed. All these signals are reminiscent of those arranged by Lysander at Aigospotami.

So it was, with great ease, that with the crews ashore, all but one of the Syrakusan ships were captured, along with their crews. The commander of the one to escape had advised his fellow officers not to disembark at that point and had chosen to remain in open waters.

Following his success, Iphikrates arranged for the majority of his crews to support themselves by working for the Kerkyrans while he sailed south to Akarnania with his peltasts and hoplites. This appears to have been more an expression of good will towards the cities there and nothing of any consequence is reported in our sources. A more positive outcome was his return to the island of Kephallenia. In a display of force, and incorporating Kerkyran vessels with his own to make a fleet of about ninety ships, he gathered considerable funds from the settlement there.[15]

Iphikrates is then described as making preparations for incursions on Spartan territories and those of its allies. Presumably these would have been coastal regions but, in the absence of any evidence of further actions, it is likely that events overtook him and he missed the opportunity.

It has already been noted that the 370s offered Thebes the opportunity gradually to regain control over the majority of the Boiotian cities. After Agesilaos' two spoiling expeditions of 378 and 377 BC, in which his enemies conducted a clever defensive war and refused to come to formal battle, there was little in this period to give Sparta comfort. The king's long illness gave command and direction of policy wholly to others. Even his return to health brought no improvement for Sparta. His part in persuading the authorities in Sparta to take no action against Sphodrias for his unilateral and lunatic attempt on Athens drove that city into continued collaboration with Thebes. The death of the skilled commander, Phoibidas, is the more to be regretted because of the appointment of Sphodrias as his successor. The ineffective expeditions of Kleombrotos and the shock of Tegyra offered no solace to Sparta. In consequence Thebes was able to establish a wider and more democratic confederacy[16] than that which had come to an end at the hands of Sparta in 386 BC. However, in the new constitution Theban control was assured in the assembly by its majority of four of the seven appointed *boiotarchs*. Two years after the brief peace of 375 BC that once again gave the cities a short-lived autonomy, the people of Plataia were driven from their city by Thebes and took refuge once more in Athens. Thespiai had earlier been overcome and its walls razed to the ground to prevent future revolt. Attacks had been made by Thebes on Orchomenos and the cities of Phokis in 374 BC. A similar campaign against Phokian cities was undertaken by Thebes in late 372 and early 371 BC. Sparta sent a large army north under Kleombroto for their protection.

Both Athens and Sparta needed a respite. The war at sea had been costly to Athens. Sparta was aware of Athens' success in building its second maritime league, had suffered defeat at Naxos in 376 BC and witnessed the ease by which successive enemy fleets were able to circumnavigate the Peloponnese virtually unchallenged in the following years. With the setback in Kerkyra and the north-west, both were now ready to recognise the other's hegemony, Sparta on land and Athens at sea. Athens also had good reason to seek to distance itself from Thebes. It had only recently been obliged to offer sanctuary to the population of Plataia following Thebes' capture of their city.

The increasing confidence and belligerence of Thebes had convinced the two protagonists to attempt some accommodation. According to Xen. *Hell.* VI. 3. 2, the Athenians took the initiative by voting for peace in their assembly, sending ambassadors to both Thebes and Sparta. Among these was Kallias, after whom the peace is named. Behind the initiative there is more than a hint that Artaxerxes was once again in the background of the negotiations, not least because of his continuing need of Greek mercenary forces (see Diod. XV. 50. 4). Shortly after the Spartan assembly voted:

> to accept the peace, with the provision that all should withdraw their governors
> from the cities, disband their armaments both on sea and land, and leave the
> cities independent. And if any state should act in violation of this agreement,
> it was provided that any which so desired might aid the injured cities, but that
> any which did not so desire was not under oath to be the ally of those who were
> injured. (Xen. *Hell.* VI. 3. 18)

All present, including Thebes, took the oath. However, on the following day the Theban delegation returned to demand that the document should be changed: 'to read that "the Boiotians" instead of "the Thebans" had sworn' (Xen. *Hell.* VI.

3. 19). In effect, Thebes was claiming to agree to the peace as leader of Boiotia. Epaminondas was one of the delegation and pressed the point. Agesilaos saw no reason to change what had already been agreed and declared that if they chose not to be party to the peace he would strike out their names from the agreement.

There had obviously been further debate within the Boiotian delegation. Behind its claim to be signatory on behalf of the cities of Boiotia lay the fact that all *boiotarch*s were elected from all Boiotian citizens and each city had its representatives to debate in the Boiotian assembly and to contribute its individual taxes and forces for the common good. Similarly, Sparta was signatory for the periokic cities of Lakonia and, as Epaminondas is reputed to have pointed out, the territory of Messenia was wholly denied its freedom.

Athens and Sparta withdrew all garrisons and governors from cities. It was anticipated by all that Thebes would be punished. To that end Sparta did not disband the forces under Kleombrotos in Phokis. There is evidence of some good advice being ignored at Sparta. This came from a certain Prothoos who urged that the army in Phokis should be disbanded in accordance to the oaths taken at the peace, thereafter to ask cities to contribute to a war fund. If any sought to deprive cities of their autonomy, those who would follow Sparta could oppose them. Behind this proposal can be seen an appropriate concern about the forces with Kleombrotos from the allied cities. Had the army been disbanded in accordance with the conditions of the peace, Sparta could, with greater justification, have called on all willing to prosecute a war against Thebes, unless the latter allowed its neighbouring cities their independence.

As it was, Kleombrotos was instructed to march to Thebes and force it to extend freedom and independence to the Boiotian cities. Within his army there were allies who resented their continued presence there and this did not bode well.

Endnotes

1   This splendid corps was annihilated to a man by Philip II of Makedon at Chaironeia, but not before they had fought so impressively that the victor raised a monument over their grave in their honour. Restored in modern times, it stands today beside the museum at the southern end of the village. A huge lion very similar to that later erected at Amphipolis surmounts the tomb. See also Plut. *Pelop.* XVIII and XIX, and J. Davidson, *The Greeks and Greek Love*, New York, Random House, 2007.

2   See also Xen. *Ages.* XXVI.

3   Plataia, which had been destroyed in the opening years of the Peloponnesian War,

was restored *c*.382 BC.

4 See also Cornelius Nepos' *Life of Chabrias*; Polyainos II. 1. 2; Demosthenes 20.

5 At Leuktra in 371 BC.

6 Although Diodoros suggests that the battle took place near the harbour of the city of Naxos, it is more likely that it was in the open waters between Naxos and its neighbouring island Paros.

7 Diodoros makes the point that this was the first naval victory achieved by an Athenian fleet since the Peloponnesian War. See also Chapter 4, n. 5.

8 Thucydides reports that Perikles warned the Athenians of the dangers of giving up empire in a manner that betrays its character: 'for by this time the empire you hold is a tyranny, which it may seem wrong to have assumed, but which certainly it is dangerous to let go' (Thuc. II. 63).

9 In giving the numbers of men in Spartan-led divisions, Plutarch cites Kallisthenes as giving 700, Polybios and others as giving 900, and Ephoros 500.

10 Beside the restored monument to the Sacred Band at the south end of the village of Chaironeia is a museum that reopened in 2010, after many years of closure.

11 Hornblower, p. 216 suggests plausibly that Sparta, after the Battle of Naxos, requested the intervention of the Persian king in order that some settlement might be achieved.

12 See also Hutchinson, *Xenophon*, pp. 132–3.

13 Xenophon had encountered this practice on his return from Asia Minor and obviously approved of it (Xen. *Anab*. VII. 2. 18). In his fictional account of Kyros the Great he also suggests a further development by making Kyros have fires at both the front and rear of his position (Xen. *Kyropaideia* III. 33). Normal practice for the time of Xenophon's service as a general seems to have been that fires were doused after an evening meal, leaving the camp in total darkness (*Anab*. VI. 3. 21).

14 Thucydides at VIII. 8. 84 describes a similar situation in which payment to men was concerned. In this case the commander had to seek sanctuary at a nearby altar.

15 Our other main source – Diodoros – agrees with much of Xenophon's more detailed description but is in error when claiming Timotheos accompanied Iphikrates. Other Athenian commanders are named by Xenophon as being Chabrias and Kallistratos (Xen. *Hell*. VI. 2. 39).

16 The Oxyrhynchos historian gives a description of this earlier Theban-led federation at XVI. 3 of the Florence fragments. Boiotia was divided into eleven areas. Each notionally elected a *boiotarch* but, with certain of the areas being under the control of others, the pattern appears to be that Thebes held four *boiotarch*ies, two for the city and two for their technically subject cities, i.e. Plataia, Skolos, Erythrai, Skaphai and others. Thespiai, Eutresis and Thisbai had two *boiotarch*s, Tanagra one, Orchomenos and Hysiai two; Haliartos, Lebadeia and Koroneia sent one, each in turn on a three-year rota, as did Akraipheion, Kopai and Chaironeia. Sixty councillors were provided

for each *boiotarch*, with its region sustaining their expenses. Each of the eleven areas had to provide 1,000 hoplites and 100 cavalry. The joint assembly of Boiotians met in the Kadmeia in Thebes. All communities paid taxes, appointed jurymen and magistrates. The above is a paraphrase of the information contained in the *Hellenica Oxyrhynchia*. For the text itself see McKechnie and Kern.

CHAPTER 10

Leuktra and the Myth Exploded

History shows how inadequate were Sparta's property laws. She was
overwhelmed by a single defeat; lack of men was her ruin . . . We are
told, in fact, that at one time Sparta had no fewer than 10,000 citizens.
Whether or not this is true, it would have been better for her to have
maintained her numbers by an equal distribution of property.

> Aristotle *Politics*, II. 3; trans. Warrington

CONTRARY TO EXPECTATIONS, KLEOMBROTOS, FROM his position in
Phokis, made his way into Boiotia via Thisbe in the west. This completely
misled the Boiotians, who had been guarding the obvious passes giving entry into
their territory from Phokis while the main part of their forces was assembled
near Koroneia. One would like to think that the king was at last showing signs
of originality when in the field. This may well have been the case, but, with his
record to date, it is more likely that his Spartiate advisers persuaded him to take
this outflanking direction. He then led his army by a mountainous, though not
too difficult, route to the seaboard where he captured twelve Theban triremes at
Kreusis (Xen. *Hell*. VI. 4. 4; ten triremes according to Diod. XV. 53. 1). Having
secured his rear on the Korinthian Gulf in this way, he proceeded north east to
encamp at Leuktra.

There, the plain nestles between rolling ridges of lowland hills. It was on those to
the south of this plain that the Spartan and allied army eventually faced the Boiotian
forces on the northern hills. Although our sources do not give figures for each army,
overall, the Boiotians were outnumbered and initially their morale suffered.

130

The account given by Diodoros is colourful but is not to be trusted in some of its detail.[1] Xenophon, our source living at the time of this action, is much the more reliable, his evidence no doubt coming from participants, but lacking important detail. The other main source, Plutarch's *Life of Pelopidas*, gives some insight to the action that displays some pride in the Boiotian tradition. It is a pity that his *Life of Epaminondas* has not also come down to us. All have problems, and it is a matter of trawling through what is available to us, while taking note of bias, omission and obvious error, to arrive at a skeletal attempt at reconstruction.

The decision to join battle with Kleombrotos proved to be a close call. Of the seven *boiotarchs*, six were present when the initial vote was taken and the result was a tie. Epaminondas, however, persuaded the lately arrived seventh *boiotarch* to cast his vote in favour of action (Diod. XV. 53. 3 and Plut. *Pelop.* XX).[2] One must conclude that Epaminondas had confidence in the likely outcome of the contest. He had urged the need to come to battle. He was not facing Agesilaos and would be aware of the relatively inconsequential record of Kleombrotos as a commander. He realised that to conduct a defensive war, in the manner of the earlier years of this decade, would probably lead to defections from the new Boiotian confederacy. He was also probably aware of the likely tactics that the Spartans would employ. Having narrowly won the vote for battle, he set about preparing the minds of his men for the coming trial. On the question of bolstering morale there is significant evidence in our main sources to suggest that Epaminondas arranged for favourable omens to be made known to his men:

> But Epaminondas, who saw that the soldiers were superstitious on account of the omens that had occurred, earnestly desired through his own ingenuity and strategy to reverse the scruples of the soldiery. Accordingly, a number of men having recently arrived from Thebes, he persuaded them to say that the arms on the temple of Heracles had disappeared and that word had gone abroad in Thebes that the heroes of old had taken them up and set off to help the Boiotians. (Diod. XV. 53. 4)
>
> Furthermore, reports were brought to them from the city that all the temples were opening of themselves, and that the priestesses said that the gods revealed victory. And the messengers reported that from the Heraklium the arms also had disappeared, indicating that Herakles had gone forth to the battle. Some, to be sure, say that all these things were but devices of the leaders. (Xen. *Hell.* VI. 4. 7)

Not that all was well within the Spartan camp at the time. One can see the microcosm of the division of opinion among Spartiatai present on the motivation of Kleombrotos. His supporters urged him to join battle to avoid yet another fruitless mission for Sparta. He was reminded of the greater success of Agesilaos. They warned him of the likely consequences to him of another relatively innocuous outcome to a mission. Exile or worse was likely if he avoided battle. Those who were severely critical of his past record and suspected him of sympathy for the Theban position suggested that now was the time to display his true colours. He could be described as being between a rock and a hard place and, given these circumstances, Kleombrotos was left with no alternative but to give to both groups what they desired.

Nonetheless, we have in Kleombrotos a commander who, although he had had sufficient time on campaign to accumulate experience, had achieved little or nothing. He had given the impression that he avoided positive contact with the enemy whenever he could, and was at times dilatory in his preparations for the invasion of enemy territory. In the absence of any direct evidence from sources, other than the stated opinions of the Spartiatai present, it is highly likely that the Spartan government had sent firm instructions that the Thebans should be brought to battle if possible. This, despite the total powers vested in a king when on campaign.

On the day of the battle Kleombrotos held his council of war at which he and his commanders took liquid refreshment: 'For it was after the morning meal that Kleombrotos held his last council over the battle, and drinking a little, as they did, at the middle of the day, it was said that the wine helped somewhat to excite them' (Xen. *Hell.* VI. 4. 8).

It was common practice to drink wine mixed with water at meal times. That Xenophon remarked on drinking alcohol at a time when perhaps no food was present, and commented on its effect, perhaps holds more significance than is immediately obvious. It could be that imbibing alcohol gave them 'Dutch courage' in face of the coming combat, but Xenophon's inclusion of this information suggests that this was not always customary before a battle. Like Agesilaos, Kleombrotos had succeeded his brother and, as he had not been directly in line to succeed to the crown, would have undergone the Spartan *agoge* training in common with other Spartiatai. That training had made him ready to serve but could in no way guarantee the original thinking on military matters required of a leader.

In the preparation for the coming battle those merchants 'who had provided the market and some baggage-carriers *and such as did not wish to fight* had set out to withdraw from the Boiotian army' (Xen. *Hell.* VI. 4.9; emphasis added). They were frustrated in their object by mercenary hoplites, Phokian peltasts and Phliasian and Herakleot cavalry who drove them back to the Boiotian camp. What is of particular interest is the suggestion in later sources that the hoplites of Thespiai were among those driven back, thereby enlarging the Boiotian army.[3] If we are to give credence to this tradition we must also question whether the Thespians were the only group to attempt to avoid the coming battle, and on what basis had such permission to withdraw been achieved. It could well be that leaders such as Epaminondas and Pelopidas, knowing the recent loyalty of Thespiai and others to Sparta, thought it better to fight without reluctant participants on their side and had approved the arrangement: 'The leaders of the Thebans, on the other hand, calculated that if they did not fight, the cities round about would revolt from them and they would themselves be besieged' (Xen. *Hell.* VI. 4. 6). This episode gives us the identity of some of the cavalry contingents and light-armed troops likely to have been stationed on the left wing of the Spartan-led army while, as is evident later, the Lakedaimonian cavalry was on the right.

In the absence of reliable numbers for each side, one must extrapolate from those present in past engagements. The most secure estimate of the Lakedaimonians present lies in the figure of four *morai* given by Xenophon (*Hell.* VI. 4. 17). If each *mora* was at full strength, which is highly unlikely, this would give a figure of 5,120 hoplites.[4] Based on thirty-five of the forty age groups being present it can be accepted that 4,480 hoplites made up the Lakedaimonian section of the army. Given the onus on the allies to provide a similar proportion to the army, an additional five to six thousand hoplites can be added to this figure. The latter is dependent on the exact number of allies present and their identity (see later). An additional 300 hoplites can be added for the *hippeis*, the king's bodyguard.

For the Boiotan side numbers are more conjectural. There is no reason to accept that Thebes could not produce 6,000 hoplites considering the numbers present at earlier battles.[5] With the addition of those from other parts of the confederacy, a further 3,000, at least, can be added to the total. The Boiotians were superior in cavalry in quality but perhaps not in number. They were able to put into the field around 700 or 800, of which 400 would have been Theban. Their main problem was that they were without allies. They may have hoped that Jason of Pherai would arrive before the onset of the battle, giving them an even greater advantage in cavalry and a welcome addition of highly trained mercenaries. However, his presence might have led to some disagreements about the conduct of the battle in terms of tactics and it may well be for this reason that Epaminondas was ready to bring on the conflict.

It is clear from previous battles that the Spartans were accustomed to win from their command position on the right, sometimes at great cost to their allies on the left. Epaminondas' expectation of the usual Spartan lead to the right persuaded him to adopt an approach to combat that manoeuvre. His intention was to limit the support available to the Spartan command position from their allies on the left. To that end he arranged his advance in such a way that his line was slanting. His left was nearer the enemy's right on approach, and Epaminondas' right was in a position to threaten without coming to contact. This was made even more effective by the swift onslaught of the Thebans that allowed Epaminondas' right to be in a position of refusal to its enemies.

The disposition of the Spartan line before the onset would have found Kleombrotos in his position between the first and second *morai* of the right wing. His 300-strong royal bodyguard, *hippeis*, would have been stationed with him. Xenophon states that the Spartan phalanx was drawn up to a depth of no greater than twelve ranks, giving a front of approximately 400 shields, i.e, the four *morai* at near full strength, plus the 300 *hippeis*.

Epaminondas set the depth of his advancing column at the surprising depth of fifty shields, which with 6,000 men would have given him a front of only 120 men. With him, but not necessarily brigaded with the main body, was Pelopidas, commanding the Sacred Band of 300 hoplites that had seen victory at Tegyra. His action proved crucial in the battle, and some indication of the Sacred Band's position in the battle line would have been welcome. On this point our sources are unhelpful.

The battle opened with a skirmish between Theban and Spartan cavalry in the plain in front of the two opposing lines and critically not on the flanks of the armies. Possibly the intention of both commanders was to use the dust storm raised by several hundred horse to disguise their initial manoeuvres. Why Kleombrotos chose to post his cavalry immediately in front of his phalanx would only be comprehensible for this reason. There is no doubt that he chose to do so for, at *Hell.* VI. 4. 10, Xenophon reports that the Thebans responded to this move in the disposition of their own cavalry arm. In effect, by his cavalry placement, Kleombrotos had confirmed his intention to attempt an outflanking on the right, thus surrendering any advantage of surprise. He could well have placed the cavalry on his wing to cover the unshielded side and still undertaken his intended manoeuvre. The terrain was conducive to such an intention. Leuktra is a small plain surrounded by low rolling hills that offer little impediment to horsemen.

Xenophon comments on the poor quality of the Lakedaimonian cavalry at that time. The richest men who owned horses sent a substitute as rider, often not in the best of physical shape, to be pitted against some of the best cavalrymen in Greece (Xen. *Hell.* VI. 4. 11–12). A further critical comment is made just a little later:

> Now when Cleombrotus began to lead his army against the enemy, in the first place, before the troops under him so much as perceived that he was advancing, the horsemen had already joined battle and those of the Lakedaimonians had speedily been worsted; then in their flight they had fallen foul of their own hoplites and, besides the companies of the Thebans were now charging upon them. (Xen. *Hell.* VI. 4. 13)

Agesilaos' experiences in command of high-quality cavalry in Asia Minor and Thessaly had no doubt been passed onto his fellow Spartiatai on his return. Despite his example, it is difficult to understand Sparta's neglect of this arm, particularly as they were going against some of the best cavalry in Greece. It is possible that they were confident that their overall hoplite numbers and quality of battleground manoeuvre would win the day.

Thus, according to Xenophon's record, at the very opening of hostilities, we have a dislocation of the Spartan battle line on the right where the best-drilled men in the whole army seemed unaware of an order to advance. By comparison, Plutarch's description suggests that the Spartans were attempting some form of reorganisation of their line in response to the Theban formation.[6] The order may have been given to effect an *anastrophe* of part of the line to shorten their front and increase the depth. The possibility that while this was happening the Spartan line made a corridor through which their defeated cavalry could escape to safety must be discounted. We know from the evidence quoted above that many of the Spartans were unaware of the order to advance or do whatever was commanded. The intended advance and the possible attempted manoeuvre were compromised

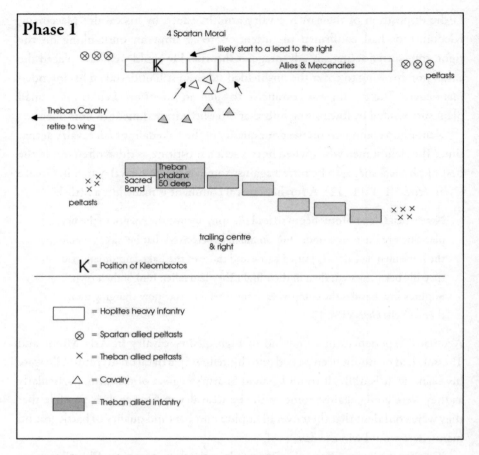

not only by this factor, but also by the confusion to their line caused by their routed horsemen. Altogether, this can only be described as a shambles.

Pelopidas can be congratulated on his speedy attack at the double to exploit his enemy's problem. That he was able to do so suggests that the Sacred Band occupied the first three ranks of the Theban massed ranks (however, see below for another possibility). What he achieved was to prevent the Spartans from reforming, by quickly entering the dislocated area, and maintaining the dislocation until the following Theban phalanx made its massed onslaught shortly after.

The area of the Spartan army most under threat was likely to have been that at which Kleombrotos himself was positioned. He was killed early in the engagement. Despite their disorganisation, it seems clear that the Spartans, near

136

ABOVE LEFT *The restored Victory Monument of the Thebans at Leuktra. It was probably surmounted by a bronze hoplite. It is significant that this is one of the earliest monuments intended to be permanent (see Diodoros quotation, p. 262).*

ABOVE RIGHT *An original section of the Leuktra monument in the form of an* aspis *(hoplite shield).*

BELOW *The battlefield at Leuktra 371 BC.*

ABOVE *The Arkadian gate at Messene. The guardhouses are situated to the left and right of the gate, to the rear of this view.*

BELOW *Typical city water storage cisterns. These were extremely useful during a siege.*

The agora at Messene, with later Roman additions.

Part of the restored stadion at Messene. It is situated to the south of the site, not too distant from the circuit walls.

ABOVE *Part of the outer defences at Messene showing one of the regularly spaced guardhouses built under the guidance of Epaminondas.*

ABOVE *View of Ancient Korinth towards Lechaion on the coast. In this area, between the ancient walls going down from the city to the sea, was fought the Battle between the Walls. The Battle of the Nemea took place a relatively short distance to the left and off the picture.*

BELOW *The massive Akropolis of Korinth, the Akrokorinth, as seen from the south.*

ABOVE *Perachora – the sanctuary of Hera Akraia – where Agesilaos met the Theban envoys just prior to the debacle of Lechaion.*

RIGHT *The Diolkos, an ancient road over the Isthmos of Korinth. Mercantile vessels were hauled on specially designed carts between the Korinthian and Saronik Gulfs. This saved having to sail around the entire Peloponnese. The Spartans once designed carts with the intention of hauling the much larger warships over this route, but never put this into practice.*

ABOVE *The theatre cut out of a natural rock face at the Boiotian city of Chaironeia. Chaironeia was the birthplace of Plutarch.*

BELOW *Some of the remains of the theatre at Megalopolis. It was the largest one in Greece, and was reputed to hold an audience of more than 20,000 people.*

ABOVE *The view towards Thermopylai from territory controlled by the Spartan colony of Herakleia in Trachis.*

BELOW *A surviving part of the superb fortifications at Aigosthena, comprising four well-preserved towers and sections of walls sometimes to the height of thirty feet. The walls originally enclosed an area of 600 feet by 1,800 feet. The Spartans retreated to Aigosthena after the Battle of Leuktra.*

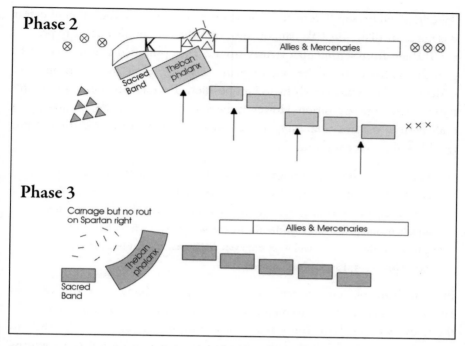

BATTLE PLAN 3 *Battle of Leuktra. The Theban cavalry in phase 1 force their enemy horsemen back on their own lines, causing disruption. In phase 2, at the double, the Sacred Band pins down the Spartan lead to the right, while in phase 3 the Theban phalanx smashes into Spartan lines already in disorder from its own cavalry. Meanwhile, Kelombrotos' initial order to lead to the right was not known to the line, and indecision occurred.*

or around the king, offered stern resistance. They withstood the Theban onslaught for long enough to retrieve Kleombrotos' body and carry it to the rear. Much has been made of the cumulative weight and pressure on an enemy phalanx by a depth of fifty ranks pushing against that of its enemy, but as mentioned in Chapter 4 this has been clearly shown to be ill-founded.[7]

Despite heavy losses to the Spartans in the initial melee, it would appear that there was no rout. Rather, a well-defended withdrawal was achieved, with the left wing of the Lakedaimonians, and their allies, seeing their colleagues on their right wing being worsted leading to that withdrawal. The Spartans grounded their arms behind the trench in front of their encampment. It is likely that they had lost the majority of the *hippeis* and senior figures such as Deinon, a *polemarch*,

Sphodrias and his son Kleonymos among many Spartiatai. Recognition of defeat was not immediate. The Lakedaimonians were vehement in their desire to prevent the Thebans from setting up a victory trophy. They proposed a further battle to gain the bodies of the fallen, rather than accepting defeat and receiving them under truce. This was a wholly logical proposition. The total Spartan-led army still outnumbered the opposition. However, the remaining *polemarch*s, on making an evaluation of the situation, came to the conclusion that a further battle was not feasible and for very good reasons:

> The *polemarch*s, however, seeing that of the whole number of the Lakedaimonians almost a thousand had been killed; seeing, further, that among the Spartiatae themselves, of whom there were some seven hundred there, about four hundred had fallen; and perceiving that the allies were *one and all* without heart for fighting, while some of them were not even displeased at what had taken place . . . (Xen. *Hell*. VI. 4. 15; emphasis added).

Faced with the obvious disinclination to fight for the bodies of those who had fallen, the remaining Spartan commanders had no option but to request a truce for the recovery of the dead. This was a formal admission of defeat and the Thebans set up a victory trophy. Although victorious, their actions thereafter are worthy of scrutiny. As far as they were concerned, they had been victorious over a section of the opposing army, but the significant numbers of the survivors, together with those of the centre and left who had not come to contact, still posed a problem for them. They remained behind their trench and, as far as the Thebans were concerned, knowing nothing as yet of the Spartan allies' reluctance to fight, still constituted a threat. It is possible that both Epaminondas and Pelopidas realised that fortune had been with them in their victory. Despite the knowledge that Sparta would send out a relief army, they seemed reluctant to press their initial advantage alone. Rather, messengers were dispatched to Athens and to their sole ally, Jason of Pherai. The requests were for support in crushing the remainder of the Spartan-led army. Those at Athens received the news with shock and made no reply to the Thebans. They were concerned that this change of fortune seemed to leave the Thebans uncomfortably dominant. Jason would receive the news while travelling south from Thessaly. He had already acted immediately in feigning to come by sea, and would probably have received the message as he made rapid progress through hostile Phokis on his way to join Epaminondas.

On his arrival he was urged to join the Thebans in an attack on the Lakedaimonians. He advised them not to risk what they had already achieved by such an act:

'Do you not see,' he said, 'that in your own case it was when you found yourselves in straits that you won the victory? Therefore one must suppose that the Lakedaemonians also, if they were in like straits, would fight it out regardless of their lives. Besides, it seems that the deity often takes pleasure in making the small great and the great small.' (Xen. *Hell.* VI. 4. 23)

His approach to the Spartans was different. Suggesting to them that some of their allies were now already engaged in negotiating with the enemy, he sowed further seeds of doubt and recommended that they forget this defeat and rebuild their strength for a future trial. He undertook to try to gain a further truce. When this had been achieved, the Spartan commanders decided to take the opportunity to withdraw and ordered their men to make ready to leave during the night. We cannot be sure of what, if any, conditions were obtained other than a continued cessation of hostilities. That they chose to go even earlier, immediately after the evening meal, indicates that, if their intentions were suspected, they sought to wrong-foot the opposition. Making their way to the coast around the western side of Mount Kithairon, they successfully reached Aigosthena[8] via Kreusis.

This would have been arduous and difficult to achieve successfully at night, all the time maintaining the secrecy of their movement. There Agesilaos' son, Archidamos, leading a relief army, met them, his father still not wholly recovered from his illness. This army was made up of the two remaining Spartan *morai* and troops from Tegea, Mantineia, Achaia, Phleious, Korinth and Sikyon. The two last states had organised triremes to transport the army across the Gulf of Korinth. The force had been speedily called up by the *ephors*. In listing the majority we have, at last, some of the names of most of those cities in the first army that may have participated in the battle: 'After this the *ephors* called out the ban of the two remaining regiments, going up as far as those who were forty years beyond the minimum military age; they also sent out all up to the same age who belonged to the regiments abroad' (Xen. *Hell.* VI. 4. 17).

News of the defeat had reached Sparta on the final day of the Gymnopaideia, a festival sacred to Sparta. In line with great piety shared by the majority of Spartans, this celebration was not to be interrupted. The messenger bringing the news

139

must have carried a highly detailed report, for the names of the fallen were made known. Women of their families were instructed not to make their grief public. By comparison, those persons whose family members were still alive appeared sorrowful in public. Strange as it may seem, they had good reason to be fearful. The surviving Spartiatai were now in danger of losing their citizen status and of being labelled as *tresantes* (cowards).

Spartan casualty figures given by Xenophon are more believable than those of Diodoros, whose description of the whole battle is almost totally flawed: 'of the Lacedaimonians almost a thousand had been killed; seeing, further, that among the Spartiatae themselves, of whom there were some seven hundred, almost four hundred had fallen' (Xen. *Hell*. VI. 4. 15).

The significant figure from this quotation is that concerning the Spartiatai present. The figure of 700 indicates that they accounted for possibly more than half of those enjoying the status of full citizen. The remainder, other than those citizens above the age of sixty and not required to serve, would be seen in the relief army that was sent out once the news had reached Sparta. What is evident is that the loss to the full citizen body would not have been only the 400 citizen casualties – which was nearly a third of the total number of citizens. To these would be added the 300 survivors who had not continued the struggle and, as observed earlier, could now under Lykourgos' law be regarded as cowards (*tresantes*). With the immediate prospect of creating further tensions in an already disaffected population by carrying out the normal legal process of disenfranchisement, Agesilaos 'allowed the laws to sleep for a day' (Plut. *Ages*. 30. 2–4). It was a ridiculous solution to a constitutional problem long overdue for resolution.

It is unclear how long there was between the arrival of the news of the battle and the junction of the two Spartan-led armies at Aigosthena. At best, the period can have been five days. The instructions given to Archidamos by the *ephors* before his departure from Sparta are not known. One can only presume that a Spartan commander outside his state and with complete control over policy in the field exercised his judgement according to the conditions that he discovered. The *ephors* may have hoped that, with the reinforcements, Archidamos might have had the opportunity to lead the combined forces against the Thebans in a renewal of the struggle. He would have been given a detailed report not only of the battle itself but also of the questionable loyalty of some of the allies. With the forces now at Aigosthena, and knowing that the Thebans had the availability of additional help from Jason of Pherai – and perhaps others, for Athens' intentions were still unclear – Archidamos wisely chose to lead the combined forces back to the Peloponnese.

Epaminondas' achievement had been to avoid the usual two-phase battle and bring on the conflict between the two strongest elements of the opposing armies. He did this by taking position on the left and made his attack on the Spartan command position. The oblique approach of his entire line made it difficult, if not impossible, for the Lakedaimonian allies on the left, threatened as they were by the Boiotian right, to assist its own right wing. They were not to know that, unengaged as they were, their direct opposition contained unwilling participants who had attempted to withdraw from the Boiotian army prior to hostilities. In such a way Epaminondas isolated the approximately 4,800 Lakedaimonians from their allies. The battle now became one between forces of near-equal strength or, indeed, of Theban numerical superiority. Aided by the initial accidental disruption of the Spartan phalanx and the speedy onslaught of the Sacred Band, this advantage was maximised. The lesson of that disruption was not lost on Epaminondas as will be seen at the Battle of Second Mantineia.

Earlier in this chapter, reference was made to the difficulties in reconstructing the Battle of Leuktra. Most battles of the ancient world provoke problems. Some prove impossible because of the lack of information other than the area in which they took place, from which the action took its name. Where sporadic detail is given, this must be sifted and the possibilities and probabilities in any perceived sequence of reported events examined. Knowledge of topography, contemporary tactics and the physical limitations faced by a hoplite carrying heavy equipment, sometimes in adverse weather conditions, must be taken into account. An appreciation of the logistical problems of food supply, its transport, the movement and safe encampment of armies and the routes taken can suggest necessary ancillary equipment such as wagons, horse or ship transport and the number of camp followers required. Although no specific studies of logistics survive from the Classical period, a trawl through Thucydides and, in particular, the writings of Xenophon can be illuminating.[9] Where sources are in conflict, common sense must prevail.

In the case of Leuktra, criticism of our sources has already been made. Diodoros' suggestion of a crescent formation for the Spartans and the presence of Archidamos is obvious nonsense. No less reprehensible is Xenophon's omission of the names of the Theban commanders and sufficient detail of the battle lines.

Plutarch is our only major source to mention the angled advance of the Boiotian battle line.

Inevitably, questions arise. Did the slanting advance of the Boiotian line reflect Epaminondas' mistrust of constituent sections of what was to be his right wing, or was it tactically based to ensure an early clash between the more equal numbers of both command wings? The critical role of the Sacred Band under Pelopidas is recognised, but where were they positioned in the Boiotian formation?

A definitive answer to the first question is impossible. It is not clear when Epaminondas' decision to take up his command position on the left wing was made. The usual disposition of the Boiotian battle line would have seen the Thespians and 'others' on the left wing directly opposite the opposing right wing, with the dominant Thebans on the right wing. This was the case at the Battle of Delion (424 BC), and at Nemea (394 BC) and Koroneia (394 BC) in the case of the Boiotian section of the last two battle lines.

Command positions on the left wing were not new but were taken to overcome local factors. That of Eurylochos at the Battle of Olpai (426 BC) was taken in consideration of topographical problems, and of Teleutias to cover the gate at Olynthos (381 BC) from which the enemy had emerged. However, those Thespians and 'others' who had been coerced into the Boiotian Federation and who were reluctant to participate in the coming battle had been given permission to leave the Boiotian army. They had been forced back, and this proved to be Epaminondas' 'local difficulty'. Their renewed presence within the battle line may well have been the issue that persuaded Epaminondas to place them as far away from the Lakedaimonians as possible, in fear that they might return to their old loyalties and go over to the other side when battle commenced. Taking command on the left solved the initial concern, and the adoption of the angled approach saw the Thespians and 'others' take little or no part in the action.

The second question is no less contentious. The position of the Sacred Band of 300 has been favoured by some as being the 'cutting edge' of the Theban phalanx. With a total of at least 5,000–6,000 hoplites to a depth of fifty ranks, the first three ranks could have been made up of the Sacred Band. As a constituent part of the main body presenting a front of 100 shields they may well have been the best troops to exploit the chaos caused to the Spartan line by their cavalry. However, even with a front of a little over 100 yards, an order from Pelopidas to charge the enemy at the double could have caused problems for the Boiotians themselves.

Inevitably, the order would have been difficult to transmit instantaeously and with clarity. Further, the likelihood of the ranks behind following their lead and joining with a charge at the double is not to be discounted. Therefore, it is unlikely that the Sacred Band could detach itself successfully from the main body force to exploit the disruption of the Spartan line while the main body of Thebans continued to advance to battle as described.

Various wild and improbable placements have been suggested for the positioning of this elite force, not least that they were in a position as a reserve. An alternative scenario is that the Sacred Band was, from the outset, given the responsibility of holding up the anticipated outflanking lead to the right of the Spartans. This would require it to be placed to the left of the main Theban phalanx. The depth would not then have been subject to the requirements of the main body and, with six ranks, would have added an additional fifty shields to the overall front.

If this were the case, the charge at the double would have been made at the already compromised attempt of the Spartans to outflank the Thebans. While the Sacred Band succeeded in this, the main body bore down on the disordered Spartan lines. The action of the Sacred Band would have been easier because a significant number of Lakedaimonians were unaware that the lead to the right had already commenced, possibly leaving only a small isolated group to face the opening onslaught.

The following closing paragraphs are conjectural but serve to illustrate that, without further evidence coming to light, we can never be secure in our judgements. Finally, following the acceptance of the remaining Spartan commanders to cede victory to the Thebans, further issues need to be addressed: first, the attempt by the Thebans to persuade the Athenians to come to help them destroy the Spartan-led army, and, second, the Theban request to Jason of Pherai, on his arrival, to join them in a concerted attack on the Spartan camp. Their suggestion was for his forces to attack from above and behind the Spartan position, while the Thebans made a frontal assault. This clearly demonstrates that the Thebans accepted that they were unable to achieve this objective alone. Unaware at that time of the mixed feelings of Sparta's allies, they were probably fearful that the Lakedaimonians would seek another engagement that could reverse the earlier Theban success. Alone, they could not make an uphill assault on the enemy's lines and would be greatly relieved at the speedy arrival of Jason.

143

While it can be accepted that, over the previous sixty years, war had become increasingly attritional, the desire to utterly destroy an opposing army shows Theban desperation, particularly when compared to Agesilaos' piety and leniency to the trapped Theban hoplites in the temple of Athena following the Battle of Koroneia. Nonetheless, the myth of Spartan invincibility had been exploded.

Endnotes

1   Diodoros suggests that an armistice was arranged during which Agesilaos' son Archidamos arrived with another Peloponnesian army and took his position on the left wing of the reinforced army. This source also has Jason of Pherai and his mercenaries present on the side of the Boiotians. The general sweep of Diodoros' description is unrealistic of Sparta manoeuvres. He describes them as advancing in a crescent formation.

2   Pausanias IX. 13 names the *boiotarch*s. He says that Epaminondas, Malgis and Zenokrates were in favour of coming to battle. Damokleidas, Damophilos and Simangelos were against, preferring the option of sending the women and children to Athens and retiring to Thebes, where they believed they could withstand a siege.

3   Polyainos II. 3. 3 and Pausanias IX. 3. 8. The 'others' are partially identified by Pausanias as being Thespians and certain others of the Boiotian forces. Epaminondas obviously had concern that they might prove treacherous in the coming action because they had been coerced by Thebes to join the federation.

4   I have always agreed with full strength numbers for *morai* and the subsidiary units of the *lochoi* and *enomotia* found in Lazenby, *The Spartan Army*.

5   Lazenby, *The Spartan Army*, pp. 151–62 gives a colourful and erudite account of the Leuktra engagement. He is perhaps a little niggardly with respect to the numbers of Thebans present at Leuktra given those present at the Nemea and Koroneia.

6   Lazenby, *The Spartan Army*, p. 158 analyses the possibilities of various potential manoeuvres suggested by Plutarch's text. Most are discounted and Lazenby offers a compromise. He suggests that Kleombrotos was attempting to achieve two manoeuvres at the same time, that of increasing the depth of the phalanx while leading to the right and round so that the Thebans could be taken in flank. This was perfectly possible for a Lakedaimonian phalanx to achieve prior to contact. As has been noted, the evidence shows that their own cavalry was driven back into their lines while these manoeuvres were in progress.

7   Du Picq, vol. 2, p. 169. Despite the loss of the integrity of the Spartan line, furious resistance saved the king's body. Assuming the original depth to have been twelve ranks, Du Picq's experiments with troops still gave the advantage of the weight to the three additional Theban ranks, and these would account for the disordered Spartans' discomfort.

8 Some impressive fortified remains can still be seen near the coastline of this small bay.
9 A very useful modern study is to be found in J. F. Lazenby, *Logistics in Classical Greek Warfare*, vol. 1 of H.Strachan and D. Showalter (eds), *War in History*, London, Edward Arnold, 1994.

CHAPTER 11

Thebes in the Ascendant

The loss of Messenia broke Sparta, and whether or not many of the *kleroi* were in Messenia, the loss must have given many individual Spartans as the Spartan state a terrible blow. But it broke Sparta because Sparta was already fragile for one reason only – there is no such thing as a caste of 'Equals' which can maintain itself when 'Equality' becomes something from which outsiders are excluded rather than something to which they can aspire.

Forrest, *A History of Sparta*

T HE GREEK WORLD WAS STUNNED. Some states, such as Athens, were understandably wary of Theban future intentions. For those in the Peloponnese League that had been under Spartan influence for centuries, the opportunity presented itself to assert their full independence of action in matters of interstate policy.

The months following Leuktra saw Thebes busily establishing its power over the whole of Boiotia. The pocket of Thespian exiles that had held out against Thebes was brought to heel, and the city of Orchomenos captured. Loyal allies of Sparta such as Phokis, now isolated from its protection, had no option but to become allies of neighbouring Boiotia. In a very short time Thebes achieved control of central Greece and even the large island of Euboia, adjacent to the mainland, came over to it. This posed an alarming threat to Athens.

Nor were these the only opportunities taken after Leuktra. Jason of Pherai destroyed the Spartan colony at Herakleia as he returned north to Thessaly. This

146

gave him easy access to the south via the pass of Thermopylai when needed in the future. He also took the peoples around the Malian Gulf into his ever-widening alliance. This was to be only a temporary worry for Thebes, removed as it was by his assassination.

With the King's Peace still unresolved, and Sparta's sponsorship now wholly compromised by the outcome of Leuktra, Athens took it upon itself to invite those cities that wished to participate in its signing. The wording of the oath is interesting, putting as it does Athens at the heart of the agreement: 'I will abide by the treaty which the king sent down, and by the decrees of the Athenians and their allies. And if anybody takes the field against any one of the cities which have sworn this oath, I will come to her aid with all my strength' (Xen. *Hell.* VI. 4. 2).

The most obvious repercussions for Sparta were felt in the Peloponnese. Mantineia took the opportunity to rebuild its city walls aided by manpower from other Arkadian cities and finance from Elis. The course of the river Ophis was reconfigured so that it could not be used again to aid the capture of Mantineia, as it had in *c.*385 BC (Xen. *Hell.* VI. 5. 5). Further, the idea of a united Arkadia was addressed. Lykomedes of Mantineia appears to have been the prime mover for this nascent dream to be realised. With such notable exceptions as Tegea, just to the north of Lakedaimon, and Peloponnesian Orchomenos and Heraia, which chose to remain loyal to Sparta, all other Arkadian cities embraced the vision and agreed to establish the new federal capital of Megalopolis. The surrounding village populations were persuaded to become its inhabitants. All citizens of the new federal state were accepted as members of the assembly that met there from the time of its completion around 369 BC.

Its constitution was democratic; interstate policy and transgressions by, or disagreements between, member cities were decided upon under its aegis. All member cities contributed to a Council of Fifty that prepared legislation and enacted the decisions of the assembly. The remains of what was, in its time, the largest theatre in the Greek world are disappointing. However, its proximity and relationship to the large hall of the assembly, the Thersilion, suggests that both structures could be used for meetings of the thousands who wished to attend on occasion.

With a newly fortified Mantineia and the ongoing building of Megalopolis in the west, Sparta was now faced with two formidable obstacles to a revival of its power. What was now deemed necessary to the Arkadians was the early inclusion of Tegea in the federal state. This was achieved, with the aid of Mantineia, by a bloody coup within Tegea whereby the pro-Spartan party was ejected from power. Some 800 exiles sought refuge and help from Sparta.

Relief for most of Greece came with news of the assassination of Jason of Pherai. His bid to be president of the Amphiktionic League and his probable future territorial ambitions had led to considerable anxiety, not least for those in Boiotia. A future conflict between the two allies, Thebes and Thessaly, had seemed inevitable in the short term. With his removal, his successors, although still powerful, did not hold power over a united Thessaly and this was to allow Thebes to develop influence in the north. Freed from a possible future threat, Thebes was able to respond to requests for help from its new Peloponnesian allies.

So it was that, when Agesilaos invaded Arkadia in response to the enforced inclusion of its long-term ally Tegea into the Arkadian League, the Arkadians appealed for help from Athens under the renewed terms of the Kings' Peace. Athens was reluctant to join a war against Sparta and its refusal led the Arkadians to turn to Thebes.

The invasion of Agesilaos in 370 BC had seen significant damage done to crops around Mantineia. Some field decisions he made are worthy of scrutiny. The forces against him were divided. The Arkadians who had been at Tegea, were moving north seeking a junction with those near, and in, Mantineia. Agesilaos was urged to attack this force. He declined to do so on the grounds that he would be exposing his flank and rear to a possible attack from the city as he marched to meet the incoming army. He preferred to allow his enemies to come together and, if they were willing to accept battle, to meet them in a normally conducted action on the plain. Some may feel that an opportunity to do damage to a divided opposition had been missed. However, like any good commander, Agesilaos preferred not to put his men at unnecessary risk. He would be well aware that their morale would still be dented after Leuktra and that this was the army's first military operation since that battle. With the arrival of peltasts from Orchomenos and some Phliasian cavalry, Agesilaos encamped in a narrow valley near to the city of Mantineia.

The following morning saw enemy forces occupying the heights to one side of the rear of his army. Considering the restricted nature of his position and the danger to his men at the rear of the column, he prepared to make a marching withdrawal (Xen. *Hell.* VI. 5. 18). From his position near the head of the column he turned this formation to face the enemy thus converting the column into a battle line ten shields deep. This ensured a readiness to meet any attack. From his position on the right wing near the mouth of the valley, his next orders were given to ensure further protection to those on the left. The manoeuvre that followed was a successful completion of the *anastrophe,* the move that had failed in Kerkyra under Mnasippos. The original rear was now the left wing of the battle line. It was now ordered to about face, march forward until it was clear of the unmoving remainder of the phalanx, left turn and march along behind the line towards the right wing until, with a further left turn, it came up behind it. In such a way the depth of the phalanx was doubled to twenty shields and its length was halved. The rear of the original column was now much safer and, from this position, much nearer to the open plain which was reached without problem.

It is likely that the manoeuvre was sequenced by *enemotia* (up to forty men) or *pentekostys* (up to 160 men) and certainly not by file. The term *anastrophe* means wheeling back and its most extravagant description is to be found in Xenophon's fictional tale of the 'Education of Kyros' where the king folds back both left and right wings towards the centre (Xen. *Kryo.* VII. 5. 3).[1]

Once out of the confines of the valley, Agesilaos extended his line of battle to a depth of ten shields. The Mantineians were persuaded not to come to battle by their Elean allies but advised to await the arrival of the promised Theban forces. In the light of no further activity from his enemies, Agesilaos led his army back to Lakedaimon.

Even though it was in the middle of winter (370/369 BC) the assembled forces of the Arkadians and their allies made a punitive expedition against Heraia and carried on with their depredations until news of the Thebans' arrival at Mantineia reached them. Xenophon gives the impression, correctly or otherwise, that the Thebans were set to return home now that the Arkadians were faced with no enemy in their territory. Even on being urged to lead the combined forces on an invasion of Lakedaimon they expressed a reluctance to do so on the grounds that entry to the country was difficult and that the Spartans would mobilise quickly. Only when some of the *perioikoi* came and promised to revolt from Sparta, saying that some of their comrades were already refusing to respond to the ban or call-up of the Spartans, did the Thebans finally agree to the enterprise (Xen. *Hell.* VI. 5. 23–5). It seems unlikely that the Theban commander, Epaminondas, and the other *boiotarchs* would have returned to Thebes without taking further action, despite it being winter. Perhaps Xenophon is painting a true picture of the unsettled conditions present in Lakonia but incorrectly infers what might have been in the mind of the Theban general.

The combined forces presented the largest army to have been assembled in Greece since the Persian War, and there would have been little danger for it in facing a much-reduced opposition. With the Thebans came Phokians, Akarnanians, Euboians, Herakliots, Malians, the Ozolian and Opuntian Lokrians, and peltasts and cavalry from Thessaly. To these were now added the Arkadians, Argives and Eleans. Plutarch (*Ages.* 31) gives the number of men as being 40,000. This is more believable than the 70,000 given by Diodoros (XV. 62).

With the coming of the Thebans, Sparta may have hurriedly dispatched messengers requesting help from those cities still within the alliance such as Phleious and Korinth. The move south by the invaders was made by four routes. This division of forces proved speedier and less difficult. Having met little effective opposition, all four groups met at Sellasia before jointly resuming the march south to Sparta.

Nature now took a hand in the defence of the unwalled city. The Eurotas was in full spate and was unfordable as the army of Epaminondas approached. The bridge to the city was obviously well guarded so the host moved south with the river on its right, burning and pillaging properties as they went. Never before had the population of Sparta even seen an enemy in their territory, let alone one causing such great damage.

With the passing of the enemy, men from Korinth, Phleious, Epidauros, Pellene and elsewhere now arrived to assist Sparta. With all routes south blocked by the invasion force, they had been forced to come by sea. Landing on the eastern seaboard of Lakonia, they were obliged to cross the Parnon range. Their arrival brought relief to the Spartans on another matter. The *ephors* had promised freedom to *helots* who volunteered to fight in defence of Sparta. The response was massive and some 6,000 *helots* enrolled, provoking some anxiety among the citizens only allayed by the arrival of their allies.

Arriving near Amyklai, Epaminondas now crossed the Eurotas at a fordable point and an advance was made on the settlement. A large advance force, seemingly of all the cavalry with some supporting foot-soldiers, reached the area of the racecourse. It seems likely that those on foot were *hammipoi*, the light infantry that normally fought in conjunction with Theban cavalry. To counter this, the Lakedaimonians drew up their small cavalry force in battle line but with a force of 300 hoplites in ambush. The last thing that the much larger enemy force would expect was that an all-out attack would be made upon it. The onset of both Spartan cavalry and the hitherto concealed hoplites proved too much for the nerve of their enemies and they fled back to their lines (Xen. *Hell.* VI. 5. 31).

Like any good commander, Epaminondas probably thought that attempting to take the settlement would lead to considerable loss of life, not least of his own men. The Spartan men of Amyklai would obviously not be foolhardy enough to accept the usual hoplite battle in the open against such odds, but would be very difficult to overcome in the physical restrictions of a conurbation.

Epaminondas had made his point. He was free to ravage Lakonia without effective resistance in the open, and this he did by moving south again to attack Sparta's port and naval dockyards at Gytheion. Perioikoi, who saw the opportunity to gain their independence, assisted him.

After attacking Gytheion for three days, he led the vast army back to Arkadia where, instead of dismissing all the allies, he moved into Messenia. There he founded and oversaw the building of the city of Messene under Mount Ithome, taking its new inhabitants, in the course of time, from the surrounding villages. The whole area of Messenia was liberated from Spartan control and all its inhabitants were given citizen rights at its new capital, Messene. Thereafter, many exiles returned to their ancestral homeland.

At a stroke Sparta's territory was cut by half, increasing the already intolerable strains on the constitution. A new fortified bulwark arose to join Mantineia and Megalopolis in a ring of containment around Lakedaimon. Today impressive sections of the large circuit wall of Messene remain.

Although Xenophon later refers to Messene as an independent state, he omits to make mention of its foundation. Another omission in his *Hellenika* concerns the name of the person charged with commanding the defence of Sparta. However, he makes good on the omission by making it clear in Xen. *Ages.* II. 24 that the old king not only took charge of the defence of the city, but also cleverly defused a plot from within against the security of the state.

Athens had been greatly concerned by the turn of events. It had voted to send an army under Iphikrates to assist Sparta. Initially he set up defences at the Isthmos using Korinth as a base, before advancing through Arkadia only to discover that the Thebans were no longer threatening Sparta. Returning to Korinth, he waited until the Theban army came back from its initial building work at Messene to make its return march. Xenophon mistakenly suggests that Iphikrates' task was to prevent the Thebans from passing the Isthmos (*Hell*. VI. 5. 51). The pass at Oneion near Kenchreion was obviously left unguarded to allow the Thebans to pass by without threatening Korinth at the other end of the Isthmos, otherwise Iphikrates would not have sent out cavalry scouts to check if the Thebans had, indeed, passed by that way.

The winter operations conducted by the Thebans in the Peloponnese had breached a constitutional protocol. The time for the hand-over of command to elected successors to office at the coming of Boukatios, the first month of the year, had passed. It is for this reason that, despite the far-reaching objectives achieved in the campaign, Epaminondas and Pelopidas were put on trial for their lives – for extending their period of command by almost four months (Plut. *Pelop*. XXV. 1). The charges were factually based, but the circumstances had been exceptional, and the gains for Thebes momentous. Consequently, the opposition to these great men proved unsuccessful. It is that very opposition which saw to it that Epaminondas, one of the two great contemporary figures of Theban history, was not always elected *boiotarch*. Pelopidas, however, continued to enjoy popularity throughout the period scrutinised. Politics, personal antagonism and envy played their usual part when later elections occurred, but there can be no doubt that Theban foreign policy was always at its most dynamic when both Epaminondas and Pelopidas were in positions of command.

Theban foreign policy now divides itself between the Peloponnese and northern Greece. The absence of reference to the latter region in Xenophon, based as he was in the former, leaves us mainly reliant on Diodoros and Plutarch's *Life of Pelopidas*. It would seem that over the coming few years Epaminondas was the architect of relations and activities in the Peloponnese and Pelopidas was concerned with those in Thessaly, Makedon and Chalkidike. The remainder of this chapter deals with matters relating to the Peloponnese and the second and third invasions of it by Epaminondas. For the contemporaneous activities of Pelopidas in the north, see the next chapter.

Early in 369 BC Athens and Sparta, with its remaining allies, entered into alliance. Diodoros XV. 68 notes that Arkadia, Argos and Elis had decided to renew the war against Sparta. To that end they also persuaded Thebes to send an army with Epaminondas in command. It is obvious that they were wary of undertaking the enterprise themselves against Sparta, with its new ally Athens and Korinth to their rear. Spartan forces managed to reach Korinth and, with its allies, prepared to hold a line near the Isthmos on the heights of Oneion. On hearing that the Thebans were marching south, the Spartans and the men of Pellene took up their position near the weakest point of the defences nearest Kenchreion.

Much of Xenophon's account (*Hell.* VII. 1. 15) is broadly in agreement in outcomes with that of Diodoros' chosen sources. There are, however, differences in the recording of detail. Xenophon, as usual, is the more critical of military matters. We gather from Diodoros that Chabrias was the Athenian commander and that the defensive works stretched from Kenchreion to Lechaion. Both sources are agreed that the Lakedaimonians were manning the weakest point of the defences.

The Thebans made camp just over three miles away, obviously to assess the positions of their opposition. Diodoros misses an essential component in his description of how Epaminondas brought his army through enemy lines:

> Accordingly, throughout the whole area heavy assaults were made, but
> particularly against the Lakedaimonians, for their terrain was easily assailed and
> difficult to defend. Great rivalry arose between the two armies, and Epaminondas,
> who had with him the bravest of the Thebans, with great effort forced back
> the Lakedaimonians, and cutting through their defence and bringing his army
> through, passed into the Peloponnese, thereby accomplishing a feat no whit
> inferior to his former mighty deeds. (Diodoros XV. 69. 5)

All very acceptable in an adventure tale for boys but it gives little or no information of the planning and the process that is covered in Xenophon's account below:

> Then, after calculating the time at which they thought they should start in
> order to finish their journey by dawn, they marched upon the garrison of the
> Lakedaimonians. And in fact they did not prove mistaken in the hour, but fell
> upon the Lakedaimonians and the Pelleneans at the time when the night watches
> were coming to an end, and the men were rising from their camp-beds and going
> wherever each one had to go. Thereupon the Thebans made their attack and laid
> on their blows – men prepared attacking those unprepared, and men in good
> order against those in disorder. And when such as came out of the affair with
> their lives had made their escape to the nearest hill, although the polemarch of the
> Lakedaimonians might have got as many hoplites as he pleased from the forces
> of the allies and might have held his position – for supplies might have been

brought in safety from Cenchreae – he did not do this, but while the Thebans were in great perplexity as to how they were to descend on the side looking toward Sycyon, failing which they would have to go back again, he concluded a truce which, as most people thought was more to the advantage of the Thebans than to that of his own side, and under these circumstances departed and led away the troops under his command. The Thebans, then, after descending in safety and effecting a junction with their allies, the Arcadians, Argives, and Eleans, immediately attacked Sycon and Pellene. (Xen. *Hell.* VII. 1. 15–18)

Without Xenophon's account we would not know of the well-planned and excellently timed operation, nor the fact that it did not initially succeed in its ultimate objective. It would appear that those who had survived the attack were sufficient in number to continue to pose a problem for the Thebans and had taken up a position that endangered their safe descent. Had the *polemarch* held that position and waited for reinforcements, the Theban breakthrough might have been thwarted. It can be inferred that an offer of safe conduct was made by the Thebans to the *polemarch*. His ready acceptance brings understandable criticism from Xenophon when measured against the consequences of his withdrawal. He notes the assaults on Sikyon and Pellene,[2] which were later to come into alliance with Thebes.[3] Both he and Diodoros agree on the extensive damage to the land of Epidauros caused by the combined forces of the Thebans, Argives, Arkadians and Eleans before they returned to the Isthmos for an attack on Korinth.

Again our two main sources give differing treatment to this assault. Chabrias, the Athenian general, is made the hero of the defence of Korinth by Diodoros. In his usual style he rather overstates the activity of the repulse of the Theban attack without giving any meaningful description. Both sources do agree that the defenders had the advantage of higher ground, but it is Xenophon's version that proves the most persuasive in its detail:

as soon as they [the Thebans] came near the city of the Corinthians they rushed
at the double toward the gates through which one passes in going to Phleious,
with the intention of bursting in if they chanced to be open. But some light
troops sallied forth from the city against them and met the picked men of the
Thebans at a distance of not so much as four plethra from the city walls; and they
climbed up on burial monuments and elevated spots, killed a very considerable
number of the troops in the front ranks by hurling javelins and other missiles, and

154

after putting the rest to flight, pursued them about three or four stadia. When this had taken place the Corinthians dragged the bodies to the wall, and after they had given them back under a truce, set up a trophy. (Xen. *Hell*. VII. 1. 18–19)

Much can be gleaned from this short paragraph. This was an opportune attack that had some possibility of success. The approach was 'at the double' in the hope that the gates were open, possibly after an unsuccessful foray by the defenders. The 'picked men of the Thebans' is an obvious reference to the Sacred Band and not merely to a group picked for the task. The attack had probably been planned well ahead of their approach to the city. The aim was that these crack troops could gain entry and hold their position until hoplites from the main army could come up in support. Peltasts made a sally from Korinth, obviously from the gateway, and took up positions on high points around the road leading to the Phliasian gates. Their distance from the walls was no more than 400 or so feet. Being more fleet of foot than hoplites they could expect covering fire from their colleagues on the walls should the necessity to retire arise. From their vantage points they poured a barrage of javelins into the advancing corps to such effect that its impetus was dissipated by significant losses in the front ranks. Being unable to come to close quarters the remainder of the Thebans turned tail and no doubt lost other men during the pursuit.

Chabrias may well have organised this response to the Theban attack but is given no mention by Xenophon. Small as the action may seem to have been, its significance cannot be underestimated. The Theban unit that had fought heroically at Tegyra and at Leuktra had been routed by peltasts and had been forced to cede defeat by regaining the bodies of their fallen comrades under truce.

This success boosted morale, which was further strengthened by the arrival at Korinth of troops and twenty triremes from Dionysos of Sicily. He was to continue to supply mercenary forces to his ally Sparta and had reason to be grateful for Sparta's support in difficult times earlier in his tyranny.[4]

Xenophon shows great interest in the tactics employed by the Syrakusan cavalry. Some fifty cavalrymen were among the expeditionary force. The day after they had disembarked the Theban-led army had occupied the coastal plain between the sea and the city of Korinth. Organised in separate units, they set about destroying property and crops throughout the area. While the Athenians and Korinthians threatened but took no action against their enemies, the Syrakusans rode along the enemy line discharging their javelins. Whenever there was a reactive move against them, the Syrakusans retreated, only to turn about to send a volley of javelins into their pursuers. At a safe distance they would dismount to rest their mounts. If their pursuers persisted, they would quickly remount and retreat further:

> On the other hand, if any pursued them far from the Theban army, they would
> press upon these men when they were retiring, and by throwing javelins work
> havoc with them, and thus they compelled the entire army, according to their own
> will, either to advance or to fall back. After this, however, the Thebans remained
> but a few days and then returned home. (Xen. *Hell.* VII. 1. 22)[5]

After this second Theban invasion of the Peloponnese there is evidence that all was not comfortable within the Theban alliance. Lykomedes' influence in Arkadian politics became paramount. Under his leadership Arkadia indulged in unilateral actions apparently without reference to Thebes. Their rescue of Argive forces blockaded in Epidauros by Chabrias commanding Athenian and Korinthian forces fed their self-confidence. More annoyingly for Thebes, perhaps, was the well-planned expedition to Asine. There, in almost the southernmost part of Messenia, the Arkadian forces defeated the Spartan garrison, killing its commander, the Spartiate, Geranor (Xen. *Hell.* VII. 1. 25). Elsewhere, their refusal to cede to Elis the cities formerly taken from them by Sparta and now part of the new unified Arkadia, led to ill-feeling between the two allies and eventually developed into open hostilities.

A year later, in 368 BC, with the arrival of a second expeditionary force from Syrakuse that also included Celts, Agesilaos' son Archidamos took the field against Karyai. This city on the borders of Lakedaimon had gone over to the Thebans in their first invasion. Archidamos carried the city and executed all prisoners. This action, extreme by Spartan standards, was obviously to demonstrate the retribution thought to be appropriate for infidelity. Moving north-west to the area of Parrhasia a little to the west of the emerging construction of Megalopolis,[6] the Spartan army laid waste the region. At the approach of an Arkadian and Argive army, Archidamos withdrew from the immediate area and encamped in the hills. While there, the general of the Syrakusans reminded Archidamos that the time had come when he and his followers must return to Syrakuse and their journey had to be to the south via Sparta.

Leaving the main body of the Spartan army, they had not gone far when a body of Messenians threatened their passage. It was probably making its way to effect a junction with the Arkadians and Argives. Kissidas, the commander of the Syrakusan expeditionary force, sent back a messenger to Archidamos requesting his help. After successfully coming to their relief, Archidamos led the reunified army south. Meantime, the Arkadians and Argives were also marching south with the intention of impeding Archidamos' return to Sparta. Archidamos possibly knew that a confrontation was inevitable and chose his ground accordingly to be on level ground 'at the junction of the road leading to the Eutresians and the road to Melea' (Xen. *Hell.* VII. 1. 29). Details of battle line positions are not given for the Argives and Arkadians but, in the case of the Spartan army, there can be no doubt that the allies of the Spartans were on the left wing. Xenophon makes the point of reporting a speech of exhortation given by Archidamos as he went along his phalanx (Xen. *Hell.* VII. 1. 30). Xenophon probably did so because it was unusual for a Spartan commander to address his soldiers prior to combat. Rather, it was the custom that the men encouraged each other. Near the right wing stood a sanctuary and a statue of Herakles. Lightning and thunder are reported to have occurred in a cloudless sky, indicating that this demigod, deemed to be the ancestor of Spartan kings, was lending his support. Given the piety and observation of ritual by Spartans, it may well be that such things were added to any reports given by participants after the battle:

> And when Archidamos led the advance, only a few of the enemy waited till his
> men came within spear-thrust; these were killed, and the rest were cut down as
> they fled, many by the horsemen and many by the Celts [mercenaries]. Then
> as soon as the battle had ended and he had set up a trophy, he immediately
> sent home Demoteles, the herald, to report the greatness of his victory and the
> fact that not so much as one of the Lakedaimonians had been slain, while vast
> numbers of the enemy had fallen. (Xen. *Hell.* VII. 1. 31–32)

Thus, for the Spartans, this military success became known as the Tearless Battle. Its significance was not lost on the rest of Greece. Sparta had clearly shown that it still had the capacity to pose a threat to its Peloponnesian neighbours. Their failure to stand firm against the Spartan phalanx showed that Sparta's centuries-long reputation still held resonance in the minds of Sparta's opponents. Without the presence of Thebes on the battlefield Sparta's enemies lacked confidence.

Xenophon remarks that the setback for the Arkadians was not unwelcome to Thebes and Elis 'so vexed had they become by this time at their presumption' (Xen. *Hell.* VII. 1. 32).

The diplomacy with Persia at Susa that occurred in the following year of 367 BC is dealt with in the following chapter on Pelopidas' activities at this time. One year later saw Epaminondas launching his third invasion of the Peloponnese.

His intention was to bring the Achaian cities into alliance. To ensure passage into the Peloponnese he requested that the Argives attempt to occupy the heights near Kenchreion. The Argive general, Peisias, with 2,000 men, succeeded in this objective and held his position until Epaminondas had passed unimpeded. Having been joined by his Peloponnesian allies, he proceeded westwards into Achaia. The ruling oligarchies of the cities collectively succeeded in coming to an agreement with Epaminondas that they would retain their form of government and become allies of Thebes. So it was that the northern Peloponnese came to be under the leadership of Thebes.

Looking at the purpose of the Theban invasion that saw little or no military activity, we can deduce certain conclusions. Among the conditions laid down at Susa had been the instruction for Arkadia to return Triphylia to Elis. Arkadia possibly viewed this as a further snub engineered by Thebes to punish it for its increasingly independent stand. As it was, Arkadia was obliged, one year later, to follow the Theban lead in the Achaian venture. Viewed geographically, Arkadia now found itself with the possibility of being surrounded by Theban allies to the north, west and east, with an enemy, Sparta, to the south. The realisation that Arkadia was no longer in the position of being able to conduct an independent interstate policy and was now obliged to follow Thebes in whatever it chose to undertake, must have been galling for the leading men. This situation was not to last long.

Very soon after, representatives of Arkadia and those of the democratic parties of the Achaian cities acted, apparently in concert, but for very different objectives: 'Their accusation, presumably made at Thebes was that Epaminondas . . . had arranged matters in Achaia in the interest of the Lakedaimonians and then had gone away' (Xen. *Hell.* VII. 1. 43).

No doubt the political enemies of Epaminondas seized the opportunity to charge him with treason. The agreement was reversed, the Achaian aristocrats were exiled and Theban garrisons under governors were established in all cities to support the new democracies. This proved to be a pivotal point in the fortunes of Thebes. Very soon after, the exiles from all the cities joined together and assailed each city in turn. Their collaborative actions were rewarded by the return of all Achaian cities to oligarchic control. A further setback for Thebes was that Achaia now openly supported Sparta; that proved to be a setback for Arkadia too.

Opportunism seemed to be the order of the day for, further east at Sikyon, a certain Euphron seized power with the help of the Arkadians and Argives. Exiling the aristocrats and confiscating their property, he set up a so-called democracy. In reality he used the proceeds of those confiscations to pay for a mercenary force whose loyalty was to him alone. In a short time he disposed of his democratically elected colleagues to become tyrant of Sikyon, initially pursuing an active pro-Theban policy. His rule was not long, but his support vacillated between Thebes and Sparta and, like so many tyrants, he was assassinated.

At about the same time another tyrant, Themison of Eretria, captured Oropos (Diod. XV. 76. 1). This city, on the border between Attika and Boiotia, then passed into the hands of Thebes. Not one of Athens' allies could, or would, offer Oropos help. Lykomedes saw this as an opportunity to attempt once again to forge an alliance with Athens. Arkadian opinion of Thebes at that time was sufficiently critical that Lykomedes had little trouble in gaining the approval of the Council of the Ten Thousand for such an approach to be made. Although Athens was in alliance with Arkadia's enemy Sparta, it was deemed advantageous to Athens that Arkadia would no longer need Theban support. Having succeeded in his objective, Lykomedes returned to the Peloponnese by boat. He disembarked at a point where there were Arkadian exiles, who killed him. Nonetheless, this great Arkadian leader had inspired the men of his state to further assert their independence of action.

There was still more disruption in this turbulent period of 367/366 BC. At the Athenian assembly, a decision was reached to take direct control of Korinth and the strategically important entry to the Peloponnese at the Isthmos. News of the covert plan reached Korinth in time for it to take countermeasures. The Korinthians defused the threat peaceably by dismissing the Athenian garrisons around Korinthia and replacing them with their own men. Shortly after, an Athenian fleet under Chares appeared just off the port of Kenchreion. He, no doubt, had come to instigate the seizure of Korinth. He claimed to have come to give help to the Korinthians because news of a plot against their state had been received (Xen. *Hell*. VII. 4. 5). His fleet was refused entry to the port and, after thanking him for his concern, he was asked to leave the area.

Korinth was now in a precarious position. Threatened from the north by Thebes, to the south by Argos, now at odds with Athens, and with no realistic expectation of Spartan help, cut off as it was by Arkadia, Korinth sought a diplomatic solution. Dispatching ambassadors to Thebes, Korinth requested consideration of peace proposals between the two states: 'The Corinthians requested that they should allow them to go to their allies also, to the end that they might conclude the peace in company with those who desired peace, and leave those who preferred war to continue war' (Xen. *Hell*. VII. 4. 7).

Accordingly, when Korinth asked for Sparta's permission to conclude a separate peace, it and other allies were given a sympathetic hearing and approval to do so. Sparta, however, would not countenance an end to hostilities until Messene was once again under its control. On returning to Thebes, Korinth and others of the allies made peace, recognising the independence of Messene, but not entering into alliance with Thebes.

Phleious is mentioned as one of those allied states, and Pellene must also have been included, because its return to the Spartan alliance in the following year is noted at Xen. *Hell*. VII. 4. 17. Another of the allies may have been Epidauros. Later, in 366 BC, with the help of mercenaries from Syrakuse, Sparta was successful in regaining Sellasia to the north.

Hostilities between Elis and Arkadia resumed in 365 BC when the former briefly retook the city of Lasion that had been taken from it by the Arkadians. Arkadia quickly struck back, retaking the city in turn and carrying the war into the Akrorian district of Elis. A little later the Arkadians took control of the area around Olympia. As was often the case in an interstate conflict, the democratic faction in Elis saw an opportunity to gain power by siding with the Arkadians. Some of the democrats had been exiled from Elis after a failed attempt to take over their city. With the help of the Arkadians, these exiles gained control of the city of Elean Pylos. This gave them a secure base from which to attract other democrats from Elis to join them. Having persuaded the Arkadians that, if the city of Elis were attacked, it would come over to them, they made the attempt and failed. Here Xenophon gives further evidence of the rapid and sometimes bewildering reconfiguration of alliances in the mid-360s. At Xen. *Hell*. VII. 4. 16 we find that the attack on Elis had been repulsed with help from Achaia, and later, at Xen. *Hell.* VII. 4. 19, an alliance between Elis and Sparta is referred to.

The hard-pressed Eleans now appealed to Sparta to attack Arkadia, thinking that they would receive respite if the Arkadian forces were faced with enemies to their front and rear. Archidamos did, indeed, reduce pressure on Elis before returning home. He captured Kromnos, leaving it with a garrison of one and a half *mora* that brought the Arkadian forces south. Strategically the capture of Kromnos threatened to cut off Messene from Arkadia and it proved sufficiently worrying to the Arkadians that they, with Argive support, erected a double stockade around the settlement.

In solving one problem, Archidamos had created another. It was now necessary for Sparta to bring succour to its own beleaguered garrison. Again Archidamos set out with an army, this time to pillage southern Arkadia in the hope that this would make his enemies give up their siege and come to the aid of their countrymen. This did not produce the desired result. The Arkadians refused to be drawn and the siege continued. Archidamos moved to the area to attempt an attack on their position. The small action that followed shows the critical part played by topography and its effect on possible formations.

Noting that the outer stockade passed over a hill, Archidamos made this his target, knowing that, if successful, he would have little difficulty in dislodging those of the enemy on the lower slopes:

> Now while he was leading the way to this place by a roundabout route, as soon
> as the peltasts who were running on ahead of Archidamos caught sight of the
> Eparitoi[7] outside the stockade, they attacked them, and the cavalry endeavoured
> to join in the attack. The enemy, however, did not give way, but forming
> themselves into a compact body, remained quiet. Then the Lacedaimonians
> attacked again. The enemy did not give way even then, but on the contrary
> proceeded to advance, and by this time there was a great deal of shouting;
> Archidamos himself thereupon came to the rescue, turning off along the wagon
> road which runs to Cromnus and leading his men in double file, just as he
> chanced to have them formed. (Xen. *Hell.* VII. 4. 22)

In the need for a speedy advance Archidamos maintained his double file until very near the enemy, who were 'massed together in close order'. The Lakedaimonian column was no match for the weight and depth of the broader Arkadian formation.

161

Losses to the Spartan army were over 30 men and a wounded commander. From the evidence there can be little doubt that the Arkadians were blocking the outlet of a restricted area of the road through which the Lakedaimonians had to pass to reach more open ground: 'But when the Lakedaimonians as they retired along the road came out into *open ground*, they immediately formed themselves in line of battle against the enemy' (Xen. *Hell*. VII. 4. 24; emphasis added).

The morale of the Lakedaimonian army was dented by their losses, and, with their commander incapacitated, they accepted a truce with their enemy, who, being fewer in number, probably did not relish conflict in the open.

With the Arkadians occupied with Kromnos, the Eleans regained control of significant areas of their state. Later that year, Sparta made a night attack on the stockade around Kromnos but was only partially successful in rescuing the garrison. Those who were unable to reach freedom and safety, numbering over a hundred, were captured by the Arkadians and divided between the besieging forces. It is here, at *Hell*. VII. 4. 27, that Xenophon describes those forces as being made up not only of Arkadians and Argives but also of Thebans.

Now that the problem of Kromnos was over, the focus of the Arkadians returned to Elis. The garrison at Olympia was strengthened and arrangements were made to hold the games of 364 BC. The Eleans with their Achaian allies marched on Olympia and a fierce battle took place, extending to the sacred precinct itself. This fell out in favour of the Eleans, until the loss of the commander of their specialist corps of 'Three Hundred'. Successfully disengaging, the Eleans returned the following day to find a strong and heavily defended stockade had been erected during the night and withdrew.

The complexities of the shifting alliances can be seen in the presence of 400 Athenian cavalry on the Arkadian side, along with 2,000 Argive hoplites (Xen. *Hell*. VII. 4. 29). This despite Athens being also allied to Sparta, an enemy of both Arkadia and Argos. It can also be assumed that Athens was with the Arkadians in the absence of Thebes. This arrangement was soon to change once more in this troubled decade.

Endnotes

1   Xenophon *Kyropaideia* VII. 5. 3–5, and appendix I of the Loeb edition describe the manoeuvre. Much of this work is based on Spartan military and organisational procedures and gives insight into training and tactical matters. Together with his

account of his command of the 'Ten Thousand' in the *Anabasis* we have details of good military practice.

2   See also Pausanias VI. 3. 3, Polyainos V. 16. 3 and Diod. XV. 69. 1.

3   At Xen. *Hell.* VII. 2. 11, Xenophon reports the Theban governor of Sikyon leading the men of that city along with the Pelleneans against Sparta's ally Phleious.

4   Hornblower, p. 189 raises the interesting idea that Spartan involvement in Sicily could have been one of the causes for the Korinthian War.

5   Xenophon could well have been an eyewitness to all that happened around Korinth at this time. Shortly after Leuktra he had left his estate in Tryphilia, which had been taken over by Thebes' ally Elis. He was now resident in Korinth.

6   Diod. XV. 72. 4 reports that the Tearless Battle was the reason for building Megalopolis to defend the area of western Arkadia.

7   Those Arkadians who undertook military training and were paid for their service, becoming the specialist core of the Arkadian army.

CHAPTER 12

Pelopidas in the North and Persia, and the Athenian Revival

I serve my master: you, and countless others,
Are governed by convention. Some again,
Obey a tyrant, ruled himself by fear.

> Philemon; T. F. Higham trans.

JUST AS IN THE PELOPONNESE to the south, Thebes took the opportunity to extend its influence to the north. Events after Leuktra worked in its favour. The possible future threat from Jason of Pherai had disappeared at his death. Jason was succeeded by his brothers Polydoros and Polyphron, and, within a year, the latter killed his brother and was then poisoned by Polydoros' son, Alexander (Xen. *Hell.* VI. 4. 33–4).

Alexander of Pherai was never able to achieve his ambition to be fully recognised as *tagos* but, in attempting to do so, created unsettled conditions in Thessaly. He had the resources, both financial and military, enjoyed by Jason prior to his elevation as *tagos*, and no doubt considered his quest for power justified. His struggle with the dynasts of Larissa, the Aleuads, for control of the Thessalian League, led them to request support from Alexander of Makedon. This monarch, the second of that name, had but recently succeeded to the throne of his father Amyntas III in 370 BC. The latter's reign of twenty-three years was unusually long for this turbulent kingdom. Despite Makedon's military weakness, he had managed to retain control by dint of a series of defensive alliances, and to regain his throne after being deposed for a period of three months early in his tenure.

Unlike Thessaly, with its large and fertile plain, Makedon's topography had dictated the settlement of its fifteen tribal areas, each with its own ruling house.

Physical barriers, mountains, large rivers and marshes made communication between tribes onerous, particularly in Upper Makedon. The country was rich in resources and it was these that attracted the attention of the Greeks. Its timber made it attractive to maritime cities such as Athens for shipbuilding, thereby bringing to it an attention from powers further south disproportionate to its importance. Makedon had been, and continued to be, regarded throughout and beyond our period as non-Greek by many Greek city-states.[1]

The dominant ruling house of the Argeadai gradually achieved its ascendancy through dynastic marriages and alliances, but the country remained weak and subject to periodic attacks from east, west and north. Two factors contributed to this weakness. The aristocracy, two centuries earlier, had resisted the adoption of the phalanx throughout Greece, in Makedon. It had been unwilling to cede some powers to a new citizenry that would have been the price of such a change. Together with the consequent military weakness, the instability of the monarchy was disruptive of development. Having no formal and agreed method of succession made for mayhem. Any member of the royal house with sufficient support could bid for the monarchy. Assassination of a king became commonplace. The habit of this dysfunctional family reached its apogee following 399 BC when five monarchs perished at the hands of assassins in six years. The problem of military weakness was later to be comprehensively solved by Philip II, but he too was to be a victim of the continuing family habit of assassination.

Now Alexander II of Makedon was given the opportunity to further cement his relationship with some of the aristocratic families in Thessaly and gain territorial advantage. Responding to the request from the Aleuadai to come to their aid, he entered the city of Larissa before Alexander of Pherai had completed his preparations to meet the army of Makedon in its own territory. Shortly after, he also took control of Krannon and placed garrisons in both cities (Diod. XV. 61. 5). This must have caused concern to the aristocratic members of the Thessalian confederacy, but all was not going well for the king. In Alexander's absence from Makedon, the exiled aspirant to the throne, Ptolemy of Aloros, had returned to exercise his claim. Meantime, the Thessalian aristocracy opposed to Alexander of Pherai, having concerns as to the motives of the Makedonian king, approached Thebes for support. Pelopidas was sent north to settle matters in the interests of Thebes. It may well be that the requests for Boiotian intervention in Thessaly and Makedon proved opportune for Thebes. Athens was becoming increasingly active in the pursuit of regaining influence in the north, with the recovery of the strategic city of Amphipolis as one of her goals.[2]

Pelopidas forced the Makedonian garrisons to leave both cities and, by his presence, diminished the threat from the tyrant of Pherai, before arbitrating between the rivals for the Makedonian throne in favour of Alexander. Of significance in the settlement was the presence, among the thirty hostages taken back to Thebes, of the boy Philip, who was to make Makedon the greatest power in the Greek world: 'This was the Philip who afterwards waged war to enslave the Greeks, but at this time he was a boy, and lived in Thebes with Pammenes. Hence he was believed to have become a zealous follower of Epaminondas, perhaps because he comprehended his efficiency in wars and campaigns, which was only a small part of the high man's excellence' (Plut. *Pelop.* XXVI. 5).

Pelopidas' arrangements proved to be only temporary. In typical Makedonian fashion, Ptolemy took power by having Alexander assassinated. Under the guise of taking the position of regent for Perdikkas, another son of Amyntas, he became ruler of the kingdom.

A number of states viewed the change of rule with interest. Influence and territorial gain were the various motivations. Olynthos had taken Sparta's defeat at Leuktra as an opportunity to rebuild its league and eagerly eyed territorial expansion at Makedonian expense. Thebes wished to reassert its influence at the Makedonian court so recently achieved by Pelopidas in the previous year. For Athens the recovery of influence in the north had become a priority, with the key aim of regaining its former colony of Amphipolis which had been freed from Athens' imperial power by the brilliant Spartan general Brasidas during the Peloponnesian War.

It was the Olynthians, in 368 BC, who seized the chance to give military support to Pausanias, yet another pretender to the throne of Makedon. They invaded the country hoping that, by setting Pausanias firmly on the throne, they would make territorial gains. Knowing his forces would be unable to withstand the Olynthians, Ptolemy called on Athens for help and, following an alliance between the two states, Iphikrates intervened, defeated the Olynthians, thereby muting their revival, and rid Makedon of Pausanias. Iphikrates was a good choice as commander, not only for his inimitable military skill, but also for his family connections with the royal house of Makedon.

While this ensued, requests came from the Thessalians for Theban intervention against the renewed activities against them of Alexander of Pherai, quickly to be followed by those who had supported Alexander, the assassinated king of Makedon.

Pelopidas and Ismenias, the son of that Ismenias who had proved so troublesome to Sparta earlier in the century, were sent as ambassadors. Pelopidas was concerned to arrive in Makedon as soon as possible and, in the absence of sufficient Boiotian hoplites being available, hired mercenaries (Plut. *Pelop.* XXVII. 1–2). At the approach of this force Ptolemy managed to bribe the mercenaries to change sides. Despite this setback, an alliance between Thebes and Ptolemy was achieved, probably because the latter feared repercussions for his actions. He agreed to be regent for the brothers of the dead king, and a further fifty aristocratic hostages, including Ptolemy's son Philoxenos, were dispatched to Thebes.

Pelopidas' next actions may well have been acceptable for a commander in the eyes of some commentators in the ancient world, but show traits that would not be applauded in later times. The desire to take revenge on his deserting mercenaries could well have been salutary had it succeeded, but its origin, even as a matter of honour, was emotional and not objective. Just as Teleutias had lost his life in an action before Olynthos provoked by anger, Pelopidas endangered his own in his pursuit of retribution.

He moved south to Pharsalos, where the possessions and families of the mercenaries were housed 'so that by getting these into his power he would sufficiently punish them for their affront to him, so he got together some of the Thessalians and came to Pharsalos' (Plut. *Pelop.* XXVII. 4). As he and Ismenias arrived at Pharsalos, so too did Alexander of Pherai with his army. Thinking that the tyrant had come to excuse his actions against the Thessalians, the two Thebans, relying on their office as ambassadors, went to meet him without attendants or bodyguard. Disregarding normal diplomatic practice and the possible danger from Thebes, Alexander took them prisoner and, soon after, occupied Pharsalos.

Reaction came quickly from Thebes. An army was immediately dispatched. Its commanders are not named but Plutarch makes the following interesting comment: 'The Thebans then, on hearing of this, were indignant, and sent out an army at once, although, since Epaminondas had somehow incurred their displeasure, they appointed other commanders for it' (Plut. *Pelop.* XXVIII. 1).

Whereas Pelopidas had held almost continuous office as *boiotarch*, Epaminondas had political enemies at Thebes, and his election was never a foregone conclusion.³ At Diodoros XV. 71. 6, he is described as serving as a private soldier on this expedition. It may well be that what follows in Diodoros is described in Plutarch's lost *Life of Epaminondas*. As the Theban army moved north the Athenians, with whom the tyrant of Pherai had just made an alliance, sent thirty ships and 1,000 men to his support. Interestingly, the Athenian fleet is described as making a circuit of the island of Euboia, no doubt to avoid any conflict with Theban warships that could easily have blockaded the narrows between the mainland and the island. It is as well to remember that Theban contributions to Spartan fleets during the Peloponnesian War had been significant. Although a longer route, once the Athenian fleet rounded Cape Artemision, it would be in waters controlled by Alexander.

On this occasion the numbers given by Diodoros of the opposing forces are almost believable. He gives those of the Boiotian army as 8,000 hoplites and 600 cavalry. The latter were joined, along with foot-soldiers, by other Thessalians opposed to Alexander. This would diminish the disparity between the cavalry fielded by Alexander, described, perhaps in exaggerated fashion, as being 'many more times more than the Boiotians'.

Having decided to come to battle, the Thebans suddenly found themselves deserted by their Thessalian forces. Diodoros' following remark that the Theban *boiotarch*s found that food, water and other supplies were giving out suggests that they had perhaps relied on such provisions being supplied to them by their former Thessalian allies. Further, the arrival of the Athenian force convinced them that a withdrawal was their only option.

The initial part of the return to Thebes was within the southern part of the plain of Thessaly. This is ideal cavalry country and Alexander took his opportunity to harass the Boiotian rear with a large cavalry force. Within the framework of Diodoros' sparse description, and aided by several clearer examples of similar actions from Xenophon, the tactical use of Alexander's cavalry and the eventual Theban response to it can be recovered: 'A number of Boiotians perished under the continuous rain of darts, others fell wounded, until finally, being permitted neither to halt nor to proceed, they were reduced to utter helplessness, as was natural when they were also running short of provisions' (Diod. XV. 71. 5).

There is nothing in this source to suggest an attempt to counter the attack by the use of the Theban cavalry, although this must have been tried and found to be ineffectual. It can be presumed that successive waves of Alexander's cavalry rode to within casting distance of the Theban rear and discharged their javelins. The attacks would be unrelenting and continuous. The constant turning of the rearguard, or indeed the whole army, to face the enemy, would have the effect of slowing the retreat until, in despair, the morale of the men slumped and progress became impossible.[4] For Alexander's men the danger was minimal, and they had the advantage of having regular periods of rest between the turn of each squadron's attack. No indication is given of the duration of Alexander's exemplary use of his cavalry. It may have lasted for hours or even more than one day.

The *boiotarchs* obviously had no answer to a crisis remarkably similar to that quickly solved by Agesilaos earlier in the century on his march through Thessaly, and the Theban hoplites elected Epaminondas as their leader. In a relatively short time he brought respite to the main body of the Theban army by using a mixed force of cavalry and peltasts. By deploying Theban cavalry supported by these light-armed troops as a screen to the rearguard, he was able to make successive offers of battle to the opposing force that was constituted of cavalry only. This buffer gave the main body the opportunity to make relatively unimpeded progress until it could reach terrain beyond the Thessalian plain where the use of cavalry was much less effective. Having returned safely to Boiotia, the Thebans saw to it that the original *boiotarchs* were tried for their ineptitude and given heavy fines.

With his reputation enhanced, Epaminondas was formally elected *boiotarch* and led another army north shortly afterwards in 367 BC. His military record may have persuaded Alexander to seek terms, as Plutarch suggests (*Pelop.* XXIX. 6). On this occasion no direct confrontation occurred, but Alexander, wisely recognising the threat to him, released Ismenias and Pelopidas under truce, and the Thebans returned home.

Pelopidas was not immediately concerned with the north. His next task was diplomatic. It took him away for a time from the concerns of Thessaly for the greater prize of achieving the support of Persia hitherto given to Sparta. This was prompted by attempts by others to clip Thebes' wings.

Since Leuktra, Sparta's forlorn aim had been to attempt to regain some semblance of its previous influence. Even after Epaminondas' next invasion of the Peloponnese (dealt with in the previous chapter), Sparta had turned again to Persia in 368 BC, with a request for the Great King's support in achieving a return to the conditions that had prevailed after the Peace of Antalkidas. In essence, it proposed an alliance with Persia for all those Greek states that agreed a return to a common peace. The meeting of states convened at Delphi proved unsuccessful. There, Sparta's demands had little prospect of success. The return of Messene to Sparta was no doubt an uncomfortable prospect for some Peloponnesian states, and Thebes would not agree to return independence to the Boiotian cities.

Despite the lack of a satisfactory outcome, Sparta was not to leave the conference wholly empty handed. Ariobarzarnes, satrap of Hellespontine Phrygia and the Great King's representative, gave funds from his own resources to Sparta for the support of 2,000 mercenaries. The Persian satrap, with an eye to the future, no doubt did this in the hope of Spartan military support in the planning of his revolt from the Great King. With the latter trying to regain control of Egypt already in revolt, Artaxerxes was to be faced by similar acts of opportunism by his western satraps in the near future.

There are explicable differences between the descriptions of Xenophon and Plutarch concerning the diplomatic meetings at Susa. Plutarch (*Pelop.* XXX) makes much of Pelopidas' reputation at the Persian court as being a leader who had defeated the Spartans and helped lay waste to their homeland. His claim is credible that the Theban proposals were simpler than those of Sparta, which would no doubt include the demand for the return of Messene, and more trustworthy than those of Athens. He also speaks of the honours done to the Spartiate Antalkidas by Artaxerxes. Xenophon (*Hell.* VII. 1. 33–8) reminds the reader of what he firmly believes to be disgraceful acts in Theban actions of the past. First he claims that Pelopidas pointed out to Artaxerxes that the Thebans had never campaigned against him. Further, the Thebans had fought against the Greeks at Plataia on the side of the Great King in the Persian Wars. They had refused to join Agesilaos on his expedition against Persia and had disrupted those sacrifices preceding his departure. Both of our main sources are agreed that the greed of one of the Athenian diplomats, Timagoras, proved to be so embarrassingly excessive that, on his return to Athens, he was tried and executed. Xenophon alone notes that representatives from Arkadia, Elis and Argos were also present.

Pelopidas' success at Susa gave Thebes the hope that, with the Great King's endorsement of its proposals, Thebes, as sponsor, could truly be the hegemon of Greece. Summoning representatives from cities, Artaxerxes' letter was read out and all were invited to give their oaths to abide by its conditions. From this point, matters began to unravel for Thebes. It is evident that those present had been sent by their cities only to listen to the content of Artaxerxes' communication and report upon it to their fellow citizens on their return. The Thebans were told to approach each city if they required a binding oath. Lykomedes, the political architect of the united Arkadia and an increasing irritant to Thebes, went even further by declaring that a meeting, such as the one they were attending, should not be in Thebes but where hostilities were prevalent in the Peloponnese. It is obvious that this went down badly with the Thebans and they accused Lykomedes of attempting to disrupt the existing alliance. He, in turn, refused to take any further part and left with his colleagues to return to Arkadia.

Xenophon describes the substance of what was agreed by Artaxerxes at the congress at Susa and eventually conveyed to those gathered at Thebes: 'Messene should be independent of the Lakedaimonians and that the Athenians should draw up their ships on the land; that if they refused obedience in these points, the contracting parties were to make an expedition against them; and that if any city refused to join in such expedition, they were to proceed first of all against that city' (Xen. *Hell*. VII. 1. 36).

Thebes' next ploy was to approach Peloponnesian cities individually. It did this, no doubt presuming that no single city would dare to go against Theban wishes when isolated from the support of a collective. However, the tactic of attempting to pick off the cities one by one fell at the first fence. At Korinth, the first city to be approached, the Thebans met with an outright refusal. Others followed its example.

Thebes was encountering problems in its alliance. The unease felt by its members was now showing itself more openly. Newly united Arkadia, in particular, was certainly less amenable. Its views, expressed in the words and, later, the actions of Lykomedes, showed Arkadia to be unwilling to accept all that Thebes asked of it. The pressure that Thebes exerted on the Peloponnese is dealt with in the following chapter along with cogent developments in the eastern and northern Aegean. Pelopidas' reputation was not diminished by this setback. He had accomplished all that was required of him on his diplomatic mission to Persia. Eventually, in 364 BC, his attention returned to developing conditions in Thessaly.

Between 366 and 364 BC little is known of Pelopidas' activities. He may well have had a hand in taking control of Oropos from the Athenians a year after his diplomacy in Persia 366 BC. This town lay opposite Eretria in Euboia, in an area long disputed between Athens and Thebes. However, elsewhere Athens was making considerable gains in its pursuit of regaining its empire. Under the guise of helping to liberate Samos from Persia, Athens was successful in its ten-month siege of the city. Further, it attained control of the cities of Sestos and Krithote in Thrakian Chersonese. Sestos was a critical gain. It controlled the passage of grain ships on which Athens depended. Control of the Hellespontine route had proved the key to Athens' survival in the past and, when it had passed to its enemies, had proved the city's undoing. All this had been achieved by Timotheos, whose intention appeared to be to extend control over the hinterland of Sestos.

With such welcome successes for Athens, Timotheos was given responsibility for the fleet that had been operating in the northern Aegean under Iphikrates. As chance would have it, a change had just occurred in the ruling house of Makedon.

In the customary habit of that kingdom Ptolemy had been assassinated and his place taken by Perdikkas. He wished to follow a policy uninfluenced by Thebes and turned for support to Athens. This proved incredibly convenient for Athens and the opportunity was assiduously taken by Timotheos. In a relatively short time the coastal cities of Methone and Pydna, immediately to the south of Makedon, came under Athenian control. Shortly afterwards the strategic city of Poteidaia, at the neck of the Pallene peninsula was taken, followed by Torone at the foot of the peninsula of Sithonia.

These acquisitions greatly improved Athens' position, but brought no benefit to the members of its league. Thebes' influence in the north was diminished, and the growing power of the Olynthian League was checked. Athens' ultimate, but elusive, goal was the recovery of Amphipolis.

Concern at these gains by Athens provoked a response from Thebes. Epaminondas was behind the suggestion that Thebes should build a fleet of a hundred ships and become a maritime power.[5] This was not, by any measure, an empty ambition. We have noted Kleombrotos' capture of twelve ships at Kreusis prior to the Battle of Leuktra, and it must be remembered that the hundred newly built vessels were in addition to those based in the Korinthian Gulf and in the channel between Boiotia and Euboia. The new fleet was to challenge Athens in the Aegean and attempt to wrest back from it some of its gains. Unopposed, the Athenian fleet could well have gone on to take control of the large island of Euboia, thereby threatening eastern Boiotia. To the north, Athens was giving support to Alexander of Pherai and had won over the support of Makedon. For Athens to regain control of Euboia would have seen a partial encirclement of Boiotia. This the Thebans correctly sought to block by taking the fight to a resurgent enemy.

As commander, Epaminondas sailed east. It is highly unlikely that his fleet approached the number originally planned. He seems to have had some success in establishing good relations with Chios and Rhodes but not to the extent that they left the Athenian League. His one major success, however, was in the Propontis. Byzantion was persuaded to secede from the league. Its geographical position on the grain route on which Athens strongly relied was more than a little cause for concern.

Athens had only itself to blame for the unrest in the league. Although not a member of that institution, Samos had been settled by Athenian cleruchies to the disadvantage of the original inhabitants. This sent an unwelcome signal to the coastal and island communities of the Athenian League. To them it appeared that Athens was up to its old tricks again and was reverting to one of the practices that had been so unpopular and had done much to change its first league into its empire. With this limited success, probably due more to the suspicions of Athens' allies than to anything else, the Theban fleet returned home, never to sail again.

Alexander of Pherai had returned to his struggle to gain supremacy in Thessaly and adjacent areas. The Thessalians again asked Thebes for armed assistance with Pelopidas as commander. As chance would have it, an eclipse of the sun occurred just prior to Pelopidas' departure. This was taken as an adverse portent by the Thebans that, according to Plutarch (*Pelop.* XXXI. 2–3), removed the compulsion for citizens to serve in the army and sent Pelopidas north with 300 foreign volunteers serving with the Theban cavalry. Plutarch leads us to believe that Pelopidas was the architect of this arrangement despite opposition from the city seers to his own involvement 'for the eclipse was thought to be a great sign from heaven, and to regard a conspicuous man. But his wrath at insults received made him very hot against Alexander.' Pharsalos was the mustering point for the Thessalians serving under Pelopidas.

Marching east towards Pherai, they were faced by Alexander's larger army. From the little information to be gleaned from Plutarch, it would appear that Alexander had significantly more hoplites whereas Pelopidas had the advantage in cavalry numbers. Hard by the place at which the initial cavalry action took place is a large upland area, most of which reaches over 1,000 feet. Known as Kynoskephalai, the stretch of hills proved to be the objective that both generals sought to occupy with hoplites detached from the main body of their armies. Pelopidas' cavalry was successful in its opening engagement and routed its opposition. It returned to harass the main body of Alexander's hoplites in the plain. With no cavalry to screen them, these forces would have been subject to javelin attack and, in consequence, mobility would have been hampered. Alexander's men, however, had won the race to occupy the heights. What followed would appear to have been a desperate attempt led by Pelopidas to dislodge Alexander's men from their position. Having eventually succeeded in doing so, Pelopidas used his vantage position to locate Alexander, who is described as being occupied 'on the right wing, marshalling and encouraging his mercenaries'.

If we are to believe Plutarch, what followed may well have seemed heroic but it would have been an act of gross irresponsibility on the part of Pelopidas: 'he could not subject his anger to his judgement, but, inflamed at the sight, and surrendering himself and his conduct of the enterprise to his passion, he sprang out far in front of the rest and rushed with challenging cries upon the tyrant' (Plut. *Pelop.* XXXII. 6).

Diodoros XV. 80. 5 supports Plutarch's view that Pelopidas lost his life while making an attack on Alexander himself and 'performing mighty deeds of valour'. From this it should not be deduced that such actions were universally approved of in the ancient world. The following comment, made by Xenophon in his description of Teleutias losing his life in an action provoked by anger, is a contemporary view made by a man with a proven record as a good commander: 'In dealing with enemies, to attack under the influence of anger and not with judgement is an absolute mistake. For anger is a thing which does not look ahead, while judgement aims no less to escape harm than to inflict it upon the enemy' (Xen. *Hell.* V. 3–7).

Despite the subsequent victory over Alexander, the death of Pelopidas could well have put his own forces at risk before victory was achieved. His action as described by Plutarch is inexcusable. Had he achieved his goal of killing Alexander he would have received plaudits. There is no doubting the man's bravery as his involvement in the liberation of Thebes, his action at Tegyra and later at Leuktra attest, but in all these there is more than a hint of the great risk taker.

Thebes sent a large army north under Malkitas and Diogeiton and forced Alexander to withdraw his garrisons and give up control of the Thessalian cities he held. Further, he was obliged to free Magnesia and Phthiotis and to vow to be an ally of Thebes. Alexander was not to survive Pelopidas for very long and was assassinated by the brothers of his wife.

Endnotes

1 Until the reign of Alexander I, all Makedonians were ineligible to participate in the Olympic Games on the grounds that they were regarded as not being of Greek blood. They were barbarians in the Greek sense of not speaking readily understandable Greek, nor sharing the common customs of the wider Greek world. It was Alexander who eventually persuaded the authorities at Olympia that the royal house was descended from Herakles and that the family had originally come from Argos. This allowed the Argeadai to compete in the games and to be accepted as a Greek family ruling over barbarians (see also Julia Heskel, 'Macedonia and the North, 400–336', in L. A. Tritle, L. A. (ed.), *The Greek World in the Fourth Century*, London, Routledge, 1997). The truth behind the claim is highly conjectural, but it was enough to bring Makedon a little closer to the Greeks in terms of more than just the southern city-states' desire to exploit the resources of Makedon. Nonetheless, the underlying attitude of the Greeks to Makedon continued. One of its most explosive expressions is to be found in the Third Philippic of Demosthenes, a speech delivered to the Athenian assembly in 340/339, a year prior to the Battle of Chaironeia: 'Yet they have no such qualms about Philip and his present conduct, though he is not only no Greek, nor related to the Greeks, but not even a barbarian from any place that can be named with honour, but is a pestilent knave from Macedonia, whence it was never yet possible to buy a decent slave' (Demosthenes, Third Philippic 31).

2 See also Hornblower, pp. 226–8.

3 At Diod. XV. 72. 1–2, we learn that Epaminondas' enemies at Thebes accused him of treason for seemingly giving favourable treatment to the Lakedaimonians when he breached the defensive line at Korinth (see previous chapter).

4 Thucydides' description of the Athenian retreat from Syrakuse towards the end of Book VII of his *History of the Peloponnesian War* paints an indelible picture of the loss of morale when under sustained attack during a retreat.

5 The fact that Athens refused to reduce its sea power was probably one of the spurs for Epaminondas to recommend the building of a fleet.

CHAPTER 13

Towards Mantineia

The perfect example of the Panhellene was Epaminondas, and it is a great
pity that Plutarch left no biography of him . . . he made up his mind to
deal with hostile Sparta only by ensuring it was harmless, determined as
always to avoid destroying Hellenic cities.

Burckhardt, *The Greeks and Greek Civilisation*

THE PREVIOUS THREE CHAPTERS WERE concerned with the growing
influence of Thebes on Greek affairs in its attempt to establish its *hegemony*
fully both on land and sea. It had been successful in central Greece but at the
cost of losing, in Pelopidas, one of its two most able commanders. The pursuit
of displacing Athens as the major sea power faltered when Thebes' attention was
drawn again to the Peloponnese. There, its ally Arkadia continued to provoke
problems which it was forced to address. The disintegration of the nascent state
of Arkadia inevitably led to yet another Theban invasion of the Peloponnese in an
attempt to impose its will on this troubled region.

Before continuing the chronological narrative it is as well to review some
causative factors that led to Sparta's decline. Following Leuktra, Sparta's slide
from being a first-rank power was not immediately appreciated by the peoples of
Greece. True Sparta had suffered a stunning reverse at the hands of the Thebans,
but its centuries-long reputation of inevitable invincibility was sufficient to sustain
it for a little longer. Its position was really only fully appreciated at the time of
Epaminondas' first invasion of the Peloponnese. The depredation of Lakedaimon,
followed by the freeing of Messene, demonstrated Sparta's inability to counter the

power of the aspiring hegemon, Thebes. Sparta now found itself able to operate only as an equal, rather than leader, within the shifting alliances that arose within the 360s. It is Aristotle, towards the end of the century, who rightly draws our attention to part of the reason for Sparta's downfall:

> We also know that the Spartans were invincible when they were the only people committed to rigorous training. However, they are now beaten in war and even in the games. And the reason for this? They were superior, not for their training methods, but because their men had discipline at a time when those that they faced had none. (Aristotle *Politics*, VIII. 1338b; trans. Warrington)

Aristotle may well be correct in suggesting that Sparta would always beat an opposition as long as its discipline was significantly better than that of any opposition it faced. However, the number of those under training must be a consideration and this too becomes an issue. Whereas a little over a century prior to our period Sparta could call on 9,000 trained citizens from which to provide the core of any Lakedaimonian and allied army, it now had a significantly lower number on which to call. At Leuktra it had fielded more than half the citizen body, possibly a higher proportion than it would have done, had it but waited for additional allies to join Kleombrotos before the start of the campaign.

The 700 Spartiatai present at that battle could be compared with other specialist corps trained and supported by other states. While a precursor of the Theban Sacred Band of 300 may well have existed in the latter part of the fifth century, the corps of 1,000 Argives trained at the city's expense certainly did so. Other trained forces came into being within the first half of the fourth century: Elis had two bodies of men numbering 300 and 400; Arkadia had formed a fully professional core to its army, the *eparitoi*, a considerable but unknown number of hoplites (Xen. *Hell.* VII. 4. 22; VII. 4. 32); Phleious also had a unit, the *epilektoi* (Xen. *Hell.* VII. 2. 10 and 12) and the increasingly common practice of hiring mercenaries and keeping them under training was taken to its apogee in terms of numbers by Jason of Pherai and continued by his successors.

There were no more than 1,400 Spartiatai in existence before Leuktra, some of whom, at sixty and over, would be above the upper age limit for military service. Having suffered 400 Spartiate casualties at that battle, Sparta was operating in the 360s with specialist forces not dissimilar to other states. The fact that after Leuktra military training was instituted for all able-bodied Boiotians was a very significant swing of the pendulum and made them the obvious dominant power. Sparta was now little different from most other states. In a populous Lakedaimon it had only itself to blame for its adherence to customs, a constitution and way of life which denied easier access to citizenship and the opportunity to build a more cohesive society. The loss of Messene proved terminal. Strive as it might, Sparta was never to regain its control over the territory or its position of dominance. There would always be stronger land powers to prevent it from doing so.

And what of Thebes? The latter years of the 370s had given it an almost heaven-sent opportunity not only to recover, but to vie with other states for supremacy. A succession of events worked to its advantage. The infamous attempt of Sphodrias to capture the port of Athens drove that city into an alliance with Thebes. With fulsome help from Athens, Thebes managed to limit the damage done by Agesilaos' successive invasions. But damage there had been, and, just when the Spartan king's depredation of Thebes' agricultural product was beginning to have its desired effect, Agesilaos suffered a severe illness from a diseased leg and was unable to take command for several years. His colleague, Kleombrotos, lacked his organisational skills and probably also Agesilaos' commitment to the task. His failure to maintain Spartan pressure on Thebes, and the incompetence of the Spartan commander to the north of Euboia in sustaining the blockade of Thessalian grain, allowed Thebes a quick recovery. Timotheos, the Athenian, diverted Spartan attention to the defence of its own coastline by making raids around the Peloponnese. Over a period of four years Thebes recovered agriculturally and consolidated its control of the cities in Boiotia. It was strong enough to threaten its neighbour Phokis despite the presence of Spartan forces stationed at Orchomenos. During this period Sparta's allies became increasingly disenchanted and irritated by the lack of direction of Spartan leadership. By the time of Leuktra some were unwilling appendages to its allied forces. Even had Epaminondas' battle plan given them opportunity to take a more active role in that battle it remains doubtful that the outcome would have been any different. As a commander, Kleombrotos showed himself to be clearly out of his depth and the kernel of the Spartan war machine was not large enough to compensate for the shortcomings of its general as it had done in the past with others. Finally, with the assassination of Jason of Pherai within a year, Thebes was in a pivotal position to exploit its newfound strength. With the invasion of Lakonia, the mirage of Spartan power had truly been broken.

Returning to our narrative, in 364 BC, the same year that had seen all Greece outraged by the battle that had taken place within the sacred precinct of Olympia, another even more horrific action was taken. A plot was uncovered at Thebes. Some 'refugees', presumably those of the aristocratic party at Thebes, approached the 300 knights of Orchomenos, now under Theban control, who were training near Thebes, with a plan to overthrow the democratic governance of Thebes. The knights (*ippeis*) obviously shared a similar aristocratic background to that of the proposers of the plot. Arrangements were made to launch a combined attack on one of the days when a review under arms was to take place at Thebes. Diodoros (XV. 4) indicates that many others joined in the enterprise. The plot could well have succeeded and overturned the democracy to replace it with an oligarchy, had not the original proposers wavered and revealed all to the *boiotarch*s in return for immunity.

The knights were arrested and put on trial, presumably for treason; the Theban assembly condemned them to death. This was not the end of the matter, however. Additional requirements called for the inhabitants of Orchomenos to be sold into slavery and their city razed to the ground. This reflects the historical enmity that had existed for centuries between the two cities. Legend has it that Thebes had once been under the control of Minyan Orchomenos, and Diodoros (XV. 79. 5) cites this as a further reason to exact revenge for perceived wrongs. To that end, Thebes marched against Orchomenos and, having captured the city, went even beyond the original brief. The Thebans proceeded to kill all adult males before razing the city and selling all women and children into slavery.

This was a barbarous and chilling act to commit against a fellow Boiotian city. It shocked much of the Greek world that such an act should take place in times of relative peace within that region. It served as a warning to others of the Boiotian federation. Epaminondas was in the Aegean with the Theban fleet at the time. Had he been present in Thebes, one can only wonder if the counsel of this philosopher soldier might have led to a more measured outcome.

The year 363 BC saw dissension in Arkadia. The use of the sacred treasures to pay the *eparatoi* was a violation of the sanctity of Olympia, and Mantineia was the first city to secede from the arrangement. The citizens voted to send their portion of payment from their own resources rather than be party to sacrilege. Having done so, the leading men were summoned to Megalopolis to appear before the Assembly of Ten Thousand and to answer the charge that 'they were doing harm to the Arkadian League' (Xen. *Hell.* VII. 4. 33). It seems obvious that the majority of the Arkadians at that time were unwilling to follow the example of Mantineia. The *eparitoi* were dispatched to arrest the leaders in Mantineia responsible for the decision, but were not permitted entry to the city. This gave others in the assembly pause for thought. When another vote was taken, conscience led them to accept that they had, indeed, been responsible for a serious breach of sanctity. It was resolved to discontinue the practice of using monies from Olympia.

Xenophon makes clear the repercussions of this decision:

> those who could not belong to the Eparitoi without pay speedily began to melt away, while those who could, spurred on one another and began to enrol themselves in the Eparitoi, in order that they might not be in the power of that body, but rather that it might be in their power. Then such of the Arcadian leaders as had handled the sacred treasures, realising that, if they had to render an account, they would be in danger of being put to death, sent to Thebes and explained to the Thebans that if they did not take the field, the Arcadians would be likely to go over to the Lacedaimonians again. (Xen. *Hell.* VII. 4. 34)

As the Thebans prepared to mobilise, the Arkadians then sent ambassadors to the Thebans, asking them not to come until summoned to do so. No doubt they were fearful that Thebes could well make Arkadia a Theban protectorate. Thebes, on its part, was aware that those aristocratic members of the Ten Thousand, who were now serving as unpaid members of the *eparitoi*, could well lead the majority of the Arkadians into an accommodation with Sparta. This was a dangerous possibility that could isolate Messenia from Thebes and endanger its newly gained independence.

With peace being made between the cities of Arkadia and Elis, and the latter now resuming the presidency of the sacred games, the shift of power within the Peloponnese was tipping away from Thebes. It was imperative that support should be readily given to those Arkadians still ready to follow Theban leadership.

When the oath of peace came to be taken at Tegea, there was great celebration and feasting among all gathered there from the Arkadian cities. However, the Theban governor in command of a 300-strong garrison made common cause with those of the Arkadians who favoured Thebes, or who were worried that their accounting for the sacred monies might be investigated. The gates of the city were closed and arrests were made of the aristocrats present. At this time most of the

Mantineians had already left to return to their city some twelve miles away. Many were captured from other Arkadian cities but, of the primary target group from Mantineia, there were notably very few.

The whole affair became an acute embarrassment to those involved in the conspiracy. The prison was now full, and the overflow of prisoners could barely be contained in the hall of assembly. Further, the reaction of Mantineia was to alert all other Arkadian cities and to demand the release of all prisoners. Faced by the possibility of concerted action being taken against him, the Theban garrison commander released the prisoners. He summoned the Arkadians within the city and told them that his action was taken because he had heard a rumour that Sparta had mobilised and was near the Tegean border. Further he had heard that there was a danger that the city was about to be betrayed to the invaders. The Arkadians knew that he was lying and, while appearing to accept his explanation, sent to Thebes demanding his execution.

Xenophon quotes what was the commonly held opinion of the time, that Epaminondas had approved the garrison commander's arrest of the Arkadians, but not their subsequent release. Epaminondas is also reported to have said to the Arkadian diplomats:

> 'For it was on your account that we entered upon war [against the Eleans and their allies], and you concluded peace without our approval; should we not, therefore, be justified in charging you with treason for this act? But be well assured,' said he, 'that we shall make an expedition to Arkadia and shall wage war in company with those who hold our side.' (Xen. *Hell*. VII. 4. 40)

We have no reason to doubt that these sentiments, or similar, were expressed, reported, as they were, by Xenophon at a time extremely close to their suggested utterance. Whether they reflect the personal views of Epaminondas, or that he was merely the mouthpiece for a Theban decision of the assembly, can never be known. In some ways Thebes could well have been pleased at the disintegration of Arkadia. It removed a unified state that had proved to be an awkward ally, and gave it an excuse for further direct intervention in the Peloponnese. Thebes' arrogance clearly emerges, and its following actions display a disquieting lack of understanding of the need for willing rather than coerced or fearful followers. Realistically, Thebes was faced by the probability of an alliance between Sparta, Athens, Elis, Achaia, and some cities from Arkadia. Athens, hitherto allied to both Sparta and Arkadia, which had been at odds one with the other, could now comfortably act in concert with both. From Thebes' point of view, the growth of a significant opposing coalition could not be tolerated if it was to preserve its *hegemony*.

The year 362 BC saw much of the Peloponnese in a frenzy of preparation for the inevitable Theban invasion. Those who, like Argos, supported Thebes prepared for the coming hostilities, while those opposed built their coalition.

The Theban-led army marched south. With it went all the forces of the Boiotian cities and significant numbers from the cities of Thessaly and Euboia. The Phokians, formerly allies of Sparta, but forced into alliance with Thebes after Leuktra, refused to participate, rightly claiming that the alliance was only defensive. However, with the expected junction in the Peloponnese with the Argives, Messenians, Megapolitans, Tegeans and other Arkadian cities still in support of Thebes, Epaminondas knew he would be at the head of a formidable army.

Xenophon records that Epaminondas stayed at Nemea longer than anticipated, hoping to engage the Athenians as they moved south into the Peloponnese to join their allies (Xen. *Hell.* VII. 5. 6). The Athenian hoplite forces, however, were transported by sea, thereby nullifying Epaminondas' plan. Therefore Tegea became his next encampment. Xenophon applauds him for making his camp within Tegea. His intentions were concealed from his opposition by the walls of the city, and he had sufficient provender for his troops there.

The allies established a strong position to the south of the city of Mantineia and alerted Agesilaos of their location. Agesilaos duly marched north to join them and had reached Lakonian Pellene[1] when a Kretan arrived to inform him that Epaminondas was marching south, with Sparta as his likely target. Fortunately, Agesilaos reached Sparta in time to ensure that the city was defended. From Xenophon's comment, 'the Spartiatai posted themselves at various points and kept guard, although they were extremely few' (*Hell.* VII. 5. 10), we must wonder who was serving under them. It may well be that contingents of Agesilaos' army dispersed to protect their own communities, having experienced the Theban depredations of the first invasion of Lakonia. Although it could be assumed that Sparta would be subject to an attack, none could have been secure that other settlements would be ignored. Certainly, the men of Amyklai would have been desirous to return to their community. It had long been the custom that the *perioikoi* did not serve in the Lakedaimonian army in any great numbers when a campaign was conducted in the Peloponnese but recent years may well have made it a necessity to do so. More evidence would have been useful for us to clarify the details.

Sparta, indeed, proved to be the object of the enterprise, and Epaminondas' army infiltrated the outlying environs of the city. He must have been surprised to find it defended, albeit by forces far fewer than his own. The description of the point of attack shows the quality of this commander. Rather than attempting to engage on level or rising ground where his men could be subject to missile attack from rooftops, he made an attempted entry to the inner city by way of an approach which descends. This is likely to have been from the north-east. Agesilaos' son Archidamos led an attack *uphill* with about 100 men against the Thebans. On all counts this was against recognised practice, and may well have been the reason for its successful outcome. The Theban attack was not merely blunted, but significant casualties were sustained by the leading ranks of the Thebans. In their exultation the Spartans, for once, indulged in an overlong pursuit and suffered the consequence of this unusual action. They lost some of their own men, but victory had been theirs. Archidamos set up a trophy and allowed the Thebans to take up their dead.

One interesting vignette comes to us from Plutarch's *Life of Agesilaos* 34. The son of the famous or infamous Phoibidas, Isadas, now in his late teens, had been busy oiling his body at the time of the attack. Taking up spear and sword, he rushed naked from his home to take his place in the midst of the thickest of the fighting. Amazingly, he killed several opponents without so much as receiving a scratch himself. His courage was duly recognised by the *ephors*, who honoured him and crowned him with a garland. They then fined him 1,000 drachmas for not wearing protective armour thereby risking his life.

After this setback, Epaminondas' next action was to make a rapid march back to Tegea. There, he intended to rest his foot-soldiers. He would have been aware too, that news of his march south would have reached Mantineia, and the allied army assembled there could well be coming south to the relief of Sparta. His cavalry, therefore, was directed to make an attack on Mantineia, where harvesting would be taking place outside the city walls. The thought behind this surprise attack was that livestock could be captured and those working in the fields could also be taken or killed as they would not have significant protection.

Fortunately for those at Mantineia, but unfortunately for the anticipated outcome of Epaminondas' plan, Athenian cavalry had but recently arrived after a long journey. They had been obliged to fight their way past the Isthmos and were taking up billets in the city when the Theban cavalry appeared.[2] Without having had time for men or horses to take food or rest, the Athenians responded to the Mantineian plea for the protection of those outside the walls. Although outnumbered, the Athenians defeated the Thebans, set up a trophy and gave back the Theban dead under truce, thereby rescuing all people and provender outside the walls of Mantineia.[3] Surprise was undoubtedly a key element in the Athenian success. To have a cavalry force issuing from a supposedly lightly defended city would have given the Athenians a significant advantage. Unfortunately for the writer of one of our sources, Xenophon lost one of his sons serving with the Athenian cavalry in the battle.

Looking at these episodes, it can be appreciated that, despite any material success, the clever and opportunistic attempts by Epaminondas to capture Sparta while it was supposedly undefended and thereafter to cause great discomfort to Mantineia while it was in a similar position had kept his opponents in reactive mode. At no time had his enemy an opportunity to wrest the initiative from him. While his routes into and out of Lakonia would have been direct, Agesilaos' initial route was via Pellene. This was to avoid contact with the Thebans based at Tegea, so that a junction could be made with the allies at Mantineia.

What Epaminondas had achieved by these operations was a diminution in the overall numbers of his opposition. Having caused his enemies discomfort, and knowing that his term of office was soon to come to an end, Epaminondas now decided to attempt to bring his opposition to battle. Having threatened both Sparta and Mantineia, it was not possible for the entire Lakedaimonian contingent to be present at the coming conflict. With the Theban-led army demonstrating admirable mobility and occupying the area around Tegea that lay between Sparta and Mantineia, it would have been unwise for the octogenarian Agesilaos to resume his march north immediately. If he had done so he would have left Sparta once more undefended. As it was, three of the twelve *lochoi* of the army had preceded Agesilaos' first march, along with mercenaries and cavalry. The king's first duty was to his city until intelligence made it clear that he could safely leave again to make the attempt to join the allies.[4]

Despite some disappointment with regard to the outcome of the two tactical marches, Theban morale was high. After due preparation, Epaminondas led his army indirectly north-north-west towards the mountains where, in sight of his enemy, he anchored his left wing. Having made this approach rather than directly to the north from Tegea where his opposition had established its line, Epaminondas gave every impression that an engagement was unlikely that day. That impression was further strengthened by the head of his column halting at the foot of the mountain, making a right turn to face the enemy, and grounding arms as if preparing to make camp. Thereafter, following companies in the column continued to march, taking up their positions behind the now immobile left wing. This continued until the depth of this wing was massively enhanced. By this time his opposition had relaxed and was preparing to stand down.

Epaminondas also arranged his cavalry in column. Supported, and among them as usual, was a number of the light-armed *hamippoi*. This force was to be thrown against the opposing cavalry, which was without foot-soldiers and was arranged, six deep, in a rectangular formation similar to an infantry phalanx. He had also posted hoplites and cavalry on rising ground on his right wing, threatening the Athenians on the opposing left wing. As at Leuktra, the rest of his battle line, the centre and part of the right wing, was to be withheld from contact for as long as possible.

Although there is some crucial detail in Xenophon's account, an unfortunate omission, among others, is that of the disposition of the constituent parts of each battle line. We know from him of the agreement that the leadership of the allies would fall to those in whose territory action was to take place (Xen. *Hell.* VII. 4. 3). This fixes the Mantineians in command on the right wing, and from the arrangement taken by Epaminondas outlined earlier to threaten his oppositions' left wing, the position of the Athenians is known.

Diodoros (XV. 85. 2) does give more detail, of which that of the actual battle should be ignored, but his account could well be accurate in the dispositions. He puts Mantineians and other Arkadians on the right wing, with the Lakedaimonians next in the line, followed by troops from Elis, then Achaia. The centre was made up of unidentified 'weaker' troops, and the left wing by the Athenians. Epaminondas' line had Thebans (and presumably other Boiotians) on the left wing, and between them and the centre, the Arkadians (Tegeates and others). The Argives occupied the right wing, and the centre made up of Euboians, Lokrians, Sikyonians, Messenians, Malians, Ainianians, Thessalians and other allies.

Diodoros' description of the battle, however, is surely fantasy, with first one side having the advantage, and then the other. He makes no mention of the surprise and consternation caused to the enemy by Epaminondas' initial advance.

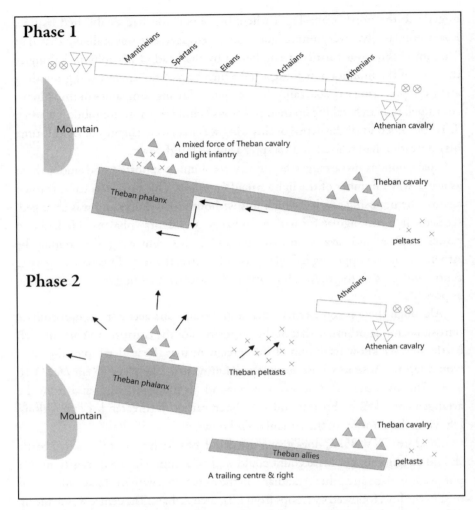

Towards the end of his extended narrative of this action, Diodoros reports that Epaminondas selected his:

> best men, grouped them in close formation and charged into the midst of the enemy; he led his battalion in the charge and was the first to hurl his javelin, and hit the commander[5] of the Lakedaimonians. Then as the rest of his men also came immediately into close quarters with the foe, he slew some, threw others into a panic and broke through the enemy phalanx. (Diod. XV. 86. 4–5)

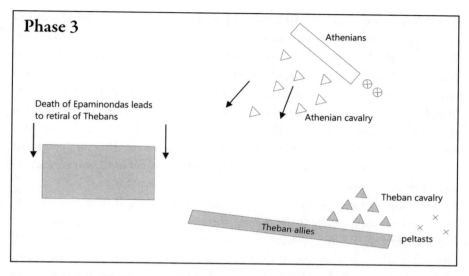

BATTLE PLAN 4 *Battle of Second Mantineia 362* BC. *In phase 1, Epaminondas halts the army on its march in column. The line right faces and grounds arms as if to encamp. Successive companies proceed to the left wing, thereby increasing its depth. Disruption and rout of right wing and centre occur in phase 2, while the Athenians destroy Theban light armed troops in phase 3. There was an inconclusive result to this battle. The Theban army became passive on the death of its leader, while the Athenians were victorious in their sector.*

This must surely have been at the outset of action, as briefly described by Xenophon. Following that writer, we have the distinct impression that the battle was, indeed, a brief one. It was when Epaminondas began his advance that:

> as soon as the enemy *saw* them unexpectedly approaching, no one among them was able to keep quiet, but some began running to their posts, others forming into line, others bridling horses, and others putting on breastplates, while all were like men who were about to suffer, rather than to inflict harm. Meanwhile Epaminondas led forward his army prow on, like a trireme,[6] believing that if he could strike and cut through anywhere, he would destroy the entire army of his adversaries. (Xen. *Hell*. VII. 5. 22–3; emphasis added)

One point in the last passage needs to be given attention. It was customary for an advance to battle to be accompanied by the troops raising the paian. If we look back for some obvious examples of hasty responses to an enemy approach,

Thucydides notes that the Athenian Hippokrates, at the Battle of Delion, in exhorting his men to valour, had only reached the centre of his line when the Boiotians raised the paian and started their advance (Xen. *Hell.* IV. 96. 1). At Nemea the Lakedaimonians could not see the enemy advance because the area was covered in undergrowth. They became aware of the enemy movement when they 'heard' the paian but still had sufficient time to order their ranks and commence their own advance (Xen. *Hell.* IV. 2. 19). In the case of Epaminondas' advance here, his enemy 'saw' (εἶδον) but did not 'hear' the advance. This surely suggests that Epaminondas ordered a delay to the raising of the paian until near contact, to maximise the surprise.

The success of his cavalry column with its intermingling of *hamippoi* was also important psychologically 'when he cut through the enemy's cavalry, he would have defeated the entire opposing army; for it is very hard to find men who will stand firm when they see any of their own side in flight' (Xen. *Hell.* VII. 5. 24). Caught unprepared, the Mantineians and Lakedaemonians on the right wing buckled under the attack and the whole right wing and centre fled. Epaminondas fell and it seems obvious from what follows that the Thebans were stunned at this:

> When, however, he had himself fallen, those who were left proved unable to take full advantage thereafter even of the victory; but, although the opposing phalanx had fled before them, their hoplites did not kill a single man or advance beyond the spot where the collision had taken place; and although the cavalry in like manner did not pursue and kill either horsemen or hoplites, but slipped back timorously, like beaten men, through the lines of the flying enemy. Furthermore, while the intermingled footmen and the peltasts, who had shared in the victory of the cavalry, did make their way like victors to the region of the enemy's left wing, most of them were slain by the Athenians. (Xen. *Hell.* VII. 5. 25)

Two other *boiotarchs* fell with Epaminondas. The shock to the Thebans is clear, but there would be other *boiotarchs* present who should have maintained the impetus of the attack. That they did not do so lays bare the proof that Theban invincibility had rested mainly with two men only, Pelopidas and Epaminondas. They, and only they, had possessed the leadership qualities to give their armies confidence.

With the death of Epaminondas, Theban power diminishes. Shocking as it may be to lose a commander-in-chief, it does not necessarily follow that all is lost, unless those who served as generals under him have no confidence in their own abilities when he is no longer present. Compare this to the conduct of the Spartans at Leuktra after Kleombrotos was killed. Not only did they retrieve his body at appalling loss, but retreated and reformed behind their trench to debate whether or not another engagement should be attempted.

This battle in many ways followed the same plan as Leuktra. The attack in close order and unusual depth on the command position of the enemy, the decisive employment of a superior cavalry arm and the speed of the advance are similar. To these may be added the clever use of dissimulation to create the opportunity for an unexpected attack on an unprepared enemy. Just as Epaminondas had used the omens and oracles which had conveniently appeared just prior to Leuktra to bolster morale in his troops, so too did he use psychology to lead his enemy into a state of mental relaxation unsuited for combat on that day.

An unexploited victory over the enemy right was balanced by the considerable losses inflicted on the Boiotians by the Athenians on the left wing. To all intents and purposes this was an inconclusive affair. Both sides set up a victory trophy and retrieved their dead under truce.

Xenophon ends his *Hellenika* at this point with the rather melancholy comment: 'while each party claimed to be victorious neither was found to be any better off, as regards additional territory, or city, or sway, than before the battle took place; but there was even more confusion and disorder in Greece after the battle than before' (Xen. *Hell.* VII. 5. 27).

In the immediate aftermath of the battle, peace was agreed by all states except Sparta. Sparta refused to take an oath that included Messenia as a participating state and still held hope of regaining the territory (Plut. *Ages.* 35). In the absence of inspired, or even firm leadership, Thebes lacked direction and ambition. It soon became obvious over the next five years that without an Epaminondas or Pelopidas, Thebes could never sustain any semblance of being a great power. Athens appeared to fare better, quickly regaining control over Euboia, unsuccessfully disputed militarily by Thebes. The Chersonese also returned to the influence of an Athens obviously hoping to recreate its maritime empire.

Agesilaos, in pursuit of the goal of recovering Messenia and regaining its dominant position in the Peloponnese, hired himself as general to successive claimants to Egypt now in revolt from Persia. For his services Sparta was paid the massive sum of 230 talents before the old king died at the age of eighty-four on his journey home.

Archidamos, his son, continued the practice of his father in hiring himself as a commander in the pursuit of raising funds to hire mercenaries, but died in combat in southern Italy, fighting for Taras.

Unfortunately for all these states, Philip of Makedon was also embarking on the reforms of his army and pursuing a continuous and successful policy of territorial expansion. The days of the wholly independent Greek city-state were numbered.

Inevitably, control of the Greek mainland passed to Philip II and was added to by the Asian exploits of his son Alexander the Great. Even with the partitioning of his empire, his successors proved massively too powerful for any city-state to resist.

To conclude the narrative section of the book it seems fairly obvious that the main reason for the shocking defeat at Leuktra lay with the citizen body. For more than a century the number of Spartiatai gradually dwindled. This decline in number can be traced from its sixth-century high of nearly 10,000 to just more than 1,000 at Leuktra, where 700 took part. In the long string of battles, victory almost always came from the right wing of a Peloponnesian army where the Spartan citizenry were brigaded. However, that success depended on the critical mass of Spartiatai present on that wing and mishaps could occur when it proved insufficient. The presence of a truly significant number of warriors, highly disciplined and under constant training, set a standard to which other states could only aspire. Those states could only hope to achieve success when that number of Spartiatai present at a battle had dropped to near parity to their own special forces.

The historical evidence must have been as obvious to the Spartans as it is to the reader and yet they continued to ignore the need to address the growing problem. Perhaps vested interests conspired to make them prevaricate. There were several ways in which citizenship could be forfeited (see Appendix 5), and as the citizen body continued to shrink, the number of demoted Spartiatai, inferior *hypomeiones*, expanded. Only a wholesale restructuring of society could replace an enduring viability to Sparta's skilled manpower.

In 479 BC, at the Battle of Plataia, the proportion of the allied Greek army contained 5,000 *perioikoi*, 35,000 *helots* and 5,000 Spartiatai from Spartan-controlled territories. It was an enormous commitment, but by no means the total manpower available. Almost without exception Sparta retained a reserve in the homeland. It can be presumed that at least 3,000 or more Spartiatai remained at home, of which 1,500 were above the normal age for military service. The number of free 'dwellers around' – *perioikoi* throughout Lakonia – was much greater than those present at the battle.

The most significant number was obviously that of the *helots*. They were present to serve the needs of the Spartiatai, seven to a hoplite, and to act as skirmishers, yet that too would have only been a proportion of this section of the population of Lakonia and Messenia. Another reason for this large number could well have been a desire to greatly diminish their presence in and around Sparta to safeguard those Spartiatai who stayed at home.

However, the *helot* population was to become a major concern to the Spartan governance as time went on and Spartan paranoia increased as their own numbers significantly reduced.

The year 465 BC proved to be significant. A great *helot* uprising occurred, supported by *perioikoi* from the Pamisos valley. Both Lakonian and Messenian *helots* were involved. This was an opportune revolt, following as it did a massive earthquake in an area that included the city of Sparta. Greatly disruptive as the natural disaster must have been, it is difficult to accept the figure of 20,000 dead and only five buildings left standing as the outcome. Even so, the rebels found it impossible to have any lasting success against the Spartans despite inflicting a little over 300 casualties upon them in the plain of Stenyklaros. They withdrew to Mount Ithome, where they were safe from heavy infantry. A siege of Ithome eventually ended in stalemate. One of the conditions was that the *helots* resettle outside the Peloponnese. In the strained relations existing between Sparta and Athens, the latter took it upon itself to settle the rebels and their families at Naupaktos.

The year 425 BC saw the surprising surrender of the Spartan force on the island of Sphakteria instead of fighting to the death as tradition and honour demanded. However, in the face of an opposition of several thousand, 120 Spartiatai and perhaps around 170 *perioikoi* were taken prisoner by the Athenians. Thereafter, their freedom became a bargaining issue in the Athenian attempt recover the strategic city of Amphipolis captured by the brilliant Spartan general Brasidas during the winter of 424/3.

Relevant to the level of insecurity and paranoia felt by the ruling class of Sparta in the mid-420s is the following edited extract from Thucydides:

> For since the Athenians kept harassing the Peloponnesians, and especially
> the territory of the Lacedaimonians, the latter thought that the best way of

diverting them would be to retaliate by sending an army against their allies, especially since these allies were ready to maintain an army and were calling upon the Lakedaimonians for help in order that they might revolt. Furthermore the Lakedaimonians were glad to have an excuse for sending out some of the helots, in order to forestall their attempting a revolt at the present juncture when Pylos was in possession of the enemy. Indeed, through fear of their youth and numbers [here, a word such as 'boldness' or 'recklessness' is missing from the MSS] – for in fact most of their measures have always been adopted by the Lakedaimonians with a view to guarding against the *helot*s – they had once even resorted to the following device. They made proclamation that all *helot*s who claimed to have rendered the Lakedaimonians the best service in war should be set apart, ostensibly to be set free. They were, in fact, merely testing them, thinking that those who claimed, each for himself, the first right to be set free would be precisely the men of high spirit who would be the most likely to attack their masters. About two thousand of them were selected and these put crowns on their heads and made the rounds of the temples, as though they were already free, but the Spartans not long afterwards made away with them, and nobody ever knew in what way each one perished. So, on the present occasion, the Spartans gladly sent with Brasidas seven hundred *helot*s as hoplites, the rest of his forces being drawn from the Peloponnese by the inducement of pay. (Thuc. IV. 80. 1–5)

Another chilling practice was the annual selection of older boys (aged eighteen to nineteen) to form the *kyypteia*. For at least a year they went into hiding in the countryside, each with a dagger and frugal supplies. While this in itself could be regarded as a form of 'rite of passage', there was a much more sinister duty for them to perform. At night they would track down and kill any *helot*s they encountered. This was not considered a crime. They had the full backing of those in governance.

With the successes of Brasidas in the north a new class emerged within the population. Those *helot*s who had accompanied him were given their freedom and settled with their families on the northern borders of Lakonia. Sparta increasingly employed bodies of freed *helot*s in future actions, particularly overseas. These *neodamodeis*, or new citizens, held positions similar to the *perioikoi*, freemen with local autonomy but without a vote in the Spartan assembly. It was certainly a step in the right direction. We find the *Brasideioi* brigaded with the *neadamodeis* at the

Battle of Mantineia in 418 BC with the number of Spartiatai present being perhaps only 2,500 with the addition of the *hypomeiones* and *perioikoi* present.

Conscious of the problem facing them in terms of a diminishing citizen body, Sparta refused to face up to the need for land redistribution and the subsequent new citizenry such a reform would produce. The eventual victors of the Peloponnesian War achieved that victory at sea and not on land, where their already-diluted army relied increasingly on allies such as Thebes, Korinth and Mantineia.

Now, within the period covered by this book, the Korinthian War saw Sparta's former allies Thebes and Korinth ranged against it, along with a revived Athens and others, with Persia as their paymaster. Two major battles later, both won by Spartan-led forces, were followed by an attritional standoff at the Isthmos. Eventually, through the negotiating skills of Antalkidas, Sparta achieved accommodation with Persia and resumed its hegemony of Greece.

All went well for a few years until the the garrison at Thebes failed to deal firmly with the liberation of the city. The campaign against Olynthos eventually proved successful but took longer than anticipated. Thereafter, Sparta, despite its reputation, achieved little of consequence except under Agesilaos and that too was somewhat disappointing. Incompetence of command played a significant part in the reduction of pressure against Thebes, as demonstrated by the inaction of the Spartiate commander on Euboia in failing to maintain the blockade against the enemy.

Of the several examples of other Spartan shortcomings two stand out as events that should have set alarm bells ringing. The first was the defeat of two *morai* of a force of around 1,000 men led by two Spartiate *polemarch*s by Pelopidas with only 300 Theban hoplites supported by cavalry in 375 BC. There, at Tegyra, the Thebans routed their enemies in an audacious attack that laid bare the lack of morale and training displayed by their opposition. The second occurred one year later when Polydamos of the Thessalian city, Pharsalos, came as envoy to Sparta to request military aid against Jason of Pherai. Jason in his campaigns to become leader of all Thessaly was threatening Pharsalos. Earlier that year Sparta had sent out Kleombrotos with four *morai* and an equal number of allies in response to a request from their ally Phokis. Thebes, fresh from the unification of Boiotia under Theban leadership, had turned to threaten its neighbour, Phokis. Sparta was now faced with a dilemma. With their reserve forces at home, the Spartans debated for three days on the subject of sending help to Pharsalos. Ultimately, paranoia prevailed and Polydamos was advised to return to attempt accommodation for his city with Jason. The fear of further stripping their city of its protection against insurrection had won the day. Evidence of the plots throughout the reign of Agesilaos that caused such paranoia can be found in Appendix 1.

Surely some response to the issues raised by these two examples concerning the numbers, training and quality of her military had become impossible to ignore. Sparta did nothing and the inevitable happened a mere three years later at Leuktra. Thereafter, stripped of half of its land holdings with the loss of Messenia, subject to invasion by Thebes, Sparta merely resorted to the device of sending out commanders like the octogenarian Agesilaos and his son Archidamos to earn funds for mercenaries.

Within forty years of the Battle of Mantineia Aristotle was to make the following observations: 'Although the country would have supported 1,500 cavalry and 30,000 heavy infantry, the total number had fallen below 1,000. History shows how inadequate were Sparta's property laws. She was overwhelmed by a single defeat; lack of men was her ruin' (Aristotle *Politics* 1270a; trans. Warrington). And:

> Whoever originated the common meals known as *phiditia* deserves little credit
> for his regulations. These gatherings should be chargeable to public funds, as
> in Crete; but at Sparta each person is expected to contribute his share, though
> some are extremely poor and cannot afford to do so. The result is to frustrate the
> legislator's intention. He devised common meals as a popular institution, but
> their present organisation is quite the opposite; the very poor find it difficult to
> take part in them, though ancient custom ordains that failure to contribute entails
> the loss of citizen rights. (Aristotle *Politics* 1271a; trans. Warrington)

It was to be almost a century later that Sparta produced men in a position of influence who would, at last, bite the bullet. As the poor became poorer and the number of Spartiatai further declined, three men appeared who had the appetite to attempt change.

First was Agis IV, who shortly after inheriting the Eurypontid kingship formulated a plan for the total redistribution of land in Lakonia, the cancellation of existing debts and a return to the Lykourgos programme for the training of citizens. His plans would have created 4,500 citizens, coming from the existing few Spartiatai, the more numerous *hypomeiones* and some of the *perioikoi*. Only debt cancellation was achieved, with the vested interests of the fortunate holding sway at Sparta until Agis' later death.

Kleomenes III came to the Agiad succession in 236 BC and proved much more successful. Land redistribution and a new citizen body of 4,000 came into being. His rule was firm and his gifted generalship threatened to make Sparta the dominant power in the Peloponnese once more. Only the intervention of Antigonos of Makedon at the invitation of Aratos of Sikyon put an end to Kleomenes' success. After a long and protracted engagement, Sparta's army of 10,000 was eventually overcome by the 30,000 men of Antigonos. Kleomenes fled into exile in Egypt.

Plutarch's treatment of the lives of both Spartan kings is sympathetic and in sharp contrast with Livy's strongly biased and negative account of Nabis. Nabis came to power in Sparta around 206 BC. Although Livy dwells on the tyrannical aspects of Nabis' rule, hints appear in his text that Nabis had a social programme, e.g land redistribution that increased the citizen body, and that the *ekklesia* were involved in very important decisions. His murder by members of the 1,000-strong force of Aitolians, ostensibly sent to help him against the Achaians, was followed by the killing of all the Aitolians by the angry Spartan citizenry. Surely this was not the reaction expected from an oppressed population as, perhaps, Livy would have wished to portray.

Brief as the coverage of this trio has been, in what is a most fascinating period in Spartan history, these kings' actions proved to be, in all three cases, a little too little in terms of citizen numbers and much too late in the new world of the superpowers of Rome and the Hellenistic kingdoms.

Endnotes

1 Diod. XV 82. 6–83. 1 confuses Agesilaos with the earlier King Agis, and Archidamos with Agesilaos. He has the king send runners to Sparta to give warning of the impending attack, reassuring Sparta that he is returning to bring them succour. In Xenophon's version, Agesilaos is back in Sparta before the attack is made.

2 Again, Diodoros (XV. 84. 2) is misleading in reporting that reinforcements from Athens to the number of 6,000 arrived at Mantineia from the north to save the day, and he makes no reference to a battle. The inference to be made from this number of men is that they were a mixture of hoplites and cavalry. Xenophon at *Hell.* VII. 5. 7, however, states that Epaminondas heard that the Athenians were preparing to send their forces by sea. This would be highly probable, knowing as they would that their passage via the Isthmos could well be impeded. A little before this passage

Epaminondas is described as having delayed at Nemea in the hope of catching the Athenians. The Athenian hoplites would embark and, after landing, pass through east and north Lakonia on their march to Mantineia. With insufficient horse transports, Athenian cavalry would proceed as described, by land.

3   After Leuktra and the freeing of Messene, Xenophon had left Skylous and taken up residence at Korinth. A little later his exile from Athens was revoked, and his sons, who had gone through the Spartan agoge, were now enlisted in the Athenian cavalry. One of them, Gryllos, was killed in the cavalry battle.

4   In his fine account, J. Buckler, *The Theban Hegemony 371–362*, Cambridge, MA, Harvard University Press, 1980, pp. 213–14 claims that Agesilaos and the whole Spartan army were present at the Battle of Second Mantineia. There is no evidence to support such a conclusion. Indeed, in Xenophon's account of the battle, Spartans are never mentioned by name. We know of only the three *lochoi* and the mercenaries which had preceded the abandoned march of the main body. At best, a few Spartiate commanders may have been present.

5   Following on from the argument of n. 4, if the Lakedaimonian commander had indeed been Agesilaos, he would have been named.

6   Here, the use in the source of the word εμβαλων is suggestive of a trireme attacking another with its beak or prow.

196

Appendices

Appendix 1

The Accession of Agesilaos and Conspiracies throughout the Period

> Looking at the individual states, at the start of this period it is Lysander
> of Sparta who combines depravity with natural gifts in a way that was
> typically Spartan and yet generally Greek . . . in short he went in for a
> series of crude stunts which would not have deceived a real child. All these
> exploits had failed by the time this universally discredited man, half-mad
> with melancholy and rage, fell in battle at Haliartus in 395.
>
> Burckhardt, *The Greeks and Greek Civilisation*

WHEN KING AGIS DIED, *c*.398/397 BC, a fascinating struggle for the
succession occurred. Fascinating not only by virtue of the circumstances
outlined by Xenophon, but by the additional information given later in the
tradition followed by Plutarch which gives detail of a rumour not covered by
Xenophon. The evidence is to be found at Xen. *Hell.* III. 3. 1–4; Plut. *Ages.* 1–3;
Plut. *Alk.* 23; Plut. *Lys.* 22.

While Xenophon was a contemporary of Agesilaos, Plutarch, who lived in the
first century AD, was very careful with his material and would have gathered it
from near-contemporary sources such as the fourth-century BC historian Duris
of Samos.

Had there been no doubts about the validity of Leotychidas' claim to
succession, history may well have taken a different course. Agesilaos would not
have been king, and his dominance over foreign policy, in which lay his strong
aversion to Thebes, would not have had the opportunity to develop. There is no

doubt that he was correct to be suspicious of Thebes and its machinations, but his hard-line stance against it probably resulted as much from personal grievance as from well-grounded suspicions of Theban political ambitions.

Throughout his life, Agis appears not to have recognised Leotychidas as his legitimate son and therefore refused to acknowledge him as his heir until his deathbed. Then, at the prolonged pleading of Leotychidas, Agis at last relented and gave the young man the recognition he desired. This was witnessed by several onlookers who were persuaded to stand as witnesses to the fact before the Spartans.

The cause of the problem lay in the claim that Leotychidas was the son of the Athenian Alkibiades, who was said to have had a liaison with Agis' wife Timaia while the king was on campaign. Alkibiades had sought refuge at Sparta to avoid the capital charges against him in Athens. Agis believed the accusation and had been told by many what had transpired during his absence. This rumoured affair was added to the fact that Agis had fled the bedchamber during an earthquake and had not slept with his wife for ten months because of his absences on campaign. As the child had been born at the end of this period, he calculated that the boy could not have been his. Whatever the truth of the matter, it should be noted that a Spartan king never campaigned continuously for such a period in Greece. However, he may have had good reason to suspect that he was a cuckold for other reasons than were proffered by his friends.

Further embellishment to the story comes from the claim that Timaia did not deny her affair with Alkibiades and, although the child's given name was Leotychidas, called him Alkibiades when in private with friends or serving women.

After the period of mourning had been observed, the half-brother of Agis, Agesilaos, with the support of Lysander, disputed the succession. It could well be that Lysander, who had been at the zenith of his power in 404/3 BC, having seen his pre-eminence decline a little over the following years, saw an opportunity to achieve greater control of Sparta's foreign policy through his protégé.[1] He had been Agesilaos' mentor and, as Plutarch claims, his lover (Plut. *Lys.* 22). To counter this, knowing that Plutarch himself was a Boiotian, we must look at Lykourgos' law. Xenophon gives the following information:

> I think I ought to say something also about intimacy with boys, since this matter
> also has a bearing on education. In other Greek states, for instance among the
> Boiotians, man and boy live together like married people; elsewhere, among

the Eleians, for example, consent is won by means of favours. Some, on the other hand, entirely forbid suitors to talk with boys. The customs instituted by Lykourgos were opposed to all of these. If someone, being himself an honest man, admired a boy's soul and tried to make of him an ideal friend without reproach and to associate with him, he approved, and believed in the excellence of this kind of training. But if it was clear that the attraction lay in the boy's outward beauty, he banned the connexion as an abomination; and thus he purged the relationship of all impurity, so that in Lakedaimon it resembled parental or brotherly love. I am not surprised, however, that people refuse to believe this. For in many states the laws are not opposed to the indulgence of these appetites. (Xen. *Constitution of the Lacedaimonians* II. 12–14)

Whatever the case, it is indisputable that he exercised influence over Agesilaos at the time and undoubtedly thought that he would secure his own position further. According to Xenophon (*Hell.* III. 4. 2), Lysander hoped to re-establish the dekarchies which he had set up at the end of the Peloponnesian War and had subsequently been overturned by the *ephors*, no doubt either proposed by, or with the support of King Pausanias. What Lysander's opponents had recognised was that he had created a 'personal empire' administered through his clients (see Plut. *Lys.* 13, supported by Nepos *Lysander* 1).

Only the direct heirs to Sparta's kingships were excused the discipline of the *agoge*, and Agesilaos had proved himself an admirable product of this institution despite being lame from birth. The exact nature of his lameness is not known. A club foot is suggested, but more probably it may well have derived from damage to an Achilles tendon, or legs of slightly differing length. Any would have made him appear lame but would not have significantly diminished his ability to succeed, or even excel, in the requirements of the *agoge*. He was held in high regard for his service and obedience to the state. Being a forty-year-old, he would have seemed an apt choice.

Obviously there were supporters for both claimants and, of those on the side of Leotychidas, one person, a certain Diopeithes, proved a formidable opponent to Lysander. Diopeithes had a reputation for accurately discerning the meanings of oracles and had uncovered one that directly placed an impediment to Agesilaos' claim. Plutarch recorded the prophecy and Ian Scott-Kilvert's translation is particularly good: 'Though *you* are sound of limb, proud Sparta, look to your ruler, lest from your stock a disabled prince should succeed to the kingdom: For then unlooked – for ordeals and unnumbered trials shall oppress you and the stormy billows of man-killing war shall roll down upon you.'[2] Unlike most oracles, this is very direct. It was with great difficulty that Lysander was able to persuade a majority of the citizen body that the reference was not to the lameness of Agesilaos, but rather to the danger to the state of permitting one not of royal stock to succeed, thereby producing a lame kingship.

One anomaly within the evidence has, to date, not been given anything but cursory examination and leaves one question unanswered. If Leotychydas was unrecognised by Agis, why was he excused the *agoge* in line with the customary practice reserved for the heir-apparent? The present writer can shed no specific light on the conundrum and can only suggest that the supporters of the other royal house, the Agiadai, would have preferred the succession to go to someone less obviously under the influence of Lysander. It must be remembered that the Agiadai king, Pausanias, had been instrumental in the dissolution of Lysander's arrangements at the end of the Peloponnesian War. The fear that Lysander could use his influence on Agesilaos to effect the reinstatement of his clients throughout the empire must have been an issue. It is ironic that the consequences of elevating Agesilaos to a kingship should see his tenure of the office bear out the predicted consequences of the oracle with Leuktra and its aftermath.

Such was the business of the succession, but now to references concerned with conspiracies during his reign. The first of these is given in unprecedented detail. While it would appear that knowledge of this conspiracy was known in the Greece of the fourth century (see below), we are indebted to Xenophon for recording the matter in such detail that would otherwise be denied today's readers. It throws light on the specific tensions within a society which was desperately in need of reform.

Within a year, while conducting a state sacrifice, the portents showed the presence of a conspiracy. Repeated sacrifices fared no better. Agesilaos and the attending seer now made offerings to the gods to seek their protection, and a favourable outcome to the danger. Eventually, a successful sacrifice was achieved. Probably amazing to us, within five days, a man appeared before the *ephors* to report that he knew of a conspiracy, headed by a man called Kinadon. This might have been sheer coincidence; it is not beyond the bounds of reason that the Spartans, known to be the most pious of the Greeks, should throw up a man who was possibly involved in the plot and who, because of this 'message from the gods', should seek to secure his own safety by giving evidence against Kinadon.

It would appear that this Kinadon was not a full citizen but one of the inferiors[3] (Xen. *Hell.* III. 3. 5). He had served the *ephors* well on several occasions and had been regarded as a dependable strong young man. However, his resentment stemmed from his status within society. He was said to have gathered around him others who shared his opinions. The informer described how Kinadon took him to the edge of the marketplace and asked him to count the number of Spartiatai (full citizens) present. On noting there were about forty, he was told by Kinadon that these men were his enemies and the other 4,000 or so of lower status who were present were allies in the plot. There followed a walk through the streets, where the few Spartiatai encountered were again heavily outnumbered. The informer added that he was told that the estate-owning Spartiatai had as enemies all those who worked for them on their land. Kinadon and his fellow conspirators knew the minds of the sub-groups in Spartan society. He claimed that *helots, neodamodeis,* inferiors and *perioikoi* would gladly eat the Spartiatai raw.

The informer was then asked by the *ephors* what weaponry was available to those in the conspiracy. His reply indicated that Kinadon had told him that those in the army had their own weapons, and the masses of the underclasses had easy access to the tools of their work. He had taken the informer to the iron market and shown him the stores of knives, swords, hatchets and sickles. Finally the *ephors* asked him the time of the intended uprising. His reply indicated that it was imminent and that he had been told to stay in the city.

No regular official body was called to decide on the matter. Only a few leading men, from the *ephors* and *gerousia,* quickly gathered together to seek a solution. Sitting as they were on a continuing powder-keg of discontent, the Spartan magistrates were well versed in handling the *helot* problem. Each year they declared war on this section of the population so that the *krypteia,* the young 'secret police', were given licence to hunt down any likely troublemakers. This current crisis was much more worrying in that it appeared to have a much broader population base. We are indebted to Xenophon who, alone of our sources, left such a detailed record of this conspiracy that gives us some insight into the continuing and developing problems of the Spartan constitution. The magistrates decided to send Kinadon on what would appear to be a fairly routine mission. The destination was to Aulon, the location of which is uncertain, but must not have been too distant from Sparta.

On being summoned, Kinadon was given a list of those who were to be arrested. He asked who was to accompany him and was given the reply: "'Go and bid the eldest of the commanders of the guard to send with you six or seven of those who may chance to be at hand.' In fact they had taken care that the commander should know whom he was to send, and that those who were sent should know that it was Cinadon whom they were to arrest' (Xen. *Hell*. III. 3. 9).

He was also told that three wagons would go with him to carry the prisoners back to Sparta. Interestingly, apart from the *helots* and Aulonians on the list, there was also a woman, said to be very beautiful, who was believed to be corrupting both young and old in the area. The magistracy had ensured that the commander was fully informed and that he should be selective in his choice of those he sent on the mission. They were to arrest Kinadon and, after 'examining' him, send back the list of his co-conspirators. They had never contemplated making the arrest in Sparta itself because at that time they had no idea how widespread the conspiracy was. Nor did they wish his confederates to have the opportunity of making their escape. Such was their concern that a contingent of cavalry was sent to give support to the arresting party.

After Kinadon's arrest, a horseman, presumably one of the cavalry, arrived in Sparta with a list of names obtained from Kinadon. It would have been informative if we had been given details of how this information was extracted. Presumably the questioning had been fairly brutal, considering the apparently short time it took to acquire answers. Selective arrests appear to have been made: 'the ephors immediately proceeded to arrest the seer Tisamenus and the most influential of the others' (Xen. *Hell*. III. 3. 11).

Kinadon, back in Sparta, was asked why he had organised his conspiracy. His reply denotes all that was wrong, and had been wrong for many years, in Sparta: 'I wished to be inferior to no one in Lakedaimon' (Xen. *Hell*. III. 3. 11). He was then bound along with his co-conspirators and dragged through the streets under constant scourge. Xenophon's closing line 'And so they met their punishment' leaves us to imagine how long this punishment went on before all the guilty finally died.

The next threat to the Spartan constitution came from no less a person than Lysander. Although Xenophon is silent on the matter, the evidence of Plutarch seems to have been drawn from more than one fourth-century writer, not least Ephoros.[4] Aristotle cites examples of circumstances which may make an individual seek to change constitutional affairs in his *Politics*, in the section on the causes of revolution in aristocracies and polities. One has been covered above: 'exclusion from honours for one of high spirits such as Kinadon'. Another, 'when great men who, in merit are inferior to none like Lysander, meet dishonour from those in higher office such as the kings of Sparta.' Here, Aristotle is referring to the undoing of Lysander's post-war settlements within the 'empire' by the *ephors* and Pausanias and particularly those at Athens, and his treatment by Agesilaos on the expedition to Asia Minor. In the case of Pausanias it is extremely likely that the king was not alone among the ruling party to have the opinion that change was necessary, and, in the case of Agesilaos, Lysander had wrongly presumed that he could himself be the power behind the throne. Such are the problems that persons of overweening ambition cause for themselves.

The sections of Plutarch's narrative are to be found at Plut. *Ages.* 20, Plut. *Lys.* 24–6 and 30. The tale is recounted as follows. A little after Lysander's death at Haliartos and after Agesilaos' return to Sparta following the Battle of Koroneia, the king found a significant number of citizens were in opposition to him. They are reputed to have been persuaded to this opinion by Lysander. Agesilaos therefore decided to investigate Lysander's previous conduct. Another version has it that some altercation at a meeting required consultation of documents that had been held by Lysander to clarify the issue in question. Agesilaos went to Lysander's house and discovered among his papers a scroll containing a speech on the constitution. This speech, by Kleon of Halikarnassos, was to serve as a model by which Lysander could bring about political change. The king had wished to make the speech public but had been persuaded by the *ephor* Lakratidas, who found the content dangerously convincing, that it would be best to keep the matter secret.

Lysander's point was that the dual kingship should be abolished and the throne be awarded on merit. Tradition has it that the descendants of Herakles came to the Peloponnese and there emerged from this clan two families, the Agiadai and the Eurypontidai, as the ruling houses. Lysander felt that all Heraklid families should have access to the position. He was of the opinion that, as it was he who had brought Sparta to its current level of power and eminence, it was wrong that he, who belonged to a family of no less consequence than the royals, should be excluded from this office. For his deeds others had given him divine honours and, in a Sparta which espoused an elective monarchy, he would be raised to this distinction.

He thought that he would be able to persuade others of the Spartiatai by addressing them along the lines laid out by Kleon of Halikarnassos. However, to be doubly sure of the outcome, he felt that he needed to prepare them by concocting oracles and prophecies supportive of his opinion. In so doing, he showed the devious side of his character which had served him well in dealing with the elements of war, but which would have weakened his position had this come to light within his lifetime. Had he made his address without the added fabrication outlined below it would at least, have given his fellow citizens something relevant to think about.

Plut. *Lys.* 30 credits Ephoros as his source for the evidence of the plot. A claim was made by a woman from Pontus that Apollo had made her pregnant. When a boy was born to her, there was an obvious division between those who believed her claim and those who did not. However, those who did give support to the claim were obviously the more influential within society and took part in his upbringing. Lysander took his opportunity to fabricate additional evidence by having some of his associates bring back news that Delphi held ancient tablets which could only be revealed when a son of Apollo appeared. One of these tablets was said to prophesy that Sparta would fare much better if it abandoned its hereditary monarchy and appointed its kings from the most illustrious citizens.

At the point when the boy, Silenos, was due to be examined on the truth of his origins, one of those in the conspiracy proved to be of faint heart and did not play his part. As a result, the machinations came to nothing. Such is the tale, but Plutarch claims that Ephoros declared that Lysander had first attempted to bribe the very person who delivered oracles, the Pythoness. Failing there, he made a similar attempt with the oracular priestess at Dodona, the oldest oracle in Greece. With no success there, a further personal approach to the priests at the Temple of Ammon in Egypt found him receive another rebuff. Not only did the priests refuse his bribe but informed the authorities at Sparta of Lysander's approach. By some means or other, Lysander managed to be acquitted of the charges laid against him.

It is difficult to believe much of the above, but we do have the evidence that two kings, first Pausanias and then Agesilaos, felt the need to diminish the control and influence that Lysander sought to exercise over Sparta. It is not beyond the bounds of possibility that Lysander did have ambitions to take the kingship for his own.

Whatever the truth of the matter, the fact that such tales could be regarded as credible shows that Spartan society was in danger of imploding just at the time when it should have been giving undivided attention to its newly acquired empire.

Much later, following the Battle of Leuktra, clear evidence of Sparta's fear of insurrection from a wide variety of sources comes to light in our ancient writers. The usual result for any Spartiate who had not held his place in battle was to be reduced from full citizenship. This loss of status for these *tresantes* required them to present themselves in public wearing patched cloaks, with uncut hair and half their moustache removed. They could be beaten by any who met them. After the battle it was discovered that 400 of the 700 Spartiatai present had fallen. To avoid demoting the 300 surviving citizens, Agesilaos suspended the traditional law for a day. Plutarch makes mention that there was a fear that, had they been shorn of their status they could have attempted a coup (Plut. *Ages.* 30).

The first invasion of Lakedaimon by Epaminondas saw Agesilaos organising the defence of unwalled Sparta. Even though the Thebans made no attempt on the city but proceeded to lay waste the area as far south as the Spartan port of Gytheion, a call went out to the *helot*s that any who volunteered to serve in the Spartan army would be given freedom. When more than 6,000 accepted the offer, the Spartan authorities were alarmed that this new force was too numerous for safety.[5] It was only when additional allies arrived that their fear was dissipated (Xen. *Hell.* VI. 5. 29).

Plutarch records two further incidents. Plut. *Ages.* 32 describes how a force of 200 men from the Spartan army had, unilaterally, taken up a position near the sanctuary of Artemis. Initially, there was a call to attack them immediately. Agesilaos resisted, being concerned that others in the army might take their side and mutiny. He chose to go up to their position, unarmed, and accompanied by a single slave. He called out to them that they had misunderstood his orders and told various groups to take their positions at different points around the city. The insurrectionists, thinking that their plot was as yet unknown, obeyed. During the night, fifteen of the leaders were arrested and executed.[6]

Not long after, information was received of a much more serious plot, this time involving Spartiatai. These men had been meeting in secret to plan a revolution. Men of their position in society posed a far greater threat to the constitution than any other group in the Lakedaimonian population. They would have their clients and personal followers, and their impending emergence would have been seen as a form of alternative governance. Dealing with them proved a sensitive problem. To have brought them to trial at such a precarious time was impossible, but some action was necessary. With the agreement of the *ephors*, Agesilaos had these men quietly disposed of, thus going against the legal rights of citizens not to be executed without trial. Although Xenophon does not record these two incidents there is no reason to deny their substance. Xenophon is selective in what he records. He does, however, make it very clear that there was considerable unrest within the population:

> But when people came from Karyai[7] telling of the dearth of men, promising that they would themselves act as guides, and bidding the Thebans to slay them if they were found to be practising deception, and when further, some of the Perioeci appeared, asking the Thebans to come to their aid, engaging to revolt if only they would show themselves in the land, and saying also that even now the Perioeci when summoned by the Spartiatae were refusing to go and help them – as a result, then, of hearing all these reports, in which all agreed, the Thebans were won over, and pushed on with their own forces by way of Karyai, while the Arcadians went by way of Oem, in Sciritis. (Xen. *Hell*. VI. 5. 25)

There were evidently a number of contemporary writers on the Spartan constitution of whom Aristotle, later in the century, was aware. These are now lost to us but, interestingly enough, Thibron, our Spartan commander in the early actions against Persia in Asia minor, figures among them.

We are led to believe that, in his exile in Mantineia, Pausanias devised alternatives to the Spartan constitution. One eminent scholar[8] claims that Pausanias made 'an attack on Lykourgos' laws'. This is technically true, and Pausanias could well have recognised that a wholesale overhaul of the constitution was needed and, indeed, sought to provide a framework for change. However, the minimal surviving evidence we have from Book V (1301b) of Aristotles' *Politics* suggests that the king's desire was to abolish the office of *ephor*. Elsewhere, in Book VII (1334a), Aristotle claims that the Spartans accused King Pausanias of attempting to seize power in Sparta. Without more specific evidence being available, only suppositions can be made.

With all that has gone heretofore we must firmly conclude that great unease was felt for decades at all levels within the population under Spartan jurisdiction.

Endnotes

1   The extent of Lysander's personal involvement in shaping Spartan foreign relations, in the years following the close of the Peloponnesian War down to his death, is well addressed in Hornblower, Chapter 14. The broad sweep of Lysander's settlement of the eastern Aegean is reasonably well documented but, using the very limited evidence available, Hornblower alerts us to probable personal diplomatic contacts and actions in relation to the northern Aegean, central Greece, Sicily and Egypt. His influence was still strong, and he must have had support for his activities from within Sparta.

2   Ian Scott-Kilvert, *The Rise and Fall of Athens*, Penguin Classics, Harmondsworth, Penguin, 1960, p. 308.

3   υπομειοσι, deriving from υπομειων (meaning lesser, or inferior), and classifying those described as not having full citizen rights or votes as opposed to those full citizens ομοιοι (peers).

4   See P. Cartledge, *Agesilaos and the Crisis of Sparta*, London, Duckworth, 1987, pp. 94–7.

5   Diodoros gives a figure of 1,000 *helots* at XV. 65. 6. Usually his figures are inflated, but this may be an exception. Xenophon's figure is to be preferred.

6   See also Nepos *Agesilaos* VI. 2–3.

7   A town to the north of Sparta but within Lakonia.

8   W. G. Forrest, *A History of Sparta*, London, Duckworth, 3rd edn, 1995, p. 112.

APPENDIX 2

Hoplites of the First Half of the Fourth Century

The Spartans meanwhile, man to man, and with their war songs in the
ranks, exhorted each brave comrade to remember what he had learnt
before; well aware that the long training of action was of more use
for saving lives than any brief verbal exhortation, though ever so well
delivered. The Spartans (advanced) slowly and to the music of many flute
players – a standing institution in their army, that has nothing to do with
religion, but is meant to make them advance evenly, stepping in time,
without breaking their order, as large armies are apt to do in the moment
of engaging.

Thuc. V. 69. 2–70.1; trans. R. Crawley

THE HUGE POOL OF MERCENARIES that had accumulated by the end of
the Peloponnesian War had the basic elements of professionalism and only
needed to be thoughtfully harnessed and improved by further training and
discipline. The standard was also to be imitated by the citizens of the city-states,
where specialist units sprang up supported and trained at a city's expense.

Apart from the Spartiatai, whose training had been a lifelong commitment
since Lykourgos' times, there had been other chosen groups, usually 300 in number,
at Argos and at Athens, the latter being trained to fight with archers from 479
BC. More recent heavy infantry examples were the Thousand Argives appearing in
the Peloponnesian War and later the Theban Sacred Band, maintained at public
expense. Before the mid-fourth century, groups such as Elis' Three Hundred and
Four Hundred (Xen. *Hell.* VII. 4. 13), the *eparitoi* of the Arkadians (Xen. *Hell.* VII.

4. 22), the *epilektoi* of Phleious (Xen. *Hell.* VII. 2. 10 and 12) had developed into full-time specialist troops. The most notable of all was the army of mercenaries and allies serving under, and trained by, the *tagos* of Thessaly, Jason of Pherai. At Xen. *Hell.* VI. 1. 5–6, Polydamos of Pharsalos describes Jason's forces as being 6,000 mercenaries. Later, at Xen. *Hell.* VI. 1. 19, when Jason had achieved his ambition to become *tagos* of Thessaly, he made an assessment of the forces then available to him from Thessaly and allies as being 20,000 hoplites, 8,000 cavalry and innumerable peltasts. Jason's early death ended the possibility of any expansionism he may have intended. Immediately after their success at Leuktra in 371 BC, the Boiotians under the leadership of Thebes are reported to be under constant military training (Xen. *Hell.* VI. 5. 23). A little later the Athenians established regular training for *ephebes* from the age of eighteen.

It is therefore not surprising that Aristotle, later in the century, observed that Sparta had always been pre-eminent on the field of battle when it alone undertook training. However, when others followed suit and practised rigorously, Sparta was regularly beaten both in war and on the playing field (Aristotle *Politics* 1338b). Aristotle does not, however, take into account that, by that time, the number of Spartan citizens was around 1,000, or even lower, and a proportion of those were over the age of sixty and therefore not available for service.

Philip II of Makedon had several models from which to choose. His establishment of a national army was the logical development of those practices that had been demonstrably successful in a century that had seen the inexorable rise of professionalism. The example of Iphikrates' reforms in the lightening of equipment and the lengthening of the spear would not be lost on him.

Hoplites

Hoplites were the heavy infantry that provided the core of a Greek army. Up to the late fifth century, when mercenaries appeared in ever-greater numbers, a phalanx of hoplites was made up of men from the citizen body. They had often fought side by side with friends and neighbours but, with the increasing purchase of mercenary services by states, the basic amateurism of such part-time citizen participation was to see changes. With the rise of standards, the physical training taken by an individual citizen became an increasingly important factor for his survival when called upon for military duties. He had to raise and maintain his own standard of fitness to survive against opponents whose stamina could well exceed his own, despite serving in the interdependent formation of the phalanx.

In battle this heavy infantry was organised in a phalanx, a rectangular formation with its length usually far exceeding its depth, the latter usually being of between eight and twelve ranks. There were exceptions to this, as has been seen at the Battle of the Nemea, where the allies had a depth of sixteen and the Thebans formed up even deeper. Earlier, at the Battle of Delion, the Thebans had adopted a depth of twenty-five and we later encounter a depth of fifty in the Theban phalanx at Leuktra.

It seems that the commonplace organisation of Greek armies was based on the *lochos*, a unit of men of variable number depending on the habit and practice of the individual city-state. The variations could be quite large, from a hundred to several hundred men. A common unit number is better suited to the needs of marching formations, column, hollow square etc., and to camping dispositions.[1] These *lochoi* were subdivisions, often based on tribal associations – in the case of Athens of tribal regiments – and, in our period, the two *lochoi* in a *morai* for Sparta.

Armed with a large and heavy circular and concave shield (*aspis*), the hoplite had admirable protection for his torso. He was protected from neck to knee. A bronze outer cover overlaid the wooden shield. It was provided with a double grip, enabling the forearm to take much of the weight. A band (*porpax*) at the centre of the shield allowed the greater part of the arm to pass through it to grasp a thong (*antilabe*) attached to the wide flat rim. In addition, the inner rim could be rested on the left shoulder thereby giving the hoplite the opportunity to gain occasional respite for his shield arm. Sometimes an apron of leather hanging from the bottom of the shield gave protection to the lower legs. By the beginning of the fourth century the use of bronze greaves for the protection of the legs became less commonplace and the more flexible linen cuirass covered with bronze plates can be found increasingly alongside the wholly metal and inflexible examples. Several layers of linen would have been used in its manufacture and acted as a protection against arrows. No doubt this lightening of the panoply would have helped the mobility of the individual. The wide variety of helmet would have had a linen lining and some gave limited vision other than to the front and a marked reduction in the ability to hear any order (if any was given) once the conflict had started. Within this period the adoption of other styles of headgear offered further reductions in weight and improvements in vision and hearing. Such examples often adopted a more open frontage and either came down to a point above the ears or incorporated cut-out sections so that the ears were uncovered. They proved increasingly popular, despite the loss of personal protection, possibly because they were more comfortable, particularly when campaigning in the heat of summer.

The spear, around six and a half feet in length, had a bronze spike on its butt. In addition to providing the weapon with balance, this proved useful for dispatching a fallen enemy, or as a secondary weapon should the spear shaft shatter. The remaining section of the shaft could be reversed to allow the butt to be used for combat. In the close order of the phalanx the use of the blade at the business end of this weapon was mostly limited by lack of space to thrusting and stabbing. However, when a more open order occurred, or the battle lines disintegrated into a series of more localised contests that gave greater space to the individual, personal skills came to the fore. This would be disastrous for the lesser skilled, whose safety relied on the integrity of the phalanx. With the loss of his spear, the only available secondary weapon available to the hoplite was a short slashing sword.

Even with the lightening of the panoply, the weight carried by the average hoplite into battle in this period must still have been considerable, particularly onerous in the main campaigning season of the summer. This equipment could prove expensive and sometimes, in states other than Sparta, a father would pass his panoply on to his son.

Only men with land or of financial substance could afford the purchase, or manufacture, of the total panoply. This could lead to a mixture of equipment styles within the phalanx, wherein some of its members would appear with older forms alongside those fortunate to be able to afford the latest type of helmet or cuirass.

On campaign, the Spartan state required uniformity in appearance from its citizens, and in this they proved the exception. Such uniformity to be seen in their section of the phalanx gave them an immediate psychological advantage over their enemies. They could be immediately identified by the lambda emblazoned on their burnished bronze shields and the deep red/purple colour of their cloaks and possibly corselets. That appearance alone could lead those opposite them in the opposing phalanx to break and run in fear before contact was made.

Generally, hoplites were the men who had a personal interest in the well-being of their state and were therefore willing to take upon themselves the duty of fighting for their city. For these citizens individual heroics, such as single combat, disappear in the desire to maintain the integrity of the phalanx formation. Personal feelings were suppressed by the need to fight for the honour of the city and its gods alongside their fellow citizens in the line.

When on the march in column, arms and armour were often carried by personal servants or on baggage wagons accompanying the army. This relieved hoplites of the necessity of always having to carry their heavy equipment. In more exposed terrain such as a plain, with the probability of cavalry harassment, a marching army could adopt a hollow square formation with the more vulnerable placed within the protection of hoplites. Only when significant hostilities were expected did the hoplites proceed under arms and adopt battle formation. The speed of any change in formation could be critical to the outcome of any confrontation, and the means by which it could be achieved had to be clearly understood by the participants:

> The prevalent opinion that the Lakonian infantry formation is very complicated is the very reverse of the truth. In the Lakonian formation the front rank men are all officers, and each file has all that it requires to make it efficient. The formation is so easy to understand that no one who knows man from man can possibly go wrong. For some have the privilege of leading; and the rest are under orders to follow. Orders to wheel from column into line of battle are given verbally by the second lieutenant acting as herald, and the line is formed either thin or deep, by wheeling. Nothing whatever in these movements is difficult to understand. (Xen. *Constitution of the Lacedaimonians* XI. 5–6)
>
> The Lacedaimonians also carry out with perfect ease manoeuvres that instructors in tactics think very difficult. (Xen. *Constitution of the Lacedaimonians* XI. 8)

There follow descriptions of deployments and countermarching. With such efficiency precious time was saved, often giving a Spartan army a tactical advantage in field operations.

Open and relatively even spaces, such as plains, had always been the preferred venues for battle but, with the adoption of the phalanx, relatively even terrain became an essential component for combat. So it is that in the great battles which are recorded from the late eighth century on, all take place at such locations. It may seem surprising that an enemy would allow its invader to cross the mountains that divided one plain from another without attempting some ambush, action, or attack on its column. Such actions were often left to the light-armed and more mobile. Hoplites were unsuited for such endeavours in difficult terrain, just as they were vulnerable when attempting to storm cities that required individual prowess when scaling walls. This is not to say that no such attempts were made.

Safety in the cohesion of the phalanx was what made the hoplite a formidable foe and, without that cohesion, the phalanx became extremely vulnerable. This is not to say that routes over high ground could not be blocked, ambushes laid and entry to a plain made more difficult, as will be seen prior to the Battle of Leuktra.

Repairing roads and bridges and removing obstacles were undertaken to make forward progress easier for the army, but equally for any easy retreat to be made should misfortune befall.

Surviving depictions on pottery give us visual clues to the activities of the front and perhaps the second rank.[2] Most fronts are calculated on the basis of a shield width, i.e. a yard. It may well be that, in the initial dressing of ranks, this was a reasonably accurate measure. However, in the advance to combat the close order became much looser when a phalanx broke into a run, not least because of any uneven terrain. The reason for an advance at the run was frequently to diminish the effectiveness of enemy missiles. Often the differing speeds of approach may have resulted in bunching before impact, as men sought security in the company of their fellows. Distances over which the charge at a run was made were quite significant for the variable ages of phalanx members. Armoured men carrying heavy shields and wearing heavy helmets running one hundred yards would inevitably lead to some dislocation in the ranks. The average speed would be little more than a trot, perhaps six to eight miles per hour. Undoubtedly the youngest of a twenty- to fifty-five-year-old assemblage would move at a quicker pace. Unless there was sufficient discipline present to keep in line with one's comrades, the timing of the onset along the line would be variable. At Kounaxa, Xenophon reports of the Greek mercenaries:

> At length the opposing lines were not three or four stadia apart, and then the
> Greeks struck up the paean and began to advance against the enemy. And when
> as they proceeded, a part of the phalanx billowed out, those who were left behind
> began to run; at the same moment, they all set up the sort of war cry which they
> raise to Enyalius, and all alike began running. It is also reported that some of them
> clashed their shields against their spears, thereby frightening the enemy's horses.
> And before an arrow reached them, the barbarians broke and fled. Thereupon the
> Greeks pursued with all their might, but shouted meanwhile to one another not

to run at a headlong pace, but to keep their ranks in the pursuit. (Xen. *Anabasis*. I. 8. 17–19)

The final sentence describes the pursuit, but even greater care would be desired for an initial clash. Xenophon is describing the professionals of his day and not the average citizen levy that made up the greater part of hoplite forces of this period.

The idea of opposing lines in absolutely even order crashing together at precisely the same instant is to be dismissed. It is easy to forget, in today's preference for combat at a distance, the psychological pressures of close combat, man on man. For the ordinary citizen the desire to get on with the job and see an end to the approaching nightmare of uncertainty would have been great, often intolerable. In his mind he would know that his greatest safety lay in maintaining the formation which afforded him the greatest protection, but, in the stress of the advance, fear may have overcome reason.

It is understandable that the phalanx sometimes 'locked shields' and, in doing so, achieved even greater protection for the individual. It was also possible that, under clear command, such sections of the line did not have their ability to manoeuvre compromised. This often occurred when an attempt to break the opposing line by brute force was made with the adoption of the *othismos* (see below). Such a tactic would be localised and not that of the entire battle line.

In an ad hoc levy for a set-piece land battle, it was difficult for commanders to have the knowledge to differentiate between dependable warriors and the more reluctant to engage. Apart from smaller actions, there had been no full-scale battles on the Greek mainland between the first Battle of Mantineia in 418 BC and that of the Nemea in 394 BC. The value of having such knowledge of those serving under them was to be recognised by some commanders as a key issue in making any deployment. However, that knowledge was likely only to be gained over time, and usually in the course of a campaign. Even so, new hoplites added to an army and thought to be dependable could cause problems. A good example is to be found in Xenophon where Derkylidas was ordered to cross over into Karia to confront the joint forces of Tissaphernes and Pharnabazos:

Now all that part of the army which was from the Peloponnesus kept quiet and prepared for battle; but as for the men of Priene and Achilleium, from the Islands and the Ionian cities, some of them left their arms in the standing grain (for the grain was tall in the plain of the Maiander) and ran away, while all those who did stand showed clearly that they would not stand very long. (Xen. *Hell.* III. 2. 17)

Good commanders recognised this and, when they had knowledge of the qualities of those who served under them, sought to take their decisions on deployment with this in mind. They also sought to bolster the confidence of new men in selective actions, so that they were better prepared for those that could prove to be more testing of resolve. Derkylidas had been remiss in such preparation for too long and perhaps should have adopted the highly successful path taken later by Agesilaos.

Again, Xenophon in both his *Memorabilia* and *Kyropaideia* gives good advice to commanders on how to arrange the ranks and files to accommodate the good and less dependable of those troops under them:

> For in war one must put the best men in the van and the rear, and the worst in the centre, that they may be led by the van and driven forward by the rearguard. (Xen. *Mem.* III. 1. 8)
>
> Behind all the rest I shall station the so-called rearguard of veteran reserves. For just as a house, without a strong foundation or without the things that make a roof, is good for nothing, so likewise a phalanx is good for nothing, unless both front and rear are composed of valiant men. (Xen. *Kyro.* VI. 3. 25)

And:

> Now you, the commander of the rearguard, as you are behind all the rest with your men, issue orders to your own division that each man watch those immediately in front of him, encourage those who are doing their duty, threaten violently those who lag behind, and punish with death any one who turns his back with traitorous intent. For it is the duty of the men in the front ranks with word and deed to encourage those who follow them, while it is your business, who occupy the rear, to inspire the cowardly with greater fear than the enemy does. (Xen. *Kyro.* VI. 3. 27)

Much of the fictional *Kyropaideia* was based on Xenophon's knowledge of Sparta, and its military practices are reflected in his novella. A description of a marching manoeuvre employed in reality by Agesilaos when seeking to withdraw his army from a weak position (Xen. *Hell.* VI. 5. 18 –19) is described also in Xen. *Kyro.* VII. 5. 3–6. The significance of this manoeuvre, the *anastrophe*, is to be found in the need to contain those regarded as the weakest within the envelope of the most reliable:

> On hearing this, therefore Cyrus took his place with his bodyguard in the centre of his army and gave orders that the hoplites should fold back the phalanx from the extremity of either wing and move toward each other behind the main body, which had been halted, until each of the extreme wings should meet in a line with him, that is, the centre. By this manoeuvre the men that remained standing in their places were at once given more courage, for the depth of the line was thus doubled; and those who had fallen back were likewise rendered more courageous, for thus those troops, which had been kept standing had now come to face the enemy, and not they. But when, as they marched in from both sides, the ends came together, they stood thus mutually strengthened – those who had shifted their position were supported by those in front of them, those in front by the men behind them. And when the phalanx was thus folded back, the front ranks and the rear were of necessity composed of the most valiant men and the poorest were drawn up between them. And this arrangement of the lines seemed well adapted both for fighting and for keeping the men from flight. (Xen. *Kyro.* VII. 5. 3–6).

Throughout history there are examples of similar arrangements to accommodate such problems. At the Battle of Zama, Hannibal arranged his army in three lines. The first line was made up of mercenaries and the third of those veterans who had served so successfully with him in Italy. Between them he placed the citizen Karthaginian levy and the Africans. These are described by Polybios (XV. 13. 3) as being given this position because they were cowardly.

Perhaps the most extreme measure taken was in the First World War, when the French shelled their own infantry positions from behind their lines to 'encourage' an advance on the enemy.

Even the Spartans, whose order would have usually been much better in their own section of the line than that of their allies or of their opponents, would not necessarily have been in close order after the initial impact. After presenting the shield wall to their opponents, the downward stabbing of the front ranks on each side, at the head, neck and shoulders of their opponents would inevitably lead to casualties and thereby a loosening of the integrity of the first ranks. Combat for the individual now required more than a yard for whatever skill was possessed in shield and spear work.

The Spartans are described as advancing steadily to battle to the sound of the aulos. This double-reed instrument had the capability to produce a penetrating sound akin to a cross between an oboe and a shawm and would be heard even by ears covered by the Korinthian-style helmet. The players would be placed at intervals all along the line, and the vase painting cited in note 2 shows one marching and playing between the first and second rank. These pipers would have the opportunity to retire to the rear of the phalanx when it stopped briefly in sight of the enemy to make its pre-battle sacrifice and also adjust its front. Spartan discipline of approach, and the maintenance of order thereafter, probably accounted more than anything for their success. Equally, their habit of limiting pursuit of a routed enemy served to preserve order.

There are, however, still questions to be answered concerning the roles expected to be played by the remaining ranks and there have been many debates over the last twenty years or so on this matter. Put in simple terms, the belief that the ranks behind the first two set their shields against the backs of their fellows and pushed (the *othismos*) is countered by the suggestion that a more open order existed wherein men in each rank replaced those to their front when death, wounds, or tiredness and retiral led to the need for the front ranks to be replaced.[3] This seems to be the safer conclusion, for the appearance of a gap in the line would afford an opportunity for the one-on-one attack to change to that of two upon one. It is at just such a point in the conflict that the opportunity to widen the gap was the occasion when the *othismos* was most effective. A hoplite could only be expected to maintain his ferocious attack for a limited time before requiring some respite. To follow one proposed idea to the exclusion of the other seems folly. The present author is of the opinion that in the course of a battle a large number of scenarios could emerge. Despite the depth of ranks, all participants could well have the expectation of being involved in face-to-face combat at some time in the battle. Even the 'reluctant' middle ranks would be 'persuaded' by those behind them to engage when necessary.

On occasions when sections of a line broke and ran early in an action, or even before engagement, it may well have been the case that the calibre of the first rank proved little different from that of their fellows. What is beyond question is that when a concerted push (*othismos*) occurred, the pressure from behind and the counter-pressure of the opposition effectively trapped the front ranks of both sides. It would be a terrifying prospect, and a front-line hoplite's chance of survival then depended on his capacity to maintain a frenzied attack on the hoplite against whom he was being pressed by his comrades behind: a true test of innate courage.

To deploy in depth gave cohesion but also left the initial direct participation only to those who could literally *reach* the enemy. Even in the unlikely event of a phalanx charging with levelled weapons, no more than the spears of the first three ranks could realistically have hoped to reach the enemy's first or second rank. It is only with Philip II's reforms later in the century that the development of the much longer and heavier *sarissa*, requiring a two-handed hold, allowed a phalanx to present an impenetrable and highly injurious front to its enemies. The Hellenistic phalangite had a more cumbersome weapon wholly unsuited, by its weight and length, to overarm use.

In Hellenic times, the initial clash of the front ranks is sometimes depicted on pottery as stabbing overarm and downwards at opponents while the following files and ranks carry their spears with the spearheads skywards (see note 2). Obviously, for the following ranks to hold them in any other way would have led to casualties among their fellows to both their front and rear.

At the onset, the front ranks of both armies would clash shield on shield while rapidly stabbing downwards at the neck and heaving or suddenly withdrawing the shield to try to unbalance their direct opponent. The second rank was likely to have been very close behind with their spears in the same overarm thrusting mode seeking to wound the front rank of the enemy. To keep spears at the level would have been an unlikely scenario. It would have necessitated a gap between the second and third rank to avoid the possibility of members of the third rank being wounded by the butt-spikes of their comrades ahead of them on their back swing. More importantly, to have such a gap between ranks would have rendered an *othismos* impossible. Only after this initial phase, and when the likelihood of a breakthrough became possible, was it likely that a shoving match occurred to widen any breach. With the winning phalanx advancing, the following ranks gave the coup de grace to any fallen enemy with a downward thrust of their butt-spikes as they passed over them. Their shields, supported by the left shoulder, were placed against the back of their comrade in front to give increased weight to the surge. With any break in the enemy line more hoplites, in close formation, would pour into the gap before loosening their order for more individual endeavour.

At the Battle of Delion in 424 BC, the break-up of the Boiotian left wing saw the Athenian hoplites surrounding the resisting Thespians who had not broken and fled. No evidence of an unbroken victorious line here; rather a disorganised melee such that Athenians sometimes fell to their death at the hand of a comrade. While this is sometimes used as evidence for the limited vision afforded to the hoplite by his helmet, it also illustrates a much less organised action by some victors once the opposing line was broken.

Thucydides noted in his description of the first Battle of Mantineia (Thuc. V. 71. 1) the desire of the man at the extreme right of the line to protect his unshielded side by edging to his right on the advance. The Spartans had converted this natural drift to the right of an advancing line to a definitive outflanking manoeuvre. It has already been noted that the Thebans adopted the same ploy at the Nemea. The outcome of the second phase of both battles shows how successful the retention of good order could be. Little or no pursuit was made by the Spartans in their initial successful phase, but a wheeling of the line and then a cross-field advance. At Koroneia Agesilaos had the same opportunity to mop up the returning Thebans by a similar advance over the field in like manner to that employed at Nemea but chose the more confrontational and, as it proved, more risky option of facing his enemy rather than taking them in flank. This decision was probably motivated more by the animosity he felt for the Thebans, an enduring hostility that, in part, was to contribute to Sparta's fall from power. Such spontaneous decisions could be devastating, as in the case of Agesilaos' half-brother, the able commander Teleutias, who lost his life at Olynthos as the result of a decision taken in anger (see Chapter 12 and below).

What gave Spartan hoplites a considerable advantage over their adversaries was the ease with which they could march, countermarch, and form and reform their ranks, even when contact with an enemy was being made. As the number of Spartiatai diminished and more states produced elite units, the difference in expertise between Sparta and others became more in balance. In practice, however, the reputation held by the Spartans on the battlefield managed to sustain their position of pre-eminence well beyond the point at which this was a reality. Knowledge of Spartan good practice can be gleaned from Xenophon's *Kyropaideia*.[4]

During the period that is the focus of the present book, Agesilaos invaded Boiotia and the vicinity of Thebes in 378 and 377 BC. Antalkidas is reported by Plutarch (*Ages.* 26)[5] as saying to Agesilaos, when the king was wounded, that the Thebans had found a splendid way to pay him for lessons in warfare, when they had been both reluctant and lacked military expertise. This was a reminder of the Lykourgos prohibition of campaigning repeatedly against the same enemy, thereby giving them the opportunity of acquiring similar skills. Whatever the validity of the attributions to Lykourgos may be, there is little doubt that, over these years, Theban military expertise in phalanx warfare radically improved, largely under the leadership of Pelopidas and then Epaminondas. Knowledge of Spartan practice was no doubt at the root of the plan by which Epaminondas defeated the Spartan phalanx at Leuktra.

At that battle we encounter an oblique advance of the Theban phalanx by its left, in great depth, in an attack upon the command position of the Spartan forces. In the later Battle of Second Mantineia, another formation is encountered, that of the *embalon*, a wedge-shaped arrangement, and the attack was made by it, again from the left, against the opposing command point. Both battles are given detailed accounts within the main text.

With modifications, the phalanx was to remain the kernel of Hellenic and Hellenistic armies for some centuries to come. This mass of men, whose individuality and mobility were subsumed to the needs of an interdependent unit, could only be secure by ensuring that the integrity of the formation was not compromised. Just prior to the period under discussion little is recorded of auxiliary arms in engagements, other than their positions in the line prior to battle. This was to change as imaginative commanders developed the discipline and skills of cavalry and the light-armed, and applied them in more prominent and productive ways (see Appendix 3).

In human terms, when the levy was called for a campaign, the young, in their ignorance of what was to come, may well have welcomed an opportunity to display the skills developed in practice. Those with experience would grimly accept their duty to fight for their city, some dreading the prospect of facing the possibility of death merely inches away when locked in combat. The average hoplite would possess the basic skills for survival if the battle line were not disrupted. His dependence on those who stood to his left and, particularly, his right for the cover of his neighbour's shield, gave him the security to do his duty.

Families dependent on the head of the house would be ever anxious of the outcome. Children of all but the rich could face a blighted future. Pensions given to the families of the fallen were not common to all cities. Perikles in 431 BC, in the opening year of the Peloponnesian War, is recorded by Thucydides as giving a guarantee to those families that suffered the loss of the head of the house: 'their children will be brought up till manhood at the public expense' (Thuc. II. 46).

Laudable as this may have been, the statement appears to exclude females from this benefice, which reflects the position of females in the democratic Athenian society. While giving much-needed help to the bereaved, the fact remains that those with female offspring were possibly left disadvantaged.

Endnotes

1 John W. I. Lee, *A Greek Army on the March, Soldiers and Survival in Xenophon's Anabasis*, Cambridge, Cambridge University Press, 2007 deals with *lochoi* of 100 men in his thematic approach to Xenophon's *Anabasis*. This common unit number is better suited to the needs of marching formations, column, hollow square etc. and to camping dispositions on a journey that covered 1,800 miles.

2 Although dating from a much earlier period of hoplite warfare *c.*625 BC, the representation on the Chigi vase of an advancing phalanx shows the front line, with spears held ready for the overarm thrust, followed by the second rank with their spears still aloft. In the interval between these ranks, an aulos player is keeping the approach in measured step. This must be the advance of a Spartan army, despite the fact that we see only the obverse of the shields. Looking closely at the vase painting, it seems that the hoplites have two spears, one slightly shorter than the other. The possibility that the shorter of the two could be used as a missile before the opposing lines clashed must be accepted.

Another fine vase from Domokos *c.*450 BC, north-north-west of Lamia, and now in the museum at Lamia shows two hoplites in combat. One figure is falling backward with his spear held in the overarm stabbing hold (thumb to the rear of the hand), while the other leans forward with his spear in a thrusting hold (thumb to the front of the hand). Both are depicted as having more than adequate space for movement. Neither scene can be imaginary but must be based on observed practice.

3 For some opposing views see W. K. Pritchett, *The Greek State at War,* vol. IV, Berkeley, CA, University of California, 1985; R. D. Luginbill, 'Othismos: The importance of the mass-shove in hoplite warfare', *Phoenix, vol.* XIVIII, no. 1; J. F. Lazenby, 'The killing zone', in V. D. Hanson (ed.), Hoplites: *The Classical Greek Battle Experience*, New York and London, Routledge, 1991.

4 Xenophon's *Anabasis* is also a veritable treasurehouse of information on all aspects of matters military. Modern studies covering the issues raised in Xenophon's writings already mentioned, but also including the *Memorabilia, The Cavalry Commander, The Art of Horsemanship, The Lakedaimonians* is J. K. Anderson, *Military Theory*

and Practice in the Age of Xenophon, Berkeley, CA, University of California, 1970; Hutchinson, *Xenophon*.

5   Reference to these invasions is made at Xen. *Ages.* II. 22, Xen. *Hell.* V. 4. 35–41 and V. 4. 47–55. See also Plutarch, *The Age of Alexander*, trans. Ian Scott-Kilvert, Penguin Classics, Harmondsworth, Penguin, 1973.

APPENDIX 3

Auxiliary Forces in the Fourth Century

> It was, then, during the confused and complicated warfare of the period
> from 394 to 386 that the Spartans perhaps most missed peltasts, possibly
> because of financial difficulties: . . . Thus at just the time when the war
> ceased to be an affair of the set-piece battle between citizen armies, Sparta
> herself still had to depend on her own regulars.
>
> Lazenby, *The Spartan Army*, p. 39

SEVERAL ACTIONS IN THE PELOPONNESIAN War had suggested useful avenues to be pursued and developed in relation to the tactical use of the various components of a Classical Greek army. Those who took these lessons to heart came to realise that inter-supportive units within an army could be used with great efficacy, and it is during this period that tactical experiments gathered pace. Those arms that during the previous century had been seen as of lesser importance than the heavy infantry phalanx now found themselves increasingly valued. Their eventual elevated status was a reward for the increasing number of tactical roles they fulfilled. A few examples of actions of these auxiliaries are given below in each section.

Cavalry

Traditionally the cavalry's use had been in screening the flanks of an army, skirmishing with opposing cavalry and other auxiliaries, or in pursuit, once the enemy had been broken. Other duties outside the sphere of a battle were scouting and reconnaissance, locating the position of the enemy, screening the rearguard of an army on the march and raiding.

The importance to a state of the cavalry arm depended greatly on the location and culture of a city-state. Areas like Makedon, Chalkidike, Thessaly and, to a lesser extent, Boiotia, with their large plains were natural horse-breeding areas. In consequence, such regions, with plenty of fodder, had the opportunity to develop better cavalry forces than other less well-endowed areas. Manoeuvres were easier to practise and refine in these places where local economies had significant reliance on horse ownership. This gave those in control of the state the opportunity to mount significant numbers of the lower social orders who could not afford to keep horses of their own.

In other areas, horse ownership was largely limited to those with the means available to afford the upkeep. Despite having control over a large geographical area, Athens falls into this category. The land of Attika was not as fertile as that of others. Athens' cavalry, of which it was proud, was therefore manned by the propertied classes. Sparta, by contrast, had a strong heavy infantry tradition. While many owned horses, these were largely raised for leisure or sporting purposes. It was only as late as around 424 BC that Sparta was forced to raise a cavalry arm in response to the need for mobility in countering Athenian attacks on the coast, rather than as a specialist unit for its armies. Sparta relied on its allies to produce such forces in times of war.

The rider had to contend with the absence of both saddle and stirrups. Control had to come from the bridle and bit and the acquisition of good balance and strength in the thighs. Contrary to some ancient relief representations, which are more aesthetic than a reflection of reality, the position taken on the horse would have been further forward than that adopted on saddled mounts today. This was to reduce the stress on the animal's back by having the rider's weight near to the forelegs of his mount, and to have a good position from which to cast a javelin. Horses of the day were fourteen hands or a little less, about the size of a robust present-day pony.

Despite these apparent limitations it was possible, given adequate horsemanship, to achieve sophisticated formations and high manoeuvrability. It is no surprise that these came about in the better-endowed areas. In Thessaly the formation adopted was that of a rhomboid that could change its direction by a lead from any of its points. This seems to have been developed from the wedge of the Thrakians, and Thebes was to use the wedge formation in the fourth century. Those like Athens,

Sparta and its Peloponnesian allies retained the older rectangular formation, similar to the phalanx and lacking the articulation of those described above.

Xenophon recommends that a cavalryman should have a well-fitting breastplate with fitted protection for the area between neck and nose. Above this a Boiotian helmet is preferred as giving a much wider view than the usual Korinthian helmet of the hoplite:

> As for the pattern of the breastplate, it should be so shaped as not to prevent the wearer from sitting down or stooping. About the abdomen and middle and round that region let the flaps be of such material and such a size that they will keep out missiles [as a protection to the thighs]. And as a wound in the left hand disables the rider, we also recommend the piece of armour invented for it called the 'hand'. For it protects the shoulder, the arm, the elbow, and the fingers that hold the reins; it will also extend and fold up; and in addition it covers the gap left by the breastplate under the armpit. But the right hand must be raised when a man intends to fling his javelin or strike a blow. Consequently that portion of the breastplate that hinders him in doing that should be removed; and in place of it there should be detachable flaps at the joints, in order that, when the arm is elevated, they may open correspondingly, and may close when it is lowered. The part that is left exposed when the right arm is raised should be covered near the breastplate with calf-skin or metal; otherwise the most vital part will be unprotected. (Xen. *Art of Horsemanship* XII. 1–7)[1]

Protection for the lower leg and foot was gained by wearing leather boots. The horse was also given protection by heavy quilting that covered the vulnerable belly. This also gave the rider a more secure seat and avoided possible chafing of the horses' back. Its head, chest and thighs were also given protection, with the last giving additional cover to the rider's thighs.

Preferred weaponry included the *machaira*, a sabre-like weapon used by Spartan and Persian armies. This was more effective in its slashing action than the thrusting action of the sword. Two Persian-style javelins with shafts of cornel wood are Xenophon's choice rather than the spear that he claims is too long and awkward to control. He suggests throwing the javelin at the limit of its range, thereby giving the rider more time to grasp his second javelin and turn his mount. On casting his weapon the rider should point his left side towards the target and pull back his right, meanwhile rising from his seat by using the grip of his legs and throwing the javelin with its point a little raised from the horizontal. This would achieve greater power and distance.

Since he gives us so much detail, we must infer from this information that this is Xenophon's ideal, and that not all cavalrymen met his criteria. Indeed both pottery and relief sculpture show representations of horsemen with spears and less protection for horses than is recommended. In the case of the latter this may be for aesthetic reasons so that the beautiful form of the horse is preserved.

Horses were unshod and care had to be taken when encountering rough ground, otherwise the animal became lame. In like fashion, dismounting from time to time when on the march gave horses periods of rest.

Within our period, small cavalry forces were used with surprising success. In 369 BC, sixty Phliasian cavalry caused the flight of the entire rearguard of an Argive and Arkadian army, after penetrating their cavalry screen (Xen. *Hell.* VII. 2. 4). The Argives had obviously not established an inter-supportive arrangement between hoplites and cavalry, or even ensured that the hoplites of the rearguard would turn to form a solid line against such an attack. No cavalry force, no matter how large, could hope for success alone, in an attack on an unbroken phalanx. The following year saw another invasion by the Argives and Arkadians. On this occasion they were attacked and defeated at a river crossing by Phliasian and Athenian cavalry supported by their 'picked troops', presumably hoplites (Xen. *Hell.* VII. 2. 10). In 369 BC, a contingent of only fifty Syrakusan cavalry, sent in support of Sparta, successfully harried the lines of the army of Thebes and its allies. Their tactic was to ride along the enemy front, discharging their javelins, after which they would retire and dismount to rest. Those of the enemy who pursued them were frustrated to find the Syrakusans remounting and retreating further. When the pursuit continued and then was abandoned, the cavalry turned and made a counterattack. This must have been repeated several times for Xen. *Hell.* VII. 1. 21 states: 'and thus they compelled the entire army, according to their own will, either to advance or to fall back'.

The ruler of Elimeia in Upper Makedon, Derdas II, proved a very capable cavalry commander.[2] Although mentioned only twice in the *Hellenika*, his exploits deserve attention. The event is described in the main text, but it is well to cover the action here to demonstrate its significance. His force was around 400 horse, and in the spring of 381 BC he had arrived in Apollonia only to discover that some 600 Olynthian cavalry were pillaging the area. He did nothing immediately but waited with his horses and men at the ready until the Olynthians had penetrated the dwellings outside the walls and come very near the city gates. Only then did he make his attack in good order. The enemy fled, but Derdas kept up the pursuit for around ten miles, killing some eighty of the enemy. The result of this action led the Olynthians to stay within their own walls and to cultivate only a very small area around the city, presumably at such times when they were aware that Derdas was in the vicinity in support of Teleutias.

The quality of Olynthian cavalry was high and they were present at Apollonia in greater numbers than those under Derdas. Obviously the surprise of the attack countered this disparity. It is evident from the distance of the pursuit that the attack was prolonged. The number of Olynthian dead proves them to have been hard pressed throughout, and not given the opportunity to reform into any cohesive order. With no report of casualties to Derdas' force it is obvious that they maintained their squadrons. The condition of mounts would have been an issue, both for pursued and pursuer. Fresher or stronger horses will have overtaken many of those they were pursuing. Lameness may have played a role in the protracted action. The unshod mounts on both sides would have had such incidents. There was no problem in this for Derdas' men, who could dismount and lead their mounts in safety behind the main force, but would be a disaster for any Olynthian rider faced with this misfortune.

Derdas would know that a long and successful pursuit would demoralise an enemy and give his cavalry an immediate advantage in any future action. The loss to the Olynthians of almost an eighth of their number further reduced the capacity of their cavalry arm.

Other actions have been described in the narrative and some examples of mutual support between different arms will be given towards the end of this appendix.[3]

Peltasts

These are the light infantry of a Greek army. This arm was to see considerable development within, and after, our period. Originally described as coming from the areas to the east of Makedon, they had a light crescent-shaped shield, javelins, a short sword and occasionally a spear. Other mountainous regions such as Aitolia had similarly armed light troops that were better suited to the terrain of their country than hoplites. Increasing use had been made of these light-armed mercenaries in the Peloponnesian War, but it is during our period that their tactical use made considerable advances.

Iphikrates, the Athenian general, is to be credited with many of these improvements. He supplied his mercenaries with oval shields, smaller than the *aspis* of the hoplite, and boots that were lighter, easy to untie and protective of the lower shin, a long sword, and a much longer thrusting spear to add to their javelins (Diod. XV. 44). This increase in spear length made the peltast much more effective both in offence and defence. Iphikrates' continual training regime made them fleet of foot, highly effective in controlled attack and retreat and, in a tight formation, with the increased reach of their spears, sometimes able opponents to less disciplined hoplites. That longer spear, sometimes half as long again as the original length of that of a hoplite, may well have required the use of both hands for efficient use. In such a case the oval shield would be slung from the neck, thereby protecting the left shoulder to leave both hands free. On rough terrain they were virtually unbeatable except by similar forces.

Earlier use of peltasts in battles had been as skirmishers prior to the main contest between opposing phalanx formations of hoplites. They could also act as a screen to the flank of a phalanx along with the cavalry, secure any heights alongside which an army might pass, and were useful in pursuit. In casting a javelin peltasts made use of a leather loop fixed about halfway down the shaft of the weapon by putting the forefinger and middle finger within it, thereby giving greater impetus to the throw.

An increase in the dedicated use of peltasts in conjunction with other arms is readily observable. The Thebans developed a tactic of having cavalry interspersed with light-armed troops (*hamippoi*) running alongside or being pulled along by the horses' tails when moving to an attack As early as 429 BC, an unusual set of circumstances gave rise to an example of the successful use of combined auxiliary forces against hoplites which was not lost on the Greek world. The Athenians had invaded Chalkidike with 2,000 hoplites supported by 200 cavalry a little before harvest time. The Athenian destruction of the crops around Spartalos led the Olynthian garrison there, together with the resident auxiliaries, to engage the Athenians in front of the city. The Chalkidian hoplites were defeated, but their cavalry and light-armed forces were successful against the Athenian cavalry and whatever local auxiliaries they had. Shortly after, additional peltasts from Olynthos joined their light-armed and cavalry allies at Spartalos, giving them the courage to make a further attack on the Athenians. The Athenian commanders seemed to have had no answer to the problems posed by the combined peltast and cavalry assaults:

> the Athenians, who now fell back upon the two companies which they had left with their baggage. And whenever the Athenians advanced, they gave way, but when the Athenians retreated they kept close at their heels, hurling javelins at them. Then the Chalkidian cavalry, riding up, kept charging the Athenians wherever opportunity offered, and throwing them into utter panic routed them and pursued them to a great distance. The Athenians took refuge in Poteidaia, and afterwards, having recovered their dead under a truce, returned to Athens with what remained of their army. (Thuc. II. 79. 5–7)[4]

This was a catastrophic defeat for the Athenians and, at that time, surprising. The terrain suited both cavalry and hoplites, but it was the tactical combination of cavalry and peltasts that won the day. The Athenians lost 430 men, including all their generals.

Although Agesilaos made effective use of peltasts in his Asiatic campaign, the Spartan practice of using hoplites of up to the first fifteen age groups, rather than peltasts in forays from the ranks is deserving of note. These young men would be fitter and fleeter than their older comrades, and were capable of overtaking peltasts over a short distance should they approach too closely. However, orders to do so had to be given by a commander who had the ability to assess the situation clearly, and not hold back after commitment. The Lechaion episode, dealt with in its own chapter, demonstrates what happens when a commander is out of his depth.

However, a thinking commander such as Agesilaos could turn a dangerous situation to his advantage. Agesilaos' success when campaigning in Akarnania in 389 BC is dealt with at the end of the chapter on the Lechaion debacle. Another example of his quick thinking and judicious action in adverse circumstances is to be encountered at Xen. *Hell.* V. 4. 39–40. In 378 BC, having laid waste to the Theban territory, he was returning to camp. Cavalry and peltasts were preparing to go for their meal. Theban cavalry burst forth from their concealment behind the long stockade they had erected to defend the land nearer to their city. Agesilaos' auxiliaries were in disarray and suffered casualties, until the king turned those forces with him to launch an attack on the Thebans. The attacking force was made up of that section of the cavalry already with him, intermingled by the first ten year classes of hoplites who ran with them: 'The Theban horsemen, however, acted like men who had drunk a little at midday; for although they awaited the oncoming enemy in order to throw their spears, they threw before they were within range. Still though they turned about at such a great a distance, twelve of them were killed' (Xen. *Hell.* V. 4. 39–40).

It is to be noted that Agesilaos' army contained peltasts, but when these were disadvantaged by the sudden Theban attack he could still rely on his younger hoplites to act in conjunction with cavalry to turn the tables on his enemy. With the overall lightening of the hoplite panoply and the increase in weight of the peltast's equipment together with the lengthening of the spear of the latter, we begin to see the embryonic form of Philip II's phalangite.

Archers and Slingers

Arms practice and javelin throwing was part and parcel of the almost daily exercise taken by the majority of Greeks. It is not difficult to see that these skills were easily transferable to cavalry and the light-armed. In the absence of Thrakian peltasts, mercenaries took their place at this period. Hunting was a very good ancillary area of training and is strongly recommended by Xenophon in his essay on that subject, so it is clear that the places in these auxiliary forces were easy to fill.

However, to acquire the skills of an archer or a slinger required equal, if not more, dedication. Therefore, we find them as highly specialised units in the ancient world. In the hoplite tradition, where men met the danger of death face to face, fighting and inflicting death at a distance was not accepted as being honourable.[5] The main areas for recruitment were therefore not on mainland Greece, but from those areas that had retained past traditions of competence, namely Krete for archers and Rhodes for slingers. Skythian archers were also available for hire as mercenaries.

Bow types were variable, and arrowheads show that the Kretans preferred a larger size than the Skythian. What is perhaps most interesting is the use of lead slingshot by the Rhodians, which gave additional distance and force to the projectile.

In his *Anabasis* Xenophon recounts the occasion when the rearguard of the Greek army was suffering severely from the missiles raining in upon them from Persian slingers and mounted bowmen. The range of the Persian archers was greater than that of the Kretans serving with Xenophon, and they wore little protective armour. Without cavalry, Xenophon had to resort to ineffectual attempts to pursue their tormentors with peltasts and hoplites, if only to gain temporary respite. They had no success, since the enemy was always beyond javelin range. In camp that evening his fellow generals censured him for his actions. Xenophon agreed with their view, but suggested solutions to their problems:

> ... we need slingers ourselves, and horsemen also. Now I am told that there are Rhodians in our army, that most of them understand the use of the sling, and that their missile carries no less than twice as far as those from Persian slings. For the latter have only a short range because the stones that are used in them are as large as the hand can hold; the Rhodians, however, are versed also in the art of slinging leaden bullets. If, therefore, we should ascertain who among them possess slings, and should not only pay these people for their slings, but likewise pay anyone who is willing to plait new ones, and if, furthermore, we should devise some sort of exemption for the man who will volunteer to serve as a slinger at his appointed post, it may be that men will come forward who will be capable of helping us. Again, I observe there are horses in the army – a few at my own quarters, others that made Clearchus' troop and were left behind, and many others as pack-animals. If, then, we should pick out all these horses, replacing them with mules, and should equip them for cavalry, it may be that this cavalry also will cause some annoyance to the enemy when they are in flight. (Xen. *Anab*. III. 3. 16–19)

The resulting force of 200 slingers and fifty cavalry proved a highly effective answer to the problem. Later, when threatened by a much larger force under Tissaphernes, the Rhodian slingers caused the enemy to withdraw beyond their range: 'And the barbarians were no longer able to do any harm by their skirmishing at long range; for the Rhodian slingers carried further with their missiles than the Persians, further even than the Persian bowmen' (Xen. *Anab*. III. 4. 16).

Soon after, an abundance of gut and lead was discovered in the villages at which they encamped. What is very obvious was the necessity to persuade the Rhodians, who were serving as hoplites, to undertake a role in the army normally regarded as of lower status. Xenophon is clear that the inducements should be of a kind that would persuade.

Apart from these specialist auxiliaries there were usually stone-throwers with most armies. These ill-protected camp followers are often disregarded in reports, but their presence could prove an annoyance to the enemy in the opening stages of a battle. Often the more prosperous of the hoplites from all city-states were accompanied by servants. Most of these would be armed and, in extremis, could make a contribution in a battle, even if not fighting alongside their masters. The Spartiatai had their *helot* servants, as did the more affluent of the *perioikoi* serving with the Spartans. Indeed, several thousand *helots* were used as hoplites by the Spartans within the period under scrutiny. When giving numbers of participants in battles, our sources usually omit the number of servants, personal slaves, muleteers, drivers of wagons and other camp followers present.

Endnotes

1   An incredible amount of information is to be gleaned from both *The Cavalry Commander* and *Art of Horsemanship*. Care for the horse is always at the heart of Xenophon's writing.

2   Elimeia was one of the kingdoms in Upper Makedon and, at the time of Derdas' reign, was in a position to dominate some of its immediate neighbours in the upland region. Lower Makedon, which constituted the lowlands and the coastal area, was under the control of the family that produced Philip II and his son Alexander the Great. Relationships between the two regions were generally good at times when a common threat appeared from external powers such as Illyria, but until the time of the unification of Makedon under Phillip II differences of policy were pursued. Derdas' daughter Phila was one of Phillip II's seven wives. The capital of Elimeia appears to have been at Aiani, where excavations started in 1983. The hill of Megali Rachi seems to have been occupied by settlements from Neolithic times before being abandoned during the first century BC. The fine museum, completed in the summer of 2002, has already had its six display rooms filled with impressive artefacts.

3   I. G. Spence, *The Cavalry of Classical Greece*, Oxford, Clarendon Press, 1995 gives a good background of the period. Although covering the subject over a much wider timescale, Gaebel, *Cavalry Operations* shows clearly the developments within the period under discussion, which led to the tactical use of this arm under Alexander and his successors.

4   In the continuation of the Loeb translation, the Athenians lost 330 men and all their generals.

5   Euripides, *Medea and Other Plays*, trans. P. Vellacott, Penguin Classics, Harmondsworth, Penguin, 1963, pp. 158–9 sets out the argument in the exchanges between Lykos and Amphytrion. The subject is Herakles, described as using the bow, 'the coward's weapon'.

APPENDIX 4

Jason of Pherai

And he himself – for I must tell you the truth – is exceedingly strong of body and a lover of toil besides. Indeed, he makes trial every day of the men under him, for in full armour he leads them, both on the parade ground and whenever he is on campaign anywhere. And whomsoever among his mercenaries he finds to be weaklings he casts out, but whomsoever he sees to be fond of toil and fond of the dangers of war he rewards, some with double pay, others with triple pay, others even with quadruple pay, and with gifts besides, as well as with care in sickness and magnificence in burial.

Polydamos of Pharsalos reporting to the Spartan assembly on Jason of Pherai at Xen. *Hell.* VI. 1. 6

XENOPHON DEVOTES THE WHOLE OF Chapter 1 of Book VI of his *Hellenika* to this personality. He is introduced at a time when the resources of Sparta were being stretched to their limits in 375/374 BC. With a resurgent Thebes making significant progress in regaining control of Boiotia and at the same time threatening Phokis, Sparta had been obliged to send Kleombrotos to central Greece with a large army for the protection of the Phokian cities.

An ambassador from Pharsalos in southern Thessaly arrived in Sparta. Polydamos had come to request military assistance against Jason of Pherai. In the course of his address to the Spartan assembly we learn of a man of extraordinary abilities and ambition.[1] Polydamos declared that he had two reasons for coming: first, as an ally who had a problem, and second, to warn the Spartans of a possible problem for them in the future. He then outlined what had recently been happening in Thessaly and, in his description, we have an example of realpolitik.

Jason had concluded a truce between Pherai and Pharsalos so that a meeting could take place between himself and Polydamos. That meeting, as the Pharsalian reported, shows Jason to have been an honourable realist. It is obvious from Jason's opening comments that he had been successful in bringing over to him most of the cities in Thessaly, even though Pharsalos had given them military aid. He now made clear to Polydamos that with his force of 6,000 highly trained mercenaries he had an army that was more than a match for any citizen army. Polydamos told the Spartans that Jason's claim was true. He could vouch that Jason led by example and accepted only the highest standards from his men and kept them under constant training. He rewarded those who served him well and honoured those who died in his cause. Jason went on to say that, given those who were already subject to him, including not only the Thessalians, but neighbouring states, it might surprise some that he did not merely attack and take over Pharsalos. His stated reason for not doing so immediately was that he preferred Pharsalos to come over to him willingly rather than by force: 'For if you were constrained by force, you, on the one hand, would be planning whatever harm you could do against me, and I, on the other, should be wanting to keep you as weak as I could' (Xen. *Hell*. VI. 1. 7).

His intention in wishing to bring over Pharsalos and the other cities under its control was because he had ambition to become *tagos* of all Thessaly. This title indicated a united state under an overlord, and would also bring other surrounding territories under his control. Thessaly had not had a *tagos* for over a hundred years and its potential power had been dissipated by rivalries between regional ruling families.

Jason predicted that once Thessaly was unified no power could overcome it. His allies, the Boiotians, would follow him if he helped rid them of their war with Sparta. He had no intention of having close ties with Athens, 'for I believe that I could obtain empire by sea even more easily than by land' (Xen. *Hell*. VI. 1. 10). This was no empty boast but a realistic intention. With Makedon under his control he would be able to deny Athens timber for shipbuilding and there was abundant manpower in terms of the serf population in Thessaly to man a strong fleet. Further, Athens was reliant on the import of corn and other foodstuffs, whereas Thessaly was not only self-sufficient, but was a net exporter. As to finance, Thessaly ruled by a *tagos* would once again draw tribute from subject territories.

He already had the Dolopians, Marakians and Alketas, king of Epiros, as subjects and would be able to draw on the resources of mainland Greece, unlike Athens, which had relied on funding for its navy from the islands.

The broad sweep of his ambition is made clear in the following:

> by drawing on the resources, not of islands, but of a continent, that the King of the Persians is the richest of mortals; and yet I think that it is even easier to reduce him to subjection than to reduce Greece. For I know that everybody there, save one person, has trained himself to servitude rather than to prowess, and I know what manner of force it was – both that went up with Cyrus and that which went up with Agesilaos – that brought the King to extremities. (Xen. *Hell*. VI. 1. 12)

To many Greeks the appeal of a Panhellenic expedition against Persia was great. To exact revenge for the depredations visited upon their ancestors at the time of the Persian wars would have brought great satisfaction. On the other hand, and this must be a matter for conjecture, Jason may have realised that to gain and maintain dominance over Greece required the elimination of the interference of Persia in Greek affairs. For too long Persia had protected itself by giving support to one or other groupings of Greek states

If all that Polydamos reported was true, it seems clear that Jason was intent on extending his sway, over not only Greece, but also Persia. He promised Polydamos that he would make him 'the greatest, next to myself, of all the men in Greece'. When Polydamos replied that as allies of the Spartans they had no good reason to go over to their enemy. Jason praised him for his loyalty and suggested that he travelled to Sparta to ask for their help against him. He would abide by the result of any ensuing war. If, however, the help offered was deemed to be inadequate, Polydamos was free to act in the best interests of his city.

Polydamos then requested that Sparta send an army sufficiently large to make war on Jason and to persuade other cities in Thessaly to revolt. He warned that it was pointless sending freed *helots* under a citizen commander. Here he is referring to the *neadamodeis* and the increasing reliance by Sparta on military service from *helots* in return for their freedom. None other than one of the kings leading a strong force of citizens, Spartan *hypomeiones*, allies and mercenaries, would suffice, for they would be going against an outstanding general with highly disciplined forces.

What follows is indicative of the desire to give help, and the growing problems facing Sparta at that time:

> As for the Lacedaimonians, at the time they deferred their answer; but after
> reckoning up on the next day and on the third their regiments abroad, to see
> how many they numbered, and the regiments which were in the vicinity of
> Lacedaimon to be employed against the triremes of the Athenians and for the war
> upon their neighbours, they replied that at present they could not send him an
> adequate supporting force, and told him to go home and arrange his own affairs
> and those of his city as best he could. (Xen. *Hell.* VI. 1. 17)

This is compelling evidence that Sparta was already overcommitted. The need
to have forces within the Peloponnese on active service to counter the coastal
forays made upon the coastline by Athenian fleets, rather than as a reserve for
such a contingency as had arisen in the case of Thessaly, while having significant
involvement in Kerkyra and Boiotia within this period, was too much to sustain.
Their response was made with regret, but realism. Had such a balanced view
prevailed into the future, matters may well have turned out differently.

As it was, Jason was elected *tagos* shortly after Polydamos came to an
accommodation with him on his return to Pharsalos. On assumption of his role,
Jason took account of those forces now available to him and discovered them to
be greater than he had initially anticipated. The numbers are impressive: 8,000
cavalry, 20,000 hoplites and innumerable peltasts from the mountainous regions
surrounding the large plain of Thessaly. He set a very fair level for the payment of
tribute. Indeed he asked for no more than that which had been paid to the last
tagos,[2] Skopas, a hundred years earlier. That tribute gave him the opportunity to
hire mercenaries to add further to his forces, and to address the enlargement of
his navy.

His ambitions have already been alluded to, but to achieve them he first had
to weaken the positions of his likely adversaries. He already had plans in place to
reduce the power of Athens at sea, as the report of Polydamos indicated, but his
first priority was to weaken Sparta further. To do this, he entered into an alliance
with Thebes.

Our next encounter with Jason in our sources is at the time of the Battle of
Leuktra. The evidence of Diodoros is flawed by more than one obvious error, not
least his numbers of casualties and the supposed joining of two separate Spartan-
led armies with the commanders, King Kleombrotos and Archidamos, son of King
Agesilaos, on each wing. Although Xenophon was not present, as a contemporary

of the action and having secure Spartan sources, he is to be the more trusted. Details of the campaign of Kleombrotos, the battle and Jason's advice to the victorious Thebans, are dealt with in Chapter 10. On his return north from Boiotia, Jason took the opportunity to destroy the Spartan colony of Herakleia, thereby securing the possibility for future unimpeded entry to central Greece.

All seemed to be going well for Jason. His power and influence now stretched over Thessaly, Epiros, Magnesia, Makedon and Perrhaibia and now, with the coming assembly at Delphi for the Pythian games, Jason planned to give a demonstration of that power. There had been an earthquake, perhaps in 373 BC, which had destroyed the temple there and, no doubt, plans would be discussed by all attending for the financing of its rebuilding. It would appear that Jason had firm plans in respect of the control of this influential site and oracle:

> Now when the Pythian festival was approaching, Jason sent orders to his cities to make ready cattle, sheep, goats, and swine for the sacrifice. And it was said that although he laid upon each city a very moderate demand, there were contributed no fewer than a thousand cattle and more than ten thousand of the other animals. He also made proclamation that a golden crown would be the prize of victory to the city which would rear the finest bull to lead the herd in honour of the god. Furthermore, he gave orders to the Thessalians to make preparations for taking the field at the time of the Pythian festival; for he was intending, it was said, to be himself the director both of the festal assembly in honour of the god and of the games. What he intended, however, in regard to the sacred treasures, is even to this day uncertain; but it is said that when the Delphians asked the god what they should do if he tried to take any of his Treasures, Apollo replied that he would himself take care of the matter. (Xen. *Hell*. VI. 4. 29–30)

The signs were ominous. It appeared that much of Greece would be coerced by a show of irresistible force to let Jason have his way at the Pythian games, and to wonder what his intentions were thereafter.

Prior to setting out for Delphi, Jason held a review of cavalry and was receiving petitioners. Seven young men approached seemingly in need of having a quarrel resolved. When they were near enough they attacked and killed Jason. Two of their number were killed by Jason's guards, but the remaining five escaped by horse and were regarded as heroes in Greek cities, such had been the fear inspired by Jason.

Endnotes

1   At Diodoros XV. 30. 3 we learn that Jason of Pherai had helped Neogenes to gain control of the city and territory of Hestaia on the northern coast of the large island of Euboia. This city had been an ally of Sparta and the action described took place c.376 BC.

2   There had been a period in the second half of the fifth century when Daochos had been elected to the position. However, at no time of his tenure was his power comfortably held or undisputed in Thessaly.

APPENDIX 5

Aspects of Spartan Society

It occurred to me one day that Sparta, though among the most thinly populated of states, was evidently the most powerful and celebrated city in Greece; and I fell to wondering how this could have happened. But when I considered the institutions of the Spartans, I wondered no longer.

Xen. *Constitution of the Lakedaimonians*

THOSE DRAWN FOR THE FIRST time to any examination of ancient Greek societies in general, and that of Sparta in particular, can often be dismayed and confused by the plethora of descriptive labels encountered. It is hoped that by showing social and political structures in diagrammatic form, some element of clarity can be achieved.

Those listed in the box (overleaf) reflect the societal elements present in the first half of the fourth century. All of them (except for the population of conquered Messene) could be described as Lakonians, i.e. coming from Lakonia the 'country' controlled by the dominant city, Sparta (Lakedaimon). However, all the categories listed in the box were domiciled within the Peloponnese, and could be described by the catch-all label, Peloponnesians.

Spartans (Spartiatai)

This was the citizen body, and the only group having the right to vote at the assembly. Spartan women of equal social status did not have voting rights but came to be very influential and, within the period of the first half of the fourth century, owned a significant proportion of land and property. They were unusual

---

Spartan citizens
known also as Homoioi, Spartiatai (equals, peers, Spartiates)
Full citizens with voting rights and the opportunity to hold office

↓

Spartan inferiors
known also as hypomeiones and subdivided into mothakes or mothones, tresantes and possibly
even including the neadamodes
All but the last could be called Spartans but not Spartiatai (full citizens)

↓

Perioikoi
Those who 'dwelt around' within Spartan territory

↓

Helots
Slaves or serfs

---

in Greece in that they held equal rights of inheritance and their position within their own society could well have made them the envy of women in Athens and other city-states. Spartans were the all-powerful members of society, devoting their lives to the state as soldiers, having estates and land with slaves to work to provide the monthly amount of produce to give to their military messes and support their families. They were not allowed to involve themselves in any other activity such as commerce. Originally, this arrangement must have been accepted by mutual consent.

Education for males followed a prescriptive pattern. In the following description not all age points can be verified but the description provides a framework for the stages within. From the age of seven to twelve a citizen's son undertook education under the *agoge*, living, thereafter, with his fellows in barracks under the supervision of a *paidonomos*. This official was appointed by the state from the very best of full citizens. He oversaw the direction of the education, the goal of which was to produce modest, self-sufficient, body-hardened, shrewd individuals skilled in the arts of war. The development of stamina and physical endurance was progressive. From twelve to eighteen years military training was given greater prominence. For much of this period youths were obliged to harden their feet by going barefoot, and to wear only one item of clothing throughout the year. They cleaned their own quarters, and were only given limited food rations to prepare them for times when supplies might be scarce on campaign. It also encouraged them to devise methods for supplementing their diet both by hunting and stealing. Theft, under such circumstances, was not regarded as a fault. Rather, being caught doing so was the crime for which severe punishment was meted out, the culprit showing himself as not having the stealth or intelligence to be successful in remaining undiscovered.

From eighteen to twenty they probably came under full-time military training commanded by others over twenty years old. They were now at the point when they could undertake field operations other than in the front line of the phalanx. These positions were reserved for those between the ages of twenty-four and thirty. From this age group were chosen the *hippeis*, 300 in number. They provided the king with his bodyguard on campaign. Three respected citizens chose them. Each chose 100 young men, giving valid reasons for each choice, no doubt based on performance in the *agoge* and personal attributes. The resulting privileged corps was subjected to continuous scrutiny by their rejected fellows in case any fell short of the standards expected of him.

Marriage was permissible from the age of twenty, but men had still to live in barracks and could only pay a visit to their wives in secrecy. This was said to promote the ardour necessary to promote both a good marriage and healthy progeny. At thirty, men had reached the age when they became full citizens with voting rights. They could now leave the barrack life and live in their homes with their families. An obligation to take a meal every night with their mess-mates still remained, however.

The *phiditia* or *syssition* was that nightly meal shared by citizens in a variety of locations, each with a membership of fewer than twenty, possibly based on some military unit. Inclusion of a newcomer could only be achieved by unanimous decision of the membership. It was essential to acquire membership if citizen status was to be preserved. One can well imagine a wide variety of machinations being undertaken by family and friends, well prior to the age of candidacy, to secure a place in a public mess. Each month every member had a duty to submit supplies from his land allotment for communal use. Failure to do so would lead to a loss of citizen status. Absence could only be excused by the necessity to undertake public duties, active service away from home or hunting, the product of which would, in all likelihood, appear as part of the monthly offering. Such regular meetings would allow conversations between a wide age range. The younger element would learn much of the traditions and history of their state, as well as respect for their elders and reliance upon them in matters of military experience.

Military service was a requirement up to the age of sixty years except under exceptional circumstances. The invasions of Lakonia by Epaminondas, or in the truly exceptional case of Agesilaos as a commander into his eighties are examples. At times when military duty was necessary, the *ephors* (see later) would undertake a call-up of age groups deemed to be sufficient for the matter in hand. This in our sources is referred to as 'calling the ban'.

Girls were also given an education. Although they continued to live at home they were organised in age bands similar to those of the boys. They often took exercise alongside the boys and became proficient in running and other field sports. The concentration on physical activities produced a healthy population with well-formed bodies. This probably accounts for Spartan women being described as being the most beautiful in the ancient world, despite the prohibition laid upon them to adorn themselves with any of the expected female accoutrements such as jewellery etc. They were wholly free of any domestic work and, despite lacking the vote, appear otherwise to have enjoyed equal status with men.

Both boys and girls were encouraged to dance and sing together with their elders in festivals throughout the year. Indeed, music was regarded as an essential in the education of both sexes. It would appear that the influence of Spartan womenfolk over husbands and sons was considerable. Unlike those in other Greek states, Spartan women enjoyed the rights of inheritance and seemed to have had some say in the choice of their marriage partners.

Spartan Inferiors (*Hypomeiones*)

Xen. *Hell.* III. 3. 6 provides a list of those groups within the population that would support an uprising against the ruling Spartiatai. Among them appears a group described as υπομειοσι and translatable as lesser citizens or lesser Spartiatai. The groups hereunder were denied full citizenship on a variety of grounds. There may well have been others to add to those already known. Those whose only transgression was an inability to sustain the monthly mess requirement would have been regarded as *hypomeines*. Those people who fell into the subdivisions described have other specific reasons for not being accepted within the citizen body. The existing strands of evidence remain debatable. What appears below contains an element of probability, rather than of absolute certainty.

Mothakes or mothones

There are a variety of explanations for this group in our sources. The most persuasive[1] is that they were the sons of good families whose forebears had lost their Spartiate status, but who were fortunate to be adopted by members of the citizen body and put through the *agoge*, probably alongside their own sons. In such a way, and with the necessary gift of sufficient land to support him, a *mothax* could become a Spartiate. Gylippos, the hero of the defence of Syrakuse during the Peloponnesian War, was described as being a *mothax*. This had probably come about with the loss of land to his family on the exile of his father. The most notable of this group is said to have been Lysander. Nonetheless, the origins remain obscure but do indicate that it was possible to achieve citizenship from the position of this subgroup of the *hypomeines*.

Tresantes

Literally 'tremblers' who had shown cowardice in action. For this dereliction of duty they lost their citizenship. There may have been a remote opportunity to regain their status, however, by some future action of bravery.

Bachelors

Curious as the inclusion of such a group under the term 'inferior' appears, there is a logical explanation. It had become the perceived duty of all adult males to marry and to raise progeny. This obligation was probably supported by law, in the hope that more male offspring would be added to the available citizen body.

Failure to marry brought about the loss of privileged rights and respect from the citizen body. The bachelors were treated much in the same way as were the 'tremblers'. Exclusion from public festivals and being the butt of public ridicule, even from younger men, was the norm. This could appear to have been a difficulty for homosexuals and those who had a genuine wish not to marry. However, the exception of Derkylidas, the highly respected general and committed bachelor, is indicative that there were some who, by their abilities, had avoided the full public consequences of the status.

Others

Under this heading are two groups. Yet more may yet come to light in the future. First, there were the sons of Spartan citizens born from an extra-marital union outside the Spartiate group. This broad category of illegitimate children probably resulted from liaisons between Spartiatai and *helot* or periokic women, but does not exclude the probability of illegitimate offspring being born of Spartan mothers and Spartan fathers.[2] Xen. *Hell.* V. 3. 9, for example, describes such a group (*nothoi*) among those who went with the army of Agesipolis to the area of Olynthos: 'and sons of the Spartiatai by *helot* women, exceedingly fine-looking men, not without experience of the good gifts of the state'.

At the time of the original distribution of common land among the newly formed citizen body, it should be appreciated that there would be variables in the quality and product of each *klaros*. The land could not be sold and was to be passed to progeny. Already it can be seen that it was possible for productive land to provide for more than one Spartan in a family. However, for those with poorer land, having too many progeny would become a problem. At that time the families of aristocrats who held estates of their own were well protected in the long term, so long as they respected the Lykourgos law. The aristocracy was also careful to limit the number of children born to their family and to intermarry within those of similar resource.

Sons of citizens from other states, now probably in exile, and living in Spartan territories, served with the army. The sons of these 'aliens' were often put through the Spartan training system and were well prepared to serve their new homeland. Xenophon, himself an Athenian exile, possibly saw to it that his sons undertook the training of the *agoge*.

Neadamodeis

Literally 'new citizens' who earned their status in the community by services to the state. Increasingly, Sparta came to rely on *helots* serving in their armies, particularly in operations outside the Peloponnese. This military service was sometimes rewarded by the gift of freedom and settlement near the borders of Lakedaimon in garrison communities. Despite their descriptive name of 'new citizens', they had no voting rights in the Spartan assembly, but would have enjoyed some form of local autonomy as freemen, similar to those in the periokic towns. The *Brasideioi*, who had served with Brasidas in northern Greece, were still brigaded together at the first Battle of Mantineia in 418 BC after achieving their freedom.

Neadamodeis served with distinction during the Peloponnesian War, and continued to do so thereafter. Within the period of this present study it will be noted that Agesilaos had 2,000 with him on his Asiatic campaign.

Perioikoi

The population of the towns and villages in Lakedaimon, and some in Messenia, were free in the normal sense of the word. Their societies reflected what could be expected of any ancient community, tradesmen, farmers, fishermen, craftsmen, aristocrats, wealthy and impoverished. Although they were self-governing, they were subject to Spartan intervention in local administrative matters. They had no representation at the Spartan assembly and were duty bound to meet Spartan requirements in time of war in terms of commissariat and as combatants. As Spartiatai were forbidden by law to engage in anything other than preparedness for the defence of the state, the periokic section of the population of Lakonia was the economic powerhouse of the state. It produced the armour and weapons for the Spartan military, building materials and all manner of manufactured goods, including building ships. The artefacts found in the area are therefore mainly of periokic or *helot* manufacture, as are the examples of fine pottery and bronzes found in various locations around the Mediterranean.

Up until the middle and third quarter of the sixth century the arts in Lakedaimon flourished. Commercial competition from Athens may well have led to a decline in the demand for Spartan pottery in much the same way as it had done for that of Korinth. Skilled bronze workers and potters thereafter sought to seek their livelihood elsewhere when they could, and Taras in southern Italy seems to have been one of the favoured locations. But external commercial pressure is not enough to explain the demise of the local production of fine artefacts.

It seems likely that the Spartan citizens were persuaded away from the disparity of outward lifestyles that gave visual evidence of the ostentation of the rich when compared to the poor. A move to simplicity and austerity seems to have been made, possibly heavily influenced by one of the seven sages of Greece, Chilon. He was *ephor* in the 550s BC and seems to have been the likely author of the reinterpretation of Lykourgos' tradition at this time. Such was his reputation, that his influence would have been felt in the years after his official magistracy. The resulting adoption of his proposals would have led to the eventual demise of the local and internal market of Lakedaimon for luxury products. It may have obscured the outward differences between the wealthy and those of lesser resource, and given a greater appearance of equality. It did not seek to remove that difference or restrict its 'invisible' growth. The behavioural change and its consequences would not have been immediate, and the decline in fine products was gradual. With its wealth lying in land and agriculture, Sparta was not reliant on commerce. There would, however, have been some effect on periokic communities as the decline in artistic products continued.

The observance of those practices of the Spartan way of life recorded by later writers such as Xenophon have led to the broadly accepted use of 'Spartan' to denote austerity. This belies what went before in the seventh and sixth centuries and laid the foundation for the modern myth that Lakedaimon was always arid in terms of artistic endeavour.[3]

Finally, it seems unlikely that, within the Spartan citizen body, there were never individuals who indulged in artistic practice even if only for personal satisfaction. Forbidden to indulge in manual labour he may have been, but this did not exclude the citizen from playing the aulos in the march to battle, or at games or at festivals.

Helots

In Athens the slave population was made up of personally owned chattels purchased from a market. Many were of barbarian origin or members of enslaved populations resulting from war. The Peloponnesian War, just prior to the period under discussion, had seen recalcitrant populations of Greek origin sold into slavery mainly by Athens.[4] By contrast, the vast preponderance of Sparta's slave population was made up of the inhabitants of local and adjacent captured territories. Over the centuries of gradual expansion up to the first Messenian War, Sparta had consolidated its position in what became known as Lakonia. The origin of the word *helot* possibly derives from the coastal town of Helos captured in the second half of the eighth century, and was to be the label used to describe all those in servitude, whatever their regional origin. Another explanation is that the meaning of the word signifies 'prisoner or captured' and points to a consequence of invasion. By the end of the eighth century Sparta had annexed the lands of Messenia and enslaved its population. With a doubling of territory under its control, Sparta became prosperous almost overnight.

What should be borne in mind is that Messenia itself would not have been under strict military domination and, provided its inhabitants conformed to their masters' requirements, they would be left to their own devices. The product of land allotment to Spartans from the newly acquired area allowed support to 9,000–10,000 citizens. The parcels of state-controlled lands were divided between citizens in the form of a small estate (*klaros*). The *helots* worked the land, and the life of the indigenous inhabitants would be akin in character to a medieval English serf, supplying the proportion of the product necessary to satisfy the needs of the citizen family and the monthly rations required for the *syssition*. All other produce was left in the hands of the *helot* and his family. In many ways the life of the *helot* was between that of a free man and a chattel. But it was that lack of self-determination emanating from the loss of freedom which, taken together with an enduring nationalism in the case of Messenia, that eventually contributed to Sparta's loss of status as a first-class power.[5]

Sitting on the smouldering resentment of an enslaved population far in excess of its own citizen body led Sparta to an extremely conservative viewpoint represented by its series of defensive alliances and repressive conduct to those within its borders. An example is the annual declaration of war made on the *helots* by the incoming *ephors* (see below). The declaration excused any Spartan of the charge of murder should he cause the death of a *helot*. Further, selected youths, probably aged between eighteen and twenty, were employed in a deadly intelligence unit called the *krypteia*, which secretly sought out probable *helot* troublemakers and did away with them. They ranged singly through the countryside, armed only with a dagger, to lie in wait for their target. These actions maintained a policy of terror. Such was the paranoia felt by Sparta in times of duress that Thucydides (IV. 80. 3–4) describes a particularly savage action taken in 424 BC against its *helot* population. The *helots* were invited to select from among their number those who had distinguished themselves in war in the service of the state. They were led to expect the gift of freedom as reward. This proved to be a ruse, so that those selected would be from those most likely to have the pride and courage to be rebellious. Two thousand came forward and, having garlanded themselves, processed around temples in celebration of their supposed freedom. Later, however, this group entirely disappeared. Probably they were picked off singly or in small groups on their return home. It is obvious that the 2,000 would not have been done to death while together in Sparta. True or false as this reported atrocity may be, it reflects the anxiety felt by the citizenry.[6]

It is likely that the *krypteia* was not traditional, but was possibly instituted following the devastating earthquake which all but destroyed the city of Sparta in 464 BC and claimed many citizen lives. The mass rising of the Messenian *helots* and some periokic communities in the west following this disaster proved to be a problem for Sparta for the next ten years. The repressive response of the murder of the 2,000 was no doubt calculated to remove any obvious men of spirit among the *helot* community. This conclusion follows the opinion expressed in Plutarch's *Lykourgos* 28. The same writer also reports in his *Life of Kimon* 16 that the earthquake at Sparta left only five houses standing in the city. With such damage it is inevitable that there was considerable loss of life.

Although the practices of the *krypteia* continued, some softening of how to deal with *helots* perceived as possible threats can be seen in the growing practice of enlisting *helots* for service outside the Peloponnese. This was done on the promise of emancipation on their return, e.g. the 700 accompanying Brasidas to Thrace and the 2,000 going to Asia Minor with Agesilaos.

Elsewhere in Greece, Thessaly treated a section of the indigenous population in much the same manner as the *helots* of Sparta. The *penestai*, as they were called, were therefore Greeks and not barbarians. So it would appear that although state owned, the status of Greeks in servitude was, in many ways, better than privately owned chattel slaves in other states. The fact that *helots* and *penestai* were both identifiable as a homogeneous section of the population of each state did, however, pose a permanent threat to the ruling caste.

Spartan Government

The Spartan constitution is difficult to define containing as it does both democratic and oligarchic elements alongside a hereditary dual monarchy. Although giving an initial appearance of being a mixed constitution or a form of constitutional monarchy, we must inevitably conclude that it was an oligarchy because those involved were members of a privileged segment of the whole population. At its greatest number, Spartan citizens probably accounted for less than 5 per cent of the total. By the beginning of the fourth century BC the dynamics of power and involvement can best be shown in the diagram below. However, in the period under discussion the direction of policy could be led by strong characters such as Lysander, Pausanias and, later, Agesilaos and, to a lesser extent, Antalkidas.

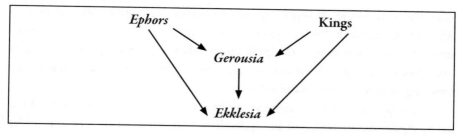

Monarchy: The Two Kings

Two families provided the kings: the Agiadai and the Eurypontidai. Over the course of centuries some of their original powers were circumscribed whereas those of the traditional priest-king and supreme military commander continued unchanged. Probably the duality came into being as the result of a political junction of two tribes. A little before 500 BC the practice of both kings leading the army on campaign was changed to one in which only a single commander took the field, while the other remained at home. On campaign the king's power was absolute and extended to the power of life and death to any individual. He was accompanied by two *ephors* available, with other accompanying Spartiatai, to give advice. The commissariat was in the charge of three Spartiatai, so that the king was free to think only of military matters and his duties as high priest:

> When the time for encamping seems to have arrived, the decision rests with the King, who also indicates the proper place. On the other hand the dispatch of embassies whether to friends or enemies is not the King's affair. All who have any business to transact deal in the first instance with the King. Suitors for justice are remitted by the King to the Court of Hellanodikae, applications for money to the treasurers; and if anyone brings booty, he is sent to the auctioneers. With this routine the only duties left to the King on active service are to act as priest in matters of religion and as general in his dealings with the men. (Xen. *Constitution of the Lakedaimonians* XIII. 8. 10–11)

The king's conduct on campaign was under observation by the *ephors*, who gave a report on their return. Any adverse criticism could be used as a means whereby a king could be deposed or exiled by the people. This would act as a curb on any extreme behaviour. Each month the kings and *ephors* undertook an oath that, providing the kings continued to act in accordance with the constitution, their positions were secure. When in Sparta the priest-kings undertook sacrifices to Apollo twice a month. Both kings employed two *pythoi* as their representatives to travel to, and consult with, the Delphic oracle and to keep safe the pronouncements made from that source. Secular duties included arranging for the adoption of the offspring of deceased citizens and the marriage of their unwed daughters.

Although a member of a *syssition,* an heir-apparent was not put through the *agoge.* Agesilaos, as described in Appendix 1, was elevated to kingship under unusual circumstances. Like all junior members of the royal houses, he had been expected to conform to the duties of the normal Spartan family and undertake membership of the *agoge.*

Ephors

The *ephors* were the chief magistrates of the state. It was an office open to any citizen and is an important democratic element in the constitution. By the time of the period under discussion, a board of five was elected by acclamation by the *ekklesia* (assembly). They were in possession of virtually all the levers of governance. Their tenure of office lasted one year, during which they formulated and introduced any legislation to be laid before the *gerousia* and *ekklesia.* All lesser magistracies were accountable to the *ephors* at the end of their tenure and any abuse of power was punished. Their ability to call a king to account has already been alluded to above. They formulated foreign policy and dealt with any ambassadors from other states. They had responsibility for the *agoge* and organised the activities of the *krypteia.* When Sparta was at war, they organised the ban or call-up by deciding on the number of age classes to be used and arranged for the necessary commissariat. If the assembly of citizens disagreed on a matter proposed by the *ephor*ate, the *gerousia* could refuse to enact it. It is more likely that the *ephors,* together with the *gerousia,* sought to adjourn the meeting of the assembly if it had produced a 'crooked' vote, or one that went against the proposal before them. At the end of their term of office they, too, had to give an account of their decisions and actions while in power. If deemed to be guilty of any significant breach they, like other magistrates, could be punished.

Gerousia

To be elected to the *gerousia* a candidate had to be over the age for military service. At sixty or older any vacancies were open to citizens, who presented themselves in random sequence before the assembly. To assure anonymity in the selection process, a group of people listened from an adjacent area out of sight of the proceeding. They listened to the volume and enthusiasm expressed by the assembly at the entry of the individual candidate. Their decision was made on the degree of approval shown by the citizens. A celebratory procession and banquet followed the result of each election. Obviously, membership would be made up of those with distinguished careers and was an honourable reward for their lifelong endeavours. As the tenure within this institution was for life, the number to be elected at any one time could be variable. It is likely that such elections followed soon after the death of members rather than at a particular time of the year.

The *gerousia* was made up of thirty members: twenty-eight citizens with the two kings also in attendance. Duties included joint sessions with the *ephor*s in adjudicating criminal cases of treason, murder, peculation etc., including those from periokic communities. A prime responsibility was in the preparation of legislation to be presented for approval by the assembly.

Ekklesia (Assembly)

This was open to all Spartan citizens of thirty years and over shown in the first tier of the first diagram. The inferiors were excluded. Monthly meetings were held at the time of the full moon. One of the *ephor*s would introduce matters on which a vote was required. No debate by its members was allowed on any issue except possibly from those elected magistrates present. The *ekklesia* then voted a simple for or against the proposal.

Although it would appear that the power of the assembly was limited, the fact that their approval was required before anything of importance could be brought into effect was significant. This meant that the *gerousia* had to prepare the framing of any proposal for new legislation, elections and decisions on war and peace with extreme care. Day-to-day governance was undertaken by the *ephor*s and *gerousia*.

The *ekklesia*'s involvement in government covered elections to offices of state described above, the emancipation of *helot*s, votes for war, agreements and treaties with other states and the resolution of problems arising in regnal succession, e.g. that of Agesilaos.

Peloponnesian League

Ostensibly, this was a defensive alliance. At its strongest, this grouping was based on the premise of mutual military support for its members. All states within the Peloponnese except Argos were included. The centuries-old enmity between Sparta and Argos led the latter to remain outside the alliance as it struggled to regain the supremacy it had lost to Sparta in the sixth century. Through the league, Sparta was secure on its frontiers and could rely for support from its allies. Any member state could raise a grievance that might involve military action at a meeting of all allies after which Sparta could choose to call a meeting of the allies. The matter would be debated, and any action proposed at this assembly was then considered again before the Spartan assembly that would take the final decision. A majority verdict had to be followed unless a state had some sacred reason for not complying with the wishes of the majority. In times of war each ally provided an agreed and proportionate number of troops which, in many instances, were allotted Spartan officers (*xenagoi*). With the pledge that all would follow where Sparta led, an effective power base existed for Sparta to wield diplomatic influence backed by military power over a wide area of the eastern Mediterranean.

An interesting picture of Spartan character emerges in a speech made by the Korinthians as they and other allies at a meeting of the league urged Sparta to declare war on Athens in 432/431 BC (Thuc. I. 68–71). The content may well prove contrary to some readers' received perceptions. Sparta is criticised for being slow to act, cautious, suspicious of the intentions of others, and apparently unwilling to go to war:

> Such is Athens, your antagonist. And yet, Spartans, you still delay, and fail to
> see that peace stays longest with those who are not more careful to use their
> power justly than to show their determination not to submit to injustice. On the
> contrary, your ideal of fair dealing is based on the principle that if you do not
> injure others, you need not risk your own fortunes in preventing others from
> injuring you. (Thuc. I. 71. 1; Crawley trans.)[7]

The Spartan Army

Like any organisation, the military machine of Sparta evolved over time. Those changes are not wholly transparent. There are mixed messages in the evidence available, and common sense on viable numbers for campaigns and battles must be applied. There is still ongoing debate, and at its crux are statements appearing in the works of Xenophon and Thucydides. One is to be found in Xen. *Hell.* at II. 4.31, where the first indication is given of a unit called a *mora* existing in the Spartan army in 403 BC. Another appears in the *Constitution of the Lacedaimonians* where, because of the number of officers given, each *mora* would appear to have four *lochoi*. At the time of its translation it was thought that the manuscript was corrupted and a copyist error had occurred in which he mistook the number of 'two' for 'four' (Xen. *Constitution of the Lacedaimonians* XI. 4; p. 172, n. 2), i.e. that the δ indicating διο (two) should be the preferred reading, rather than the τετταρασ (four) chosen by the copyist. This conclusion is firmly supported by Xen. *Hell.* VII. 4. 20 and VII. 5. 10, which describe the *lochoi* (battalions) as numbering twelve. Given that there were six *morai* (regiments), this fits easily into the graphic representation given below. By the end of the Peloponnesian War and throughout the period under review, it can be assumed that the structure outlined below suggests its makeup and constituent numbers.[8]

Thucydides (V. 66. 3–V. 68. 3), in his description of the first Battle of Mantineia, 418 BC, would appear to have mistaken the largest unit of the Spartan army as being a *lochos*. The resulting estimate of numbers of Spartan forces in the battle is insufficient for the task it took upon itself. One can only assume that by doubling his numbers we would arrive at a more appropriate total. This will permit a *mora* to be made up of two *lochoi*.

The largest unit in the Spartan army was the *mora*, of which there were six. Each was further subdivided as follows into the named units below. The bracketed numbers relate to those to be found in a single *mora*.

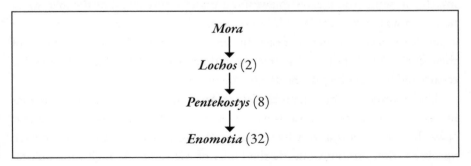

A *mora* contained 1,280 men at full strength, a *lochos* 640 men, a *pentekostys* 160 men and an *Eenomotia* 40 men. The above numbers indicate those available to serve but do not reflect the numbers actually committed to campaigns (see below).

A *mora* was commanded by a *polemarch* and the remaining subordinate commanders are easily identifiable by the relationship of their title to that of the unit they led, e.g, *lochagos, pentekoster, enomotarch.*

Additional units can be identified in the form of Skiritai, *hippeis,* and *neadamodeis.* A force of Skiritai was usually placed on the left of the Spartan battle line. They came from the north-eastern border of Lakonia and sometimes operated as light-armed skrmishers, but as hoplites occupied the prestigious position on the left wing of a Spartan-led army. The *hippeis* could be described as the cream of the Spartan hoplite force and acted as the king's bodyguard while on the march and in battle. Already described above, *neadamodeis* were increasingly used throughout our period. They continued to be brigaded together as they had been in 418 BC at the first Battle of Mantineia, when they are described as being alongside the Brasideioi.

The overall size of the army in the field depended on the number of year groups called up for service and on the number of *morai* committed. If four *morai* were committed, with the other two remaining at home as a reserve, and the call-up, or ban, was for the first thirty-five of the forty age groups, the total serving would be 4,480. Such exactitude in numbers allowed the commissariat to plan for provisions and the requisite number of sacrificial animals to be taken for the number of days allotted for a campaign or operation. Wagons would therefore accompany the march and some would carry the weapons under secure guard of the men when no action was imminent. In addition *helots* up to the number of seven would be available to service the needs of each citizen hoplite and often to act as bearers of their shields and bedding. Craftsmen would be in attendance for all foreseeable repairs and fittings of replacement equipment.

Unless protected by a natural feature, Spartan encampments were circular in design. Sentries faced inwards with a clear view of the weapons store so that *helots* had no opportunity to gain access. As long as light held, cavalry took up observation positions outside the limits of the camp. At night, the Skiritai undertook these duties.

Up to the Battle of Second Mantineia, the Spartans always took the command position on the right, with their allies to their left.

Spartan citizen hoplites differed from those in other Greek states in one significant aspect until well into our period. Their lives were totally focused on military training to the exclusion of all other occupations. They were the wholly dedicated section of the Spartan army to the practice of arms. In the sixth and early fifth centuries they had been the predominant part of the armies put into the field by Sparta. With the marked decrease in citizen numbers, changes were inevitable. It is probable that they had to be brigaded with 'inferiors' and the *perioikoi* to make the requisite numbers in units (see above). Nonetheless, Spartiate officers would command them. Despite the marked fall in Spartiate numbers, the overall population of Lakedaimon was buoyant.

Equipment was supplied by the state and led to a uniformity of appearance within the Spartan phalanx not shared by any other city's army. Their enemies of the fourth century would face a wall of burnished bronze shields emblazoned with the famed *lambda* (Λ), and an overall background of the martial reddish/purple colour of their tunics. Under the tunic a lighter form of corselet of quilting or leather was hidden. This had replaced the much heavier and cumbersome bronze breast and back protections. Metal helmets had possibly also been replaced by a conical leather version and the offensive weapons were the spear and short sword, shorter and straighter than elsewhere in Greece. The overall lightening of body armour was an obvious response to the increasing use of peltasts by their enemies. It was a common practice of the younger and more mobile of Spartan hoplites to be ordered to leave their line to repel and pursue attacking light troops.

It can be seen that there were checks and balances in Sparta's constitution that had evolved over time. After the rather didactic descriptions above, it must be asked how this constitution came into being. The tradition that a certain Lykourgos set down a constitution, that was to be followed by the Spartans may have some credibility. Myth or man, Lykourgos is named as the personality responsible for the revolutionary changes that were set in place to govern Spartan life thereafter. What was proposed depended greatly on the agreement of a large number of people; there must have been significant contemporary issues that persuaded them to accept such a radical change in their lifestyle. This probably helps us to suggest an approximate date for the change. Following the successful appropriation of Messenia, which doubled the area under Spartan control, just prior to the foundation of the colony at Taras in southern Italy in the last decade of the eighth century BC, there would be a need to apportion the new territory. This would require firm planning. It seems most likely that the Lykourgos reforms were put in place in the first third of the seventh century. In the so-called Great *Rhetra*, which Lykourgos is credited to have given the Spartans as the basis of their constitution, there is no mention of the office of *ephor*. Whether it developed from the accretion of further powers being given to a minor magistracy, or was instituted later, remains an open question.

What seems possible is that the content of the Great Rhetra derives from a Delphic oracle and was used as a means of tidying up existing traditions and practices to accommodate the needs of a society which had adopted phalanx warfare. The shared experience of being part of an interdependent formation facing the same danger on the basis of equality within the constitution, whether a man was rich or by comparison poor, aristocrat or of less notable stock, was to be an aspect of democracy or at least a broad oligarchy.[7] The interdependence and risk were equal, and the equality was recognised within the constitution in terms of basic rights and land holdings. This constitution also acknowledged and formalised customs that had already existed for a considerable time, such as communal meals and the organisation of young males into age groups for the purpose of education.

By the first half of the fourth century BC, Spartan society had become ossified within its Lykourgan tradition. It had desperately needed reform and modification for decades. The continuing reduction in the number of Spartiatai, citizens, equals, or whatever one may wish to call them, posed an ever-increasing threat to the stability of the state. The adherence to the strict codes of citizen conduct by the many was loosening, and the roguish attempts of the very few to attempt change, brought with them tensions which are not difficult to understand. Intermarriage between landed gentry, the flouting of the law of accumulating wealth in anything other than land (which proved a problem in itself) brought the Spartan state to a condition, just prior to the Battle of Leuktra, of citizen numbers of perhaps 1,300. By 371 BC, around a third of privately held land was owned by Spartan women.[9] This resulted in an increase in the number of disenfranchised men. The constitution needed to evolve. Under the continued conservatism of Sparta, the seeds of its downfall were already sown.

Of course there had been attempts to change the system of governance, but these had been mainly the work of individuals who had pretensions arising from inflated opinions of their own worth and a desire for greater recognition of their achievements reflected in an office of state. The case of the regent Pausanias, the victor at Plataia that settled the Persian War, is an example. He possibly believed that he could wrest the monarchy to his own devices in the early fifth century. More worrying was the plot of Kinadon in the early fourth century. It showed clearly the ever-increasing tensions between sections of Spartan society. Following on quickly from this, the intrigue that emerged after the death of Lysander (see Appendix 1) should have focused the minds of those who governed. Eminent figures could seek to cloud the issue but at the heart of Spartan society was a worm that ate at the entrails of its existence: the ever-diminishing numbers of the citizen body. Despite the massive reduction in citizen numbers over the years, the overall population remained buoyant. Fewer Spartiatai resulted in greater numbers of *hypomeines*. Apart from the occasional recorded item of disaffection and personal ambition, there is evidence of possible endeavours to seek resolution to the growing constitutional crisis. It has been suggested that around 401/400 BC an *ephor*, Epitadeos, set before the assembly a law on behalf of the *gerousia* which, after acceptance, allowed any citizen to give or bequeath his estate to any other, citizen or inferior.[10] Well intentioned as this and possibly other as yet unknown items of legislation may have been, succeeding years were to prove that it probably accelerated the concentration of property in even fewer hands, thereby leading to further reductions in citizen numbers. The problem had become too big to be solved by mere tinkering.

At Leuktra 400 or so of the 700 Spartiatai present were killed. After receiving the news Agesilaos suspended the laws for the day. In such a way the surviving citizen element was saved from being demoted as *tresantes*.

Near the close of Xenophon's *Constitution of the Lacedaimonians* the writer's profound disappointment with those who continued to flout Lykourgan tradition is in stark contrast with the admiration he had shown hitherto. The quotation below lists the ills Xenophon perceived as being directly a cause for their decline:

> For I know that formerly the Lakedaimonians preferred to live together at
> home with moderate fortunes rather than expose themselves to the corrupting
> influences of flattery as governors of dependent states. And I know too that in

former days they were afraid to be found in possession of gold; whereas nowadays there are some who even boast of their possessions. There were alien acts in former days, and to live abroad was illegal; and I have no doubt that the purpose of these regulations was to keep the citizens from being demoralised by contact with foreigners; and now I have no doubt that the fixed ambition of those who are thought to be first among them is to live to their dying day as governors in a foreign land. There was a time when they would fain be worthy of leadership; but now strive earnestly to exercise rule than to be worthy of it. Therefore in times past the Greeks would come to Lakedaimon and beg her to lead them against reputed wrongdoers; but now many are calling on one another to prevent a revival of Lakedaimonian supremacy. Yet we need not wonder if these reproaches are levelled at them, since it is manifest that they obey neither their god nor the laws of Lykourgos (Xen. *Constitution of the Lacedaimonians* XIV. 1. 1–7).

Endnotes

1   See Lazenby, *The Spartan Army*, pp. 19–20.
2   See Forrest, *A History of Sparta*, p. 61.
3   L. F. Fitzhardinge, *The Spartans*, London, Thames and Hudson, 1980. This is a very useful study covering a wide variety of artistic endeavours, including poetry.
4   Among several instances of the male members of a captured population being killed, and the women and children being enslaved, the fates of the cities of Melos, Skione and Torone display a significant brutality on the part of Athens. Thebes, within the period presently being addressed, meted out the same fate to the inhabitants of Orchomenos in Boiotia. It is well to remember that such acts were carried out by democracies.
5   Paul Cartledge, *The Greeks*, Oxford, Oxford University Press, 1993, Chapter 6, 'Of Inhuman Bondage', proves to be a very thoughtful overview of the subject.
6   See also Plutarch's *Lykourgos*.
7   Robert B. Strassler (ed.), *The Landmark Thucydides: A Comprehensive Guide to the Polponnnesian War*, trans. Richard Crawley, New York, NY, Touchstone Books, 1998.
8   I have accepted the conclusions on numbers given in Lazenby, *The Spartan Army*, Chapter 1. In view of the conflicting evidence, this gives credibility to the size of armies and the duties given to its components when not directly concerned with the battlefield. More recently, Lazenby is supported by Lee, p. 81: 'The Lacedaimonian *lochos* was clearly a durable tactical and administrative entity, some 600 strong in the late fifth and early fourth centuries.' See also Cartledge, *Sparta and Lakonia*, pp. 217–20 supporting six *morai* each having two *lochoi*. He concludes: 'In 425,

therefore, Sparta would have called up thirty-five of the forty age classes, and the presence of *perioikoi* in the garrison was a consequence of the fact that they were now brigaded with Spartiates in the twelve *lochoi* of the "moral" army (two *lochoi* to each of the six *morai*). Thus the *terminus ante quem* for the army reform would be 425.'

9   For property rights of Spartan women, see Stephen Hodkinson, *Property and Wealth in Classical Sparta*, London, Duckworth with the Classical Press of Wales, 2000, pp. 94–103.

10 In the Loeb translation of Plutarch's *Lives* this amendment to the laws is to be found in *Life of Agis*, X, p. 12. Cartledge, *Sparta and Lakonia*, Chapters 10 and 14 give magisterial treatment to *helot*s and *perioikoi* and the progressive decline in the number of Spartiates.

APPENDIX 6

Piety in Warfare

For what reason did the ancestors of all the Greeks ordain that the
trophies set up in celebrating victories in war should be made, not
of stone, but of any wood at hand? Was it not in order that the
memorials of the enmity, lasting as they would for a brief time, should
quickly disappear?

Diod. XIII. 24. 5–6

TODAY, IT SEEMS STRANGE TO have a sizeable group of gods of such
capricious nature. The Greeks saw their gods in the mirror of their own
human condition, sharing the same virtues and weaknesses in character. In the
Iliad they are depicted as partisan, interfering and displaying recognisable human
characteristics. However, there was a difference. To the Greeks the gods were
immortal and possessed supreme powers.

It is sometimes difficult to appreciate the degree to which Greek society was
permeated by religious observance. Such observance, often translated into ritual
and dedicated to specific objectives, appeared in all aspects of life, both personal
and communal, from the simple action of pouring a libation of wine, to rituals
followed in matters of state. Such dutiful devotion to belief and the principles in
what was deemed appropriate attitudes and actions defined the qualities of those
who could be described as pious. Respect for the gods, in whatever local aspect
they were viewed, was an essential component in all Greek city-states and proved
to be the glue that bound Hellenes together and separated them from others.
While each city held certain deities to possess great local significance, all held Zeus
and Athena, Hera, Apollo and Poseidon as paramount deities.

Men and gods were inextricably linked in all aspects of public life. The rituals followed were on behalf of a community, be it city or some representative section of it such as the army. Those of appeasement were rarer than is imagined and often claimed. Most often, they sought approval and endorsement for proposed action or were of celebratory substance. What was of prime importance to the Greeks was their everyday existence, lived in the knowledge that their individual and collective proposals had the approval of their deities. Not for them were the rituals and subsequent actions premised on the basis of reward in some possible afterlife. The need for any ritual was more immediate. An afterlife was acknowledged but did not depend upon, nor was unduly affected by, good or bad actions made when mortal. Retribution for an act deemed wrongful could well be recognised and explained by an observer well after the event yet still in the lifetime of the perpetrator (see below in Xenophon's comments following Leuktra).

A temple built to a god was not used or regarded as we do churches or mosques. It was not a place within which a community would gather to worship. Rather it was the home of the god or goddess. Certainly, ceremonials occurred in its vicinity.

Despite the unpredictability of the plethora of gods, the Olympian pantheon provided the basis for an ethical code that bound a community together. Myth had fewer connections than is often realised and the predilection for myth continues to mislead. A myth and its variants recounting the actions of the gods permitted the Greeks to rationalise their own condition and to make fundamental choices in life. Agreed values emerged within society as a consequence. As in all societies, there were levels where the higher moral ideals were not wholly shared, or even fully understood, and superstition remained in place. The last showed itself in times of extreme adversity and could sway the better counsels, particularly in a democratic society (as in the final stages of the Athenian siege of Syrakuse in the Peloponnesian War).

When the invading Greek tribes took control of areas from previous inhabitants it was not unusual for them to adopt the local deities into their pantheon, or attribute their aspects to their own. Hence we have the Spartan town of Amyklai celebrating the Hyakinthia, a festival involving the Greek god Apollo and the previous non-Greek god giving its name to the celebration. Who, originally, would have been behind such decisions? Inevitably, the answer must be the aristocratic section of the invading population. This is reflected in the epics passed down in the oral tradition before the reappearance of literacy in the Greek world in the eighth century.

Moving to the purpose of this appendix, a variety of examples of piety are given here. Although by no means exhaustive, they cover the categories encountered in our sources. Xenophon is found to be a veritable treasure-trove of examples of contemporary practices when involved in the study of military matters. In his *Constitution of the Lacedaimonians,* the duties of the king when leading the army are made clear: 'the only duties left to the King on active service are to act as priest in matters of religion and as general in his dealings with the men' (Xen. *Constitution of the Lacedaimonians* XIII. 11). The king is therefore relieved of any duties unrelated to the requirements of the campaign. However, from the above we observe that his role as priest-king seems to be of equal value, or even to take precedence over those of his actions as general.

Before he led forth his army the king conducted sacrifices at home to Zeus and the gods of Sparta associated to him, namely the twin gods Kastor and Pollux. If those sacrifices seemed encouraging, an appointed bearer took flame from the altar and led the way for the army to the borders of the state. There the king made further sacrifice to Zeus and Athena and, only if these appeared propitious, proceeded over the border. The fire taken from these sacrifices then took the van, along with a large herd of animals for future sacrifices, and was kept alight throughout the campaign. Daily sacrifice was usually made before dawn and the king conducted the ceremony in the company of representatives from all sections of the army. Two *ephors* observed that the behaviour of all present in no way detracted from the solemnity of the occasion. Such is Xenophon's description of the rites followed by a Spartan army as it left its territory (*Constitution of the Lacedaimonians* XIII. 2–5).

The staff accompanying the army contained seers and aulos players whose presence was essential to battlefield sacrifice (Xen. *Constitution of the Lacedaimonians* XIII. 7). The sacrifice by the Spartans at the Nemea was hasty and barely had time to conform to the usual practice as laid down by Lykourgos. Ideally, the usual preliminaries for battle held that all Lakedaimonians attended the sacrifice wearing a wreath, with all aulos players performing as the goat was dispatched in full view of the enemy (Xen. *Constitution of the Lacedaimonians* XIII. 8). As was the Spartan custom, the sacrifice would be made to Artemis Argotera. She was a goddess associated with hunting who, together with Apollo, was given a pledge that the hunters would share an offering from a successful hunt. Although appearing initially to be unconnected, the dangers of both battle and boar hunt were significant.

The desire to keep malignant forces at bay and to proceed with the act of killing the enemy with the support of divinities was matched by the hope of their protection in the conflict. Once the sacrifice was completed, an immediate order to advance was made, with the sound of the double reed instruments and the singing of the paian giving the pulse necessary for good marching order to be maintained.

The paian, or marching chant, seems to have been a predominantly Dorian custom. It served as a collective prayer, sung by an entire army approaching its enemy, and provided the focus of all minds to the coming task. Morale and good marching order would be preserved and even enhanced.

Here, distinction must be made between a sacrifice conducted without haste and those immediately before hostilities, where time was indeterminate and limited. The pre-battle ceremony, quick and in sight of all, was a rite that took place when battle was unavoidable. The signs emanating from the victim's demise, if indeed they were sought on every occasion, did not give those sacrificing any choice of whether to engage or avoid battle. It could not be taken to have any effect on the outcome. It was made to propitiate the gods in the hope that continued support would be given, not to seek some indication of the ultimate result. Other sacrifices, when on campaign, were made at border and river crossings, or more usually when the army was in camp, where the ceremony could be more elaborate. There, they required an altar – wholly impractical on the battlefield. The presence of an altar permitted ceremonies in which divination rather than propitiation was the prime objective. They involved fire and smoke.

Further distinctions are necessary. Two specific words, *hiera* and *sphagia,* and associated forms thereof are common in our sources. The first, *heira,* covers all aspects of the sacrifice, of which *sphagia* is a part. *Heira* saw the sacrificial animal being led to an altar, quickly dispatched, certain organs such as the liver extracted, examined and placed in the sacred altar fire. Signs such as the health of organs, the direction of the altar smoke, possibly the way in which the animal fell at its death and, importantly, the direction and flow of the blood at its death would be considered. Any additional signs such as the flight of birds or natural phenomena at the time of sacrifice would be noted. Within this sequence is *sphagia,* relating to the plunging of the sacrificial weapon into the throat of the animal and the subsequent flow of its blood. This is the swift action that was transposed to the battlefield, as described above at the Nemea, occurring before the opposing phalanxes crashed together and often taking place after initial skirmishing of light-armed troops and cavalry had already commenced.

An example of a successful camp sacrifice is given in Xenophon's *Anabasis*: 'Xenophon arose early and sacrificed with a view to an expedition. And with the first offering the omens turned out favourable. Furthermore, just as the rites were nearing the end, the soothsayer, Arexion the Parrhasian, caught sight of an eagle in an auspicious quarter, and bade Xenophon lead on' (Xen. *Anab.* VI. 5. 2).

Having recovered and buried the bodies of fallen comrades, which was the purpose of their mission, the Greeks were confronted by the enemy in battle order, at a distance of one and two-thirds of a mile away: 'Hereupon Arexion, the soothsayer of the Greeks, immediately offered sacrifice, and at the first victim the omens proved favourable' (Xen. *Anab.* VI. 5. 8).

The Greeks advanced but came to a halt on encountering a ravine that would inevitably bring disorder to their line. They were persuaded by Xenophon to cross it, by reminding them that the sacrifices had been wholly favourable: 'Gentlemen, our sacrificial victims were favourable, the bird omens auspicious, the omens of the sacrifice most favourable; let us advance upon the enemy' (Xen. *Anab.* VI. 5. 21).

Bolstered by his words, and now convinced that the divinities were with them, the Greeks crossed the ravine and continued their advance. The first sacrifice made in the security of camp would have been *heira* and all aspects would have been present. The second made in open country could have been only *sphagia* but, as it was made some distance from the enemy, it is more likely that, even if they were not burnt, the opportunity to examine the organs would have been taken.

Just as a border crossing was an issue, so too was the crossing of water. At rivers the taking of the *sphagia* is more likely. There, the divination would be made on the basis of signs emanating from the mixing of the victim's blood with the water. Xenophon uses the term *sphagia* in preparation for a river crossing that was made under missile fire, at *Anab.* IV. 3. 19. When successful, the Greeks raised the paian and then the war cry. This was the conclusion of a sequence of incidents. The problem of making the river crossing in safety had presented itself earlier. The river had appeared to be too deep to effect a safe passage. On the bank opposite was an army of Karduchians and another force to their rear, ready to attack them when they attempted to make the crossing (Xen. *Anab.* IV. 3. 7). Having already suffered seven days of continuous fighting on their march through Karduchian territory, their plight had now become critical. The Greeks were obliged to remain where they were until the following day. During the intervening night Xenophon had a dream in which he found himself severely restricted by leg-irons. Soon, however, the irons fell off, leaving him free to take normal strides. The verb he uses, διαβαίνω, can also be used to convey the meaning 'to cross over'. That he shared his experience with his colleague generals demonstrates how seriously dreams were taken as a source for divination. Soon after, the *heira* proved favourable at the first sacrifice. While he was taking breakfast, two young men came to Xenophon. They reported that, while foraging, they had discovered a fordable point where the water level was below waist level and the ground opposite was rocky enough to be unsuitable for enemy cavalry.

This was interpreted as an answer to the meaning of his dream. He gave the young men wine and poured some of his own as a libation to the gods who had given him the dream and its solution to the problem of a crossing place. Xenophon took the young men to the commander-in-chief, Cheirisophos, where they repeated their discovery and the commander too made libation. Thereafter, plans were made to attempt what was, eventually, to be a successful crossing.

Crossing a sea was another matter and often there was sufficient time to undertake a more elaborate ceremonial in which both *sphagia* and *hiera* were present. One such occasion is reported by Xenophon. Prior to Agesilaos' departure from Greece to Asia:

> he desired to go and offer sacrifice at Aulis, the place where Agamemnon had sacrificed before he sailed to Troy. When he had reached Aulis, however, the *boiotarch*s, on learning that he was sacrificing, sent horsemen and bade him to discontinue his sacrificing, and they threw from the altar the victims which they found already offered. Then Agesilaos, calling the gods to witness, and full of anger, embarked upon his trireme and sailed away. (Xen. *Hell.* III. 4. 3–4)

Aulis lay within Boiotia, and the elected leaders of Thebes, the *boiotarch*s, had chosen to disrupt the sacrifices because their own seers should have conducted any ceremony taking place within their territory. They were probably happy to do so, and saw an opportunity to cause discomfort to the Spartans by their action. Thebes had been a firm ally of Sparta during the Peloponnesian War. It had been angered by what it saw to be Sparta's relatively lenient treatment of Athens at the end of the conflict. Thebes had not contributed men to Agesilaos' expeditionary force and was soon to be the leading member of the anti-Spartan alliance in the Korinthian War. Without his army, Agesilaos could only protest at what he believed to be a sacrilegious act before sailing off to join his forces at Gerastos.

A relatively rare occurrence was the act of purification carried out by an army. A prime example is to be found in the *Anabasis*. Following a series of acts of indiscipline, and dangerous rumours after the murder of Kerasuntian ambassadors to the Greeks, it was necessary to cleanse the entire army of guilt. It is not clear what this ceremony entailed. At *Anab*. V. 7. 35 Xenophon baldly states that the rites of purification were performed. That they are given in the plural perhaps indicates more than the mere taking of *sphagia*, and the ceremonial will have been more elaborate.

Sacrifice by the commander on campaign did appear to have some limitations by either custom, or a view that the number three held some particular significance not wholly understood as yet. The latter seems most strongly to have been the case. In the examples that follow, the last proves to be the most extreme and will be given the most attention.

The first two come from the *Anabasis*. It was to become a serial problem of having successful endorsement for departure: 'But though he sacrificed a second and a third time with a view to departure, the victims would not prove favourable' (Xen. *Anab*. VI. 4. 16). This was the second day on which they had not been given signs that were supportive of their proposed intention. Even with a changed framing of intention of leaving camp only to search for provisions: 'With this object in view Xenophon again sacrificed, going as far as three offerings, and the victims continued unfavourable' (Xen. *Anab*. VI. 4. 19).

Another example of three being significant is seen when Kleander, the Spartan governor of Byzantion, was to have taken command of what remained of the army of the 'Ten Thousand'. He was delighted to have the opportunity to do so but, on making unsuccessful sacrifices over a period of three days, he gave up the opportunity saying to their generals:

> The victims do not prove favourable to me as the man to lead you onward; but
> it is not for you to be despondent on that account, since to you, as it seems, is
> given the office of delivering these soldiers. To the road then! And we shall give
> you, when you have reached your journey's end, as splendid a reception as we can.
> (Xen. *Anab*. VI. 6. 36)

With that he took ship and returned to Byzantion.

The most extreme example comes in 413 BC, a little before the period under discussion. Nonetheless, it is close enough in time to indicate how seriously soldiers within an army, its attendant soothsayers and their commander regarded the occurrence of natural phenomena.

At Syrakuse the Athenians were secretly preparing to abandon their attempted siege of the city in view of the unprecedented resistance they had encountered. Daily, their position had worsened:

> But after all was ready and when they were ready to make their departure, the moon, which happened then to be at the full, was eclipsed. And most of the Athenians, taking the incident to heart, urged the generals to wait. Nicias also, who was somewhat too much given to divination and the like, refused even to discuss further the question of their removal until they should have waited thrice nine days, as the soothsayers prescribed. (Thuc. VII. 50. 4)

The period recommended is clearly 3 x 3 x 3 days and obviously carried significance. To wait an additional twenty-seven days after that on which the eclipse had occurred equates to a lunar month. Some may find this a highly superstitious response to what was taken to be an omen. From the source quoted above a significant majority had no desire to attempt the withdrawal, and it may well be that the soothsayers were either like-minded or sought to satisfy the common desire to make no change to their position in fear that some disaster would occur. The prescription itself suggests that there may have existed an agreed tariff of responses to natural phenomena, although there is no direct evidence of this. Obviously, the Syrakusans were subject to the eclipse and may, at first, have been as alarmed as the Athenian forces. However: 'The Syracusans on their part, on learning about this, were far more aroused than before and determined not to give the Athenians any respite, seeing that these had now of their own act confessed themselves no longer superior either with their fleet or with their land-force, for otherwise they would not have laid plans for their departure' (Thuc. VII. 51. 1).

Thereafter, the Syrakusans pressed the Athenians on land and sea, virtually trapping the fleet in the Great Harbour. Great losses in material and morale followed, until the sailors of the Athenian fleet refused to make a last attempt to force the blockade. This left only a land retreat as an option. It is at this point that pious observances were abandoned, such was the diminished morale of the desperate Athenians. Numbering 40,000 men, they left their fallen comrades unburied and abandoned the wounded, marching off to final defeat and eventual servitude.

Within the narrative of this book the reader will have noted the return of the men of Amyklai from the port of Korinth, Lechaion, for the celebration of the local festival to the gods, the Hyakinthia. This was acceptable practice even at time of hostilities and had been planned: 'Accordingly Agesilaos had on this occasion left behind at Lechaeum all the Amyclaeans in the army' (Xen. *Hell.* IV. 5. 11).

So too the conduct of the *ephors* on hearing of the Spartan defeat at Leuktra shows the pious regard for the gods even at a calamitous time: 'on the last day of the festival of the Gynopaediae, when the chorus of men was in the theatre. And when the *ephors* heard of the disaster, they were indeed distressed, as, I conceive, was inevitable; yet they did not withdraw the chorus, but suffered it to finish its performance' (Xen. *Hell.* VI. 4.16).

Xenophon believed that the Spartans had brought their defeat at Leuktra upon themselves. He regarded the taking of the Kadmeia in 379 BC as a violation of their oath to ensure that all Greek city-states were to be independent (Xen. *Hell.* V. 4. 1). Further, the Spartan assembly had compounded that action against Thebes by not following the common pledge of 371 BC to disband their forces in the field (Xen. *Hell.* VI. 4. 2). On the latter point it is quite possible that Sparta could have fielded a much larger force against Thebes had they waited for other states, such as Athens, that had taken the oath to contribute forces.

Within the period under review it would appear that acts of sacrilege increase. Possibly one of the most obvious is the battle between the Eleans and the Arkadians in the sacred precinct of Olympia with the roofs of temples being peopled by missile throwers (Xen. *Hell.* VII. 4. 30–1): a clear example of piety being swept aside by expediency.

Another example, of greater significance to this narrative, relates to the aftermath of the Battle of Leuktra. When taken together with the quotation at the head of this excursus the following is illuminating:

> The Thebans, having defeated the Lakedaimons in battle, set up a trophy of *bronze*. They were accused before the Amphictyons, the common Council for Greece. The charge was: 'It is not right?' The question is: 'Was it right?' The defendants' reason was: 'By our valour we won such glory in war that we wished

to leave a perpetual memorial of it to our descendants.' The counter-argument is: 'Still it is not right for Greeks to set up a permanent memorial of their quarrel with Greeks' (Cicero *De Inventione* 2. 23; emphasis added).

Further Reading

Cartledge, P., *The Greeks*, Oxford, Oxford University Press, 1993, chapters 2 and 7

Hutchinson, G., *Xenophon and the Art of Command,* London, Greenhill, 2000 has three sections on piety, which restrict their concern to the period that is the subject of the current book

Jameson, M. H., 'Sacrifice before battle', in V. D. Hansen (ed.), *Hoplites: The Classical Greek Battle Experience*, New York and London, Routledge, 1991 is more far ranging and, like Pritchett, covers the whole of the Classical period

Pritchett, W. K., *The Greek State at War,* vols I–VI, Berkeley, CA, University of California, 1965–1989; vol. 1, Chapter 8 'Sacrifice before battle' gives a succinct account, while vol. 2, Chapter 8, 'The Battlefield Trophy', gives wide-ranging examples

APPENDIX 7

Anabasis and Kounaxa

The *Anabasis* is valuable, furthermore, for the information it yields regarding the art of war among the Greeks, and as a real contribution to military science. Xenophon was, or became in the course of the retreat, an exceedingly able strategist and tactician, approaching each problem in the spirit of a scholar and thinker and then translating his reasoned solution into terms of military method, always resourceful in meeting new situations with new tactics, and never fettered by the lore of accepted practice.

From the Introduction to the Xen. *Anabasis*, C. L. Brownson trans.

WITH THE DEATH OF THE Great King Dareios, Artaxerxes secured the succession around the time of the surrender of Athens to Sparta. It had not been a wholly straightforward affair. From Plutarch we learn that as his father lay dying, Kyros returned to the Persian court in the hope that his mother had secured the succession for him. Her argument was as follows:

> For Parysatis had a specious argument (the same that Xerxes the Elder employed on the advice of Demaratus), to the effect that she had borne Arsicas to Dareius when he was in private station, but Cyrus when he was king. However, she could not prevail, but her elder son was declared king under the new name of Artaxerxes, while Cyrus remained satrap of Lydia and commander of the forces in the maritime provinces. (Plut. *Artaxerxes* II. 2. 3)[1]

Hints of plots by Kyros against his brother's life followed, but the evidence that he returned to his satrapy thereafter can discount these. What is certain is that,

272

such was his disappointment, he started making arrangements for an attempt on the throne shortly after his return to the Aegean littoral.

As satrap and enabler of the Spartan victory, Kyros had come to see how much more effective Greek hoplites were than any other form of infantry available at that time.[2] With the ending of the war, considerable numbers of men had come to rely on military service for their livelihood. From this pool of available mercenaries Kyros secured their recruitment through a certain Klearchos. This Spartan had held commands both on land and sea in 412/411 BC and in 408 BC was governor of Byzantion. He appears to have served Sparta well in the war against Athens and was sent out again to Byzantion in 403 BC at a time of factionalism in the city and hostilities with their Thrakian neighbours. On the face of it this would seem to have been a good choice for Sparta to make. He obviously had good knowledge of the area and would have opportunities to re-establish personal contact with citizens and those in control of adjacent areas, such as the Persian satrap Pharnabazos. Unfortunately, rather than settling matters in reasonable fashion, Klearchos made himself tyrant of the city and also of neighbouring Selymbria. We have two conflicting views. If Diodoros is to be wholly believed, Klearchos did this by committing a series of atrocities and misappropriating the properties of his victims (Diod. XIV. 12. 2–9). Initially, Sparta sent out ambassadors with orders that he abandon his tyranny. Klearchos ignored them and was eventually forced to flee to Ionia in the face of a Spartan army sent out to depose him. Now in the territory governed by Kyros he found himself in the employ of the Persian prince as an army commander and as the covert recruiting officer of Greek mercenaries. Again, if Diodoros' evidence is to be believed, Klearchos is another example of a Spartan serving overseas who succumbed to personal ambitions of wealth and power. However, in the contemporary evidence of Xenophon, Klearchos is shown in a much better light.[3]

We come now to an account that has fascinated generations and which, until about the middle of the twentieth century, was the favourite text of schoolboys learning ancient Greek. It remains so today for the few fortunates who still have the opportunity to learn the language. Xenophon's *Anabasis* recounts the march to the interior of the Persian Empire by Kyros' army, the battle for the throne, the loss of the Greek command structure by treachery and the return of the undefeated 'Ten Thousand' Greek hoplites under new commanders through hostile country. Xenophon himself was one of those replacement generals and, eventually, supreme commander. His first-hand narrative is a mine of information on strategy, tactics, military innovation, man management and all aspects which contribute to successful command.[4] His account has been the subject of study in many military academies and essential reading for anyone interested in the warfare of this period.

Klearchos was successful in his enterprise. For Kyros' army over 10,000 Greek hoplites were recruited with another 2,000 or so auxiliaries. In an attempt to conceal his true purpose, Kyros first made as if he was marching against the Pisidians. Thereafter, as the army moved further inland, the Greeks became increasingly uneasy. Throughout the long march towards Babylon, Kyros managed to retain the goodwill of the Greeks by dint of dissimulation and increases in pay. Eventually the aim of the enterprise became abundantly clear to all and it was with great difficulty that the mission continued. Eventually, at Kounaxa, a few miles from Babylon, battle was joined. An attempted reconstruction of the battle is given below.

On reading Xenophon's account, what can be recognised is Kyros' organisational ability. To arrange the accumulation of troops and the desired commissariat to fulfil the needs of the army, along with the adroit arrangements made for overcoming topographical obstacles such as the Cilician and Syrian gates was achievement enough. But to do this in the utmost secrecy, while keeping his true objective from the Greek troops – and from his brother – until he was sufficiently far from the sea was incredible.

We learn more details of hoplite warfare and the adaptive use of forces to changing conditions from the first half of the fourth century than from elsewhere in the Classical period. Xenophon's writings are awash with observations on military practices and the innovative thinking of the time. His observations are the more useful for being those of a proven and highly successful commander.

Coming now to the Battle of Kounaxa, it would appear that Kyros the Younger's penetration so deep into the empire had been initially aided by his concealment of intention. This allowed his brother Artaxerxes less than the usual time expected to gather his forces to meet the threat. No doubt elated at the apparent lack of opposition, Kyros continued his advance past a newly dug trench some forty miles long from the huge defensive Wall of Media to the north and almost to the Euphrates river. The trench, possibly thirty feet wide and around eighteen feet deep, fell short of the river by about seven yards and it was through this narrow passage that the army made its way. It has been suggested that Kyros' advance had not allowed the completion of the work.[5] Had the trench been completed, the waters of the Euphrates would have formed a canal-like impediment. As it was, the constriction of the passageway could have been purposely designed to deny comfortable retreat or withdrawal by an invading army following engagement.

Kyros and his commanders made their first error in concluding that the Great King had abandoned the thought of fighting (Xen. *Anab.* I. 7. 19). For three days thereafter the advance continued, but in a much more relaxed manner. Xenophon goes so far as to describe the advance as being lacking in care, with weapons being carried on wagons and the marching column in casual disorder. On the third day, when the vanguard had made its morning halt for victuals, and the remainder of the column was coming up to join it, an officer of Kyros' staff, who had presumably been with a scouting party ahead of the column, came riding up at full speed. His news was that a large enemy army was approaching in battle order. Immediate consternation took hold of Kyros' forces as they scrambled to form up in battle line, thinking that the enemy was already upon them. Luckily, this proved not to be the case.

Kyros' order of battle was still incomplete by midday, with Klearchos taking the right, Proxenos the centre and Menon the left wing of the Greek forces. Shielding Klearchos' flank were peltasts and a thousand Paphlagonian cavalry hard against the river. Thus, the Greeks made up the right wing of the army. Kyros himself was at the centre with 600 cavalry and the left wing was made up of the Asiatic forces under Ariaios. Kyros' cavalry is described as being heavily armoured with breastplates, thigh pieces and helmets, and the horses had frontal protection on head and chest. Spears and the Greek short sword made up the armament of this crack unit. Only Kyros went unhelmeted, possibly for identification purposes, or as an act of heroic bravado.

Early in the afternoon dust was seen in the distance and, shortly after, the dark shape of the oncoming army appeared, spreading widely over the plain. It is described as advancing in national divisions in solid squares preceded by chariots fitted with scythes at the wheel axles and under the floors. It soon became obvious that the Great King's army hugely outnumbered that of Kyros. As the enemy advanced, Kyros' line of battle was still being formed as men continued to arrive at the halting place. It is uncertain that by the time the battle started that all Araios' Asiatic foot-soldiers had joined their cavalry in the line.

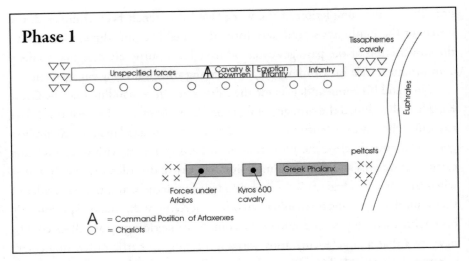

BATTLE PLAN 5 *Battle of Kounaxa. Note the Greeks' position with the river on their right flank. In phase 2, chariots were ineffectual. Tissaphernes breaks through the peltasts. The Greek phalanx is victorious on its wing, while Ariaios is forced to retire as the attempted encirclement begins. In phase 3, after pursuing Ariaios, capturing the Greek camp and being rejoined by the successful Tissaphernes, Artaxerxes turns to meet the returning Greek phalanx. Both armies face each other in a direction opposite to that in which the battle began. The Persians took to flight before contact.*

Contrary to Kyros' warning that the enemy would try to intimidate the Greeks by the volume of their shouting, Artaxerxes' men came on slowly and in total silence. It seems obvious that Kyros had always envisaged his Greek mercenaries attacking the Great King's position at the centre of his army for he rode down his line to direct Klearchos to lead his men against the centre, saying that victory at that point would decide the battle. Herein lies a critical issue. Kyros was probably correct in his assumption, but Klearchos, while saying he would ensure that all would go well, had seen that the centre of the Great King's army was at a position beyond the left wing of Kyros' army. He was unwilling to move his right wing away from the protection of the river, fearing that, in so doing, Kyros' army would be encircled on both flanks. With the enemy closing and the two battle lines about seven hundred yards apart, the Greeks raised the paian and started their advance at a run. This quick approach reduced the risk of damage from arrows. Their opposition broke and ran before contact and the Greeks pursued them, all the

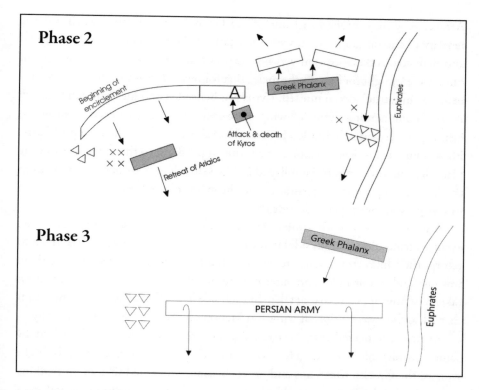

while maintaining their unbroken ranks. Some unmanned chariots were allowed to pass through the Greek lines, which parted on their approach. Other chariots added to the mayhem of the troops fleeing from the Greeks as they crashed through their own lines. Only the satrap Tissaphernes had charged through the Greek peltasts and the Paphlagonian cavalry adjacent to the river but, rather than turning to attack the phalanx in the rear, carried on with his cavalry to the Greek camp. He is reported to have suffered casualties on his passage through the Greek lines from the javelins of the peltasts and did little or no damage to them in return. It was total victory for the Greeks on this wing of Kyros' army.

Meantime, while being congratulated by those around him, Kyros became concerned when he saw the Great King begin to wheel his right wing with the intention of making an encirclement. At the head of his 600 cavalry, Kyros led them in an oblique attack on the command point of the enemy centre, which still lay beyond his own left wing. There, 6,000 cavalry under the command of

Artaxerxes were stationed in front of the Great King's position. Such was the ferocity of the onslaught that, with the death of their general, the 6,000 turned and fled. Artaxerxes' position was now exposed and Kyros, on catching sight of him, made straight for him. In the melee that followed, Kyros wounded Artaxerxes before being struck down himself. Kyros was beheaded and his right hand cut off. Ariaios, commanding Kyros' left wing, appears not to have attempted to engage on hearing of Kyros' death, but led his section of the army from the field post haste. He was pursued to Kyros' camp but continued his flight to the previous stopping place, leaving the camp to be pillaged by the Great King's troops. The Greeks in the camp put up a spirited resistance and the majority managed to survive but not to save persons or property outside their lines.

With sections of both armies victorious in the first phase of the battle, the eventual realisation of both sides that the conflict was not yet over caused them to reform their lines and advance towards each other. The distance separating them was just under four miles and, after countermarching the phalanx, the direction taken was now opposite to that taken by each side in the first phase. This now meant that Klearchos was on the left wing and Menon on the right of the Greek army.

At first it appeared that Artaxerxes' army would pass the Greek phalanx by some considerable distance. However, when they were about to pass the right wing of the Greeks, Klearchos and others became concerned that an outflanking movement by the Persians would place them in a perilous position. Therefore, a debate arose as to whether it would be better to pull the right wing back and wheel the whole line so that that it would be parallel to the river, instead of being at right-angles to it. The Persian command had other ideas and brought their line to a position directly opposite that of the Greeks. Once again, the Greek phalanx advanced to the paian. The Persians are reported to have fled the field even earlier than they had done on the first occasion. After a considerable pursuit, the Greeks assured themselves that the battle was over and returned to their ravaged camp.

Such is the account set down by Xenophon. There are, however, details that are in conflict with the evidence of others. For example, Diodoros XIV. 23. 6 claims that, when he was wounded, Artaxerxes was carried from the battle and command was taken over by Tissaphernes. His version in this matter is to be preferred and probably follows the lost account of Ktesias. Artaxerxes would be in need of medical attention and his personal physician, who wrote of the battle, is to be believed. Similarly, he would probably know better than Xenophon of the command structure of the Persian army and it is likely that Tissaphernes was at the centre with the Great King and not on the left wing as Xenophon reports. This is not to suggest that Xenophon intended to mislead. One has to consider the positions of the two reporters. Ktesias was at a distance from the engagement as a passive observer and would later be busy tending to Artaxerxes after his fall. We must take his word on the fact that the Great King did not take further part in the battle and did not go on with his forces to pillage the Greek camp. Xenophon, by comparison, was a participant in the battle. He would be aware of the broad sweep of what happened but, such would have been his involvement that details could only have been garnered from others after the event. He is to be trusted on the manoeuvres of the Greek phalanx and the general disposition of both battle lines even if he made mistakes over commanders of divisions of the Persian army.

It is easy in hindsight to suggest that matters might have turned out otherwise in the battle. Returning to the dispositions made for the conflict, it may well be that these were at fault. If Kyros had wished the Greeks to face Artaxerxes' command position they should not have been arrayed on the right wing of his army. He would know the customary position of the monarch to be always at the centre of his armies so that the distance for commands to reach left and right wings would be equitable. His request that Klearchos should attack the king's centre from the wing would have led to an oblique movement over the field and was correctly ignored. While Klearchos' reluctance to move his wing from the protection given to his flank by the river is understandable, he must still share the blame for the defeat of the rest of the army. As a Spartan he would know that his countrymen did not indulge in extended pursuits of a routed enemy. What is clear is that this happened to be the case at Kounaxa. It would have been far better if he had allowed only a short pursuit and then, in the customary Spartan fashion of moving to the second phase, wheeled his line to the left and rolled up the Persian line. In such a way Kyros would not have been put in the position of distracting a possible attack on the Greek rear by his heroic assault on the centre.

The rest of the *Anabasis* recounts the treachery of Tissaphernes that led to the loss of the Greek command structure and its replacement by new men, including Xenophon himself. Thereafter, we read of the return of the Ten Thousand from the heart of the Persian Empire, encountering all forms of hardships, formidable problems and fighting for much of the remainder of their 2,500-mile march. It gives details on morale, training, discipline, day and night marches and encampment, intelligence gathering, tactics, provisions, deceptions, special forces, martial religious practices, modified battle lines for changing conditions, leadership by example and the first recorded example of dedicated reserves.[6]

Apart from giving a great deal of information on areas not familiar to those back in Greece and offering instruction on the avoidance of snow-blindness, it served as an inspiration, as it was realised that the power of Persia had been exposed as grossly exaggerated. The fact that a force of Greek hoplites, very small in number by Persian standards, had marched through the Persian Empire, defeating all who came against it, laid bare the weakness of what had, hitherto, been regarded as a formidable opponent. The fervent desire for retribution for the Persian invasion of Greece by Xerxes almost a hundred years earlier was now given new impetus. We have seen in Chapter 2 that Agesilaos was aware of the example and seemed to be intending to make the attempt, before machinations back in Greece brought about his recall. A divided Greece, kept busy with its own interstate conflicts, continued to preserve Persia from terminal harm. Artaxerxes cleverly guarded his empire by the use of money, thereby ensuring that the Greeks were constantly concerned with interstate rivalries at home. It was not until Philip II of Makedon had brought all Greece – except for a much-reduced Sparta – under his control and prepared the bridgehead over into Asia Minor, that Persia faced its nemesis. Philip's assassination left the glory of its conquest to his son Alexander.

Endnotes

1   Plutarch uses a variety of sources and in his *Life of Artaxerxes* the names of Xenophon, Deinon and Ktesias are cited. The last was the Greek physician to the Great King, and snippets of his lost account of these years survive in other sources. Plutarch is carefully selective in what he takes from Ktesias, and shows himself to be aware of some of the gross reportage that he encounters in this source. What is reported here has great credibility and, given Ktesias' close association with the royal household, and what was to follow after the succession, must be accepted.

2   Hutchinson, *Xenophon*, part 1 gives a detailed analysis of the solutions to tactical problems encountered. Very useful information is to be found in J. K. Anderson, *Military Theory and Practice in the Age of Xenophon*, Berkeley, CA, University of California, 1970 and J. K. Anderson, *Xenophon*, London, Duckworth, 1974.

3   Xenophon, however, paints a different picture of Klearchos to that given in Diodoros. At *Anab*. I. 1. 9 the Greek cities of the Hellespont are described as willingly contributing funds to Klearchos for the payment of his mercenaries in thanks for his actions against the Thrakians. Later he states: 'he (Klearchos) persuaded his state that

the Thracians were injuring the Greeks, and, after gaining his point as best he could from the *ephors*, set sail with the intention of making war upon the Thracians who dwelt beyond the Chersonese and Perinthus. When, however, the *ephors* changed their minds for some reason or other and, after he had already gone, tried to turn him back from the Isthmus of Korinth, at that point he declined to render further obedience, but went sailing off to the Hellespont. As a result he was condemned to death by the authorities at Sparta on the ground of disobedience to orders' (Zen. *Anab*. II. 6. 2–3).

4 *Anabasis* covers the journey of the Ten Thousand deep into the Persian Empire and the tribulations encountered on their return. It proves to be a textbook in the imaginative resolution of military problems. *Kyropaideia* presents a fictional picture of the ideal ruler in the life of Kyros the Great. It shows political resonance with Athenian political ideology and Spartan tactical practices in martial matters. *Constitution of the Lacedaimonians* also gives details of Spartan practices in the preparation for and conduct of war. Xenophon's essays on *The Cavalry Commander*, *The Art of Horsemanship*, *On Hunting*, and *Ways and Means* are cumulatively informative, while his *Memorabilia* is well worth reading for the regular nuggets of information on matters such as generalship.

5 C. L. Brownson, in his translation for the Loeb edition of the *Anabasis (Cambridge, MA, Harvard University Press, 1986)*, p. 68 n. 1 suggests that Kyros' rapid advance had prevented completion. Bury, p. 521 puts forward the idea that the narrow passage was left undefended because the Great King had not yet mustered a force sufficient in strength to meet that of Kyros in battle. This is a highly unlikely hypothesis given the restrictions of the area for an invader.

6 For a detailed analysis of such matters see Hutchinson, *Xenophon*, pp. 42–99.

References

Loeb Classical Library, Cambridge, MA, Harvard University Press

Anderson, J. K., *Military Theory and Practice in the Age of Xenophon*, Berkeley, CA, University of California, 1970
— 'The Battle of Sardis in 395 BC', *California Studies in Classical Antiquity*, vol. 7 (1974), pp. 27–53
— *Xenophon*, London, Duckworth, 1974
Andrewes, A. A., 'Two notes on Lysander', *Phoenix*, vol. 25 (1971), pp. 206 ff
Aristotle, *Politics*, trans. J. Warrington, London, Dent, n.d.
Bowra, C. M. (trans.), 'Terpander', in T. F. Higham and C. M. Bowra, *The Oxford Book of Greek Verse in Translation*, Oxford, Clarendon Press, 1938
— (trans.), 'Tyrtaios', in T. F. Higham and C. M. Bowra, *The Oxford Book of Greek Verse in Translation*, Oxford, Clarendon Press, 1938
Buckler, J., *The Theban Hegemony 371–362*, Cambridge, MA, Harvard University Press, 1980
Burckhardt, J., *The Greeks and Greek Civilisation*, ed. O. Murray, trans. S. Stern, London, Fontana Press, 1998
Bury, J. B., *A History of Greece to the Death of Alexander the Great*, London, Macmillan, 3rd edn 1961
Cartledge, P., *Agesilaos and the Crisis of Sparta*, London, Duckworth, 1987
— *The Greeks*, Oxford, Oxford University Press, 1993
— *Sparta and Lakonia*, London, Routledge, 2nd edn 2002
Davidson, J., *The Greeks and Greek Love*, New York, Random House, 2007

DCDC, *Operations: Army Doctrine Publication,* Vol. I, Army Publications, Marlborough, 2010, available at www.dcdc.dii.r.mil.uk

Du Picq, A., *Battle Studies,* vol. 2 *Roots of Strategy*, trans. J. N. Greely, Mechanicsburg, PA, Stackpole Books, 1987

Euripides, *Medea and Other Plays*, trans. P. Vellacott, Penguin Classics, Harmondsworth, Penguin, 1963,

Fitzhardinge, L. F., *The Spartans*, London, Thames and Hudson, 1980

Forrest, W. G., *A History of Sparta*, London, Duckworth, 3rd edn 1995

Gaebel, Robert E., *Cavalry Operations in the Ancient Greek World*, Norman, OK, University of Oklahoma, 2002

Gray, V. J., 'Two different approaches to the Battle of Sardis in 395 BC', *California Studies in Classical Antiquity*, vol. 12 (1979), pp. 183–200

Hamilton, C. D., in Laurence A. Tritle (ed.), *The Greek World in the Fourth Century: From the Fall of the Athenian Empire to the Successors of Alexander*, London and New York, NY, Routledge, 1997

Hanson, V. D. (ed.), *Hoplites: The Classical Greek Battle Experience*, New York and London, Routledge, 1991

— *A War Like No Other*, London, Methuen, 2005

Heskel, J., 'Macedonia and the North, 400–336', in L. A. Tritle (ed.), *The Greek World in the Fourth Century*, London, Routledge, 1997

Hodkinson, S., *Property and Wealth in Classical Sparta*, London, Duckworth with the Classical Press of Wales, 2000

Hornblower, S., *The Greek World 470–323 BC*, London, Methuen, 1983

Hutchinson, G., *Xenophon and the Art of Command*, London, Greenhill, 2000

— *Attrition: Aspects of Command in the Peloponnesian War*, Stroud, Spellmount, 2006, pp. 194–5

Kagan, D., *The Fall of the Athenian Empire,* Ithaca, NY, Cornell University Press, 1987

Lazenby, J. F., *The Spartan Army*, Warminster, Aris & Phillips, 1985

— 'The killing zone', in V. D. Hanson (ed.), *Hoplites: The Classical Greek Battle Experience*, New York and London, Routledge, 1991

— *Logistics in Classical Greek Warfare*, vol. 1 of H. Strachan and D. Showalter (eds), *War in History*, London, Edward Arnold, 1994

— *The Peloponnesian War – A Military Study*, London, Routledge, 2004

Lee, John W. I., *A Greek Army on the March, Soldiers and Survival in Xenophon's Anabasis*, Cambridge, Cambridge University Press, 2007

Lendon, J. E., *Soldiers and Ghosts: A History of Battle in Classical Antiquity*, New Haven, CT and London, Yale, 2005

Luginbill, R. D., 'Othismos: The importance of the mass-shove in hoplite warfare', *Phoenix*, vol. XIVIII, no. 1

McKechnie, P. R. and Kern, S. J. (trans.), *Hellenica Oxyrhynchia*, Warminster, Aris & Phillips, 1988

Morrison, J. S., Coates, J. F. and Rankov, N. B., *The Athenian Trireme*, Cambridge, Cambridge University Press, 1986

Murray, G., *Five Stages of Greek Religion*, London, Watts, n.d.

Plutarch, *Agesilaos*, trans. R. Waterfield, Oxford World's Classics, Oxford, Oxford University Press, 1998

Plutarch, *The Age of Alexander*, trans. Ian Scott-Kilvert, Penguin Classics, Harmondsworth, Penguin, 1973

Powell, D., *An Affair of the Heart*, London, Hodder & Stoughton, 1958

Pritchett, W. K., *The Greek State at War*, vols I–VI, Berkeley, CA, University of California, 1965–1989; vols VII and VIII, Amsterdam, Gieben, 1991 and 1992

— *Studies in Ancient Greek Topography*, vols I–VI, Berkeley, CA and Los Angeles, CA, University of California Press, 1965–1989; vols VII and VIII, Gieben, Amsterdam, 1991–1992

Scott-Kilvert, I., *The Rise and Fall of Athens*, Penguin Classics, Harmondsworth, Penguin, 1960

Sealey, R. A., *A History of the Greek City States 700–338* BC, Berkeley, CA, University of California Press, 1976

Spence, I. G., *The Cavalry of Classical Greece*, Oxford, Clarendon Press, 1995

Strassler, Robert B. (ed.), *The Landmark Thucydides: A Comprehensive Guide to the Polponnnesian War*, trans. Richard Crawley, New York, NY, Touchstone Books, 1998

Sun Tzu, *The Art of War*, trans. Y. Shibing with a foreword by N. Stone, London, Wordsworth Editions, 1993

Tod, M. N., *Greek Historical Inscriptions*, Oxford, Clarendon Press, 1933, rev. edn 1948

Vaughan, P., 'Identification and retrieval of Hoplite battle dead', in V. D. Hanson (ed.), *Hoplites: The Classical Greek Battle Experience*, New York and London, Routledge, 1991

Xenophon, *Anabasis*, trans. C. L. Brownson, Loeb edition, Cambridge, MA, Harvard University Press, 1986

Xenophon, *A History of my Times (Hellenica)*, trans. R. Warner, intro. and notes G. Cawkwell, London, Penguin, 1979

Select Bibliography

THE LIST OF PUBLICATIONS BELOW is by no means exhaustive. It is selected from the available mass of publications as those which the author thinks to be invaluable to the reader who considers extending their knowledge of the period. Mine is, of course, a personal choice but, within the titles chosen, the reader will occasionally encounter some minor, but cogent, differences of opinion from those expressed in this book.

Anderson, J. K., *Military Theory and Practice in the Age of Xenophon*, Berkeley, CA, University of California, 1970
— *Xenophon*, London, Duckworth, 1974
Andrewes, A. A., 'The generals of the Hellespont', *Journal of Hellenic Studies*, vol. 73 (1953)
Barry, W. D., 'Roof tiles and urban violence in the ancient world', *Greek, Roman and Byzantine Studies*, vol. 37, no. 1 (1966), pp. 55–74
Barron J. P., *Silver Coins of Samos*, London, Athlone Press, 1966
Bodil, D., *The Cyropaedia: Xenophon's Aims and Methods*, Aarhus, Aahus University Press, 1989
Bruce, I. A. F., *An Historical Commentary on the Hellenica Oxyrhynchia*, Cambridge, Cambride University Press, 1967
Buck, R., *Boiotia and the Boiotian League 432–371*, Edmonton, Alberta, University of Alberta, 1994
Buckler, J., *The Theban Hegemony 371–362*, Cambridge, MA, Harvard University Press, 1980
— 'Epaminondas and the *Embolon*', *Phoenix*, vol. 39 (1985)

Bury, J. B., *A History of Greece to the Death of Alexander the Great*, London, Macmillan, 3rd edn 1961

Campbell, D. B., *Spartan Warrior 735–331 BC*, Oxford, Osprey, 2012

Cartledge, P., 'Hoplites and heroes', *Journal of Historial Studies*, vol. 97 (1977), pp. 11–27

— *Agesilaos and the Crisis of Sparta*, London, Duckworth, 1987

— *The Greeks*, Oxford, Oxford University Press, 1993

— *Sparta and Lakonia*, London, Routledge, 1979, 2nd edn 2002

— *The Spartans*, London, Macmillan, 2002

Cawkwell, G. L., 'Epaminondas and Thebes', *Classical Quarterly*, vol. 22 (1972)

— 'Agesilaos and Sparta', *Classical Quarterly*, vol. 31 (1981), pp. 69–83

— 'The decline of Sparta', *Classical Quarterly*, vol. 33 (1983), pp. 385–400

David, E., *Sparta between Empire and Revolution 404–243 BC*, Salem, NH, Ayer, 1981

Delbruck, H., *The History of the Art of War Vol. 1, Warfare in Antiquity*, trans. W. J. Renfroe, Bison, NE, University of Nebraska Press, 1990

Devine, A. M., 'Embolon: A study in tactical terminology', *Phoenix*, vol. 37 (1983)

Dillon, M., *Pilgrims and Pilgrimage in Ancient Greece*, London, Routledge, 1997

Du Picq, A., *Battle Studies Vol. 2, Roots of Strategy*, trans. J. N. Greely, Mechanicsburg, PA, Stackpole Books, 1987

Ducat, J., *Spartan Education: Youth and Society in the Classical Period*, trans. E. Stafford, P. J. Shaw and A. Powell, Swansea, Classical Press of Wales, 2006

Figuera, T. J., *Spartan Society*, Swansea, Classical Press of Wales, 2004

Fitzhardinge, L. F., *The Spartans*, London, Thames and Hudson, 1980

Forrest, W. G., *A History of Sparta*, London, Duckworth, 3rd edn 1995

Gaebel, Robert E., *Cavalry Operations in the Ancient Greek World*, Norman, OK, University of Oklahoma, 2002

Georgiadou, Aristoula, *Plutarch's Pelopidas: A Historical and Philological Commentary*, Stuttgart and Leipzig, Teubner, 1997

Goodman, M. G. and Holliday, A. J., 'Religious scruples in ancient warfare', *Classical Quarterly*, vol. 36 (1986)

Hamilton, C. D., *Sparta's Bitter Victories: Politics and Diplomacy in the Corinthian War*, Ithaca, MI, Cornell University Press, 1979

— *Agesilaos and the Failure of Spartan Hegemony*, Ithaca, NY, Cornell University Press, 1991

Hammond, N. G. L., *Studies in Greek History*, Oxford, Oxford University Press, 1973, rev. edn 1993

Hanson, V. D., *The Western Way of War*, New York, Hodder & Stoughton, 1989

— (ed.), *Hoplites: The Classical Greek Battle Experience*, New York and London, Routledge, 1991

— *Warfare and Agriculture in Classical Greece*, Berkeley, CA, University of California, 1998

— 'Hoplite obliteration: The case of the town of Thespiae', in J. Carman & A. Harding (eds), *Ancient Warfare*, Stroud, Sutton Publishing, 1999

Heskel, J., 'Macedonia and the North, 400–336', in L. A. Tritle, (ed.), *The Greek World in the Fourth Century*, London, Routledge, 1997

Hodkinson, S., *Property and Wealth in Classical Sparta*, London, Duckworth with the Classical Press of Wales, 2000

Holladay, A. J., 'Hoplites and heresies', *Journal of Hellenic Studies*, vol. 102 (1982). pp. 94–103

Hornblower, S., *The Greek World 470–323 BC*, London, Methuen, 1983

Hutchinson, Godfrey, *Xenophon and the Art of Command*, London, Greenhill, 2000

Kagan, D., *The Fall of the Athenian Empire*, Ithaca, NY, Cornell University, 1987

Kern, P. B., *Ancient Siege Warfare*, Bloomington, IN, Indiana University Press, 1999

Kelly, D. H., 'Agesilaos strategy in Asia Minor 396–395 BC', *Liverpool Classical Monthly*, vol. 3 (1978), pp. 97–8

Krentz, P., *The Thirty at Athens*, Ithaca, NY, and London, Cornell University Press, 1982

— 'Casualties in hoplite battles', *Greek, Roman and Byzantine Studies*, vol. 26 (1985), pp. 13–21

—*Xenophon, Hellenika I–II. 3. 10*, Warminster, Aris & Phillips, 1989

—*Xenophon, Hellenika II. 3. 11–IV. 2. 8*, Warminster, Aris & Phillips, 1995

Lazenby, J. F., *The Spartan Army*, Warminster, Aris & Phillips, 1985

— *Logistics in Classical Greek Warfare*, vol. 1 of H. Strachan and D. Showalter (eds), *War in History*, London, Edward Arnold, 1994

Lee, John W. I., *A Greek Army on the March: Soldiers and Survival in Xenophon's Anabasis*, Cambridge, Cambridge University Press, 2007

Lendon, J. E., *Soldiers and Ghosts: A History of Battle in Classical Antiquity*, New Haven, CT and London, Yale, 2005

Lipka, Michael, *Xenophon's Spartan Constitution: Introduction, Text, Commentary*, Berlin and New York, Walter de Gruyter, 2002

McKechnie, P. R. and Kern, S. J. (trans.), *Hellenica Oxyrhynchia*, Warminster, Aris & Phillips, 1988

Perleman, S., 'The causes and outbreak of the Corinthian War', *Classical Quarterly*, vol. 14 (1964), pp. 64–81

Powell, A. and Hodkinson, S. (eds), *Sparta and War*, Swansea, Classical Press of Wales, 2006

— (eds), *Sparta: The Body Politic*, Swansea, Classical Press of Wales, 2010

Powell, D., *An Affair of the Heart*, London, Hodder & Stoughton, 1958

Pritchett, W. K., *The Greek State at War*, vols I–VI, Berkeley, CA, University of California, 1965–1989; vols VII and VIII, Amsterdam, Gieben, 1991 and 1992

— *Studies in Ancient Greek Topography*, vols I–VI, Berkeley, CA and Los Angeles, CA, University of California Press, 1965–1989; vols VII and VIII, Gieben, Amsterdam, 1991–1992

Rhodes, P. J. and Osborne, R. (eds), *Greek Historical Inscriptions 404–323 BC*, Oxford, Oxford University Press, 2003

Rice, D. G., 'Agesilaos, Agesipolis, and Spartan politics 386–379 BC', *Historia*, vol. 23 (1974), pp. 164–82

Rusch, S. M., *Sparta at War: Strategy, Tactics, and Campaigns, 550–362 BC*, London, Frontline Books, 2011

Sage, M. M., *Warfare in Ancient Greece*, London, Routledge, 1996

Seager, R., 'Thrasybulus, Conon and Athenian Imperialism 396–386 BC', *Journal of Hellenic Studies*, vol. 87 (1987)

Sealey, R. A., *A History of the Greek City States 700–338 BC*, Berkeley, CA, University of California Press, 1976

Snodgrass, A. M., *Arms and Armour of the Greeks*, Baltimore, MD and London, Johns Hopkins University Press, 2nd edn 1999

Spence, I. G., *The Cavalry of Classical Greece*, Oxford, Clarendon Press, 1995

Stylianou, P. J., *A Historical Commentary on Diodorus Siculus Book 15*, Oxford, Oxford University Press, 1998

Tatum, J., *Xenophon's Imperial Fiction*, Princeton, NJ, Princeton University Press, 1989

Tod, M. N., *Greek Historical Inscriptions*, Oxford, Clarendon Press, 1933, rev. edn 1948

Tritle, L. A. (ed.), *The Greek World in the Fourth Century*, London, Routledge, 1997

Trundle, M., *Greek Mercenaries from the Late Archaic Period to Alexander*, New York, Routledge, 2004

Tuplin C. J., 'The Leuktra campaign: Some outstanding problems', *Klio*, vol. 74 (1987), pp. 72–107

— *The Failings of Empire: A Reading of Xenophon Hellenica 2.3.11–7.5.27*, Historia Einzelschriften, Stuttgart, Steiner, 1993

Vaughan, P, 'Identification and retrieval of Hoplite battle dead', in V. D. Hanson (ed.), *Hoplites: The Classical Greek Battle Experience*, New York and London, Routledge, 1991

Wees, H. van, *War and Violence in Ancient Greece*, London, Duckworth with the Classical Press of Wales, 2000

— *Greek Warfare Myths and Realities*, London, Duckworth, 2004

Westlake, H. D., *Thessaly in the Fourth Century*, London, 1935, reprint by Ares, 1993

Winter, F. E., *Greek Fortifications*, Toronto, University of Toronto, 1971

Worley, L. J., *Hippeis: The Cavalry of Ancient Greece*, Boulder, CO, Westview Press, 1994

Zaidman, I. B. and Pantel, P. S., *Religion in the Ancient Greek City*, trans. P. Cartledge, Cambridge, Cambridge University Press, 1992

Index

A

Agesilaos II xiii–xvii, 13, 15, 18–30,
33–4, 38, 43, 45–60, 61–2, 71–5,
77–82, 85–6, 88, 95, 97, 99, 100,
103–5, 110, 113–16, 118, 125,
127, 131–2, 135, 139, 140, 144,
148–9, 156, 169–170, 178,
182–4, 189, 193–6, 199–209,
217–21, 231–2, 237–8, 244, 247,
250, 252–3, 259, 267–8, 270, 280

Agesipolis 103–5, 108, 246

Agis II 10, 11, 13, 30, 38, 199, 200,
202

Agis IV xvi, 194–5

Alexander II of Makedon 164–9, 174,
280

Alexander of Pherai 164–9, 172, 173

Alexander the Great 190, 234

Alketas 116, 237

Alkibiades xvi, 83, 200

Alkimenes 64

Alkisthenes 33

Amyntas 101, 105, 164, 166

Anaxibios 87–8

Antalkidas xv, xviii, 69–70, 85, 89–90,
92–4, 170, 193, 221, 250

Antalkidas, Peace of 94, 98, 121, 169

Aratos of Sikyon 195

Archidamos III 139–41, 144, 156–7,
161, 183, 190, 194, 195n, 238

Aristodemos 34–5

Artaxerxes xvi, 12, 15, 24, 26, 70, 85,
94, 126, 170–1, 272, 274, 277,
278–80, 280n

B

Battles (of significance)
Battle between the walls of Korinth
xvii, xxiv, 59, 64–8
Haliartos 26–30, 32, 103, 205
Knidos 49, 57–8, 60n, 61, 84, 109
Koroneia xvii, 41–9, 50–1, 58, 60n,
71, 76, 94, 119, 142, 144, 205,
221
Kounaxa xvii, 12, 17, 24, 215,
274–9
Lechaion xv, 71–2, 74–8, 81, 83n,
97, 231

293